Kantian Ethics

Kantian Ethics

Value, Agency, and Obligation

Robert Stern

OXFORD UNIVERSITY PRESS

OXFORD
UNIVERSITY PRESS

Great Clarendon Street, Oxford, OX2 6DP,
United Kingdom

Oxford University Press is a department of the University of Oxford.
It furthers the University's objective of excellence in research, scholarship,
and education by publishing worldwide. Oxford is a registered trade mark of
Oxford University Press in the UK and in certain other countries

First Edition published in 2015
Impression: 1

Published in the United States of America by Oxford University Press
198 Madison Avenue, New York, NY 10016, United States of America

British Library Cataloguing in Publication Data
Data available

Library of Congress Control Number: 2015936892

ISBN 978–0–19–872229–8

Printed and bound by
CPI Group (UK) Ltd, Croydon, CR0 4YY

Contents

Acknowledgements

The papers in this collection also appear in the following places, and where necessary I am grateful for permission to reprint the relevant material:

Chapter 1: 'Kant, Moral Obligation, and the Holy Will', in Mark Timmons and Sorin Baiasu (eds.), *Kant on Practical Justification: Interpretative Essays* (Oxford: Oxford University Press, 2013), pp. 125–52

Chapter 2: 'Constructivism and the Argument from Autonomy', in James Lenman and Yonatan Shemmer (eds.), *Constructivism in Practical Philosophy* (Oxford: Oxford University Press, 2012), pp. 119–37

Chapter 3: 'The Value of Humanity: Reflections on Korsgaard's Transcendental Argument', in Joel Smith and Peter Sullivan (eds.), *Transcendental Philosophy and Naturalism* (Oxford: Oxford University Press, 2011), pp. 74–95

Chapter 4: 'Moral Scepticism and Agency: Kant and Korsgaard', *Ratio*, 23 (2010), pp. 451–74

Chapter 5: 'Moral Scepticism, Constructivism, and the Value of Humanity', in Carla Bagnoli (ed.), *Constructivism in Ethics* (Cambridge: Cambridge University Press, 2013), pp. 22–40

Chapter 6: 'Does "Ought" Imply "Can"? And Did Kant Think It Does?' *Utilitas*, 16 (2004), pp. 42–61

Chapter 7: 'Why Does Ought Imply Can?', in Marcel van Ackeren and Michael Kühler (eds.), *The Limits of Moral Obligation: Moral Demandingness and Ought Implies Can* (Abingdon: Routledge, 2016), pp. 100–15

Chapter 8: 'On Hegel's Critique of Kant's Ethics: Beyond the "Empty Formalism" Objection', in Thom Brooks (ed.), *Hegel's Philosophy of Right* (Oxford: Wiley-Blackwell, 2012), pp. 73–99

Chapter 9: 'Does Hegelian Ethics Rest on a Mistake?' in Italo Testa and Luigi Ruggiu (eds.), *I That Is We, We That is I: Contemporary Perspectives on Hegel* (Leiden: Brill, 2015)

Chapter 10: '"My Station and its Duties": Social Role Accounts of Obligation in Green and Bradley', in Nicholas Boyle, Liz Disley, and Karl Ameriks (eds.), *The Impact of Idealism: Volume 1 Philosophy and Natural Sciences* (Cambridge: Cambridge University Press, 2013), pp. 299–322

Chapter 11: 'The Ethics of the British Idealists: Perfectionism after Kant', in Sasha Golub and Jens Timmermann (ed.), *The Cambridge History of Ethics* (Cambridge: Cambridge University Press, 2015)

Chapter 12: 'Round Kant or Through Him? On James's Arguments for Freedom, and their Relation to Kant's', in Gabriele Gava and Robert Stern (eds.), *Pragmatism, Kant, and Transcendental Philosophy* (Abingdon: Routledge, 2015)

Chapter 13: '"Duty and Virtue Are Moral Introversions": On Løgstrup's Critique of Morality', in Hans Fink and Robert Stern (eds.), *What is Ethically Demanded? Essays on Knud Ejler Løgstrup's 'The Ethical Demand'* (Notre Dame: Notre Dame University Press, 2016)

Chapter 14: 'Divine Commands and Secular Demands: On Darwall on Anscombe on "Modern Moral Philosophy"', *Mind* 123 (2014), pp. 1095–122

Many people have helped me to produce the work collected in this volume; some (but I fear not all) are thanked in the relevant papers. Colleagues and students at Sheffield have also been particularly supportive, as has my family, for which I am extremely grateful once more. Thanks also go to Peter Momtchiloff of OUP for again supporting another collection of my papers, which is a kind of companion volume to my earlier *Hegelian Metaphysics* (Stern 2009).

I would like to dedicate this volume to the memory of my father, a good man.

List of Abbreviations

In general, I have used the author/date system of referencing. However, in the case of Kant and Hegel, I have used a system of abbreviations (see below), where details of the works are given in the Bibliography.

Works by Kant

References are given to one of the following translations, followed by references to the volume and page number of the Akademie edition of Kant's works (Kant 1900–), except for references to *CPR*, which are given to the pagination of the first (A) and second (B) editions in the standard manner.

CBHH *Conjectural Beginning of Human History*, translated by Allen Wood, in Kant 2007: 160–75

CJ *Critique of the Power of Judgment*, translated by Paul Guyer and Eric Matthews, in Kant 2000

CPR *Critique of Pure Reason*, translated by Paul Guyer and Allen Wood, in Kant 1998

CPrR *Critique of Practical Reason*, translated by Mary J. Gregor, in Kant 1996a: 133–272

CS 'On the Common Saying: That May Be Correct in Theory, but It Is of no Use in Practice', translated by Mary J. Gregor, in Kant 1996a: 273–310

GMM *Groundwork of the Metaphysics of Morals*, translated by Mary J. Gregor, in Kant 1996a: 37–108; and on occasion revised in the light of Kant 2011

LE *Lectures on Ethics*, translated by Peter Heath, in Kant 1997

LR *Lectures on the Philosophical Doctrine of Religion*, translated by Allen W. Wood, in Kant 1996b: 335–452

MM *The Metaphysics of Morals*, translated by Mary J. Gregor, in Kant 1996a: 353–604

OCS *On the Common Saying: That May Be Correct in Theory, But It Is of no Use in Practice*, translated by Mary J. Gregor in Kant 1996a: 287–8

PP *Toward Perpetual Peace*, in Kant 1996a: 311–52

Relig *Religion within the Boundaries of Mere Reason*, translated by George di Giovanni, in Kant 1996b: 39–216

Schulz 'Review of Schulz's *Attempt at an Introduction to a Doctrine of Morals for all Human Beings Regardless of Different Religions*', translated by Mary Gregor in 1996a: 7–10

Works by Hegel

References are given to one of the following translations, and then to the volume and page number of the *Theorie Werkausgabe* edition of Hegel's works (Hegel 1969–71). Where appropriate, references are also given to section numbers (where 'Z' indicates a reference to a 'Zusatz' or student note).

EL *Logic: Part I of the Encyclopaedia of the Philosophical Sciences,* translated by T. F. Geraets, W. A. Suchting, and H. S. Harris, in Hegel 1991b

ILHP *Lectures on the Philosophy of World History: Introduction,* translated by H. B. Nisbet, in Hegel 1975

LHP *Lectures on the History of Philosophy,* translated by E. S. Haldane and Frances H. Simson, in Hegel 1892–6

NL *On the Scientific Ways of Treating Natural Law, on its Place in Practical Philosophy, and its Relation to the Positive Sciences of Right,* translated by H. B. Nisbet in Hegel 1999: 102–80

PR *Elements of the Philosophy of Right,* translated by H. B. Nisbet, in Hegel 1991a

PS *Phenomenology of Spirit,* translated by A. V. Miller, in Hegel 1977b

SC 'The Spirit of Christianity and its Fate', translated by T. M. Knox, in Hegel 1948: 182–301

Introduction

In his essay 'On the Basis of Morality', Schopenhauer raises a number of fundamental difficulties for Kant's ethics, one of which is the following:

> Conceiving ethics in an *imperative* form, as *doctrine of duties*, and thinking of the moral worth or unworth of human actions as fulfilment or dereliction of *duties*, undeniably stems, together with the *ought*, solely from theological morals and in turn from the Decalogue. Accordingly it rests essentially on the presupposition of the human being's dependence on another will that commands him and announces reward or punishment, and cannot be separated from that.[1]

The difficulty may be put this way: How can Kant have an ethics of duty and obligation on the one hand, which is compatible with the emphasis he wants to place on our autonomy as agents on the other? For, Schopenhauer argues, duty and obligation are notions which have an essential basis in a theological context, and so require there to be commands from God who attaches rewards and punishments to those commands; but then how can the dutiful agent ever be considered to be autonomous in Kantian terms? As I will explain in what follows, and as several papers in this collection discuss further, I think Schopenhauer is correct to see this tension between obligatoriness and autonomy as an issue for Kant; but as I will also explain, and as other papers also discuss further, I think Schopenhauer is correct to focus on the question of *obligation* or *duty* as raising the problem here, not what makes actions right and wrong as such, so that many prominent contemporary followers of Kant who fail to see this are led astray in their understanding of what Kant might take our autonomy to require.

Schopenhauer's raises the difficulty because he adopts what is in many respects an intuitive and straightforward account of what it is to be under an obligation or duty, which he thinks makes perfect sense against a theological background: namely, that this obligatoriness involves sanctions or incentives imposed by a divine law-giver, where these are what bind the will in one direction or another, making it the case that some action is genuinely required. He quotes Locke in support of this view: 'For since it would be utterly in vain, to suppose a Rule set to the free Actions of Man, without annexing to it some Enforcement of Good and Evil, to determine his Will, we must,

[1] Schopenhauer 1988, vol 4: 125/2009: 129.

where-ever we suppose a law, suppose also some Reward or Punishment annexed to that Law'.[2]

Clearly, as Schopenhauer urges, if this account of obligation were correct, it would create immediate difficulties for Kant, as it would reduce all such obligations to hypothetical and not categorical imperatives, as their basis would now lie in the end to be achieved in following them as bringing satisfaction or avoiding dissatisfaction, thus rendering ethics conditional on our desire for that end in a way that Kant takes to be heteronomous. Indeed, this is precisely one of the objections Kant himself raises against theological ethics conceived of in this manner, as laid down by a divine ruler who attached punishments and rewards to certain actions and not others.[3]

It might be said, however, that Kant does not have a lot to fear from Schopenhauer's worry here. For, Schopenhauer may seem to be just confusing obligation with coercive force, in a way that was nicely brought out by H. L. A. Hart in his critique of related views proposed by Jeremy Bentham and John Austin: for, while the highway robber may *oblige* me to hand over my money by using a threat of injury, he cannot be said to have put me under an *obligation* to do so, because he is not in a position to exercise *legitimate authority* over me.[4] It could therefore be argued that there is no threat to my autonomy as far as obligation proper is concerned, as punishment and reward are not sufficient conditions for genuine obligatoriness, where it is to this other feature of legitimate authority that the theorist can turn in order to explain the binding force of obligation.

However, even if Schopenhauer were to accept this, he could still argue that what is essential for this bindingness is that this authority resides in the will of another, who thereby exercises authority *over me*, and this in itself results in a loss of autonomy, in a perfectly intuitive sense: I am no longer 'self-ruled', but find myself constrained in my actions by someone else. It is thus the connection between duty or obligation and 'the presupposition of the human being's dependence on another will that commands him' that creates the difficulty with respect to autonomy, regardless of the issue of punishment and reward and their link to our desires.

One response to this challenge might be to question the assumptions on which it rests: namely, that following the orders of a legitimate authority is sufficient to take away one's autonomy. After all, it could be argued, this is precisely the force of the *legitimacy* of the authority in question, which implies that it is *entitled* in some way to

[2] Locke 1975: Book II, Chapter XXVIII, §6, p. 351; cited Schopenhauer 1988, vol. 4: 123/2009: 128, where the wrong reference is given for the Locke text.

[3] Cf. *GMM*: 91 [4:443], and the parallel discussion in *CPrR*, where Kant notes that 'the will of God, if agreement with it is taken as the object of the will without an antecedent practical principle independent of this idea, can become motives of the will only by means of the happiness we expect from them', in a way that makes the position of following God's will 'quite unfit to be the supreme moral law'. Cf. also *CPrR*: 244 [5:129]: 'Here again, then, everything remains disinterested and grounded only on duty, and there is no need to base it on incentives of fear and hope, which if they became principles would destroy the whole moral worth of actions'.

[4] Hart 1958: 95–6.

exercise that authority over others, where this entitlement means that they are not coerced or constrained in a way that deprives them of autonomy—any more than I lose my freedom by following the laws of a properly constituted and legitimate state.

Whatever the virtues of this response in some contexts, however, it would seem difficult for Kant to deploy it here, as it is hard to see on his account of ethics how any being could *acquire* this legitimate authority over us in the first place. There are, of course, many possible models of how authority can be legitimated, but none would seem to fit the ethical situation as Kant conceives it. Thus, for example, it is hard to see how we could think of this as a transfer of sovereignty from us to a legislator via some sort of contract, while it is also hard to see how it could fit a Razian 'service conception'[5] which would require a kind of moral inegalitarianism, whereby some are better placed to get us to conform to moral reasons than we are ourselves, which is something that Kant would want to deny. On the face of it, therefore, it looks difficult to find a way of legitimating the authority of one will over another that can render that authority compatible with our autonomy.

It is at this point in the dialectic, I would argue, that we can see how Kant arrives at the account of duty and obligation which I propose in some of the papers in this book, which I suggest can best be approached by the contrast Kant draws between the holy and human will. On this account, I argue, Kant did not attribute the obligatory or imperatival force of morality to the commands of an external law-giver, but to the fact that we are not holy wills, and thus experience morality in an imperatival way, in a way that a holy will does not. For, while a holy will has no sensuous nature that stands in opposition to what it is morally right to do, we have inclinations that pull in the other direction, and so must be constrained by our reason in order to act morally, thus giving morality its obligatory character in our case. Thus, Kant argues, while other theorists have held that 'another person must be present, who necessitates us to duty' and have found this person in God (as Schopenhauer does), this is not needed to explain the nature of obligation or duty, as in fact this stems from 'man considered solely as an intelligible being, who here obligates man as a sensory being, and we thus have a relationship of man *qua* phenomenon towards himself *qua* noumenon'.[6]

It is this model, I argue, that lies at the heart of Kant's picture of obligation, which thus transfers the commanding force of morality from the external will of God to our own reason, as it compels us to act in the face of countervailing inclination. This then explains how morality binds us in a way that it does not bind a holy will, while also making this compatible with our autonomy, as there is now nothing outside us on which this obligatoriness is seen to depend. Considerations of autonomy, therefore, play an important role in driving Kant towards this picture of obligation, and away from the more traditional theological conception proposed by Schopenhauer and

[5] Raz 1986: Chapters 1 and 2. [6] *LE* 274–5 [27:510].

others. I develop an account of this picture in more detail in the paper on 'Kant, Moral Obligation, and the Holy Will'.

However, while I maintain that such considerations of autonomy play a vital role here, in helping us to understand Kant's conception of obligation and duty, many commentators on Kant have wanted to go further, and claim that his account of autonomy rules out not only an external source for obligation, but also any realist account of value in his ethics as such, so that instead Kant must be viewed as a thoroughgoing constructivist. I have dubbed this the 'argument from autonomy' for constructivism, and it forms the focus of the second essay in the collection, 'Constructivism and the Argument from Autonomy'. Here, I argue, the 'argument from autonomy' goes too far, both as an interpretation of Kant, and as a position in its own right. As a result, I suggest, it is possible to take Kant's concern with autonomy with full seriousness, while still taking him to be a moral realist at the level of value, even while accepting that he sees the *obligatoriness* of morality in a more anti-realist manner, as something we bring about by imposing morality on ourselves. Thus, I propose what I call a 'hybrid view' of Kant's position, which combines a realism about the value of rational agents and thus what is right or wrong to do in the face of that value, with an anti-realism about the obligatory force of that rightness or wrongness as it figures in our relation to the moral. If I am correct (and of course many would still dispute this),[7] attempts to read Kant as a constructivist about value are both undermotivated in Kantian terms, and mistaken.

However, interpretative issues concerning Kant notwithstanding, the constructivist approach to ethics is of great interest in its own right, where in this tradition Christine Korsgaard is perhaps the most prominent current representative; her work therefore forms a focus for the next few papers. The first of these concentrates on a well-known argument in her influential book *The Sources of Normativity*, which she presents in a transcendental form, to the effect that agents must see value in their humanity. While many have found her position here intriguing, it has also not been made entirely clear, and has frequently been criticized. In my discussion in 'The Value of Humanity: Reflections on Korsgaard's Transcendental Argument', I set her claims against the background of debates concerning transcendental arguments more generally, and also emphasize the anti-realist conception of value that is meant to underline her position as I understand it; I then suggest that given the latter assumption, the argument she offers is more compelling than is often recognized.

One issue this discussion raises, however, is what in fact the role of any such transcendental argument in ethics is really meant to be: suppose Korsgaard were

[7] The issue of whether or not to read Kant as a constructivist remains a lively one, largely sparked off by Rawls 1980. For notable contributions on the constructivist side, see: Rauscher 2002, Reath 2006a and 2006b, Johnson 2007, Formosa 2013. For notable contributions criticizing the constructivist view, see Ameriks 2003b, Kain 2004, Irwin 2004, Langton 2007, Hills 2008, Galvin 2010. Of course, some of these contributions as well as others also cast doubt on the terms of the debate: see e.g. Sensen 2013.

right, and it could be shown that to be an agent at all, one must take oneself to have a certain value, but where this argument will only work if this value is understood in constructivist and not realist terms; does this show that the constructivist is in a better position than the realist to answer certain sorts of challenges to ethics, and thus resolve what Korsgaard calls 'the normative question'? If so, it might be felt, that would give the constructivist a decisive advantage over the realist, even if the earlier argument from autonomy is rejected on the basis suggested previously. This might then instead be called 'the argument from anti-scepticism' for constructivism.[8]

A difficulty with this approach, however, is that when it comes to ethics, there is a well-known trap identified by H. A. Prichard and others, who claim that in some sense it is in fact impossible to *answer* the sceptic, and indeed folly even to try. For if the 'normative question' the sceptic is raising is why they should be moral, the only morally adequate answer is to give them a moral reason, for example if they didn't act in a certain way they would be lying, or stealing, or committing murder; but if they are asking the question at all, they presumably don't find such reasons compelling and so will be left unsatisfied. But then to satisfy them, it would seem they need a non-moral reason, such as that ultimately acting in these ways is in their interest or will lead to their good; but while that kind of response may get them to act in a way that *conforms* to morality, it will not turn them into *proper moral agents*, who do the right because it is the right, not because it is in their interest to behave rightly. So, it may seem that (paradoxically) by promising to answer the sceptic, the Korsgaardian puts herself in a weaker position, rather than a stronger one, and so faces difficulties that the realist can avoid. And, insofar as Korsgaard presents herself as following Kant's lead here, then he too might be said to fall into the same trap.

My paper 'Moral Scepticism and Agency: Kant and Korsgaard' starts from this Prichardian challenge to Korsgaard and her handling of the 'normative question' by making an appeal to the conditions for agency. I suggest, however, that if we look first at Kant, it is clear that he took himself to be engaging with moral scepticism of a very different kind, to which the Prichardian challenge raised above does not so readily apply. Focusing mainly on Section III of the *Groundwork of the Metaphysics of Morals*, I suggest that Kant's concern with scepticism was not with the amoral agent who is looking for reasons to be moral, but with a kind of *transcendental* sceptic, who cannot see how morality can even be possible for agents such as ourselves, and thus finds morality puzzling from within. I argue that this puzzlement may arise in relation to three related concerns that are covered in Section III of the *Groundwork*: first, whether we are free, and thus whether we are the kind of beings to

[8] Some might think the better term to use in relation to Korsgaard is 'constitutivism' rather than 'constructivism'. While I would agree that they can be understood as different positions, they are still closely enough linked that I would see the former as a species of the latter, for the purposes of the discussion here. Cf. also Korsgaard 2008b, where she seems happy to characterize her fundamental outlook in the terminology of constructivism. For a trenchant critique of the constitutivist variant of constructivism, see Enoch 2006.

whom morality can apply; second, how the apparently binding force of morality on us is to be explained; and thirdly how the psychology of moral action it to be understood, given that (on Kant's account, at least) it cannot be based on any 'interest' we take in it. In raising these issues, the person who fears that morality might be a 'chimera' is asking a different kind of 'normative question' from the one which Prichard rejected as illegitimate, as these are questions that the individual who is perfectly well-disposed towards morality could intelligibly raise, in the sense that at one level they fully accept the special claims morality is meant to make on us, but they just don't understand how such claims are to be rendered intelligible given certain apparently plausible assumptions in metaphysics and human psychology. I then argue that it is Kant's transcendental idealism that is meant to undercut those assumptions, or at least make room for morality, even if they are held to be true within a certain domain. Finally, I suggest, while Korsgaard is perhaps not as clear as she could be on these matters, the possibility is then also open for reading her 'normative question' along different lines, thereby avoiding the challenge that Prichard raises for that question as it arises in a more limited form.

If this is correct, however, Korsgaard's earlier challenge to realism comes back on the table for reconsideration: namely, that the realist is unable to properly deal with moral scepticism, where now the scepticism in question is taken in a form that avoids the Prichardian trap. In the next paper on 'Moral Scepticism, Constructivism, and the Value of Humanity', I address this issue, suggesting that the scepticism Korsgaard has in mind might be best understood as a kind of 'debunking scepticism' that can be associated with thinkers like Mandeville, Nietzsche, and Marx, who argue that behind the façade of morality lie other kinds of interests and powers, in a way that should undermine our allegiance to the norms that are enforced in its name.[9] Korsgaard's challenge, then, is that faced with scepticism of this sort, the realist is not in a position to offer any adequate response as all she can do is insist that our moral system properly fits some pre-existing ethical order; but the constructivist is said to be in a better position, as she can show why allegiance to that system constitutes a necessary condition for our rational agency and thus our identity, in a way that makes it inescapable. Moreover, using her constructivist reading of Kant, Korsgaard contends that something like this strategy is adopted in Kant's ethics as well, particularly in his treatment of the Formula of Humanity in the *Groundwork*, which she reads as offering a response to the moral sceptic along these lines (as do others). Korsgaard thus seeks to reinforce her constructivist approach to Kant by claiming to show how he rightly uses this constructivism to engage with the debunking sceptic in the manner she recommends, thus offering a significant challenge both

[9] Another thinker whose questioning may be taken in the same spirit is Emmanuel Levinas, when he famously writes at the start of *Totality and Infinity*: 'Everyone will readily agree that it is of the highest importance to know whether we are not duped by morality' (Levinas 1969: 21).

to realist readings of Kant of the sort I prefer, and to the philosophical capacities of that realism when it comes to dealing with scepticism of this kind.

In the rest of the paper, I seek to respond to this challenge, by in effect turning it on its head: I argue that in this part of the *Groundwork*, there is no engagement by Kant with scepticism along the lines Korsgaard suggests, and thus that none of the constructivist arguments that she attributes to Kant here can really be made to fit the text. In fact, I argue, Kant's position here corresponds much better to exactly the kind of realist perspective which Korsgaard takes to be disallowed because she reads Kant's target here in an anti-sceptical manner. I then conclude by considering Korsgaard's broader worry that any such realism leaves us vulnerable to the debunking sceptic, where I suggest that there are strategies that the realist can perfectly well adopt in responding to this scepticism, so that her fears on this score are exaggerated. In the end, then, I conclude that 'the argument from anti-scepticism' is in fact no better than the earlier 'argument from autonomy' in motivating a turn from realism to constructivism, either in reading Kant or in ethics more generally.

In the following two papers, I turn away from the consideration of debates between constructivism and realism as such, but move on to an issue which still relates to the earlier discussion of the distinction between the right and the obligatory: namely to a consideration of the thesis that 'ought implies can', and the place of this thesis in Kant's ethics. In this first of these papers entitled 'Does "Ought" Imply "Can"? And Did Kant Think It Does?' I consider the position of those (such as James Griffin) who wish to use the principle to claim that morality must be such as to fit our capacities, as otherwise the principle of 'ought implies can' would be violated. However, I argue that an argument of this sort overlooks the distinction between what we may be under an obligation to do, and what it is right to do, where a lack of capacity may undercut the former but not the latter; and thus if we take morality to encompass the right, and not just the obligatory, then it may still be wider than what our capacities for action make possible. So, to take a simple example, while it may be impossible for me to keep a promise to you because I am at present tied to a chair, and therefore under no obligation to do so, it may still for all that remain *right* for me to keep the promise and wrong of me not to do it, even while recognizing that I cannot. I then turn to a discussion of Kant, and by looking at various relevant passages, I argue that nothing shows that he would have understood the principle in the strong way that Griffin and others want to use it; on the contrary, they show that while Kant may have held we cannot be under an obligation to do what we cannot do, they do not show that he held that what is right for us to do is circumscribed by what we can do, and thus that our capacities place any constraint on the moral law as such, even if they may influence the extent to which we stand under its obligations. By turning on the distinction between the right and the obligatory in this way, this discussion also fits and reinforces the hybrid account of Kant's position presented earlier, which distinguishes between the moral law on the one hand, and its obligatory force on the other.

Some of these difficulties in understanding 'ought implies can', and what it involves, arguably stem from a lack of clarity concerning what it is that makes the principle plausible in the first place, and thus what grounds it. In the paper 'Why Does Ought Imply Can?' I raise this issue, which has been surprisingly little discussed. I set the principle in the context of the kind of theories of obligation that might go with it (where I consider divine command accounts, natural law accounts, self-legislation accounts, and social command accounts), and explore the way that each offers a rather different perspective on the principle, and why it might hold. My aim here is not to defend the principle as such, but to explore the kind of commitments that might be required to make it plausible, where it turns out that they can be interestingly various.

These first seven papers have largely focused on themes raised by Kant's ethics as such; the second part of the collection widens the canvas to include consideration of post-Kantian developments, beginning with Hegel's influential critical response to Kant's moral theory. In this section, in the paper 'On Hegel's Critique of Kant's Ethics: Beyond the Empty Formalism Objection', I start by considering Hegel's well-known 'empty formalism' objection to Kant's first formulation of the categorical imperative, the so-called Formula of Universal Law: '*act only in accordance with that maxim through which you can at the same time will that it become a universal law*'. Hegel's claim that this principle is merely formal, and hence unable to provide any content to the moral law in a way that will actually enable us to distinguish right from wrong, has persuaded many that it is unworkable on its own, including many Kantians. However, those Kantians have rightly pointed out that Kant offers other related formulations, particularly the Formula of Humanity, which seem precisely designed to provide the content that is arguably missing in the Formula of Universal Law, so that in the end the Hegelian critique can be blunted, once the full Kantian picture is brought into play. This dialectic has led to an uneasy truce between Kantians and Hegelians, the former conceding that there is some force to Hegel's concerns, but that in the end Kant has the resources to deal with them; while the latter have been satisfied to have those concerns taken seriously, and so not taken the critique much further, where Hegel doesn't seem to have offered any objections to the Formula of Humanity as such.

I argue, however, that there is a deeper issue underlying Hegel's critique of Kant here, which is that he wants to reject the whole project of which Kant's attempt at formulating an ethical principle is an instance, namely the project of searching for *the* 'supreme principle of morality', as a single principle we can adopt in guiding us in moral matters, whether that be the Formula of Universal Law, the Formula of Humanity, or some suitably subtle union of the two. For, while the value of such a project may seem to have been taken for granted by Kant, I argue that Hegel's particularism and contextualism in moral matters leads him to question it, as based on a false rationalism in ethics that will lead us astray. Thus, to settle the differences between Kant and Hegel here it is not enough to just bring in the Formula of Humanity as a response to the empty formalism objection: something more radical is required. I suggest, however, that a rapprochement between the two philosophers may still be possible, if we have a suitable understanding of *why* it was that Kant thought we might need a single 'supreme principle of morality' in the first place, which is not to resolve puzzling moral questions as such, but rather to help us see through our temptations to act in a non-moral way, by making clear what it is at stake in acting morally in an admittedly artificial but suitably stark manner.

If this first paper deals with a possible Hegelian critique of Kant, the next one entitled 'Does Hegelian Ethics Rest on a Mistake?' deals conversely with a possible Kantian critique of Hegel, based around the concerns raised by H. A. Prichard that were discussed earlier, which may be said to have a Kantian pedigree. For, the worry considered in this next discussion is whether, from a Prichardian perspective, ethics of an Hegelian kind may be said to fall into the trap of offering non-moral reasons to be moral, and thus to rest on a fundamental mistake. This objection may seem plausible, insofar as an Hegelian approach to ethics makes ethical life within a community of others essential to our self-realization as individuals, thus seeming to provide agents with a motivation to live ethically that is in the end self-interested, as Prichard feared. This paper considers this worry as it applies to T. H. Green, F. H. Bradley, and Hegel himself, arguing that while Green perhaps finds it hard to avoid, Bradley sticks to a more genuinely Hegelian approach, and as such is in a better position to address it, as is Hegel himself.

The next paper, entitled '"My Station and its Duties": Social Role Accounts of Obligation in Green and Bradley', also draws a contrast between these two thinkers from the British Idealist tradition. The aim of the paper is to consider what account of moral obligation best fits their approach, where this is often summarized in the slogan 'my station and its duties'. According to some commentators, this slogan is to be read as what I call an 'identificatory account' of obligation: namely, the directive force of an individual's duties comes from the fact that these individuals identify themselves with a certain social role, which then constrains them to act as a result. By contrast, I argue that Green's position is closer to the Kantian account suggested in the first paper in the collection, while Bradley holds what I have elsewhere identified as the kind of social command account to be found in Hegel.[10]

In the paper that follows entitled 'The Ethics of the British Idealists: Perfectionism after Kant', I consider some broader questions raised by the ethics of the British Idealists and where they stand in relation to Kant, again focusing primarily on Green and Bradley. The aim of this paper to consider their place in the perfectionist tradition in ethics, and what their positions might tell us about Kant's impact on that tradition. By 'perfectionism' here, I mean the suggestion (often associated with Aristotle in particular) that following the moral life will lead to human

[10] See Stern 2012: Chapter 5.

self-realization and thus well-being. As we have already noted in discussion of Prichard, one concern is that taking this idea seriously will reduce moral motivation to self-interest, where Prichard may be seen to be following Kant's general objection to this approach, which is that it makes morality heteronomous by grounding it in our desire for happiness. In this paper, I suggest that Kant's critique of perfectionism led the British Idealists to develop this tradition in two contrasting directions, which before Kant had been conjoined, but which under Kantian pressure came apart. The first, exemplified by Green, saw perfection in terms of the successful development of certain capacities of the individual, while the second, exemplified by Bradley, saw the perfection of the individual in holistic terms, as constituted by a unity of different elements within a single coherent self. I suggest that Bradley's model of perfectionism is better placed than Green's to respond to the Kantian objections to the perfectionist tradition that lead to this bifurcation in its elaboration at the hands of these British Idealists.

In the next paper ('Round Kant or Through Him? On James's Arguments for Freedom, and their Relation to Kant's'), I turn from the idealist response to Kant, to the pragmatist one, where the focus is now on William James. I argue that while James claimed it is best to go 'round Kant' rather than 'through him', a consideration of James's arguments against determinism in fact display a clear Kantian pedigree, particularly in the light of Kant's famous claim that the moral law is the *ratio cognoscendi* for freedom. However, exactly what this claim amounts to, both in Kant and in James, is a much disputed matter, where for some it has seemed to put our belief in freedom beyond the pale of rationality, or perhaps to make it something other than a belief at all. I suggest, however, that both Kant and James can be seen as evidentialists about this issue, but where they are distinctive is in taking practical reason to provide us with the evidence for freedom that is required, thus giving it primacy over theoretical reason in this quite specific (and more defensible) sense.

Having dealt with debates in the post-Kantian tradition that concern mainly the nineteenth and early twentieth century, I turn finally to two discussions that are more contemporary, one concerning a critique of Kant's ethics offered by the Danish philosopher and theologian K. E. Løgstrup in the 1950s and 1960s, and one concerning an essentially Kantian critique of divine command ethics offered recently by Stephen Darwall.

In the paper '"Duty and Virtue are Moral Introversions": On Løgstrup's Critique of Morality', I consider Løgstrup's claim that Kant's emphasis on duty distorts his account of the properly functioning moral agent, who should act out of concern for the other rather than with doing her duty as such. While Løgstrup's critique does raise genuine issues, I suggest that the Kantian is nonetheless able to show that it rests on an over-simplified account of what Kant's position amounts to, and that in the end Løgstrup's criticisms are misplaced. Nonetheless, I argue, there is a sense that Kant himself would share Løgstrup's misgivings about the role of duty in our moral lives, as is shown by the contrast between the human and the holy wills discussed previously: it is precisely because the holy will does not experience the moral in terms of duty that such wills count as ethically superior to our forms of willing, where on this matter it is arguably Kant's and Løgstrup's shared Lutheran heritage that comes through, in a way that illuminates Løgstrup's fundamental misgivings concerning an ethics of duty.

In the final paper 'Divine Commands and Secular Demands: On Darwall on Anscombe on "Modern Moral Philosophy"', I consider a very interesting recent contribution by Stephen Darwall to the critique of divine command ethics, which incorporates some important Kantian claims. Darwall argues that divine command ethics can be criticized in an internal or immanent manner, in such a way that it must give way to something more like a social command conception of moral obligation instead. The key move here is that divine command cannot be merely coercive, but must instead involve the exercise of legitimate authority, but where the conditions for that (Darwall argues) require the acknowledgement that we can also exercise authority over one another, thus displacing God from his supposedly unique position as the source of moral obligation, and transferring it to ourselves. Thus, Darwall argues, he can turn on its head Anscombe's famous claim in her article 'Modern Moral Philosophy' (which echoes Schopenhauer's position outlined previously), that moral obligation only makes sense if commanded by God; on the contrary, he suggests, that idea of divine command itself only makes sense if the basis of moral obligation turns out to be the moral community of rational agents of which we are all part.

However, while acknowledging the attractiveness of Darwall's project,[11] I suggest that in fact his attempt to offer an *internal* critique of the divine command position is misplaced, and that his claim to have done so breaks down at certain fundamental points. I also argue that some of the difficulties which Darwall raises for the divine command theorist can be met if we take seriously the place of gratitude to God in their account, where this attitude is importantly seen as a virtue rather than as itself falling under a duty or obligation.

The hope is, therefore, that this series of connected papers bring out a strand of inter-related issues that form a 'spine' in Kantian ethics, concerning Kant's particular understanding of obligation, value, agency, autonomy, and rationality, and how this has influenced certain key figures in what has come after him. Despite occasional protestations to the contrary, it seems to me that there is little doubt that Kant's ethics will always form one of the key positions in our philosophical reflection on our moral lives, even if just as a point of contestation; my intention here has been to take that reflection a little further.

[11] Though for some further reservations, see Stern 2014.

PART I
Themes from Kant's Ethics

1

Kant, Moral Obligation, and the Holy Will

> O Duty,
> Why hast thou not the visage of a sweetie or a cutie?
> Ogden Nash, 'Kind of an Ode to Duty'

Compared to many other aspects of his rich and complex practical philosophy, Kant's discussion of the holy or divine will, and the distinction that he draws between that will and one such as our own, has been little discussed. In some ways this is surprising, as it is a distinction that Kant draws frequently, and which he uses to do important work in his ethical theory. On the other hand, this neglect in the literature on Kant is also readily explicable—for in a context where the predominant mood of ethical theorizing is secular, talk of 'the holy will' may in itself cause misgivings; and at the same time, at the core of Kant's discussion seems to lie one of those notorious 'Kantian dualisms' (here between reason and desire), where sympathetic commentators have perhaps been understandably wary of making too much of the notion as a result. It may seem best, then, to treat this distinction as of no great significance both to Kant and to philosophy in general, and to pass over it in somewhat embarrassed silence.

In this paper, by contrast, I want to argue that this attitude is mistaken, and that in fact there are valuable insights to be gained by reflecting on the distinction in the way that Kant does, so that when it comes to Kant's practical philosophy, it should be given as much prominence as the related distinction in Kant's theoretical philosophy between the intuitive and discursive intellects.[1] I will begin by setting out the way in which Kant conceives of the distinction between the holy will and our own, and what work he uses it to do (sections 1.1 to 1.3), and then try to settle some misgivings that may arise concerning it (section 1.4). I will then explain how, when it comes to familiar debates in ethics between realism and anti-realism, and between externalism and internalism, we can see Kant's distinction as enabling him to combine elements of both sides in a way that may fruitfully resolve these controversies, and so

[1] Lewis White Beck makes this comparison: see Beck 1960: 50.

contribute to the contemporary discussion (sections 1.5 and 1.6). Thus, I will try to show, far from being an element in his thought that we would do best to ignore, Kant's conception of the holy will is therefore one that deserves to be taken seriously, as well as being integral to a proper understanding of his ethical views.

1.1 On Kant's Distinction between the Divine and Human Wills

Kant draws a distinction between the holy will and a will such as ours throughout his ethical writings, and in his lectures on ethics. The actual difference he points to is in essence a simple one, and obviously relates to standard theological conceptions of our 'fallen' nature: whereas a divine will acts only in line with the good, and has no inclinations to do otherwise, we have immoral desires and inclinations, that mean we find ourselves drawn to adopt immoral courses of action. As Kant puts it: 'The dispositions [*Gesinnungen*] of the deity are morally good, and those of man are not. The dispositions or subjective morality of the divine are therefore coincident with objective morality',[2] but ours are not.

While the contrast Kant draws is itself perhaps not unusual, however, the way Kant uses it is considerably more distinctive. For, he deploys it in order to explain the particular force that morality has for us, which takes the form of a *command* or *imperative*, as telling us that there are things that we *must* or *must not* do—what Kant calls 'constraint' or 'necessitation' (*Nötigung*). In many passages, Kant explains this obligatoriness in terms of the distinction between the holy will and our own, arguing that it is because we have dispositions to do things other than what is right, that the right for us involves a moral 'must'; but for a holy will, which has no inclination to do anything other than what is right, no such 'must' applies. A typical statement of Kant's view is the following from the *Groundwork of the Metaphysics of Morals*:

A perfectly good will would, therefore, equally stand under objective laws (of the good),[3] but it could not on this account be represented as *necessitated* to actions in conformity with law since

[2] Kant *LE*: 56 [27:263]. Cf. Kant *LE*: 68 [27:1425]: 'The divine will is in accordance with the moral law, and that is why His will is holiest and most perfect... God wills everything that is morally good and appropriate, and that is why His will is holy and most perfect'; and *LE*: 229 [29:604]: 'In the Gospel we also find an ideal, namely that of holiness. It is that state of mind from which an evil desire never arises. God alone is holy, and man can never become so, but the ideal is good. The understanding often has to contend with the inclinations. We cannot prevent them, but we can prevent them from determining the will'; and *LR*: 409 [28:1075]: 'A holy being must not be affected by the least inclination contrary to morality. It must be *impossible* for it to will something that is contrary to the moral law. So understood, no being but God is holy. For every creature always has some needs, and if it wills to satisfy them, it also has inclinations which do not always agree with morality. Thus the human being can *never* be *holy, but of course* [he can be] *virtuous*. For virtue consists precisely in *self-overcoming*.'

[3] The 'good' here can be broader than the moral good as it may include things that are good qua means; on the other hand, as Timmermann observes (2007: 62–3 note 27), 'it is most likely that Kant first and foremost has the *moral* law in mind when he says that the same objective laws of the good hold for both kinds of will [viz. human and holy] alike'.

of itself, by its subjective constitution, it can be determined only through the representation of the good. Hence no imperatives hold for the *divine* will and in general for a *holy* will: the 'ought' is out of place here, because volition is of itself necessarily in accord with the law. Therefore imperatives are only formulae expressing the relation of objective laws of volition in general to the subjective imperfection of the will of this or that rational being, for example, of the human will.[4]

Thus, the principles that determine what it is good and bad to do apply to the holy will, where these principles are laws because they hold of all agents universally, and of such agents independently of the contingencies of their desires and goals, and thus necessarily.[5] However, because the holy will is morally perfect, these laws lack any necessitating force for it, whereas our lack of moral perfection means that they possess such force for us.[6]

This, I take it, is the basic outline of Kant's position; but before adding some complexities to the discussion, let me next set out what issues Kant was concerned to address in putting it forward.

1.2 Explaining the Moral 'Must'

In making the distinction he does between the holy will and one like our own in the way we have outlined, Kant is offering part of a solution to a fundamental transcendental or 'how possible?' question in ethics: namely, how are categorical imperatives possible?[7] Unless we have a convincing answer to this question, Kant fears, we may doubt the intelligibility of the moral, where an aspect of the problem is that it can be hard to see what gives the commands of morality their special imperatival force, and thus what makes them necessitating: for, if we explain the source of the demand by appeal to a demander, such as God, then we would seem to undermine our freedom as moral agents, in making moral obedience into obedience to the will of another,

[4] Kant *GMM*: 67 [4:414].

[5] On universality, see: Kant *GMM*: 65 [4:412]: 'moral laws are to hold for every rational being as such'. On necessity, cf. Kant's distinction between *principles* and *laws*, where the former are what govern 'what it is necessary to do merely for achieving a discretionary purpose', and so can be 'regard as in [themselves] contingent and we can always be released from the precept if we give up the purpose', whereas a moral law 'leaves the will no discretion with respect to the opposite, so that it alone brings with it that necessity which we require of a law' (Kant *GMM*: 72 [4:420]). Cf. also Kant *GMM*: 44–5 [4:389].

[6] Cf. Kant *MM*: 377 [6:222]: 'An imperative is a practical rule by which an action in itself contingent is *made* necessary. An imperative differs from a practical law in that a law indeed represents an action as necessary but takes no account of whether this action already inheres by *inner* necessity in the acting subject (as in a holy being) or whether it is contingent (as in a human being); for where the former is the case there is no imperative. Hence an imperative is a rule the representation of which *makes* necessary an action that is subjectively contingent and this represents the subject as one that must be *constrained* (necessitated) to conform with the rule.'

[7] I say 'part of a solution', because the problem is not just that categorical imperatives are imperatival, but also that they are *categorical* and not merely hypothetical, where this is not an issue that concerns us here.

whilst also making morality conditional;[8] but if we treat the world in itself as exerting an obligatory force, we would seem to attribute to it a mysterious capacity for exerting authority over us. Thus, just as in the theoretical case, where Kant is concerned that worries about metaphysical necessity might lead us (as it did Hume) into doubting that synthetic a priori knowledge is possible, so in the practical case, Kant is concerned that doubts about the necessitation involved in the moral 'must' might lead us into doubt concerning the moral law. As Kant puts it: 'This question does not inquire how the performance of the action that the imperative commands can be thought, but only how *the necessitation of the will*, which the imperative expresses in the problem, can be thought [or conceived, or made sense of: *gedacht*]' (*GMS* 4:417, my emphasis).[9] If the 'must' in 'you must not tell lies' is not explained, therefore, this can leave us wondering how there can be any such necessity[10]—just as in the case of metaphysical necessity, we can be left wondering how it can be the case that every event *must* have a cause.

It can therefore be seen how Kant's distinction between the holy will and ours is designed to resolve this puzzle, by appeal to the fact that our will is divided between reason and inclination in a way that the will of the divine being is not, a division that Kant characterizes in the terms of his transcendental idealism as mapping onto the distinction between the noumenal and phenomenal realms (or the 'intelligible world' and 'the world of sense'):

> And so categorical imperatives are possible by this: that the idea of freedom makes me a member of an intelligible world and consequently, if I were only this, all my actions *would* always be in conformity with the autonomy of the will; but since at the same time I intuit myself as a member of the world of sense, they *ought* to be in conformity with it; and this *categorical* ought represents a synthetic proposition a priori, since to my will affected by sensible desires there is added the idea of the same will but belonging to the world of the understanding—a will pure and practical of itself, which contains the supreme condition, in accordance with reason, of the former will... The moral "*ought*" is then [the person's] own necessary "*will*" as a member of the intelligible world, and is thought by him as "ought" only insofar as he regards himself at the same time as a member of the world of sense.[11]

[8] Cf. *GMM*: 91 [4:443]. The extent to which this passage shows Kant to be opposed to divine command theories in this way has been disputed recently by John Hare, however. See Hare 2000a, Hare 2000b, Hare 2001a: 87–119, and Hare 2009: 122–75. Whilst I believe that Hare's position is mistaken, I do not have space to challenge it here, and will simply follow what I take to be the more orthodox line without any further defence. I respond to Hare at greater length in Stern 2012: 58–67.

[9] For a helpful discussion of the background to this issue in Wolff and Baumgarten, see Schwaiger 2009.

[10] Cf. Garner 1990: 141 and 143: 'How could *any* feature of something outside us make it the case that we are objectively required to do something?... It is the peculiar combination of objectivity and prescriptivity... that makes moral facts and properties queer... It is hard to believe in objective prescriptivity because it is hard to make sense of a demand without a demander, and hard to find a place for demands and demandingness apart from human interests and conventions. We know what it is for our friends, our job, and our projects to make demands on us, but we do not know what it is for *reality* to do so.' Garner is of course here explicating one aspect of J. L. Mackie's famous 'argument from queerness'.

[11] Kant *GMM*: 100–1 [4:454–5]. Cf. also *LE*: 274–5 [27:510]: 'Although the obligation is established by reason, it is nevertheless assumed that in the performance of our duty we have regard to ourselves as

Kant thus uses his transcendental idealism, and his dualistic picture of the will, to help address the transcendental question he raises concerning the imperatival nature of morality, in order to explain hereby how that is possible. Kant's distinction between the holy will and ours therefore forms a crucial part of his answer to the problem of accounting for the moral 'must', in a way that explains its possibility (unlike a view that simply treats the 'must' as a feature of the world), but without recourse to the problematic notion of a divine legislator as the source of that 'must' (thus avoiding any need to adopt a divine command theory).

1.3 Analysing the Distinction

Having shown the way Kant sets out the distinction, and indicated the role he gives it within his practical philosophy, I now want to examine it in a little more detail. For, although in some ways Kant's position is fairly straightforward, it is nonetheless not without its ambiguities.

One issue concerns what it is about the holy will, exactly, that makes it the case that there is no moral obligation for a will of this kind. The simplest answer to this question, which I have largely adopted in sketching Kant's position above, is to think that morality lacks any obligatory force for the holy will because it has no *resistance* to morality: unencumbered as it is by any non-moral desires and inclinations, it feels no *constraint* in acting morality, because nothing in its will fights against the moral course of action as determined by reason, and so no part of its will has to be restrained or held back in any way. This picture fits with many passages from Kant, such as when he says that if we had a holy will 'the [moral] law would finally cease to be a command to us, since we would never be tempted to be unfaithful to it';[12] or characterizes a '*holy* (superhuman) being' as one 'in whom no hindering impulses would impede the law of its will and who would thus gladly do everything in conformity with the law';[13] or states that '[God is] unlimited only in this, that no moral necessitation can be supposed in Him, in regard to the determination of His will, since he lacks the limitations imposed on human nature, of an inclination to contravene the laws'.[14]

However, as well as this way of characterizing what is distinctive about the holy will, as being a will that lacks any non-moral inclinations, Kant also characterized the

passive beings, and that another person must be present, who necessitates us to duty. Crusius found this necessitating person in God, and Baumgarten likewise in the divine will, albeit known through reason, and not positively, and on this principle a particular moral system has been erected. If, however, we pay heed to self-regarding duties, then man is presented in his physical nature, i.e., insofar as he is subject to the laws of nature, as the obligated, and rightly so; but if the obligator is personified as an ideal being or moral person, it can be none other than the legislation of reason; this, then, is man considered solely as an intelligible being, who here obligates man as a sensory being, and we thus have a relationship of man qua phenomenon towards himself qua noumenon. The situation is similar in obligations towards others.' For a closely related passage, see *MM*: 543–4 [6:417–18].

[12] *CPrR*: 206 [5:82]. [13] *MM*: 533 [6:402]. [14] *LE*: 304 [27:547].

holy will in terms that deploy more of his technical machinery, particularly the idea of a *maxim*. Unfortunately, however, there is some ambiguity in Kant's account of what maxims are, where this is then reflected in apparently contradictory claims Kant makes about how the holy will stands in relation to maxims—for, Kant sometimes states that the holy will (unlike us) has *no* maxims,[15] and sometimes that it has maxims, but unlike us, its maxims always coincide with the moral law.[16]

The difficulty here arises, because of an underlying unclarity in what Kant means in characterizing maxims as 'subjective principles of acting'.[17] At times he seems to mean by this nothing more than the idea that a maxim is a principle on which an agent acts or proposes to act, in which case there is no difficulty for him in attributing maxims to the holy will, and claiming that the principles on which it acts will always be ones that conform to the moral law. However, Kant also characterizes the 'subjective' nature of maxims in a further way, not just as principles employed by subjects in acting, but as principles that have merely subjective *validity*, in contrast to the objective validity of the practical law, where the subjectivity of a maxim in *this* sense mean that it holds only for the subject insofar as it relates merely to his or her 'conditions', such as what he or she is inclined to do, and thus does not apply to those whose 'conditions' are different. So, out of concern for my health, I might make it my maxim to drink less coffee because I think drinking coffee leads to insomnia; but this is merely a subjective rule, as it does not profess to be valid for anyone else, relating as it does to my particular inclinations, and my views about the effects of coffee on my sleep and insomnia on my health. By contrast, on this picture, a moral principle has an objectivity that maxims lack, because they do indeed apply to others, where here the relevant grounds or conditions are not confined to the individual subject.[18] Thus, while in both cases, because they are general principles, maxims and practical laws are determined by reason, in the former case it is reason working on the basis of the

[15] Cf. *CPrR*: 204 [5:79]: 'All three concepts, however—that of an *incentive*, of an *interest* and of a *maxim*—can be applied only to finite beings. For they all presuppose a limitation on the nature of a being, in that the subjective constitution of its choice does not of itself accord with the objective law of a practical reason; they presuppose the need to be impelled to activity by something because an internal obstacle is opposed to it. Thus they cannot be applied to the divine will.'

[16] Cf. *GMM*: 88 [4:439]: 'A will whose maxims necessarily conform with the laws of autonomy is a *holy*, absolutely good will'; and *CPrR*: 165 [5:32]: 'a *holy* will... would not be capable of any maxim conflicting with the moral law'.

[17] Cf. *GMM*: 73 note [4:420], and also *GMM*: 56 note [4:401].

[18] Cf. *CPrR*: 153 [5:19]: 'Practical *principles* are propositions that contain a general determination of the will, having under it several practical rules. They are subjective, or *maxims*, when the condition is regarded by the subject as holding only for his will; but they are objective, or practical *laws*, when he condition is cognized as objective, that is, as holding for the will of every rational being.' Cf. also *LE*: 263 [27:495]: 'The *maxim* of an action differs, that is, from an objective principle in this, that the latter occurs only insofar as we consider the possibility of the action on certain rational grounds, whereas the former includes all subjective grounds of action whatsoever, insofar as they are taken to be real. N.B. The principle is always objective, and is called a maxim *quoad subjectum* [as to the subject]. It is understood as the rule universally acknowledged by reason, while the maxim is the subjectively practical principle, insofar as the subject makes the rule by which he is to act into the motive of his action as well.'

particular agent's particular preferences and so framing principles with limited applicability, while in the latter it is reason arriving at genuine laws that apply to all, independent of these circumstances. Now, given *this* conception of maxims, as having only subjective validity in this sense, it is understandable why Kant might come to say that the holy will lacks them altogether: for, if none of the 'conditions' that give merely subjective validity to maxims apply to the holy will, and if instead the only principles that guide it are the principles of the objectively valid practical law, then it becomes clear why Kant might claim that we cannot think of the holy will as having maxims—but it also becomes clear why, given the *other* way in which the notion of a maxim is also used by Kant, he might allow that the holy will can have maxims, and speak of the holy will in these terms.[19]

Having resolved the apparent contradictions in Kant's position with regard to the holy will on the issue of maxims, we can now turn to another area where there also might appear to be some ambiguity: namely, on what basis does Kant claim that the holy will cannot be obligated to act, or stand under a duty? In the first section, I suggested that Kant's reason for this claim is that he thought that for these notions to apply to an agent, what it is right for them to do must exert some necessitating force, which is impossible in the case of a holy will, as it lacks the inclination to do anything other than the moral action; but there is another way of taking Kant's position here that should be considered.

On this alternative view, the reason why the holy will has no duties or obligations, is that duties and obligations require the agent to be able to *fail* to act as they are obligated to do, so that in this sense 'ought implies might not'. Kant's position has been presented along these lines by Samuel Kerstein, who writes that

> According to Kant, one can be obliged to do something only if there is some possibility that he will fail to do it. Yet some beings, for example, God, might be such that they cannot fail to obey the supreme principle of morality. It would thus make no sense to say that they have an obligation to obey it.[20]

Kerstein cites evidence that Kant believed in the 'ought implies might not' principle by pointing to a passage in the *Metaphysics of Morals*, where Kant is discussing whether we could have a duty to pursue our own happiness, which Kerstein reads as saying that 'an agent cannot have an obligation to promote the end of his own happiness, since each agent unavoidably has this end' (Kerstein 2002: 193 note 4).

[19] Cf. Paton 1967: 61: 'Kant speaks at times as if all maxims are grounded on sensuous inclinations, and consequently as if a divine or holy will could have no maxims. A holy will would have no maxims which were not also objective principles; but to say this is not to deny that it acts in accordance with maxims, if we interpret "maxims" to mean principles manifested in action. It is all-important to recognize that while maxims are commonly based on inclinations . . . it may nevertheless be possible to act on maxims which are not so based.'

[20] Kerstein 2002: 2.

Now, the principle 'ought implies might not' is perhaps plausible, and there is some additional textual evidence that Kant held it as a necessary condition for obligatoriness.[21] But in fact the passage Kerstein cites seems to suggest that Kant also believed that more was required to account for obligatoriness as it applies to us; for here Kant says that we cannot have the duty to pursue our happiness because this happiness accords with our desires, and thus there is no experience of *resistance* in aiming at happiness as an end (in contrast, say, to our own perfection, where we do experience resistance from desire, and where therefore it makes sense to speak of a duty to self):

His own happiness is an end that every human being has (by virtue of the impulses of his nature), but this end can never without self-contradiction be regarded as a duty. What everybody already wants unavoidably, of his own accord, does not come under the concept of *duty*, which is *constraint* to an end adopted reluctantly. Hence it is self-contradictory to say that he is *under obligation* to promote his own happiness with all his powers.[22]

Here Kant clearly seems to make the conceptual claim that I am interested in, and not just the one attributed to him by Kerstein, namely that '*duty*... is *constraint* to an end adopted reluctantly', where it is precisely this lack of 'reluctance' and hence constraint that seems to make the concept of duty 'self-contradictory' in this context—and thus, equally contradictory in the case of the holy will.[23] In the light of this

[21] See for example: *LE*: 256 [27:486]: 'In God the nature of action is likewise that it accords with the moral laws which are formed by the concepts of the highest reason; save only that since no subjective possibility of contravening such laws is possible in His Case, His actions being morally necessary both objectively and subjectively, no imperative is appropriate to Him either, since however He acts, He does so in accordance with the moral laws, and will at all times act freely and unconditionally'; *GMM* 67 [4:414]: 'Hence no imperatives hold for the *divine* will and in general for the *holy* will: the "ought" is out of place here, because volition is of itself necessarily in accord with the law'; *GMM*; 96–7 [4:449]: 'this "ought" is strictly speaking a "will" that holds for every rational being under the condition that reason in him is practical without hindrance; but for beings like us—who are also affected by sensibility, by incentives of a different kind, and in whose case that which reason by itself would do is not always done—that necessity of action is called also an "ought," and the subjective necessity is distinguished from the objective'; and *MM*: 377 [6:222]: 'An imperative differs from a practical law in that a law indeed represents an action as necessary but takes no account of whether this action already inheres by an *inner* necessity in the acting subject (as in a holy being) or whether it is contingent (as in the human being); for where the former is the case there is no imperative.'

[22] *MM*: 517 [6:386]. Cf. also *CPrR*: 170 [5:37]: 'A command that everyone should seek to make himself happy would be foolish, for one never commands of someone what he unavoidably wants already.' Of course, 'foolishness' is a weaker notion than self-contradictoriness, but is a negative mark against such a command nonetheless.

[23] Kant seems to have this view in several other passages, e.g. *MM*: 512 [6:379]: 'The very *concept of duty* is already the concept of a *necessitation* (constraint) of free choice through the law. This constraint may be an *external constraint* or a *self-constraint*. The moral *imperative* makes this constraint known through the categorical nature of its pronouncements (the unconditional ought). Such constraint, therefore, does not apply to rational beings as such (there could also be *holy* ones) but rather to *human beings*, rational *natural* beings, who are unholy enough that pleasure can induce them to break the moral law, even though they recognize its authority; and even when they do obey the law, they do so *reluctantly* (in the face of opposition from their inclinations), and it is in this that such *constraint* properly consists'; and *LE*: 236 [29:616–17]: '*Necessitas actionis invitae* [necessity of action against one's will] is a compulsion. For this it is

textual evidence, I think it is reasonable to conclude that there is more to Kant's position here than just an appeal to the 'ought implies might not' principle, and that the account I offered in the first section should be allowed to stand.

1.4 Concerns about Kant's Distinction

Having further clarified Kant's position on the distinction between the holy will and our own, and how this relates to his account of duty and obligation, I now want to briefly consider concerns that might be raised about it, and about the work that Kant uses it to do.

1.4.1 The holy will and the good will

A first such concern might be to wonder whether Kant can in fact make the idea of the holy will, as he conceives it, consistent with his own philosophical position, and in particular with his conception of the good will. For, in the *Groundwork* and elsewhere, Kant famously characterizes the good will as a will that acts out of duty; but if the holy will cannot act in this way, how can it be good?

I think this worry underlies H. A. Prichard's claim, in his unpublished lectures on the *Groundwork*, that '[Kant's] idea of a holy will is untenable'.[24] Prichard argues that Kant must explain how the holy will is moved to action, where (Prichard states) the mere goodness or rightness of some state of affairs cannot explain this in itself. However, Kant has ruled out using a 'sense of obligation' as the explanation for action by the holy will, as this will is not supposed to have any such sense. Thus, Prichard argues, Kant is forced to say that the holy will acts out of a 'good desire'. But then, it seems, Kant has contradicted his own analysis of the good will, which is a will that acts out of a sense of duty, not inclination, no matter how beneficent: 'For though it is possible to perform duties from some good motive other than a sense of obligation, e.g. a desire arising from affection or public spirit, and though such an act will manifest goodness, the goodness manifested will not be moral goodness'.[25] The question Prichard is pressing, therefore, is the internal coherence of Kant's position: 'having formulated the spirit in which a moral being will act, viz. the sense of obligation',[26] but having deprived the holy will of any such sense, how can the holy will be a moral being?

While interesting and prima facie plausible, I think however that Prichard's concern can be allayed.

required, not only that our will be not morally good, but also that it have hindrances. A compulsion always presupposes a hindrance in the will. A man often has inclinations which conflict with the moral law. So duty we regard as a compulsion. A compulsion occurs when we have an inclination to the opposite of an action. The necessitation to an action, such that we have an inclination to its opposite, is therefore compulsion'. Cf. also *CPrR*: 165–6 [5:32]; 206–7 [5:83]; *LE*: 229–30 [29:605]; 234–5 [29:611]; *LE*: 282 [27:519]; 365 [27:623].

[24] Prichard 2002d: 55. [25] Prichard 2002d: 55–6. [26] Prichard 2002d: 56.

A first point to note, regarding Kant's conception of the good will itself, is that it is a mistake to think that Kant *identified* the idea of the good will with the will that acts from duty, as if goodness must always involve dutifulness. In fact, when introducing his conception of the good will at the beginning of the *Groundwork*, Kant says that dutifulness only characterizes the good will when thought of 'under certain subjective limitations and hindrances'; he just wants to stress that these 'subjective limitations and hindrances' do not take away its goodness altogether—indeed, 'far from concealing it and making it unrecognizable, [they] rather bring it out by contrast and make it shine forth all the more brightly'.[27] These 'subjective limitations and hindrances' are obviously the non-moral inclinations that prevent us from being holy wills, but where we can still display goodness through acting out of duty: but it is clear from the outset of the *Groundwork* that Kant did not *identify* being a good will with acting out of duty, but merely thought of this as a way of being good, under special constraints and conditions. There thus seems to be no incoherence, from a Kantian point of view, in holding that the holy will acts from the thought that doing this act would be good, and not from the thought that it is its duty.

Second, there are two possible responses one might give to Prichard's worry concerning the actions of a holy will, where Prichard thinks this is a worrisome issue because such actions cannot be explained as arising from a sense of duty (as a holy will has no such sense) or from desires (because a holy will has none). One response is to accept that Prichard is right to be puzzled here, but to argue that Kant would have not have seen anything problematic in such puzzlement; rather, it is just what we would expect, given our limited understanding of any such will (where, of course, this kind of response would fit with Kant's more general emphasis on our cognitive limitations regarding questions of this sort). Even if this kind of reply is in some ways unsatisfying, it is not clear why this still doesn't allow Kant's conception of the holy will to do the work he requires of it, namely to provide a contrast class to a will such as our own.

A more positive response, however, would be to challenge Prichard's claim that the holy will is a 'being without desire'[28] in *any* sense. For, of course, while holy wills must lack any desire to do what is wrong, we might still think of the holy will as having inclinations that are in accord with what is right, in a way that would explain the contrast with our own case, while making the agency of the holy will less inchoate than on the first response. So, if we first consider what moral action involves in our own case, Kant's account seems to be that we have various inclinations (such as the desire to commit suicide, or keep some money that has been borrowed), but where conscience then leads us to question such inclinations, and test their associated maxims, where the various formulae that Kant proposes are the tests we use to determine the rightness or wrongness of the actions we feel inclined to perform.[29] We

[27] *GMM*: 52 [4:397]. [28] Prichard 2002d: 55. [29] Cf. *GMM*: 73–5 [4:421–4].

can therefore think of the holy will as also having inclinations,[30] which are what lead it to act, but only inclinations that are moral; but when it acts on them, it does so because they have been assessed in accordance with the formulae and thus in moral terms, so it is not acting *merely* out of feeling or on the basis of inclinations. However, unlike us, because the holy will has no *non*-moral inclinations, these formulae do not constitute imperatives, or what it *ought* to do, but rather what it *will* do, in a way that makes the holy will exempt from duty and obligation, as Kant claims.

I will not attempt to adjudicate between these responses to Prichard here, but both seem available to Kant in ways that suggest the Prichardian worry can be defused. In fact, although Kant does not introduce this distinction very often or with much emphasis,[31] he might be said to draw the contrast between us and the holy will in *both* these ways, when he distinguishes between the human will on the one hand, and two *types* of holy will—namely *finite* holy wills and *infinite* ones. The former seem to have inclinations arising from their sensuous natures, but where these inclinations (unlike ours) are always in harmony with reason or at least offer no temptation to it, where the infinite holy will then appears to contrast with the finite holy will in having no inclinations at all. One might then worry, in a Prichardian manner, how such an infinite holy will could operate—but where again it may seem plausible to respond that such understanding is beyond us, while pointing to the finite holy will as a perhaps more intelligible but no less significant contrast class to the human case, on whom the imperatival force of morality still falls.

1.4.2 The holy will and 'Kantian dualism'

A second concern to consider is one that was mentioned at the outset: namely, that Kant's account of obligatoriness as it relates to a will that (like ours) is not holy, seems to be symptomatic of the sort of dualistic picture which his critics in the idealist and romantic traditions imputed to Kant, and which so troubled them—this time between reason and desire, duty and inclination. In searching for a more unified picture of the human agent, and in their unwillingness to accept any stark differentiation between the human and the divine, it is unsurprising that this issue of the holy will proved a sticking point for Kant's contemporaries and successors, from Schiller to Hegel.

Now, in order to get this issue into focus, it is important not to exaggerate or misidentify the concerns of Kant's critics here: in fact, there were significant areas of agreement. Thus, both Schiller and Hegel accepted that we are not immediately or spontaneously inclined to moral action, in the manner of the holy will, and that to acquire these moral inclinations require effort and work for us, through the results of education and habit-forming, in a broadly Aristotelian manner.[32] Indeed, Schiller

[30] For a defence of the view that we should see the holy will as having inclinations, see Willaschek 2006: 130–2.

[31] Cf. *MM*: 515 [6:383].

[32] For Schiller, cf. Schiller 1967: 15, where Schiller characterizes man's 'natural character' as 'selfish and violent'; and pp. 173–9, where Schiller characterizes man's natural state in amoral terms: 'Unacquainted as he is with his *own* human dignity, he is far from respecting it in others; and, conscious of his own savage

was prepared to follow Kant in taking this process to be one of endless striving, while even for Hegel it would require the coming into being of the rational State to be properly achieved.[33] Moreover, both Schiller and Hegel fully appreciated and sympathized with the motivations behind Kant's position, as required to redress the balance in ethics in favour of rationalism and notions of duty, and against feeling and eudaimonism.[34] It would be wrong to say, therefore, that Schiller and Hegel rejected the very distinction between the holy will and our own, and treated us simply as equivalent in moral character and dispositions to such a perfect moral agent.

However, while accepting the distinction, and even while accepting this makes it hard or even impossible to say that we could be compared to a will that is divine, by going without any non-moral inclinations, Schiller and Hegel nonetheless disagreed with Kant about the *difficulty* that a properly brought up human moral agent will find in resisting his or her non-moral inclinations, and thus Kant's tendency to make the idea of *struggle* and *resistance* central to his account of moral obligatoriness, and of human moral experience. Thus, while Schiller accepts that (unlike the holy will) we have non-moral inclinations, and these may always be part of our nature, he thinks we are also capable of 'inclinations to duty', of the sort that he associates

greed, he fears it in every creature which resembles him' (p. 173). For Hegel, cf. Hegel *PR*: §151, p. 195 [VII: 301]: 'But if it is simply *identical* with the actuality of individuals, the ethical [*das Sittliche*], as their general mode of behaviour, appears as a *custom* [*Sitte*]; and the *habit* of the ethical appears as a *second nature* which takes the place of the original and purely natural will and is the all-pervading soul, significance, and actuality of individual existence [*Dasein*]'; and §18 Z, p. 51 [VII: 69]: 'The Christian doctrine that man is by nature evil is superior to the other according to which he is good. Interpreted philosophically, this doctrine should be understood as follows. As spirit, man is a free being [*Wesen*] who is in a position not to let himself be determined by natural drives. When he exists in an immediate and uncivilized [*ungebildeten*] condition, he is therefore in a situation in which he ought not to be, and from which he must liberate himself. This is the meaning of the doctrine of original sin, without which Christianity would not be the religion of freedom.'

[33] Cf. Schiller 1967: 111; and Schiller 1962: 289/2005: 154: 'Human beings do have the task of establishing an intimate agreement between their two natures, of always being a harmonious whole, and of acting with their full human capacity. But this beauty of character, the ripest fruit of humanity, is only an idea that they can valiantly strive to live up to, yet, despite all efforts, can never fully attain'. Cf. also Schiller 1962: 293/2005: 158: 'In the emotions, agreement with the law of reason is only possible by contravening the demands of nature. And since nature, for ethical reasons, never withdraws her demands, and therefore everything on her side remains the same, no matter how the will behaves in relation to her, so here there is no agreement possible between inclination and duty, between reason and sensuousness; so humans cannot here act with their whole nature in harmony, but only with their reason.'

[34] Cf. Schiller 1962: 282/2005: 148: 'In common experience... pleasure is the reason for acting rationally. We have to thank the immortal author of the Critique, to whom fame is due for having reestablished healthy human reason out of philosophical reason, for the fact that morality itself has finally stopped using this language'; and cf. Hegel *PR*: 15–17 [VII: 18–20], and Hegel *EL*: §54 Z, p. 101 [VIII: 139]: 'This prevalent moral theory [prior to Kant] was, generally speaking, the system of *Eudaemonism* which, in response to the question of the vocation of man, imparted the answer that he must posit his *happiness* as his aim. Insofar as happiness was understood to be the satisfaction of man's particular inclinations, wishes, needs, etc., what is accidental and personal was made into the principle of his willing and its exercise. In reaction against this Eudaemonism, which lacked any firm footing, and opened the door to every sort of caprice and whim, Kant set up practical reason; and by so doing he expressed the demand for a determination of the will that is universal and equally binding upon all.'

with 'grace'.[35] And likewise, Hegel holds that while human beings are susceptible to 'natural drives' that go against morality, they are also capable of gaining emotional and affective satisfaction in moral action, and thus experiencing no necessary exertion in exercising the will when acting ethically.[36]

It might be said, however, that if this is the issue that underlies their residual worries concerning Kant's apparent 'dualism', it is an exaggerated one and does not really apply: for, it could be argued, nothing in Kant's picture of obligation actually *requires* any such struggle of this sort. Instead, it could be claimed, all Kant needs and all he is appealing to is a weaker notion, namely the idea that non-moral action is always *possible* for us in a way that it is not for the holy will; this means that morality serves to constrain us to the extent that it prevents us from taking this option, but where this need not involve any great inner battle between the forces of duty and inclination, reason and desire. That this is the best way to understand Kant's position has been argued by Philip Stratton-Lake:

> The moral law appears to us as an imperative because we do not necessarily will in accordance with it. It appears, therefore, as a *constraint* for a finite rational will. It is easy to take the notion of a constraint as implying that our natural inclinations are in some way essentially opposed to the requirements of the moral law. But Kant thinks that the moral law appears to us as necessitating, or constraining, not because our natural inclinations are intrinsically immoral, but because of the *contingency* of the connection between what we are inclined to do and what we ought to will. The notion of a constraint should not, therefore, be understood as presupposing a conception of inclination as essentially opposed to morality (a view that Hegel and Hegelians are fond of ascribing to Kant), but as expressing the fact that the moral law places a rational *limit* on the practical possibilities open to us in certain circumstances, and is recognised as such. The moral law does not appear to a perfectly rational being as a rational *constraint* because it does not limit the possibilities open to such a will. This is because such a being does not have possibilities open to it which can conflict with, and hence can be limited by, the moral law.[37]

[35] Cf. Schiller 1962: 297–308/2005: 160–70. Schiller's position is made more complicated, however, by his equal (and perhaps more Kantian) insistence of the significance of *dignity*, which consists in a greater degree of self-overcoming. For a fuller discussion of Schiller's position than I can give here, see Stern 2012: 103–35.

[36] Cf. Hegel *PR*: §151 Z, p. 195 [VII: 302]: 'Education [*Pädagogik*] is the art of making human beings ethical: it considers them as natural beings and shows them how they can be reborn, and how their original nature can be transformed into a second, spiritual nature so that this spiritual nature becomes *habitual* to them', and §124, p. 152 [VII:233], where Hegel (mis)quotes Schiller, and objects to the way in which 'abstract reflection... produces a view of morality as a perennial and hostile struggle against one's own satisfaction'.

[37] Stratton-Lake 2000: 37–8. Cf. also Stratton-Lake 1996: 50:

> I do not, however, think Kant did conceive of morality as essentially opposed to sensibility. The main textual evidence in support of the view that he did is his conception of duties, or obligations as constraints. Duty, according to Kant, is essentially a constraint for a finite will, and a finite will is a sensible will. But what can morality be constraining if it is not our sensible nature? And, it may be asked, what does it mean to say that morality is essentially a constraint on sensibility unless sensibility is conceived of as essentially opposing it?

On this sort of account, therefore, we can explain why Kant used the language of constraint and necessitation, insofar as morality limits our options in a way that it does not for the holy will, but not in a way that introduces the sort of dualistic picture that so concerned Schiller, Hegel, and many others.

However, while this reading of Kant might make his position more palatable to some tastes, the textual evidence is against it. Stratton-Lake cites in his support the following sentence from *The Metaphysics of Morals*, which may indeed seem to make nothing more than the point he attributes to Kant, that morality constrains us merely to the extent of limiting the various options proposed to us by our inclinations: 'The very *concept of duty* is already the concept of a *necessitation* (constraint) of free choice through the law'. However, Kant immediately continues:

> This constraint may be an *external constraint* or a *self-constraint*. The moral *imperative* makes this constraint known through the categorical nature of its pronouncement (the unconditional ought). Such constraint, therefore, does not apply to rational beings as such (there could also be *holy* ones) but rather to *human beings*, rational *natural* beings, who are unholy enough that pleasure can induce them to break the moral law, even though they recognize its authority; and even when they do obey the law, they do it *reluctantly* [*ungern*] (in the face of opposition from their inclinations), and it is in this that such *constraint* properly consists.[38]

Kant seems unequivocal here in emphasizing the element of struggle and consequent reluctance involved in obligation, and so exactly the element in his view that Schiller and Hegel found so problematic. And this is by no means an isolated passage, so that while he may have thought we could develop inclinations to be moral, Kant also seems to have held that where we are conscious of a duty, we must invariably experience reluctance, resistance, and a sense of hindrance—not just an awareness of the existence of possible non-moral options, but also the thwarted desire to take them.[39] For Kant, it seems, the concept of duty only makes sense in this context.

Moreover, if we downplay these aspects of Kant's view, we also arguably lose much of the explanatory power of Kant's position, which is to account for the felt necessity of morality, the way it exercises a certain authority or control over us—where Kant seems to rely on the 'clash' between the forces of reason and desire, duty and

But moral constraint need not be interpreted as overpowering the opposing force of sensibility. Moral constraint may be interpreted as a *rational limitation* of the possibilities open to one in certain situations... It is for this reason that duty is inapplicable to a holy will. Such a will is not constrained, or limited by morality because it necessarily wills what is right. Since it is not possible for a holy will to set itself to bring about anything other than a moral end, morality cannot be conceived of as a limitation on the possible courses of action open to it. It is, however, *possible* for a finite will to set itself to bring about some end other than the one required by morality. On this interpretation, then, Kant's view does not commit him to the view that morality and sensibility are essentially opposed, but only to the view that they *may* be opposed.

[38] *MM*: 512 [6:379]. [39] Cf. the passages cited above, note 23.

inclination, to account for this experience.[40] If we go too far in depriving Kant of his 'dualism', therefore, we will arguably lose this aspect of his account, which is required if he is to do justice to what he is setting out to explain.[41] Conversely, Kant's critics such as Schiller and Hegel are not in a good position to make sense of this feature of our moral life, and so attempt to downplay it or do away with it altogether: but it is arguable that this leaves them failing to leave room for the demandingness that ethics must require, if it is not to become complacent and ask too little of us. Thus, while Kant can be accused by Schiller and Hegel of seeming to make morality go against the grain of our dispositions, Schiller and Hegel can in their turn be accused of compromising the critical force of morality and potentially radical nature of its demands, by trying to prevent morality from going beyond them in this way.[42]

1.4.3 Accounting for necessitation without the distinction

However, even if it is accepted that it is important for an account of obligation to explain the imperatival force that morality has for us as a feature of our moral experience, it might be said that alternative and better ways of doing this can be found, that can do without Kant's distinction between the holy will and our own.

An alternative strategy of this sort has been put forward recently by Christine Korsgaard. On the one hand, she has little sympathy with attempts to downplay the role of necessitation as a psychological force in our moral lives,[43] and to replace it with what she calls the 'Good Dog' picture of the virtuous agent, as someone 'whose

[40] Cf. Sidgwick 1907: 77 (my emphasis): 'Such cognitions [of the rightness and wrongness of conduct], again, I have called 'dictates', or 'imperatives'; because, insofar as they relate to conduct on which anyone is deliberating, they are accompanied by a certain impulse to do the acts recognised as right, *which is liable to conflict with other impulses*'. As Sidgwick makes clear on pp. 34–5 (to which he is referring back here), it is this conflict which he makes crucial to the commandingness of morality, and which he sees as distinctive to us as moral agents, much like Kant—where also much like Kant (I will argue in §1.5) he treats this picture as compatible with a realism about what is right: 'In fact, this possible conflict of motives seems to be connoted by the term "dictate" or "imperative," which describes the relation of Reason to mere inclinations or non-rational impulses by comparing it to the relation between the will of a superior and the wills of his subordinates. This conflict seems also to be implied in the terms "ought," "duty," "moral obligation," as used in ordinary moral discourse: and hence these terms cannot be applied to the actions of rational beings to whom we cannot attribute impulses conflicting with reason. We may, however, say of such beings that their actions are "reasonable," or (in an absolute sense) "right."' Cf. also Schneewind 1992: 317: '[For Kant] The term "ought" is central to our moral vocabulary because the tension between reason and desire is central to our moral experience.'

[41] Cf. Kant's response to Schiller in *Relig*, where Kant makes clear that he is unwilling 'to associate *gracefulness* with the *concept of duty*... For the concept of duty includes unconditional necessitation, to which gracefulness stands in direct contradiction' (*Relig*: 72 note [6:23]). Some commentators have taken Kant's subsequent talk of the joyous temperament that should go along with duty as a sign that he is in fact closer to Schiller's model of grace than this first comment suggests. But it is important that the joy taken is in the successful doing of one's duty and hence in the self-mastery that this has involved, not a joy that will somehow take this element of mastery away, in the manner of Schiller's model of grace.

[42] For further discussion of this and related issues, see Stern 2012: 247–52.

[43] Cf. Korsgaard 2009: 3: 'The normativity of obligation is, among other things, a psychological force. Let me give this phenomenon a name, borrowed from Immanuel Kant. Since normativity is a form of necessity, Kant calls its operation within us—its manifestation as a psychological force—*necessitation*.'

desires and inclinations have been so perfectly trained that he always does what he ought to do spontaneously and with tail-wagging cheerfulness and enthusiasm'.[44] On the other hand, she does not think necessitation can be accounted for by adopting the opposite model of the 'Miserable Sinner', which treats human beings as 'in a state of eternal reform, who must repress [their] unruly desires in order to conform to the demands of duty'.[45] Korsgaard claims that 'the opposition between the two pictures is shallow, for they share the basic intuition that the experience of necessitation is a sign that there is something wrong with the person who undergoes it', and thus they both 'denigrate the experience of necessitation'.[46] She also argues that both pictures fail to give an adequate account of how we are necessitated, or how it is we come to be bound to what is right or good.[47]

Now, Korsgaard sees Kant's attempt to offer an account of necessitation which employs the contrast between us and the holy will as fitting into the flawed 'Miserable Sinner' model; and though she accepts that therefore Kant in part adopted this model, she thinks he was wrong to do so, for the reasons outlined above.[48] But she thinks we can use different Kantian materials to develop a better and less shallow way of understanding necessitation, which traces the issue back to the struggle for self-constitution, and what is involved in that:

> I believe that these theories [associated with the 'Good Dog' and 'Miserable Sinner' models] both underestimate and misplace the role of necessitation in our psychic lives. There is work and effort—a kind of struggle—involved in the moral life, and those who struggle successfully are the ones whom we call "rational' or "good". But it is not the struggle *to be rational* or *to be good*. It is, instead, the ongoing struggle for integrity, the struggle for psychic unity, the struggle to be, in the face of psychic complexity, a single unified agent. Normative standards—as I am about to argue—are the principles by which we achieve the psychic unity that makes agency possible. The work of achieving psychic unity, the work that we experience as necessitation, is what I am going to call *self-constitution*.[49]

Korsgaard thus develops what she still thinks of as a Kantian account of necessitation, but one that makes no appeal to his conception of the holy will, and the contrast that conception allows Kant to draw with a finite will such as ours.

It is not possible here to work though Korsgaard's position in any detail, as she offers a complex view that requires extensive consideration to do it justice. However, I think there is an obvious potential difficulty for it, which does not seem to afflict the Kantian position which she rejects as based around the 'struggle to be good'. For, that position locates duty and obligation as arising from the way in which the goodness and rightness present themselves to us, and thus as residing in the moral situation, so

[44] Korsgaard 2009: 3. [45] Korsgaard 2009: 3.

[46] Korsgaard 2009: 3–4. [47] Korsgaard 2009: 4–7.

[48] Cf. Korsgaard 2009: 4 note 5, and Korsgaard 2008c: 52 note 39, where she states that 'the view that the will's imperfection is what makes us subject to an *ought*... is a red herring here'.

[49] Korsgaard 2009: 7.

that it is what is right and good that obligate and necessitate; but, by contrast, the worry about Korsgaard's account is that it puts this necessitation in the wrong place (so to speak), where it is the struggle of the subject to unify itself that is responsible for this as a 'psychic force', where this would seem to lack any underlying connection to anything normative. Someone might well think, therefore, that if there is any degree of struggle in morality, and if this is to be used to explain its obligatory force, then this struggle should revolve around the good and the right, not on the difficulties faced by the self-constituting subject—and this is more readily available on the picture of Kant's position that Korsgaard rejects, than on the one with which she replaces it.

Having now tried to clarify Kant's account of obligation, and shown how it rests on his distinction between the holy will and our own, and having responded to possible objections to my reading of that account, and to the account per se, I now want to go on to suggest two respects in which the account can be used to do some useful work, in enabling us to find a way out of two seemingly intractable disputes in ethics: those between realism and anti-realism, and between externalist and internalist accounts of motivation.

1.5 Applying the Distinction: Realism and Anti-realism

It is scarcely surprising that the dispute between realists and anti-realists in ethics is long-standing and ongoing, as both sides have their clear attractions, while also having their drawbacks, where each is often mirrored in the views of the other. In the recent literature on Kant, these respective advantages and disadvantages have been highlighted in competing interpretations of Kant himself, where both realist and anti-realist constructivist accounts have emerged.[50] Very broadly speaking, the contrast here is that the realist claims that moral facts (such as the fact that lying is wrong) hold independently of human attitudes, responses or choices (for example, of whether we disapprove of lying, or would reject lying in a contractual situation, or would in some way be irrational to adopt lying as a form of behaviour), while the anti-realist claims that these facts obtain precisely *because of* these attitudes, responses or choices—where for the *constructivist* anti-realist, what matters is that agents operating under certain real or ideal conditions would endorse or accept or choose some behaviours or outcomes over others, thereby making them right or good.

Now, given these contrasting views, there is then a familiar dialectical back-and-forth between them. On the one side, the realist will argue that the constructivist cannot accepting endorsing realism at some point, for unless some moral facts are

[50] On the constructivist side, these readings originate with John Rawls's seminal article Rawls 1980, and can be found in work by (for example) Korsgaard, O'Neill, and Reath. On the realist side, see for example, Kain 1999; Hare 2001a: 87–119; Ameriks 2003b; Irwin 2004; Kain 2004, 2006; Langton 2007; Hills 2008. There is also a realist aspect to Allen Wood's reading of Kant: see Wood 1999: 157 and pp. 374–5, notes 4 and 5; this is even clearer in Wood 2008 (see e.g. pp. 112–14).

taken to obtain *prior* to the choices we make as agents, where these choices are then governed by these facts, then the constructive procedure will be utterly unconstrained and its results morally arbitrary and relative. On the other side, the constructivist will argue that any such independent moral facts are too mysterious to be treated as explanatorily basic but are not in any way explained by the realist, while their independence from us makes them a threat to our autonomy as agents. Each side thus raises concerns (of emptiness and relativism on the one hand; and of 'queerness' and heteronomy on the other) that appear genuine and serious, but which neither can wholly address left to itself.

At this point, therefore, it is natural to look for a way out of the impasse: and I would argue that Kant's account of obligatoriness using his position on the holy will provides us with such a way forward. For, this account can be viewed as having two levels, and thus as a kind of 'hybrid' position that combines elements of realism with elements of anti-realism, to the advantage of both.

The realist level concerns the content of morality, what is right and wrong, and the value of freedom on which this rests. Kant is insistent in many passages that not even God can determine by an act of will or choice what this content is to be, as this is not contingent and chosen but fixed and necessary, and so obtains independently of any relation to an agent.[51] He also speaks in many passages as if he conceives of the value

[51] Cf. *LE*: 76 [27:282–3]:

> The lawgiver is not always simultaneously an originator of the law; he is only that if the laws are contingent. But if the laws are practically necessary, and he merely declares that they conform to his will, then he is a lawgiver. So nobody, not even the deity, is an originator of moral laws, since they have not arisen from choice, but are practically necessary; if they were not so, it might even be the case that lying was a virtue. But moral laws can still be subject to a lawgiver; there may be a being who is omnipotent and has power to execute these laws, and to declare that this moral law is at the same time a law of His will and obliges everyone to act accordingly. Such a being is then a lawgiver, though not an originator; just as God is no originator of the fact that a triangle has three corners.

and *MM*: 381 [6:227]:

> A (morally practical) *law* is a proposition that contains a categorial imperative (a command). One who commands (*imperans*) through a law is the *lawgiver* (*legislator*). He is the author (*autor*) of the obligation in accordance with the law, but not always the author of the law. In the latter case the law would be a positive (contingent) and chosen law. A law that binds us a priori and unconditionally by our own reason can also be expressed as proceeding from the will of a supreme lawgiver, that is, one who has only rights and no duties (hence from the divine will); but this signifies only the idea of a moral being whose will is a law for everyone, without his being thought of as the author of the law.

and cf. also *LE*: 302 [27:544]:

> Were we to conceive of the legislator as *auctor legis*, this would have reference only to statutory laws. But if we ascribe an *auctor* to laws that are known, through reason, from the nature of the case, he can only be an author of the obligation that is contained in the law. Thus God, too, by the declared divine will, is *auctor legis*, and precisely because natural laws were already in existence, and are ordained by Him.

For further discussion of this material and related passages, see Acton 1970: 38–9; Kain 1999: 177–99; Hare 2001a: 94–7; Irwin 2004; and Timmermann 2007: 106–7.

of the free rational agent in realist terms.[52] However, as we have seen, Kant does not treat the *obligatoriness* of what is right and wrong as independent in this way, for we give the content of morality its obligatory form, insofar as this depends on our limitedness as finite creatures, so that this obligatoriness is just the way in which what is right and wrong presents itself *to us*, from our human (all too human) perspective; from the perspective of a divine will, and so from the 'absolute standpoint', there *is* no duty and obligation, but only what is right and wrong, because the divine will has none of the non-moral inclinations which (as we have seen) means that what is right is represented to us in the form of duties and obligations, and thus as the moral 'must'.[53] Kant is thus able to side with the realist about the right, and thus avoids the spectre of emptiness and arbitrariness that threatens constructivism; but he is able to side with the anti-realist about the obligatory, and thus avoid much of the 'queerness' associated with the idea that the world in itself makes *demands* on us, and also avoid the threat to our autonomy that any such purely 'external' demand might seem to imply. Kant thus offers us a hybrid view, that is neither fully realist nor fully anti-realist 'all the way down', but combines elements of both to the advantage of his position as a whole.[54]

To a significant degree, therefore, I would argue that the basic structure of Kant's ethics resembles that of his theoretical philosophy, which equally employs a form/content distinction to combine realism with idealism. Thus, while Kant rejects an idealism that goes 'all the way down' and leads to a Berkeleyan subjectivism that would be unconstrained by the world, he also rejects a full-blown realism that aims to treat all our experience of that world as if it conformed to reality as it exists in itself, wholly independent of our perspective on it. And equally, of course, Kant hoped that this would enable us to escape the fruitless oscillation between empirical idealism on the one hand, and transcendental realism on the other. In ethics, it can therefore be argued, Kant could use his distinction between the divine will and our own to settle a similar kind of impasse, in a way that promises some of the similar dividends of his 'Copernican revolution' in theoretical philosophy.

[52] Cf. *GMM*: 78–9 [4:428]:

> But suppose there were something *the existence of which in itself* has an absolute worth, something which as *an end in itself* could be a ground of determinate laws; then in it, and in it alone, would lie the ground of a possible categorical imperative, that is, of a practical law.
>
> Now I say that the human being and in general every rational beings *exists* as an end in itself, *not merely as a means* to be used by this will or that will at its discretion.

[53] Cf. *CJ*: 273 [5:403–4]: 'It is clear that it depends only on the subjective constitution of our practical faculty that the moral laws must be represented as commands (and the actions which are in accord with them as duties), and that reason expressed this necessity not through a *be* (happening) but through a should-be.'

[54] I think Irwin also sees Kant as adopting this sort of hybrid view: '[Kant] recognizes intrinsic rightness without any acts of commanding or obligating... In Kant's view, commands and act of binding are [only] relevant to finite rational agents, who are also subject to other incentives and so have to be instructed and urged to follow the moral law' (Irwin 2004: 149).

1.6 Applying the Distinction: Externalism and Internalism

I now want to turn to a second area where again I believe that Kant's account of obligation also enables him to take a distinctive 'middle path', this time between externalism and internalism concerning the relation between the normative status of certain actions and the motivations of agents.[55]

This terminology is used in a number of different ways, but at the heart of the dispute I am interested in here is the question whether (as the internalist claims), for someone's actions to possess the moral status they have (of being right or wrong, or good or bad, or a duty, or an obligation, or something they ought to do, and so on), it is necessary for the agent to have (actually or dispositionally) a motivation so to act, so that the former depends on the 'internal states' of the latter; or whether on the other hand there is no such link or dependence, as the externalist claims. Thus, on the internalist view, the moral features of actions are said to be essentially related to considerations concerning motivation, thereby bringing in the motivational states of agents, not just features of the action that stand outside the agents concerned and are 'external' to them (for example, whether the action would maximize happiness, or is divinely commanded, or is 'fitting', or whatever).

One's stance on this dispute can be influenced by a variety of considerations, but perhaps three are central: the relation between cases of moral judgement and action; the threat of moral scepticism and how to deal with it; and the relation between this issue and meta-ethical disputes concerning realism and various forms of anti-realism.

On the first issue, internalists have been struck by the fact that in making a positive moral judgement concerning some action, it then seems very curious not to act or to at least admit to some inclination to doing so: surely, the internalist argues, (absent weakness of will and other complicating factors),[56] in these circumstances we would be forced to conclude that the agent did not really have the moral concept in the first place or had not genuinely made a judgement involving it[57]—where this then suggests (the internalist will claim) that what makes the moral judgement true partly concerns their motivational state and not just some fact 'external' to this. By contrast,

[55] This is to be distinguished from a different debate in ethics where the vocabulary of externalism and internalism is also used, which centres on *reasons*, where the internalist argues that for an agent to have a reason to act, that action must in some way relate to the agent's desires, interests, and concerns, in a way that the externalist denies. The debate I will discuss is also to be distinguished from another more closely related internalism/externalism dispute, which concerns motivations, but which focuses on whether making a positive moral judgement about an action can in itself give one a motivation to so act (internalism), or whether it can only do so in conjunction with some additional factor (such as a desire to act morally). Following Darwall, this position is often called *judgement internalism*, whereas the one I will discuss is called *existence internalism*: see Darwall 1992.

[56] For example, that there is a greater obligation to do something else.

[57] Cf. Smith 1994: 67–71.

externalists have thought that such cases, while in fact (thankfully) rare in practice (perhaps because most of us possess an antecedent disposition to act on our moral judgements, or that these judgements bring about such motivations in themselves), nonetheless do not involve any conceptual incoherence as such, as they would if to make a first-personal moral judgement about an action is to already attribute to oneself some motivation to so act.

On the issue of moral scepticism, internalists have taken it as an advantage of their view that a certain sort of moral sceptic is ruled out, namely a sceptic who makes a moral judgement concerning some action ('this is right', 'this is what I ought to do'), but denies any motivational connection to the action, and so still asks to be given some motivating reason to act in this way. Insofar as dispensing with the threat of scepticism is always desirable in a philosophical position, internalists have therefore claimed it as an advantage of theirs that it does so.[58] Against this, however, externalists have claimed that the internalist position is in fact implausibly strong when it comes to scepticism, in seeming to make amoralism of this kind incoherent, when in fact it is not—the amoralist, the externalist argues, is a perfectly conceivable creature, and we are not guilty of any conceptual error in taking him seriously as a threat.[59]

And on the background meta-ethical issue, philosophers have often been attracted to internalism because it seems most naturally to go along with an anti-realist position in ethics, as this most easily explains why the truth of a moral judgement depends on the motivational status of the agent: for example, on an expressivist view, moral facts are themselves grounded in the attitudes, desires, and passions of agents, where these are states that motivate the agent to act, so it is clear why the internalist claim might hold. On the other side, therefore, realists have generally been wary of accepting internalism in this form, fearing that to do so will push them into an anti-realist stance.

Here, then, we again have a debate where it is possible to be pulled both ways. For, even if the externalist is right to claim that there is not something wholly inconceivable in a person forming a moral judgement about an action and yet not being moved to act, on the other hand the internalist seems right to point out that there is *something* curious in this situation that needs to be explained. And even if the externalist is right that amoralist moral scepticism is not incoherent in every respect, on the other hand it would be good to have something to say to such a sceptic along internalist lines. And while the realist might be right to be wary of internalism, this does not in itself count as an argument against it, so that to anyone who is *not* a realist, it might instead count in its favour.

Now, from the perspective of Kant's position as I have characterized it, I think we are in a position to diagnose this debate, and see how it is that there is something

[58] For a thorough discussion of the relation between internalism and moral scepticism, see Superson 2009: 127–59.

[59] Cf. Brink 1989: 46–50.

plausible in both sides. This diagnosis hinges on the distinction we have drawn between rightness or goodness on the one hand, and obligatoriness or duty on the other, a distinction which (as we have seen) relates closely to Kant's contrast between the holy will and a will such as ours. For, I will argue, this enables Kant to be an internalist at the level of obligation and duty, while being an externalist about the right and the good, and thus once again allows him to combine elements from both positions, and so resolve the impasse between them.

When it comes to obligation or duty, as we have seen, Kant holds that these arise for wills such as ours because our non-moral inclinations are in some sort of tension with our moral motivations, in a way that does not happen for a holy will, which is only ever motivated to act morally. It follows from this account, therefore, that for a person to have an obligation or duty to ϕ, they must have at least some motivation to ϕ, as otherwise no such tension could arise. Kant's position on obligation and duty is therefore at least weakly internalist, in the sense that it is committed to there being at least some degree of motivation to ϕ in the agent who has ϕ-ing as their duty or obligation, whether or not that motivation will always ultimately be the one that wins out. To this extent, therefore, the Kantian can agree that there is something indeed incoherent in acknowledging a duty or obligation and failing to acknowledge any motivation to do it, which fits with the internalist's intuitions about some of the cases; and he can agree about the absurdity of the sceptic who claims to see he ought to do ϕ or that ϕ is his duty, but not to have any motivation to ϕ: to grasp the former, he must have the latter, for the former involves a tension between *that* motivation, and some other.

On the other hand, Kant can also accommodate externalist concerns that embracing internalism can take us too far: for, as we have seen, Kant's hybrid account allows him to distinguish between moral notions like duty and obligation on the one hand, and notions like the right and the good on the other, and so to hold that while the internalist may be right about the former, the externalist is right about the latter. For, while the internalist's position might well fit with imperatival concepts like duty and obligation, for Kant it is possible also to conceive of moral concepts that do not take this imperatival form, so that judgements involving such concepts need assert or imply nothing about the agent's motivations, but can be employed and made true in an externalist manner. This, then, allows room for an externalist treatment of actions that are right and good for the agent to do, while combining this with an internalist treatment of actions that are obligations or duties for the agent. Moreover, this means that Kant can respect internalist intuitions about the sceptic who ascribes moral properties like duty and obligatoriness to her actions, as such properties would seem to have motivational considerations 'built in'; at the same time, however, it can also make space for externalist intuitions concerning the sceptic who only ascribes to them properties like rightness or goodness: for nothing in the moral properties of the right or the good involves this internal relation to motivational forces, in the way that it does for obligatoriness and duty, on Kant's picture. And Kant need not therefore claim that the amoralist about the right and the good, who accepts that an act has these features but lacks any motivation to so act, can be ruled out on the grounds of misusing the relevant concepts or failing to make a judgement.

Moreover, we can also see how Kant can offer a more complex treatment of the relation between internalism and externalism on the one hand, and anti-realism and realism on the other. For, just as his anti-realism operates at the level of obligatoriness but not at the level of the right and the good, so too his internalism operates only at that level and not the second; he therefore shows how the realist can safely embrace internalism about some aspects of the moral, insofar as this does not in itself force him to become an anti-realist all the way down.

In these respects, it is interesting to compare Kant's position with that of W. D. Falk on such issues. Falk, of course, is generally credited with first crystallizing the whole externalism/internalism debate, both in terms of the distinction itself, and also how it relates to wider meta-ethical issues, such as the contrast between realism and anti-realism. However, it has less often been noted that Falk seems to adopt a view that, like Kant's, operates at different levels and so is equally hybrid in defending an internalism and anti-realism about obligation and duty, and an externalism and realism about the right and the good. This has been obscured, I think, because the subsequent debate has often focused on moral properties or judgements in general rather than on duty and obligation in particular, in a way that means this distinction of levels gets lost—so that it is not properly appreciated that when Falk talks about internalism, it is really an internalism about *obligation* that he is speaking about, not about *all* moral properties.

This feature of Falk's position comes out particularly clearly in his article 'Obligation and Rightness'.[60] In this paper, Falk's basic aim is to question whether Ross (and to a lesser degree Prichard), in providing an account of rightness, can also claim to have accounted for moral obligation. Falk does so by contrasting rightness and goodness as states of affairs external to the subject, with duties and obligations, which involve the subject feeling '*internally constrained* to do the act in question'.[61] It is for this reason that Falk thinks that 'when we try to convince another that he ought to pay his bills, we expect our argument if accepted to affect a change of heart in him, though it may still not change his outward actions'.[62] Falk therefore argues that the good and the right can be no more than the *ground* of what is obligatory, and should not be confused with obligatoriness as such:

> The nature of the things which we are obliged to do contains only the *grounds*, but not yet the *essence* of moral obligation. What alone can render a prospective action obligatory is that an agent is in some manner impelled to do it, or that he thinks he would be so impelled if he reflected... Hence what makes the good act a duty is not the bare fact that it would be good

[60] Falk 1945. This is one of Falk's earliest papers, and perhaps for this reason it was not included in his collection of papers Falk 1986—and therefore is correspondingly little discussed.

[61] Falk 1945: 138. [62] Falk 1945: 141.

when done, but the fact that the thought of it is related to ourselves in a special manner; and even if it were the case that ultimately none but good acts were obligatory, their goodness would be no more than the *ground* of a separate obligation to do them... The same argument applies to rightness or fittingness.[63]

In distinguishing the right and the good from duty and obligation in this way, Falk like Kant appears to adopt a hybrid view; and this means his position can contain both internalist and externalist elements.

Thus, Falk is willing to accept an externalist position like Ross's and Prichard's when it comes to the right and the good. He argues, however, that this should not be confused with obligation and duty, which has a different logical form from the right and the good, which involves taking into account the motivations of the agent when attributing to them any obligation and duty:

Here it is interesting to note that the belief that obligations are independent existents is in some manner fostered by the suggestiveness of language. "Having an obligation" or "being under an obligation" suggests a state of affairs existing for an agent, yet not merely in relation to him. But to "have an obligation" is not like "having money in the bank"; to be "under an obligation" is not like being "under a shower" or 'in the water." If anything it is like "having an impulse," "having an obsession," or "being in trouble." For the second set of expressions we can substitute assertions about individual states of mind, like "being impelled," "being obsessed" or "being troubled," for the first we cannot. I have no doubt that "having an obligation" ranks with the second. The possibility of substituting for it the expression "being obliged" is a clear clue to this. Strictly speaking, there is nothing that can be called *an obligation*. What we think of when we use the term is *that agents are obliged by the thought of them*, or *that the thought of actions obliges agents to do them*. We think not of an *entity*, but of a *relation* between agents, the thought of actions, and the doing of actions.[64]

Falk therefore argues that 'To oblige is to affect, to be obliged is to be affected'.[65] But it is important to note that he is talking *only* about obligation here, not the right and the good as such, where he raises no objection to the realist accounts of this offered by Ross and Prichard; his objection is just to treating the two normative levels in the same manner, and so treating law and duty as if they were inherent 'in the nature of things'.[66] Falk rightly (on my view) characterizes his position as Kantian, both to the extent that 'to Kant the very existence of a duty was inseparable from the existence of a motive', as providing 'some real check on [a person's] freedom to act otherwise',[67] and because like Kant he traces the 'must' of obligation back to the conflict between reason and desire, and the limitations of the human will.[68] Thus, when Falk comes to argue in his later papers that there is a certain incoherence in moral scepticism that the externalist cannot acknowledge, and that the externalist cannot account for the absurdity of being faced with someone who accepts that ϕ-ing is their duty but

[63] Falk 1945: 145. [64] Falk 1945: 143. [65] Falk 1945: 143.
[66] Falk 1986: 180. [67] Falk 1986: 29. [68] Cf. Falk 1986: 184 and 168–9.

questions whether they have any motivation for doing so, it is important to remember that Falk (like Kant) is pressing the force of these internalist considerations just at the level of duty and obligation, so that nothing here commits him to internalism about the 'ground' of obligation, which is the right and the good; and insofar as internalism has any affinity with anti-realism, nothing commits him to anti-realism about this 'ground' either.

1.7 Conclusion

My aim in this paper has been to explicate Kant's distinction between the holy will and one like our own, and to show how that distinction plays a significant role in his account of duty and obligation. I do not here pretend to have resolved or anticipated all the objections that might now arise to this position, both as an explication of Kant, and as a position in its own right—indeed, much like the empirical realism/transcendental idealism combination adopted in Kant's theoretical philosophy, to which I have compared it, one can anticipate comparable puzzlements and expressions of dissatisfaction about the overall coherence and stability of the view. However, much as that view in Kant's theoretical philosophy has proved remarkably durable and attractive in the face of such puzzlement and dissatisfaction, so, perhaps, it might in the end turn out similarly here in Kant's practical philosophy, by reflecting a higher wisdom than either of the sides it tries to steer between.[69]

[69] I am grateful to the following people who provided me with helpful comments on previous drafts of this paper: Karl Ameriks, Sorin Baiasu, Daniel Elstein, Paul Franks, Charles Larmore, Oliver Sensen, Philip Stratton-Lake, Oliver Thorndike, and Marcus Willaschek.

2

Constructivism and the Argument from Autonomy

My aim in this paper is to consider a particular line of criticism that has been used by constructivists to argue against moral realism, which is to claim that if moral realism were true, then this would threaten or undermine our autonomy as agents. I will call this *the argument from autonomy*. The basic criticism can be found in the work of many constructivists, where the core idea is helpful summarized by Stephen Darwall as follows: 'For a Kantian such as Korsgaard, the idea of an independent order of normative fact is inconsistent with *the autonomy of the will*. Practical reasoning is not a matter of orientating oneself properly in relation to some external source of value. Rather it is a *self*-government or autonomy—the agent determining herself in accord with principles she can prescribe for herself as one rational person among others.'[1]

Now, I take it that if this line of criticism could be successfully substantiated, this would be of great philosophical significance in relation to the debate between constructivists and realists. For, while the constructivist can and has raised other kinds of criticism against the realist, most especially perhaps the familiar objection of being 'anti-naturalist', such criticisms have brought equally familiar responses, where either the charge is accepted with equanimity,[2] or the whole naturalism/anti-naturalism distinction is questioned by the realist,[3] so that in this way the objection is side-stepped.[4] On this and other issues, therefore, the constructivist/realist controversy may perhaps be said to have petered out, as each side seems to just talk past the other. The interest of the argument from autonomy, therefore, might be felt to lie in its potential to offer a criticism of the realists that will be harder for the realist to shrug off, as autonomy looks on the face of it to be something that the realist will want to preserve as much as the constructivist, making it harder for her to respond by biting the bullet, or denying that the notion of autonomy makes any clear sense. This is not to deny that in this debate, too, such evasive tactics can be adopted by the realist;[5] but the price of adopting them is perhaps higher and more worrying to the neutral

[1] Darwall 1997: 310. [2] Cf. Larmore 2008. [3] Cf. McDowell 1994.

[4] This is not to deny, of course, that the realist can also respond more directly, by defending the claim that realism is compatible with naturalism.

[5] Thus, some have responded to the worry about autonomy raised in this and other contexts, by arguing that what matters instead is a weaker notion that can more easily be accommodated by their view, such as *self-governance*, *orthonomy*, or *theonomy*. See, for example, Hare 2001a: 114–15.

than it is when it comes to the naturalism/non-naturalism issue, thereby making the argument from autonomy of great potential value to the constructivist.

However, despite this potential, when one comes to consider the argument from autonomy in any detail, and just what it amounts to, it is in fact surprisingly hard to find it spelled out in any significant way in the literature; and likewise, it is correspondingly hard to find any detailed response to it by realists. I think the reason for this is that, curiously, each side takes it as so obvious that they are right, that they feel no real need to say much more in defence or elaboration of the argument. Thus, constructivists just take it as obvious that realism *is* a threat to autonomy and that this is a serious count against it, while realists take it to be just as obvious that this threat is non-existent, and that the argument can be ignored. So, on the one side, constructivists such as Rawls, Schneewind, Korsgaard, and Reath have often deployed the argument from autonomy,[6] but not done much to explain it or defend it against criticisms, while on the other side realists have not put themselves to much trouble to dismiss it.[7] Thus, debate on this important issue has not in fact really got very far.

My aim in this paper, then, is to try to flesh out in more detail than is usual what the basis for the argument from autonomy might actually be, and to consider then what strategies the realist might use in response. I will therefore consider three different broad types of 'argument from autonomy' that might underlie the constructivist position on this issue, and what line the realists could best take to deal with arguments of these types. I will call the three types in question: *Kantian arguments from autonomy*; *Rortyean arguments from autonomy*; and *arguments from obligatoriness*.

A final preliminary remark: While obviously relevant, I do not have the space here to consider in any detail how the constructivist/realist distinction is best elaborated. But just to give some general and basic characterization of the distinction as I am understanding it for the purposes of this paper, I think the following account by Sharon Street is helpful:

> The key point at issue between realists and antirealists is the answer to the central question of Plato's *Euthryphro* (in roughly secular paraphrase), namely whether things are valuable ultimately because we value them (antirealism), or whether we value things ultimately because

[6] Rawls's position will be discussed in section 2.1. Cf. also Schneewind 1986: 66: 'The defining feature of an autonomous agent, in Kant's view, is its ability to guide its own action by the choices of a will that is such that whatever it wills is good simply because it is willed by it'; Korsgaard 1996b: 5: 'If the real and the good are no longer one, value must find its way into the world somehow. Form must be imposed on the world of matter. This is the work of art, the work of obligation, and it brings us back to Kant... The ethics of autonomy is the only one consistent with the metaphysics of the modern world, and the ethics of autonomy is an ethics of obligation'; Reath 2006b: 164 note 17: 'A constructivist account of Kant's moral theory offers one way to spell out what it is for the "rational will" to have autonomy'.

[7] So, for example, Russ Shafer-Landau dismisses it in one page, calling it the weakest of the constructivist's arguments against realism: see Shafer-Landau 2003: 44.

they possess a value independently of us (realism). In the final analysis, in other words, is normativity best understood as conferred or recognized?

Metaethical constructivism falls squarely on the antirealist side of this divide... [M]etaethical constructivism asserts a counterfactual dependence of value on the attitudes of valuing creatures; it understands reason-giving status as conferred upon things by us. According to metaethical constructivism, there are no facts about what is valuable apart from facts about a certain point of view on the world and what is entailed from within that point of view.[8]

Working with this general characterization of the two sides in this debate, I will now consider a first type of argument from autonomy that the constructivist might use against the realist, which has a broadly Kantian inspiration.

2.1 The Kantian Argument from Autonomy

There is widespread consensus amongst constructivists that Kant should be credited as holding a constructivist position in ethics at least partly on the strength of his commitment to autonomy, and thus that Kant was committed to something like the constructivist's autonomy argument. This is pretty clearly Rawls's view, and I think it is his view which has influenced so many others. Thus, Rawls comments in *Political Liberalism*:

Another and deeper meaning of autonomy [than 'doctrinal autonomy'] says that the order of moral and political values must be made, or itself constituted, by the principles and conceptions of practical reason. Let us refer to this as constitutive autonomy. In contrast with rational intuitionism, constitutive autonomy says that the so-called independent order of values does not constitute itself but is constituted by the activity, actual or ideal, of practical (human) reason itself. I believe this, or something like it, is Kant's view. His constructivism is deeper and goes to the very existence and constitution of the order of values. This is part of his transcendental idealism. The intuitionist's independently given order of values is part of the transcendental realism Kant takes his transcendental idealism to oppose.[9]

and his position is echoed in passages from others such as the following:

Kant's conception of autonomy precludes such a [realist] conception of morality. Human beings cannot be dependent upon anything distinct from their will for the moral law that binds them... If the distinctive feature of Kant's moral theory is autonomy, and if autonomy requires the dependence of moral principles upon the human will, and if this dependence on the human

[8] Street 2010: 370–1. For similar accounts of the distinction, cf. also Cullity and Gaut 1997b: 4; and Hills 2008: 182–3.

[9] Rawls 1993: 99–100. Cf. Neiman 1994: 33: 'Having declared that reason is in the world, Leibniz is stuck with the fact that reason is *in the world*—to be read off of, rather than put into, the objects of experience. Naturally, those objects are not the everyday ones to which empiricists appeal but the supersensible truths of an intelligible world. For Kant, however, the determination of reason by eternal truths is as fundamentally heteronomous as its determination by any other object'; and Lafont 2004: 28: '[Kantians] agree with the anti-realist that our normative judgments do not purport to describe a pre-given moral order, heteronomously imposed on us independently of our practical reason'.

will is idealist, then the distinctive feature of Kant's moral theory is its idealism. Kantians ought to embrace moral idealism as the distinctive feature of Kant's moral theory.[10]

We might therefore expect to find in Kant some material by which the argument from autonomy is to be elaborated.

Now as it happens, however, the interpretative position taken here by the constructivists has in fact been strongly challenged by realists, who have argued instead that Kant is best understood as being on their side in meta-ethics, at least to a significant degree.[11] If this is indeed so, then of course constructivists are wrong to look to Kant for their inspiration for an argument from autonomy. While myself sympathizing with the realist reading,[12] however, I do not intend here to enter into this complex interpretative debate, and will take it for granted that the constructivist can appropriately look to Kant as some sort of ally in this area.

A first argument we might consider, then, under the broad heading of Kantian constructivism, is one that has been put forward by Robert Johnson, which is modelled on the argument for voluntarism that has been put forward by theists:

First, let me give you an intuitive sense of why autonomy commits Kantian ethics to denying that value is a source of reasons. Consider a parallel example: the Divine Command theory's resolution of a Euthyphro-style dilemma. That dilemma begins with the assertion that God loves (or responds in some appropriate way to) all and only good things. This raises the question, Why? Is it because their value provides a reason for God to give them their due, His love? But if God loves a good thing only because its goodness gives him a reason to love it, then its goodness explains the appropriateness of God's love for it, and this is incompatible with God's omnipotence. The value that provides a reason for God to love it would be a constraint on God's love in the sense that God must respond to reasons provided by the value of things or else fail to have the requisite response. The alternative is to say that those things are good because of God's love for them. God's love explains their value. But then goodness looks like an arbitrarily distributed shadow cast by God's attention. For if God loved some entirely different set of things, then those other things would have been good. The Divine Command theorist opts for the second horn, and then is saddled with the problem of explaining why goodness isn't arbitrarily distributed after all.

Kantians must resolve a similar Euthyphro-style dilemma in the same way as the Divine Command theory. What possess value on the Kantian view are all and only the objects of rational agency. Now if value is the source of the reasons for the pursuits of rational agents, then the authority governing rational agency is external to that agency itself, in the value of things that are its objects. But on the Kantian view, rational agency must be autonomous, in the sense that the requirements binding it are wholly self-generated and self-imposed. The autonomy of reason, the central guiding idea behind Kantian moral theory, is thus the very

[10] Rauscher 2002: 496.

[11] See, for example, Hare 2001a: 87–119; Ameriks 2003b; Kain 2004; Kain 2006; Langton 2007; Hills 2008.

[12] See Stern 2012, esp. Chapter 1.

foundation of the case against the claim that there is some value that provides reason to conform to moral obligation. Autonomy requires that value not be a source of reasons.[13]

The central claim seems to be, then, that just as value realism would clearly undermine God's omnipotence in the theistic case, so it would clearly undermine our autonomy in the case of human beings.

However, the realist can I think argue in response to this challenge that there is a significant difference between *omnipotence* and *autonomy*, however we exactly spell out the latter, and that this is apparently being overlooked by Johnson. Thus, while it may indeed be plausible to hold that God's *omnipotence* would be undermined if values obtained independently of his will (though of course even this could be denied), given that autonomy is a much weaker notion that omnipotence, nothing so far shows that the parallel argument has any such plausibility and that to model the argument on the theistic case is highly misleading for that reason. The realist may therefore grant that Johnson is right that realism would undermine omnipotence in the theistic case, but still feel she has been given no grounds on which to think it undermines autonomy in ours. For, suppose the goodness of something did indeed provide God with a reason to love it, such that he would be rationally criticizable were he not to do so; there would then be some sense in which he 'must' respond to that thing with love, based on this reason. Perhaps Johnson is right that then God would then have to fulfil certain requirements in a way that would limit his 'powers' in some way and thus threaten his omnipotence; but (the realist will argue) how can it be that having to follow a reason in this manner in his actions would make him less *autonomous*, any more than having to follow what there is reason to *think* does so?

The constructivist could respond, however, by suggesting that if we look a bit more closely at Kant's position, a better argument from autonomy can be constructed on Kantian materials—and in particular, on Kant's discussion of the heteronomous nature of what Kant calls *material* moral principles which (in contrast to his own formal formula of universal law and related formulae) employ some notion of value and the good as their basis—for example, the good of happiness or perfection. These principles, it could be argued, involve a realist notion of value, so we might look to Kant to show how it is that this realism would lead to heteronomy were such principles to be adopted.

What, then, makes these material moral principles heteronomous for Kant? The answer seems to be that in acting from them, the will is determined by our inclinations and desires, not solely by our reason, so that it is because we want or desire our happiness or perfection that we are led to follow the principles of a hedonistic or perfectionist ethics. So we can take Kant as arguing that because certain ethical positions ground their position in some conception of what is good for us, and motivate our attachment to that good by appeal to our desires, that they result in an

[13] Johnson 2007: 140–1.

outlook that is heteronomous. The constructivist's claim might be, therefore, that *any* form of realism will have to end up giving a priority to desire over reason in this way, and thus end up in a heteronomous position. An argument of this sort has been proposed by Cristina Lafont, where she writes that:

> The standard reason that Kantian constructivists adduce against any kind of moral realism is always the concern that any concession to realism unavoidably involves introducing heteronomous considerations about what human beings happen to want or desire which are incompatible with the crucial role that the notion of autonomy plays in Kantian moral theories.[14]

Thus, following someone like Lafont, Kant might be interpreted as saying that if we adopt value realism, then one will be forced to claim that this value gives one reason to act and motivates one's actions only because of the satisfaction to be gained thereby; but then reason can only play a subordinate role, in working in the service of desire to help it find the best means of attaining this end; so reason loses its autonomy; so the will as a whole is no longer autonomous.

Now, Kant certainly does seem to have thought that if reason is just used by a person to 'service' or in subordination to their desires, such a person is not fully autonomous;[15] and this would seem to be one premise that the Kantian constructivist needs here. Another premise she needs is that the value realist must end up treating reason in this way, as a general claim about *all* values the realist might propose. Thus, in response to the Kantian constructivists argument here, the realist can object to either of these claims.

To resist the first premise, the realist might adopt a more Humean picture of reason as 'the slave of the passions', and argue that there is nothing in this picture that undermines our autonomy as agents, provided other more familiar Humean constraints relating to our desires are met (for example, that our second-order desires are in line with our first-order ones). Of course, it may be true that (so to speak) the faculty of reason *itself* is not autonomous here, because it is working 'in subordination' to desire; but the Humean response might be that this is irrelevant to whether

[14] Lafont 2004: 35.

[15] Cf. Kant *GMM*: 90 [4:441]: only when it does 'not merely administer an interest not belonging to it' can practical reason 'show its own commanding authority as supreme lawgiving'.

Kant *MM*: 189 [5:61]: '[The human being] is nevertheless not so completely an animal as to be indifferent to all that reason says on its own and to use reason merely as a tool for the satisfaction of his needs as a sensible being' (cf. Kant *GMM*: 50–2 [4:395–6]).

Kant *LE*: 266 [27:499]: 'If, for example, the principle of universal happiness were to be the basis for determination of the moral law, it would be a question of how far our needs were satisfied in their entire totality by following these laws; but here laws of nature are involved, and the moral laws would have to be subject to them, so that reason would have to obey the laws of nature and sensibility, and that in a necessary fashion (for in the physical order this is so anyway). But this would obviously put an end to the autonomy of reason, and thus be heteronomy.'

Kant *LE*: 263 [29:625–6]: 'Reason attends either to the interest of the inclinations, or to its own interest. In the first case it is subservient, but in the other, legislative.'

the person *as a whole* is autonomous, where it is this that really matters here. Now, obviously, this raises a host of highly complex issues in the philosophy of mind and action, which I do not propose to go into here: but it does suggest that there is a possible line of response open to the realist, at least, even if it is one that the Kantian might find objectionable.

When it comes to the second premise, however, some Kantians *themselves* have seemed to question it: namely, so called 'teleological' Kantians who think Kant himself was a realist who had a conception of the good underlying his moral position—namely the good of freedom, rational agency, or the good will which forms the basis of the principles of morality.[16] Kantians of this sort therefore hold that there are some things of objective value, where these things make Kant's principles of morality valid, but where the will is not thereby rendered heteronomous, as it is not related to these values through desire but through reason instead. Thus, on this 'teleological' reading of Kant, it is the value of rational nature that gives you reason to respect it in yourself and others; and as a rational agent, and hence respecter of reasons, this gives one the motivation to act accordingly, without appeal to the heteronomous motivations of desire and inclination.

Now, again, I do not want to enter into the complex interpretative debate between 'teleological' interpreters of Kant and their opponents.[17] But in general, these teleological Kantians are simply exploring an option that seems to be open to the realist, whether or not it is one Kant himself took: namely, of denying that the realist can only relate value to the will through desire, in a way that would inevitably push realism into this kind of heteronomy. The constructivist might say, of course, that without some appeal to desire then the realist response here will leave moral action *mysterious* in some way; but again there are familiar realist responses to this sort of worry, which hold that only a misplaced Humeanism concerning the sources of moral motivation could make it seem that any sort of gap here really arises. If this is right, therefore, there would again seem to be resources that the realist can use to resist this form of Kantian argument from autonomy, once the relation between reason, desire, and action are seen in the way the realist is likely to favour.

We are therefore yet to find a convincing argument from autonomy that can be built on Kantian resources; but it may be that the constructivist can look elsewhere, so that I now turn to some ideas found in the work of Richard Rorty.

[16] Cf. Langton 2007; Hills 2008. Cf. also Wood 1999: 46–7, 111–55; and Guyer 2000. Wood makes the general view clear when he writes: 'The content of the [moral] law is not a creation of my will, or the outcome of any constructive procedure on my part. The law of autonomy is objectively valid for rational volition because it is based on an objective end—the dignity of rational nature as an end in itself' (Wood 2008: 108).

[17] For some responses, see Dean 2006 and Sensen 2009. For further discussion, see Stern 2012, esp. Chapter 1.

2.2 The Rortyean Argument from Autonomy

Rorty has argued that realism in general (not just *moral* realism) is *authoritarian*, as it puts something over and above us to which our beliefs or actions are required to conform, thereby leaving us in the position of being subordinated to something else outside and beyond us. Rorty argues that just as we should learn to give up thinking that we have a duty to follow God's will as a sign of our greater intellectual maturity and self-confidence, so too we should learn to give up thinking that we should conform our thoughts or actions to 'how the world is' or Reality (with a capital 'R'), which is somehow prior to us and governs how we should act or think. Rather, Rorty claims, what we should really care about is not this independent order of things, but our fellow human beings, and how we get along with them and secure agreement with them—in his slogan, we should look for solidarity, not objectivity. Thus, Rorty writes:

> There is a useful analogy to be drawn between the pragmatists' criticism of the idea that truth is a matter of correspondence to the intrinsic nature of reality and the Enlightenment's criticism of the idea that morality is a matter of correspondence to the will of a Divine Being. The pragmatist's anti-representational account of belief is, among other things, a protest against the idea that human beings must humble themselves before something non-human, whether the Will of God or the Intrinsic Nature of Reality.[18]

Given his general claim about the authoritarianism of realism in general, then, we can see quite easily how be might extend this claim to moral realism in particular, and thus argue that the latter is a threat to our autonomy.

It is not clear, however, that Rorty would take constructivism to be much better than realism in this regard, at least when it comes to *Kantian* constructivism. In general, Rorty tends to see Kant as a 'transitional' figure, whose own notion of pure practical reason is still tainted with the same motivations as realism, to set something 'above' us—where in Kant's case this is the rational or noumenal self:

> We are often told by contemporary moral philosophers that Kant made a breathtaking discovery, and gave us a vitally important new idea, that of moral autonomy. But I suspect that when Kant is given credit for this discovery, we are using the term ambiguously. Everybody thinks autonomy in the sense of freedom from outside imposition is a fine thing. Nobody likes either human or divine tyrants. But the specifically Kantian sense of autonomy—having one's moral decisions made by reason rather than by anything capable of being influenced by experience—is quite a different matter...
>
> As Dewey saw these matters, the Kantian split between the empirical and the non-empirical was a relic of the Platonic distinction between the material and the immaterial, and this of the

[18] Rorty 2006: 257. See also Rorty 1991: 21–34; and Rorty 2000: 217–18. Cf. Nietzsche 1974, §344, p. 283: 'Even we seekers after knowledge today, we godless anti-metaphysicians still take our fire, too, from the flame lit by a faith that is thousands of years old, that Christian faith which was also the faith of Plato, that God is the truth, that truth is divine.'

theologico-metaphysical distinction between the human and the divine. Dewey thought this "brood and nest of dualisms," as he called it, should be swept aside, taking Plato and Kant with it.[19]

For Rorty then, it seems, Kantian constructivism is at root as authoritarian in its outlook as moral realism.

However, it might be said, some Kantian constructivists (such as Onora O'Neill) could be held to be closer to Rorty than others (such as Christine Korsgaard, who does seem inclined to hang on to the hierarchical view of the self that Rorty wants to reject).[20] Moreover, some constructivists (such as Sharon Street)[21] are closer to Hume than to Kant, and so may be more palatable to Rorty in this regard as a result (though whether moves towards Hume makes it hard for the constructivist to avoid collapsing their position into some sort of expressivism or subjectivism is currently a subject of much discussion).[22]

But what about Rorty's argument as such, whether or not constructivism itself would fall foul of it? Is moral realism 'authoritarian' and undermining of our autonomy because it treats values in a realist manner? What one thinks about this depends, as we have seen, on how plausible one finds Rorty's argument against realism in general, and his claim that any position that makes it necessary to conform our minds or actions to a subject-independent world is authoritarian as a result. John McDowell has argued against Rorty that this argument does not hold, and that realism only becomes an authoritarian position if it becomes a form of *transcendent* realism, that treats what is real as an unknowable beyond to which we have no cognitive access, thereby cutting us off from how things are:

The world as it figures in mainstream epistemology is a counterpart, not to just any idea of the divine as non-human and authoritarian, but to the conception of *deus absconditus*, God as withdrawn into a mysterious inaccessibility. A telling Deweyan protest against epistemology, as practised in the Cartesian and British-empiricist style, can be cast as a protest against the idea of philosophy as priestcraft, supposedly needed to mediate between this *mundus absconditus* and ordinary human beings who aspire to knowledge of it.

The idea that inquiry is answerable to the world does not by itself commit us to believing that there is a need for philosophy as priestcraft. We can accept that inquiry is answerable to the things themselves and still suppose, correctly, that the resources of ordinary investigative activity can suffice to put us in touch with the subject matter of investigation, without need of special philosophical mediation. That is: we can follow Dewey in rejecting philosophy as priestcraft, without needing to abandon the very vocabulary of objectivity. What we need to dislodge is the idea of the world as withdrawn into inaccessibility, and that is quite another matter.[23]

[19] Rorty 2007: 188–9.

[20] Cf. Rorty 2007: 195, who quotes Korsgaard as writing that 'the relation of the thinking self to the acting self is one of legitimate authority' (Korsgaard 1996b: 165).

[21] Cf. Street 2008.

[22] Cf. Street 2010 and the discussion of her position in Ridge 2012.

[23] McDowell 2000: 110–11.

So, McDowell argues, there is nothing authoritarian in realism as such, just a transcendent realism which treats reality as a distant, unreachable realm, to which we are expected to conform without knowing quite how or whether we have done so. If we abandon realism in this form, however, McDowell argues that the realism we are left with is thoroughly unobjectionable, and indeed a normal part of common sense. As he puts it: 'Acknowledging a non-human external authority over our thinking, so far from being a betrayal of our humanity, is merely a condition of growing up.'[24] My sympathies are with McDowell in this debate, and indeed it is notable than when Rorty himself comes to spell out what he finds objectionable about realism, it is the *inscrutable* nature of reality as conceived of by the realist that he seems to be picking up on, rather than its subject-independence per se.[25]

However, even if this sort of response to Rorty is right, it might still be felt that a problem can be raised here for the realists along Rortyean lines. For, it could be argued, it is a feature of realism that, because it treats what is real here as mind-independent, the possibility of our being in radical error always arises, so that moral realism must always leave open the sceptical worry that our beliefs about moral matters are in error, given the independence of the moral domain—and doesn't this make the moral epistemically transcendent in just the way that raises the authoritarianism worry for Rorty? Conversely, the constructivist might argue that it is an advantage of their position that no such gap can arise.[26]

Now, of course, the realist can respond in turn that this is precisely one thing that makes constructivism (and other forms of anti-realism) in ethics implausible, because any sensible view must in fact allow for the possibility of error of this kind. I do not wish to pursue this line here, however, as it is unlikely that either side will feel that its opponent can avoid begging the question in their favour—the intuitions one has on this matter tend to reflect too closely the intuitions that make one a realist or anti-realist in the first place, in my experience. I think, however, the realist can take a less ambitious line, and argue that while it is indeed true that according to realism, we have no a priori guarantee that no gap between our moral convictions and moral reality might not exist, this in itself is too weak a basis to generate any genuine moral scepticism and thus any real doubt that the moral realism in fact *is* transcendent in a way that would lead to Rorty's authoritarian worries. For, the sceptic here is raising a mere logical possibility that follows from realism, and not giving any evidence that we have *in fact* got things wrong, for which some arguments to establish a source of error in our moral convictions would have to be provided—where here it is not realism *simpliciter* that would be generate the sceptical doubt, but those arguments

[24] McDowell 2000: 120. Cf. also Larmore 1996: 87–8. [25] Cf. Rorty 2006: 257, 258.

[26] Cf. Rauscher 2002: 496: 'Kant's notion of autonomy distinguishes Kant's cognitivism from other cognitivist moral theories... [On these latter theories] it might be the case that humans are wrong about every moral belief they hold, since the truth of moral propositions is independent of human knowledge. Kant's conception of autonomy precludes such a conception of morality.'

themselves. Thus, just as in the external world case, realists have responded to sceptical worries based on the mere fact of mind-independence by dismissing such doubts as unreal and groundless in themselves (even though the possibility of error cannot be ruled out by the realist as a logical possibility),[27] so the same strategy (I am suggesting) can be applied here, in a way that shows how one can endorse realism, without spiralling into the kind of sceptical doubt that would generate the concern about epistemic opacity that might trigger and substantiate Rorty's worry about authoritarianism. To that extent, therefore, it would seem that the Rortyean argument from autonomy against realism falls flat.

2.3 The Argument from Obligatoriness

We can now then turn, finally, to the third type argument from autonomy that I wish to consider, which I take to be more promising than any of those we have discussed so far, but where again I think the realist has resources with which to challenge the argument.

The intuitive idea behind this sort of argument, I take it, comes from a challenge posed by the apparently special obligatory nature of morality and the moral 'must': morality is taken by many to be a matter of *obligation*, and to that extent a matter of laws or principles that *bind* or *command* us, and thus have *imperatival force*. It may therefore seem to follow that morality as a system of laws requires a *legislator*, so that morality can only come about as a result of some act of legislation which this legislator undertakes—as Korsgaard has put this view, 'Obligation must come from law, and law from the will of a legislating sovereign; morality only comes into the world when laws are made'.[28] But then, if we accept this line, it may then seem that we are left with only two options: either morality is legislated by *us*, or by some *other* sovereign authority, such as God. Now, if we opt for the second alternative, the link with heteronomy may seem very plausible,[29] because now it will seem that in following the dictates of morality as these are conceived to exist independently of us, we are following the directions of *another* will, as the institutor of that moral law. Faced with that alternative, it may then appear that the Kantian constructivist is right, and that the only way to preserve our autonomy is to endorse the first option,

[27] This approach can be found, for example, in the fallibilist pragmatism inspired by C. S. Peirce, and his distinction between 'real' and 'artificial' doubt: see Peirce 1992c.

[28] Korsgaard, 1996b: 23. Cf. also G. E. M. Anscombe's discussion of the 'special "moral" sense' of 'ought' and its connection with the '*law* conception of ethics' in Anscombe 1958: 5.

[29] Even taking this option, however, I do not deny that the divine command theorist may find a way to preserve some conception of our autonomy; but for the sake of the discussion here, I will not consider the issues any further, taking it that the worry has at least a prima facie force, and might well persuade people to think they need to opt for the second, constructivist, option—where I am mainly concerned below with challenging the exhaustiveness of this dichotomy and so avoiding the dilemma, rather than ways dealing with the first (theistic) horn of it. For some further discussion of how the divine command theorist might response to the problems, see Hare 2001a.

and to make *us* the legislators of the moral law, in a way that takes us from considerations of autonomy to constructivism. Thus, as Robert Pippin has put the general thought here: 'Laws, to be laws, require legislators, and once a divine legislator is excluded, "we" are the only candidates left'.[30] The realist would thus seem to face the problem of accounting for the obligatoriness of morality, in a way that makes this obligatoriness compatible with our autonomy, if they reject constructivism and the Kantian idea of 'self-legislation' and so deny that this obligatoriness stems from our own legislative act.

I now want to turn to a consideration of ways in which I think the realist can respond to the argument from autonomy that takes this form. Some sorts of responses are 'offensive', in trying to show that the constructivist option here is itself incoherent or deeply problematic in some way, so that there is really no constructivist route out of the problem either, and so no grounds in this respect to prefer constructivism to realism. Other sorts of response are 'defensive', and try to show that really the issue of obligatoriness does not arise as a problem for realism in the way that the argument from autonomy tries to suggest.

Going on the offensive, the realist can try to claim that the constructivist position is itself unable to show that it makes sense to treat *self*-legislation as a source of obligatoriness, and thus as a coherent alternative to realism. The first problem often raised by realists here is the problem of *emptiness*: if moral reasons and norms do not exist prior to the legislative acts of the will, how is such a will to be guided or constrained in any way in its legislative activities, and thus how can those activities be anything other than empty and arbitrary?[31] However, constructivists have perhaps found a reasonable answer to such concerns in the idea that some constraints are constitutive of the will or practical reasoning itself, so that there is some content built into the activity of legislating by such a will from the outset.[32] What those constitutive constraints exactly are, and whether they are still sufficiently contentful to do much guiding, will still remain an issue for the constructivist to resolve; but in principle, at any rate, this might be thought to provide an adequate response to the emptiness problem.

At least two further problems for the constructivist remain, however, relating to the *authority* of norms that are self-legislated in this way. The first of these remaining problems concerns whether *self*-legislating can ever really amount to a genuine kind of *legislating* or binding—for if I bind myself, can't I *unbind* myself at will, leaving it unclear how I was ever really *bound* in the first place? And the second, related,

[30] Pippin 2005: 219.

[31] Cf. Larmore 2008: 44: 'When we do impose principles on ourselves, we presumably do so for reasons: we suppose that it is fitting for us to adopt them, or that adopting them will advance certain of our interests. Self-legislation, when it does occur, is an activity that takes place in the light of reasons that we must antecedently recognize, and whose authority we therefore do not institute but rather find ourselves called upon to acknowledge.'

[32] Cf. Korsgaard 1996b: 235–6.

problem is raised by Elizabeth Anscombe in the claim that 'the concept of obligation requires superior power in the legislator'.[33] But if it is right that some such hierarchical relation is needed here, how can that be the case if *I* am legislating over *myself*, where it would seem that both sides are on a par, so making the act of legislation impossible?

In response to the first of these worries, the constructivist might, I think, appeal again to the idea of the norms in question being constitutive of reason or practical agency in some way, where as a result of being constitutive, it is not clear that reason or practical agency could ever 'withdraw' or alter them; but nonetheless, the constructivist could argue, it still makes sense to think of them as *self*-legislated, as they get their normative force through being constitutive of *our* agency.

In response to the second of these worries, Kantian constructivists have often appealed to the hierarchical structure of the self that Kant himself seems to employ, which puts the rational aspect of the person in a position of 'superior power' over other aspects, which enables it to have this legislating role. Thus, in this vein Korsgaard writes: 'We might say that the acting self concedes to the thinking self its right to government. And the thinking self, in turn, tries to govern as well as it can. So the reflexive structure of human consciousness establishes a relation here, a relation which we have to ourselves. And it is a relation not of mere power but rather of *authority*. And *that* is the authority that is the source of obligation'.[34] A difficulty here, however, that might well be raised by Anscombe, is that Korsgaard still talks about one part of the self *conceding* authority to the other, which Anscombe might think greatly dilutes the kind of power required, arguably again making talk of legislation inappropriate. Nonetheless, Korsgaard might reply that we are familiar with democratic models of sovereignty, where legislative authority arguably is transferred from the people to democratically appointed legislative bodies in this way, and perhaps this is the model that the Kantian could use here.

We have seen, then, that notwithstanding the criticisms of the constructivist's 'self-legislation' model put forward by Anscombe and others, it can perhaps be made coherent, so that the realist cannot rely on ruling out constructivism as a strategy for defending her own view, and must instead seek to defend it from the argument from obligatoriness in its own right. I will here discuss two possible lines of defence, both of which take the general line of denying that the realist must be committed to there being an external law-giver as essential to their realist conception of morality; so the claim is that it is possible to remain a realist in ethics while denying that this realism commits the realist to holding that the obligatoriness of morality has its basis in any external law-giver, and thus in any source that might seem to threaten our autonomy.

The first such approach is in many ways the simplest, and just questions the argument's assumption that obligation requires a legislator at all, where the claim is

[33] Anscombe 1958: 2. [34] Korsgaard 1996b: 104.

that just as values are independent features of the world, so too are the duties and obligations to which they give rise. This would seem to be the position adopted by Samuel Clarke:

> These eternal and necessary differences of things make it fit and reasonable for creatures so to act; they cause it to be their duty, or lay an obligation on them, so to do; even separate from the consideration of these rules being the positive will or command of God; and also antecedent to any... particular private and personal advantage or disadvantage, reward or punishment, either present or future.[35]

Clarke seems to see no difficulty in being a realist about duties and obligations in a way that does without the need for *any* legislating will, and thus without a law-giver who might threaten our autonomy; for, he held, just as it makes sense to speak of laws in arithmetic and geometry without postulating a legislator for them, so the same can be said of moral laws.[36] By dispensing with the role of an external law-giver in this way, therefore, the argument from obligatoriness based on the threat of such a law-giver is simply inapplicable to a position of his sort.

Now, the constructivist will no doubt feel, that just as there is something peculiar and 'queer' in the realist's conception of moral values, so there is something even more peculiar and 'queer' about treating duties and obligations in this realist manner, where any explanation or account of this remarkable feature of the world would appear to be lacking on the realist's picture. This, however, is to move from considerations of autonomy, to the more standard naturalistic and explanatory concerns which (as we have noted at the outset) have for some time formed part of the realist/anti-realist debate in ethics, where the outcome of this controversy remains to be seen. What is more relevant to our purposes here, is to ask whether, giving the realist the benefit of the doubt on these questions, there are any special considerations of *autonomy* that can be used against a position like Clarke's, once the role for an external law-giver has been dropped out of the realist's picture and the need for any such law-giver has been rejected? It would seem that the argument from obligatoriness *itself* would not bite here, as that did rely on an appeal to such an external law-giver; and given the realist's apparently cogent responses to the other arguments from autonomy we have considered, it would therefore appear that a realist's position such as Clarke's is immune to the constructivist's concern with autonomy—at least until an argument somehow different from the ones we have discussed comes along.

[35] Clarke 2003: 295. Cf. also Price 1948: 105–6: 'virtue, *as such*, has a real obligatory power antecedently to all positive laws, and independently of all will; for obligation, we see, is involved in the very nature of it'. And cf. also Roger Crisp: 'Oddly, Anscombe appears never to consider the view that claims that we have such obligations might be self-standing, requiring no justification from elsewhere, though she does consider, as alternatives to divine legislation, the norms of society, self-legislation, the laws of nature, Hobbesian contractualism, and the virtues. Perhaps, like the early Greeks, she also felt that a *nomos* had to be *nomizetai* ("dispensed")' (Crisp 2004: 86 note 33).

[36] Clarke 2003: 295–6.

Nonetheless, we may assume that many will find Clarke's treatment of the obligatoriness of morality unenlightening at the very least, in seeming to have nothing to say about how it comes about and what it consists in. Can the realist therefore do any better on this front, without on the one hand postulating some sort of external law-giver and thus raising the threat of heteronomy, or treating morality as stemming from some sort of *self*-legislation and thus abandoning realism?

Now, ironically enough given his influence on constructivism, it could be argued that one option for the realist to explore here is offered by Kant's treatment of the contrast he draws between the holy or divine will, and one such as our own. For, in drawing this contrast, Kant takes himself to be explaining the way in which for us, what is morally right takes on an obligatory force, as we are faced by inclinations and desires that go against the correct action, and which makes it appear to us that this right action is *demanded* of us in an imperatival manner ('you *must not* tell lies', and so on). Thus, on the one hand, Kant offers an account of obligation that does not rest on any appeal to an external law-giver, while treating it as a result of our limited and human moral perspective, where from the perspective of a divine or holy will, morality has no such character; to that extent, therefore, his position might be seen as anti-realist. On the other hand, however, unlike constructivism this is arguably not an anti-realism that goes 'all the way down' but incorporates an important element of realism—not about how it is that morality appears obligatory to us, but about what it is that so appears, where this is held in common between us and the holy will, as the thing that it is right for both wills to do (tell the truth, for example), but where this is a something that we feel obliged to do but which the divine will does not, as it lacks the non-moral inclinations that create the sense of obligation that we experience in our moral lives.

Kant can therefore be held to offer what might be called a 'hybrid' view that contains both anti-realist and realist elements, the former at the level of obligation and the latter at the level of the right, where this enables the realist to avoid the threat of the argument from obligation on the one hand, while avoiding anti-realism 'all the way down' on the other, while also offering some sort of account of the nature of obligation in a way that eluded Clarke. The realist level concerns the content of morality, what is right and wrong, and the value of freedom on which this rests. Kant is insistent in many passages that not even God can determine by an act of will or choice what this content is to be, as this is as fixed and necessary as the fact that a triangle has three corners, which obtains independently of any relation to an agent.[37]

[37] Cf. Kant *LE*: 76 [27:282–3]:

> The lawgiver is not always simultaneously an originator of the law; he is only that if the laws are contingent. But if the laws are practically necessary, and he merely declares that they conform to his will, then he is a lawgiver. So nobody, not even the deity, is an originator of moral laws, since they have not arisen from choice, but are practically necessary; if they were not so, it might even be the case that lying was a virtue. But moral laws can still be subject to a lawgiver; there may be a being who is omnipotent and has power to execute

He also speaks in many passages as if he conceives of the value of the free rational agent in realist terms.[38] However, as we have seen, Kant does not treat the *obligatoriness* of what is right and wrong as independent in this way, for we give the content of morality its obligatory form, insofar as this depends on our limitedness as finite creatures, so that this obligatoriness is just the way in which what is right and wrong presents itself *to us*, from our human (all too human) perspective; from the perspective of a divine will, and so from the 'absolute standpoint', there *is* no duty and obligation, but only what is right and wrong, because it has none of the non-moral inclinations which Kant thinks render us subject to duties and obligations, and thus the moral 'must'.[39] Kant is thus able to side with the realist about the right; but he is able to side with the anti-realist about the obligatory, and thus avoid much of the 'queerness' associated with the idea that the world in itself makes *demands* on us, and also avoid the threat to our autonomy that any account of such a demand that postulates an external law-giver would seem to imply.[40] Interpreted in this way,

> these laws, and to declare that this moral law is at the same time a law of His will and obliges everyone to act accordingly. Such a being is then a lawgiver, though not an originator; just as God is no originator of the fact that a triangle has three corners.

and Kant *MM*: 381 [6:228]:

> A (morally practical) *law* is a proposition that contains a categorial imperative (a command). One who commands (*imperans*) through a law is the *lawgiver* (*legislator*). He is the author (*autor*) of the obligation in accordance with the law, but not always the author of the law. In the latter case the law would be a positive (contingent) and chosen law. A law that binds us a priori and unconditionally by our own reason can also be expressed as proceeding from the will of a supreme lawgiver, that is, one who has only rights and no duties (hence from the divine will); but this signifies only the idea of a moral being whose will is a law for everyone, without his being thought of as the author of the law.

and cf. also Kant *LE*: 302 [27:544]:

> Were we to conceive of the legislator as *auctor legis*, this would have reference only to statutory laws. But if we ascribe an *auctor* to laws that are known, through reason, from the nature of the case, he can only be an author of the obligation that is contained in the law. Thus God, too, by the declared divine will, is *auctor legis*, and precisely because natural laws were already in existence, and are ordained by Him.

For further discussion of this material and related passages, see Hare 2001a: 94–7; Ameriks 2003b; Kain 2004; Irwin 2004; Kain 2006; Wood 2008: 106–16.

[38] Cf. Kant *GMM*: 78–9 [4:428]:

> But suppose there were something *the existence of which in itself* has an absolute worth, something which as *an end in itself* could be a ground of determinate laws; then in it, and in it alone, would lie the ground of a possible categorical imperative, that is, of a practical law.
>
> Now I say that the human being and in general every rational beings *exists* as an end in itself, *not merely as a means* to be used by this will or that will at its discretion.

[39] Cf. Kant *CJ*: 273 [5:403–4]: 'It is clear that it depends only on the subjective constitution of our practical faculty that the moral laws must be represented as commands (and the actions which are in accord with them as duties), and that reason expressed this necessity not through a *be* (happening) but through a should-be.'

[40] I think Terence Irwin also sees Kant as adopting this sort of hybrid view: '[Kant] recognizes intrinsic rightness without any acts of commanding or obligating... In Kant's view, commands and act of binding are [only] relevant to finite rational agents, who are also subject to other incentives and so have to be instructed and urged to follow the moral law' (Irwin 2004: 149).

therefore, Kant might provide a model for the sort of position that can claim to incorporate a significant element of realism on the one hand, while on the other hand showing how (if this Kantian account of obligatoriness can be accepted) the argument from autonomy based on obligation can be avoided.

2.4 Conclusion

In this paper, I have set out to explore in some detail the threat to realism posed by considerations of autonomy. I have argued that the best way to understand argument from autonomy is to relate it to the issue of obligatoriness; but that there are a variety of strategies to be explored concerning obligation before it is clear that the right response to this issue is a constructivist one, or that the realist is hereby compelled to surrender their position.

3

The Value of Humanity

Reflections on Korsgaard's Transcendental Argument

The purpose of this paper is not to consider the worth of transcendental arguments in general (which I have done at length elsewhere),[1] but instead to focus on a specific example of the genre. However, this is an example taken not from epistemology or metaphysics where (in Anglo-American philosophy at least)[2] such arguments have most usually found a home, but rather from ethics. Nonetheless, I hope that what I have chosen to do will not prove valueless, as although specific and in some ways untypical, the argument I set out to discuss is important and influential, but not much considered as a transcendental argument as such. The argument in question is Christine Korsgaard's, from her book *The Sources of Normativity*. My aim is to try to understand what role her transcendental argument for the value of humanity is meant to play in her project, and whether the argument succeeds. Rather to my surprise, and rather against the run of the critical literature on Korsgaard's book, I will suggest that in one of its forms, the argument can be made to work—at least in its own terms[3] and when its rather limited place in Korsgaard's overall strategy is understood. And in the end, of course, it may also turn out that there are general lessons to be gained from the examination of this argument after all.

3.1 Korsgaard's Anti-sceptical Strategy

Taken as a whole, Korsgaard's aim is to show that we stand under moral obligations, by constructing an argument to that effect. But only part of the overall argument is meant to be a transcendental one—roughly, the middle part. How that specifically transcendental argument is understood therefore depends on how one conceives of what precedes it, and

[1] Most particularly in Stern 2000.

[2] Transcendental arguments have of course been used by Habermas, Apel and others as part of their projects in social philosophy. For a discussion of current uses of transcendental arguments in ethics, but which curiously hardly mentions Korsgaard, see Illies 2003.

[3] For example, as we shall see, I think the argument relies heavily on other arguments Korsgaard gives against realism, where in this discussion I allow her to take these for granted (but cf. Chapter 5, where some of these arguments are questioned).

what work its conclusion is supposed to do in what follows. Let me begin by setting out in broad terms what I take the three phases of Korsgaard's overall argument to be.

3.1.1 *Phase One: From free agency to the categorical imperative*

Korsgaard starts from a Kantian antinomy: that we conceive of ourselves as free on the one hand, but also as agents with a certain stability of purpose and character on the other, which means we take our actions to be governed by principles or laws. Korsgaard's Kantian solution to this antinomy is to argue that these principles or laws must be self-imposed.[4] But now we seem to face a second antinomy: on the one hand, unless a principle or law already binds the will, on what basis can the will rationally legislate a law to itself; but on the other hand, if the will is already bound by a law, how can this count as self-legislation?[5] Korsgaard's proposal is that Kant's notion of the categorical imperative is designed to resolve this second antinomy: on the one hand, the free will is not completely lawless, because it must act in accordance with a law or principle; but on the other hand, this does not constrain it or make it less free, because it is just constitutive of free legislation that it has this structure,[6] while which law it chooses is left open.[7] The conclusion of this first phase of the argument is therefore that in order for the will to be free, it must act on the basis of something that has the nature of a law or principle.

Before moving on to Phase Two of Korsgaard's overall argument, it may be worth pausing to emphasize that (at least as I see it) Phase One is not a transcendental argument: rather, it is an argument that works by showing how the antinomies of free agency and of self-legislation need to be resolved, leading to the categorical imperative, to act only on a maxim that I can will as a universal law.

[4] Cf. Korsgaard 1996b: 97–8: '[Kant] defines a free will as a rational causality which is effective without being determined by an alien cause, including the desires and inclinations of the person. The free will must be entirely self-determining. Yet, because the will is a causality, it must act according to some law or other. Kant says: "Since the concept of a causality entails that of laws... it follows that freedom is by no means lawless." Alternatively, we may say that since the will is practical reason, it cannot be conceived as acting and choosing for no reason. Since reasons are derived from principles, the free will must have a principle. But because the will is free, no law or principle can be imposed on it from the outside. Kant concludes that the will must be autonomous: that is, it must have its *own* law or principle.'

[5] Cf. Korsgaard 1996b: 98: 'And here again we arrive at the problem. For where is this law to come from? If it is imposed on the will from outside then the will is not free. So the will must make the law for itself. But until the will has a law or principle, there is nothing from which it can derive a reason. So how can it have any reason for making one law rather than another?'

[6] Cf. Korsgaard 1996b: 235: 'Cohen makes it sound as if autonomous lawmaking were one thing, and universal autonomous lawmaking another, and this in turn makes it sound as if universalizability is a rational constraint which is imposed on what would otherwise be the arbitrary unconstrained activity of autonomous lawmaking. But I think Kant himself means something else, namely autonomous lawmaking just *isn't* autonomous lawmaking unless it is done universally. The requirement of universalization is not imposed on the activity of autonomous lawmaking by reason from outside, but is constitutive of the activity itself.'

[7] Cf. Korsgaard 1996b: 98: 'The problem faced by the free will is this: the will must have a law, but because the will is free, it must be its own law. And nothing determines what that law must be. *All that it has to be is a law.* Now consider the content of the categorical imperative, as represented by the Formula of Universal Law. The categorical imperative merely tells us to choose a law. Its only constraint on our choice is that it has the form of a law. And nothing determines what the law must be. *All that it has to be is a law.*'

3.1.2 Phase Two: From the categorical imperative to the moral law, step 1: the value of your own humanity

In a way that she represents as a departure from Kant,[8] Korsgaard says that the strategy of Phase One cannot in itself take us as far as the *moral* law: that is, it cannot establish that the law we must abide by is one that constrains our treatment of others in any recognizably moral way, in either a positive or negative sense, in terms of our obligations to do things for them, or to avoid acting against them. For example, the rational egoist acts on a practical law, in as much as she adopts the principle of always acting to promote her interests, and that seems sufficient to provide the kind of coherent structure to the will that is constitutive of free agency on this account. Korsgaard therefore allows (in a way that a more traditional Kantian might not)[9] that nothing she has said so far establishes that the principle the agent needs to adopt is anything we would recognize as a moral principle, 'the law of what Kant calls the Kingdom of Ends, the republic of all rational beings'.[10] To get to *this* law, Korsgaard holds, she must first argue that you must place a value on your own humanity (which is what she does in Phase Two), and then that you must value the humanity of others (which is what she does in Phase Three); once this is established, then the agent cannot adopt the principle of self-interest or any other such non-moral principle as her law, because this would violate the value of humanity. As Korsgaard puts it: 'The argument... aims to move from the formal version of the categorical imperative to moral requirements by way of the Formula of Humanity.'[11]

On this approach, then, the role of Phase Two is to be a stepping stone to establishing the value of humanity, which is a conclusion of the whole argument in Phase Three; and that stepping stone is to establish to the agent the value of her humanity. To see why Phase Three is required, we can ask how Phase Two falls short: why isn't establishing the value of the agent's own humanity sufficient to lead the agent to adopt the moral law? The answer, of course, is that even if the agent recognizes the value of her own humanity, to be moral she needs to respect the value of others, and it is this shift from agent-relative to agent-neutral reasons that Phase Three is designed to achieve.

3.1.3 Phase Three: From the categorical imperative to the moral law, step 2: the value of humanity in general

As with Phase One, this phase of the argument is not a transcendental one;[12] and it is perhaps the part of Korsgaard's overall approach that has been most brusquely

[8] Cf. Korsgaard 1996b: 98–100, 221–2, 233, 237. As she also points out (e.g. p. 99, n. 9), this is also a departure from her earlier self in papers reprinted in Korsgaard 1996a, where she moves straight from her solution to the Kantian antinomy of self-legislation to the moral law: cf. pp. 166–7.

[9] Cf. Ginsborg 1998: 8. [10] Korsgaard 1996b: 99. [11] Korsgaard 1999: 28, n. 23.

[12] At least, I don't think it is, and Korsgaard doesn't claim it is either. But for the suggestion it should be seen in this way, see Skidmore 2002: 135.

dismissed by critics. Korsgaard's strategy here is to claim that the egoist's agent-relative reasons are private, and then to use considerations from Wittgenstein's private language argument to show that this would make them incoherent as reasons, for this argument shows that reasons must be public to be reasons at all.[13] But Korsgaard's critics have been unimpressed by the suggestion that agent-relative reasons are in fact private ones, in any sense that brings in Wittgensteinian considerations: as Skorupski puts it, 'others can "share" the normative force of the egoist's reasons; that is, they can understand his reasons and, if egoism were right and they were rational, could acknowledge their force (as agent-relative reasons)'.[14]

This completes my outline of Korsgaard's overall argument. I will not say anything more about Phase One or Phase Three, and in particular I will not attempt to defend Korsgaard from her critics over the latter, because my focus here is intended to be on the transcendental part of her strategy, which is in Phase Two. It is therefore now time to look in more detail at what the transcendental argument in Phase Two is meant to be.

3.2 Transcendental Arguments for Value

On the account I have given of Phase Two, the aim here is to establish the value of your humanity, as a way of moving to the establishment of the value of humanity in general in Phase Three, in order to show why the law that the agent chooses in Phase One cannot violate the dignity of persons.

To those familiar with debates surrounding transcendental arguments, this may immediately raise concerns. For, it may seem that Korsgaard is straightaway making claims for her transcendental argument that have been famously rendered problematic by Barry Stroud, by using that argument to establish a conclusion about how things are, namely, that your humanity has value. As has been much discussed, Stroud suggested in his 1968 article that such world-directed claims can invariably be resisted by the sceptic, and weakened to appearance or belief directed ones, so that the conclusion of a plausible transcendental argument will only tell us how things must appear to us or how we must believe them to be, in order to make possible thought, language, experience or whatever.[15] If Korsgaard's transcendental argument is making a world-directed claim, therefore, it may seem that this Stroudian worry needs to be addressed.

Of course, if Korsgaard wanted to defend a world-directed transcendental argument, she could perhaps do so by questioning Stroud's reasons for thinking that such

[13] Cf. Korsgaard 1996b: 132ff.

[14] Skorupski 1998: 348–9. Skorupski is here echoing Nagel's complaint in his response to Korsgaard in Nagel 1996: 208; and cf. also Skidmore 2002: 135–7.

[15] Stroud 1968: 255–6. For further discussion of Stroud's position, see Stern 2000.

arguments can always be weakened by the sceptic to what we must believe or how things must appear. But even if Stroud's position is questionable in general,[16] it may seem that there is something especially problematic in taking Korsgaard's argument in a strong or ambitious form: for it may just seem incredible to think that you could be given an argument to establish that your humanity has value, in a world-directed sense. This incredibility is clearly felt by Skorupski when he writes: 'It would be gratifying to have it demonstrated by pure philosophy that one is important . . . But in the absence of contagious magic the demonstration seems less than cogent.'[17] The worry here, I think, is hubris: how can it be established that we have value as such, when seen in the scheme of things it seems we have no more significance than anything else—when, as Hume put it, 'the life of man is of no greater importance to the universe than that of an oyster'.[18] Thus, even if a case could be made for world-directed transcendental arguments in general (contra Stroud et al.), is it reasonable to think that such a case can be made concerning my value as a human being?

However, whatever the force of these concerns, it is not clear that they are worries that need apply to Korsgaard. For, she herself does not propose any such ambitious, world-directed transcendental argument,[19] but instead puts forward a modest argument, combined with a kind of anti-realism or perspectivism about value, that does get to the stronger conclusion that your humanity has value, but only where that value is conceived of in this perspectival way.[20]

That Korsgaard sees herself as approaching things this way is clear from what she says when she summarizes her transcendental argument:

> The argument I have just given is a transcendental argument. I might bring that out more clearly by putting it this way: rational action exists, so we know it is possible. How is it possible? And then by the course of reflections in which we have just engaged, I show you that rational action is possible only if human beings find their own humanity to be valuable. But rational action is possible, and we are the human beings in question. Therefore we find ourselves to be valuable. Therefore, of course, we are valuable.[21]

[16] In Stern 2007b, I argue that Stroud's argument is not as compelling as is usually assumed, but that a better argument can be offered to the same modest effect.

[17] Skorupski 1998: 350.

[18] Hume 1965: 301.

[19] I would therefore contrast Korsgaard's position with Allen Wood's, who follows a similar argument to Korsgaard, but to a more realist conclusion, but without attempting to address Stroudian concerns: cf. Wood 1999: 125–32; and his review of Korsgaard's *Creating the Kingdom of Ends* in Wood 1998.

[20] Skidmore accepts this defence of Korsgaard's transcendental argument in Phase Two, but as we have seen, thinks Korsgaard also has a transcendental argument in Phase Three, which is more ambitious, and so which falls foul of Stroud's criticisms: see Skidmore 2002: 134–40. But as I have mentioned, Korsgaard herself doesn't present Phase Three as a transcendental argument, so it is debatable whether these issues apply to it. In her more recent rehearsal of the argument in Korsgaard 2009: 22–5, she also distinguishes clearly between these phases, and again only talks of the second in transcendental terms.

[21] Korsgaard 1996b: 123–4.

Korsgaard then goes on:

> You might want to protest against that last step. How do we get from the fact that we find ourselves to be valuable to the conclusion that we are valuable?[22]

And here is Korsgaard's response to this worry:

> There's a good reason why the argument must take this form after all. Value, like freedom, is only directly accessible from within the standpoint of reflective consciousness. And I am now talking about it externally, for I am describing the nature of the consciousness that gives rise to the perception of value. From this external, third-person perspective, all we can say is that when we are in the first-person perspective we find ourselves to be valuable, rather than simply that we are valuable. There is nothing surprising in this. Trying to actually see the value of humanity from the third-person perspective is like trying to see the colours someone sees by cracking open his skull. From the outside, all we can say is why he sees them.
>
> Suppose you are now tempted once more to say that this shows that value is unreal just as colour is unreal. We do not need to posit the existence of colours to give scientific explanations of why we see them. Then the answer will be the same as before. The Scientific World View is no substitute for human life. If you think it is unreal, go and look at a painting by Bellini or Olitski, and you will change your mind. If you think reasons and values are unreal, go and make a choice, and you will change your mind.[23]

Korsgaard is thus agreeing with the central Humean idea, that from the point of view of the universe nothing really has value; but Korsgaard doesn't claim to be operating from that point of view. Rather, she is engaging with agents who have a perspective on the universe that involves the experience of values and making judgements about them, just as much as they have a perspective that involves experiencing colours and making judgements about them too. So, she holds, if we can establish that from our perspective we must experience or judge that we ourselves have value, that is good enough for this exercise. Korsgaard can therefore agree with the Humean point that to think that we could establish anything more about this world is absurd, and can likewise claim that her transcendental argument doesn't have to be ambitious in this sense, while still insisting that no more than this is required, once this conception of value is accepted.

Now, of course, this approach to the notion of value, and whether it is substantive or realist enough, will be controversial;[24] but I take it here that enough people will

[22] Korsgaard 1996b: 124. [23] Korsgaard 1996b: 124–5.

[24] In his response to Korsgaard in Korsgaard 1996b, G. A. Cohen expresses some misgivings on this score: see Cohen 1996: 186; and for a defence of Korsgaard's approach, see Gibbard 1999: 153: 'One aspect of Korsgaard's argument will be controversial, but not with me. It is transcendental: it takes something we can't act without accepting, derives a consequence, and then embraces the consequence... [But] if the argument goes through as intended, its conclusion doesn't follow logically from its premises—that's the worry. Mightn't it be that although merely acting at all commits us to *thinking* that humanity has value, in fact it doesn't *have* value? Korsgaard, though, say I, has every right to rely on such arguments. Suppose she is right, and in settling whether to act, I've settled whether to believe humanity valuable. I'll then act and voice the conviction to which acting commits me: Humanity is valuable. What other conceivable access can

find it congenial to serve as an adequate way of allowing Korsgaard to present her transcendental argument in modest terms.[25] We are now in a position to see what that modest transcendental argument is meant to be, where all that it intends to establish qua transcendental argument is that we must value our own humanity. I will offer two accounts of this argument, and claim that the second is to be preferred.

3.3 The Regress of Identities Argument

The first account of the argument I will consider runs as follows:

1. You cannot act unless you can take some impulse to be a reason to act.
2. You cannot take some impulse to be a reason to act unless it conforms to some way in which you identify yourself (a practical identity).
3. You cannot adopt a particular practical identity unless you also adopt humanity as a practical identity.
4. You cannot adopt humanity as a practical identity unless you value your humanity.
5. Therefore, you must value your humanity, if you are to be an agent.

Let me consider in more detail what this all means.

As with most transcendental arguments, Korsgaard is trying to begin with a premise that the sceptic can be expected to accept, where here the premise is that he is capable of agency. Now, by this Korsgaard doesn't just mean behaviour or bodily movement, but some exercise of the will. Moreover, she holds, to exercise the will and so act in this way, it is not sufficient that whenever an impulse to act or a desire assails you, you will follow it, for then you are not deciding to act at all. Rather, the way to act is to act for a reason: to decide that this impulse (for example, to buy this toy) is a good one (for example, because it will make my daughter happy).

I have, after all, to the question of whether humanity is valuable, but to reflect on what to do? The value of humanity or its lack isn't a feature of nonnatural space, glimpsed by intuition. Thinking humanity valuable, if Korsgaard is right, is an inseparable part of thinking what to do and why. Whether to think humanity valuable is just the question, whether to value humanity.' Cf. also Bittner 1989: 24: 'Now actually we may disregard the difference between showing that moral demands are valid and showing that they must be considered valid. For the realization that given certain basic features of our lives we cannot help but acknowledge moral demands is tantamount to having their validity demonstrated to us.'

[25] Skorupski seems to think that even such a modest transcendental argument is as problematic as a more ambitious one, when the full quotation from him cited earlier runs: 'It would be gratifying to have it demonstrated by pure philosophy that one is important. *Or even—to put it with due Kantian caution—that one must take oneself to be.* But in the absence of contagious magic the demonstration seems less than cogent' [my emphasis]. This is because Skorupski does not see why there might not be valuable things to be done independently of our having value (cf. Skorupski 1998: 350: 'Even if humanity is worthless might there not still be valuable things to be done?'), or how our having value can 'magically' confer value on other things. I think Korsgaard's response, however, would be to say that the alternative is equally 'magical'—namely, how can things have an intrinsic value in themselves? For this sort of worry concerning intrinsic value, cf. also Street 2008.

The second step is to introduce a more distinctively Korsgaardian idea: that if action requires the having of reasons, those reasons are not 'out there' in the world, but come from the way in which doing certain actions would relate to the kind of person you are. Thus, it is qua my daughter's father that I have a reason to buy her this toy, if it would make her happy. As Korsgaard puts it: 'It is necessary to have some conception of your practical identity, for without it you cannot have reasons to act. We endorse or reject our impulses by determining whether they are consistent with the ways in which we identify ourselves.'[26] Unless we had some such practical identity, Korsgaard claims, there would be no reason for us to act on one impulse rather than not, and thus no possibility of rational agency at all.

Obviously one way to resist Korsgaard's argument at this point would be to opt for a more realist conception of reasons, and to claim that for us to have a reason to act on an impulse is just a feature of the situation, independently of whether or not this relates to our practical identity: for example, it is just the potential happiness of my daughter that constitutes a reason for me to obey my impulse to buy the toy. But much of the first two chapters of *The Sources of Normativity*, as well as related papers, is spent arguing against realism of this kind.[27] Korsgaard's position here is complex, and has several strands. One strand is that realism is unable to explain the felt obligatoriness of moral reasons,[28] where by relating this to the person's sense of self, we can see why she must act, to preserve her sense of who she is.[29] Another strand is that the realist faces a regress of justification or an arbitrary foundationalism, as either one reason is grounded on another, or the regress is brought to a stop by fiat;[30] by contrast, on her position the reasons that apply to the agent can be explained in terms of her practical identity, where (as we shall see) Korsgaard thinks that the regress can be brought to a satisfactory end. Korsgaard thinks that both of these features mean that her position is better placed that the realist's to deal with the moral sceptic, who asks why she should act morally. A final strand in Korgaard's case

[26] Korsgaard 1996b: 120.

[27] See Korsgaard 1996b: 7–89; and Korsgaard 2008b.

[28] 'According to . . . realism . . . there are facts, which exist independently of the person's mind, about what there is reason to do; rationality consists in conforming one's conduct to those reasons . . . The difficulty with this account in a way exists right on its surface, for the account invites the question why it is necessary to act in accordance with those reasons, and so seems to leave us in need of a reason to be rational . . . we must still explain why the person feels it *necessary* to act on those normative facts, or what it is about *her* that makes them normative *for her*. We must explain how these reasons get a grip on the agent' (Korsgaard 2008c: 52–3).

[29] Cf. Korsgaard 1996b: 100–2.

[30] Cf. Korsgaard 1996b: 33: 'As these arguments show, realism is a metaphysical position in the exact sense criticized by Kant. We can keep asking why: "Why must I do what is right?"—"Because it is commanded by God"—"But why must I do what is commanded by God?"—and so on, in a way that apparently can go on forever. This is what Kant called a search for the unconditioned—in this case, for something which will bring the reiteration of "but why must I do that?" to an end. The unconditional answer must be one that makes it impossible, unnecessary, or incoherent to ask why again. The realist move is to bring this regress to an end by fiat: he declares that some things are *intrinsically* normative . . . Having discovered that he needs an unconditional answer, the realist straightaway concludes that he has found one.'

against realism is an argument from autonomy: if the reasons we have to act are independent of us, then in acting on those reasons we are not acting freely.[31] On the other hand, if reasons stem from our practical identity, then that makes them intrinsic to who we are, and so compatible with our agency.

Now, of course, all these points against realism can be and have been resisted by realists.[32] But perhaps again we can give Korsgaard the benefit of the doubt here, as many would share her conviction that realism is indeed problematic in the ways that she suggests.

Let us move, then, to the third premise of the argument, where having shown that to have a reason to act this must relate to a particular practical identity, Korsgaard tries to show that no particular practical identity can be adopted unless you adopt the practical identity of being human. I think the idea here is as follows.

Suppose you take an impulse like wanting this toy to be a reason to act because it conforms to your particular practical identity of being a father. But as a reflective agent, you can then ask: what reason have I got to adopt this particular practical identity of being a father? You cannot give as a reason: because then I will go around doing good things like buying toys for my daughter, because doing those things are only reasons for you from the perspective of this identity, which is precisely what is in question. And you cannot give as a reason some further particular practical identity, like being a husband, because the same questions can be raised about that. If you are to halt the regress of reasons, therefore, you must appeal to some reasons that are not grounded in any particular practical identity and so an identity that is likewise not so grounded or 'conditioned': and the only identity of which this is true is the identity of humanity, for without that identity, you could not see yourself as an agent with reasons at all, so it itself does not rest on any reasons given to it by some further particular practical identity. As Korsgaard puts this, beginning with the passage we quoted earlier covering premises 1 and 2:

> It is necessary to have some conception of your practical identity, for without it you cannot have reasons to act. We endorse or reject our impulses by determining whether they are consistent with the ways in which we identify ourselves. Yet most of the self-conceptions which govern us are contingent... What is not contingent is that you must be governed by some conception of your practical identity. For unless you are governed by some conception of your personal identity, you will lose your grip on yourself as having any reason to do one thing rather than another—and with it, your grip on yourself as having any reason to live and act at

[31] Korsgaard 1996b: 5: 'If the real and the good are no longer one, value must find its way into the world somehow. Form must be imposed on the world of matter. This is the work of art, the work of obligation, and it brings us back to Kant. And this is what we should expect. For it was Kant who completed the revolution, when he said that reason—which is form—isn't in the world, but is something we impose on it. The ethics of autonomy is the only one consistent with the metaphysics of the modern world, and the ethics of autonomy is the ethics of obligation.'

[32] For some notable responses, see Gaut 1997; Regan 2002; Fitzpatrick 2006; Crisp 2006: 49–56; Parfit 2006; Wallace 2006: 71–81. I consider Korsgaard's argument from autonomy further in Stern 2007a; and Chapter 1, this volume.

all. But this reason for conforming to your particular practical identities is not a reason that springs from one of those particular practical identities. It is a reason that springs from your humanity itself, from your identity simply as a human being, a reflective animal who needs reasons to act and to live.[33]

I think we can view Korsgaard's position here this way. My practical identity is my sense of who I am. As a reflective agent, I can see that I could be brought to give up any particular practical identity I may have, such as being a father, husband, Englishman, university lecturer, and so on, as I come to see that they are not really essential to me as such, in a way that 'alienates' me from them. But I cannot give up my sense of being a person who can think about who he is in the same way, because to do this I would have to be thinking about who I am—and it is this which Korsgaard thinks is distinctive of the practical identity of humanity. In this case, therefore, no more basic identity can supply me with a reason to adopt this identity, any more than some more basic logical principle can supply me with a reason to believe the principle of non-contradiction, in which case I am entitled to treat it as just the sort of 'unconditioned' stopping point that is able to bring the regress of reasons to a principled end.

Now let's consider the final premise: you cannot adopt humanity as a practical identity unless you value your humanity. Thus far, Korsgaard has shown that you are required to adopt humanity as your practical identity if you are to adopt any practical identity at all, as this identity brings a halt to the regress. But suppose you didn't value your identity as human—meaning here being a reflective agent—but just saw it merely as a necessary fact about yourself, which nonetheless you felt neutral about, or even rather regretted and despised?[34] In this case, however, humanity would not bring a halt to the regress, because unless you saw humanity as valuable, it could not give any reasons to act in itself or to adopt any other particular practical identity, where unless it does so, you cannot continue to think of yourself as a rational agent with reasons. It is therefore a necessary condition of having such reasons that you value your humanity: according to Korsgaard, the price of denying this is to see yourself as living in a world in which there are no reasons to act and thus no way to be an agent at all. In a sense, Korsgaard admits, she cannot prevent the sceptic paying the price if he is determined to do so, in a kind of suicidal abandonment of agency;[35] but in another sense we have little choice but to see ourselves as agents, and so (she thinks) to accept the conclusion of this part of her argument, that you must value your humanity.

[33] Korsgaard 1996b: 121.

[34] Cf. Gibbard 1999: 154: 'Why, though, couldn't I think of reflective choice as a burden, only mitigated by some admirable way that people like me handle it? ... couldn't I still disvalue the sheer state of being a reflective chooser?'

[35] Cf. Korsgaard 1996b: 160–4.

3.4 An Objection to the Regress of Identities Argument

Let us call this version of Korsgaard's argument the regress of identities argument. I now want to consider an objection to it.[36]

This concerns whether Korsgaard is right to think that if we work merely with our particular practical identities, we will be threatened with a regress. Now Korsgaard admits, of course, that as a matter of psychology some of us may not reflect on our particular practical identities, and so not face the regress in our daily lives; but that, she argues, just shows that we can be insufficiently reflective and doesn't show we ought not to feel the regress.[37] But, why ought we to feel the regress? Korsgaard's idea seems to be that our particular practical identities are contingent, and that we could therefore always be brought to give them up by finding other identities that are more compelling:

> You may cease to think of yourself as a mother or a citizen or a Quaker... This can happen in a variety of ways: it is the stuff of drama, and perfectly familiar to us all. Conflicts that arise between identities, if sufficiently pervasive or severe, may force you to give one of them up: loyalty to your country and its cause may turn you against a pacifist religion, or the reverse. Circumstances may cause you to call the practical importance of an identity into question: falling in love with a Montague may make you think that being a Capulet does not matter after all. Rational reflection may bring you to discard a way of thinking of your practical identity as silly or jejune.[38]

Now Korsgaard is of course correct that this sort of thing can occur, and when it does, in a way that should lead you to question your particular practical identity. But Korsgaard seems to think that she can generalize from this, to show that it can apply to every particular practical identity for every agent. But I think that the kind of self-doubt that Korsgaard sees as pervasive is in fact harder to achieve than she realizes—where I don't just mean psychologically harder (which I agree with her is irrelevant here), but rationally or normatively. I think one can see this by looking at her examples. It is important to the persuasiveness of her examples, that the competing identity is not just different from the one you hold, but can itself supply reasons in its favour: for example, the pacifist can nonetheless come to see some value in fighting for his country. But might there not be particular practical identities which nonetheless seem invulnerable to competing reasons in this way, despite being identities we accept are contingent, in the sense that we can see we might not have had the identity in question? For example, suppose that I am a loving son. I am certainly conscious that I might not have been, had I been raised in a different way or in a

[36] I also have my doubts about the step from (4) to (5), but will leave these aside for now.

[37] Cf. Korsgaard's comments on the member of the Mafia brought into the discussion by G. A. Cohen: see Korsgaard 1996b: 257–8.

[38] Korsgaard 1996b: 120.

different time or place, so it is a contingent identity in that sense. But suppose someone offers me an alternative identity. Unless they can supply me with reasons to think being a loving son is wrong or mistaken in some way, why should I be brought to doubt my identity? But it might seem that the only reasons that would count as reasons to give up that identity are ones that would only do so once that identity has been given up. So, for example, you might say I should become a ruthless city trader, and so stop wasting my time visiting my sick mother and spend it arranging profitable deals instead. But what reason could you give me for taking this seriously as an identity, given that you are asking me to betray everything I hold dear? It seems that you would need to give me some internal grounds for giving up my identity (for example, that my loving regard for my mother is making her life worse and not better), which even in the case of an identity which is contingent may not be forthcoming. Or you would need to appeal to common ground between being a son and the values that leads to, and being a ruthless city trader, just as the values of the pacifist and non-pacifist may be said to coincide at certain points, from which the divergences can be explored. But in so far as this is possible, then we can continue to operate with reasons at the level of converging particular practical identities, rather than moving to the kind of universal and necessary identity that Korsgaard thinks is required. So, if this is right, Korsgaard has arguably not done enough to show that it is only the identity of humanity that is invulnerable to the regress issue and hence 'unconditioned', and not also certain particular practical identities; and if this is right, her transcendental argument in this form collapses at step (3).[39]

3.5 The Regress of Value Argument

I now want to look at a second transcendental argument that can be found in Korsgaard's work, which I think fares better than the first one.

This second argument is modelled on an argument that Korsgaard finds in Kant, and which she outlines as follows:

> [Kant] started from the fact that when we make a choice we must regard its object as good. His point is the one I have been making—that being human we must endorse our impulses before we can act on them. He asked what it is that makes these objects good, and, rejecting one form of realism, he decided that the goodness was not in the objects themselves. Were it not for our desires and inclinations—and for the various physiological, psychological, and social conditions which gave rise to those desires and inclinations—we would not find their objects good. Kant saw that we take things to be important because they are important to us—and he concluded that we must therefore take ourselves to be important. In this way, the value of humanity itself is implicit in every human choice. If complete normative scepticism is to be

[39] For similar sorts of objections, see Schneewind 1998a: 43–8. See also Korsgaard's reply in Korsgaard 1998.

avoided—if there is such a thing as a reason for action—then humanity, as the source of all reasons and values, must be valued for its own sake.[40]

This argument can be laid out as follows:

1. To rationally choose to ϕ, you must regard ϕ-ing as good.
2. You cannot regard ϕ-ing as good in itself, but can only regard ϕ-ing as good because it satisfies your needs, desires, inclinations, and so on.
3. You cannot regard your desiring or needing to ϕ as making it good unless you regard yourself as valuable.
4. Therefore, you must regard yourself as valuable.

Consider this example. To rationally choose to eat this piece of chocolate cake, I must think that the eating cake is good in some way. How can I regard it as good? It seems implausible to say that eating cake is good in itself, of intrinsic value. It also seems implausible to say that it is good just because it satisfies a desire as such: for even if I was bulimic it might do that, but still not be regarded as good. A third suggestion, then, is that it can be seen as good because it is good for me, as satisfying a genuine need or desire of mine. But if I think this is what makes eating the piece of cake good, I must value myself as, otherwise, I could not hold that satisfying me is sufficient to make something good enough for it to be rational for me to desire it; so I must regard myself as valuable. Put conversely: suppose that you thought that you and your life were utterly worthless, pointless, meaningless—that in your eyes, you were valueless. And suppose that you are faced with a piece of cake: on what basis would you choose to eat it? It seems unlikely that there is something intrinsically good about eating it, or that you should do so just because you find yourself with a desire to do so, even while finding your existence valueless. It seems that the only reason to do so would be if you thought eating the cake brought you some genuine benefit—but if you thought your life was worthless, how could you see this as a reason either? Why is bringing benefit to something that in your eyes is so utterly without value a reasonable thing to do?

There are some dangers in this argument, however. One, which Korsgaard considers, is that it might lead to 'self-conceit':[41] that is, I might conclude from this that I am supremely valuable, simply as Bob Stern, which could obviously then get in the way of my ethical treatment of others. But, this worry might be lessened by the thought that while the argument gets me to see that I must find something valuable about me, it need not be anything about me in particular, and perhaps could instead be something about me that is more general—such as my humanity or personhood. However, while Korsgaard says that reflection will indeed lead us in this more general

[40] Korsgaard 1996b: 122. Korsgaard claims to take her inspiration from Kant's *Groundwork of the Metaphysics of Morals* (*GMM*: 77–9 [4:427–8]), which she discusses further in her paper 'Kant's Formula of Humanity', reprinted in Korsgaard 1996a: 106–32. I leave aside here whether or not Korsgaard is correct in her reading of Kant; but for some doubts on this score, see Timmermann 2006; and Chapter 5, this volume.

[41] Korsgaard 1998: 54. Cf. also Korsgaard 1996b: 249–50.

direction, we will need to see how. A second, perhaps related, worry is that this argument has a troubling parallel in the case of Satan, where Satan goes through 1 to 4 above, and concludes that he must regard his devilish nature as valuable. If this argument somehow entitles us to regard our humanity or personhood as valuable, why doesn't it entitle Satan to think the same about his nature? This is not the same as self-conceit, because he is not valuing himself as Satan just qua Satan; he is valuing his nature, just as we are valuing ours. Nor does devilishness seem any less central to his nature than humanity is to ours. So it is hard to see how the Satanic parallel can be avoided by the argument as it stands.

Nonetheless, it is possible that something can be built on the central idea of the argument, which I take to be this: As long as we think we can act for reasons based on the value of things, but at the same time reject any realism about that value applying to things independently of us, then we must be treated as the source of value and in a way that makes rational choice possible. We can therefore see Korsgaard's second argument as attempting something along these lines, using her notion of practical identity to perhaps avoid the two problems we have identified with the Kantian argument.

Here, then, is an outline of Korsgaard's second argument:

1. To rationally choose to ϕ, you must take it that ϕ-ing is the rational thing to do.
2. Since ϕ-ing in itself gives you no reason to ϕ, you can take it that ϕ-ing is the rational thing to do only if you regard your practical identity as making it rational to ϕ.
3. You cannot regard your practical identity as making ϕ-ing the rational thing to do unless you can see some value in that practical identity.
4. You cannot see any value in any particular practical identity as such, but can regard it as valuable only because of the contribution it makes to giving you reasons and values by which to live.
5. You cannot see having a practical identity as valuable in this way unless you think your having a life containing reasons and values is important.
6. You cannot regard it as important that your life contain reasons and values unless you regard your leading a rationally structured life as valuable.
7. You cannot regard your leading a rationally structured life as valuable unless you value yourself qua rational agent.
8. Therefore, you must value yourself qua rational agent, if you are to make any rational choice.

The first step is now familiar: To act is to do or choose something for a reason. The second step is also now familiar: Korsgaard thinks that we have reasons to act because of our practical identities, not because acts have reasons attached to them in themselves. Once again, realists might demur,[42] claiming that some actions are

[42] See, for example, Scanlon 1998: 55–72; and Kerstein 2002: 70–2.

rational things to do, because some things have value as such: so, perhaps knowledge is valuable in itself, thereby making it rational to seek it.[43] But as before, let us leave such worries aside and assume with Korsgaard that nothing is objectively rational for us to do.

The third step asks how a practical identity can make something into a reason for an agent: how can the fact that I am a father make it rational for me to buy my daughter this toy? The thought here is that it can only do so if I see value in that identity. Korsgaard stresses this when she writes:

> The conception of one's identity in question here is not a theoretical one, a view about what as a matter of inescapable scientific fact you are. It is better understood as a description under which you value yourself, a description under which you find your life to be worth living and your actions to be worth undertaking.[44]

So, being a father, whether contingently or essentially, gives one no reason to be a caring or devoted father of a sort that would have good reason to buy a daughter a gift; rather, valuing one's fatherhood does this.

But (moving on to step 4), how can I see my particular practical identity as valuable? I think Korsgaard's position here is that I cannot see any value in any particular practical identity as such, and this might seem to rest on something like the sort of regress argument we looked at and criticized above: one will always be faced with requiring a reason for valuing any particular practical identity, and this regress cannot be halted by any such identity. But, as we saw, this thought can perhaps be resisted. However, I think that even without a regress argument, Korsgaard can make her point here, more by using the objections to realism considered previously: namely, that to see value in any particular practical identity as such is to be committed to realism, to thinking that being a father, an Englishman, a university lecturer or whatever matters as such; or (in a way that is in the end equally realist), it matters because of the intrinsically valuable things it leads you to do. But, as we have seen, Korsgaard also takes such realist positions to be problematic, so can perhaps use such arguments here, without appealing to the regress considerations at all.

So suppose we allow that no particular practical identity can be seen to have value in itself; Korsgaard then offers as the only remaining explanation of its value to the agent that has that identity, that such identities have the general capacity of enabling the agent to live a life containing reasons: because I have whatever particular practical identities I do (father, Englishman, university lecturer ...), I can then find things to be valuable and act rationally accordingly, in a way that gives me unity as a subject. As Korsgaard puts it: 'To be a thing, one thing, a unity, an entity; to be anything at all: in the metaphysical sense, that is what it means to have integrity. But we use the term for someone who lives up to his own standards. And that is because we think that living up to them is what makes him one, so what makes him a person at all.'[45]

[43] Cf. Regan 2002: 272. [44] Korsgaard 1996b: 101. [45] Korsgaard 1996b: 102.

But then (step 5), to think that this makes having some sort of particular practical identity important, you must think that it matters that your life have the sort of rational structure that having such identities provides; but (step 6), to see that as mattering, you must see value in your leading a rationally structured life. And then, finally, to see value in your leading such a life, you must see your rational nature as valuable, which it to value your humanity.

Does this Korsgaardian argument avoid the pitfalls of the Kantian one discussed earlier? I think it avoids the problem of self-conceit, because it does seem that what you end up valuing is not yourself simply as such, but yourself qua rational agent. And I think as I have presented it, it avoids the problem of the Satanic parallel, because all it shows is that Satan must value his rational nature, not his devilishness.

For both these problems to be avoided, however, it is important to run the argument as I have done, not as it is sometimes presented by Korsgaard, which is via the notion of need.[46] This would follow the same premises as before for 1–5, and then go as follows:

6*. You cannot regard it as important that your life contain reasons and values unless you take your need to lead this sort of life as important.
7*. You cannot take this need to be important unless you take yourself to be valuable.
8*. Therefore, you must value yourself, if you are to make any rational choice.

The difficulty with 6*–8*, I think, is that 8* does not stipulate what it is about yourself that you are required to value, so that this could be my sheer particularity (self-conceit), or if I am not in fact human, my non-human nature (Satan). This is because 6* just identifies a need, and says that this need could not be important unless the agent who has the need were seen to be valuable somehow—whereas the previous argument narrows value down to rational agency, and so rules out both self-conceit and devilishness.

3.6 Conclusion

I have therefore reconstructed that part of Korsgaard's strategy which offers an argument to the effect that you must value your humanity, as a transcendental argument. It turns out that if it is to be made plausible in this way, a lot depends on accepting Korsgaard's arguments against realism; but then, many have suspected

[46] Cf. Korsgaard 1996b: 121: 'Most of the time, our reasons for action spring from our more contingent and local identities. But part of the normative force of those reasons spring from the value we place on ourselves as human beings who need such identities. In this way all values depends on the value of humanity; other forms of practical identity matter in part because humanity requires them'; and Korsgaard 1996b: 125: 'Our other practical identities depend for their normativity on the normativity of our human identity—on our own endorsement of our human need to be governed by such identities—and cannot withstand reflective scrutiny without it. We must value ourselves as human.'

that some commitment to anti-realism is required to make a transcendental argument convincing. A worry then is that it can appear to make the argument redundant in the standard anti-sceptical case, because anti-realism appears sufficient as a response to scepticism on its own;[47] but in this ethical case, this does not seem to be the issue, so that here this worry is less of a concern. Of course, as Korsgaard herself allows, this transcendental argument in itself is not meant to be sufficient to complete her project, which still requires a third phase, which I have not considered, and which may still be found to be problematic.[48] Nonetheless, I hope to have shown something, which is to have established how the transcendental argument of the second phase can be seen to work, and how it is more plausible than many of Korsgaard's critics have found it; and this I think is an achievement of sorts.[49]

[47] For more discussion of this issue, see Stern 2000: 49–58.

[48] There is another objection which I also cannot address in this paper, and which is not considered directly by Korsgaard: namely that if 'valuing your humanity' comes down to 'valuing your rational agency', will that cover enough of what morality is usually meant to cover? Allan Gibbard puts the point this way: 'If valuing my humanity is taking pride in being a reflective chooser, how does that constrain what I do, what I reflectively choose? Perhaps I must nurture my powers of reflective agency… Still, if that's all we must do as human beings, then enlightenment morality is far too narrow: we'll need to oppose pain and seek fulfilment and enjoyment only when they affect our powers of reflective agency' (Gibbard 1999: 156). I am not sure the Kantian would in fact see much of a worry here. Perhaps a deeper concern, however, is that even if the argument I have considered works, there is a problem with Korsgaard's whole *strategy* of attempting to respond to moral scepticism in the way she does, as in the end the reason to be moral becomes grounded in the interest we have in being agents, which is to distort the nature of genuine moral action which should not be grounded in anything *outside* morality itself. I discuss this issue further in Chapter 4.

[49] I gave a first version of this paper at one of the *Transcendental Philosophy and Naturalism* workshops, under the AHRC funded project run by Mark Sacks. Mark offered very useful and characteristically generous comments on that occasion, the last on which I was to see him. I am therefore particularly grateful to Joel Smith and Peter Sullivan for undertaking the publication of this paper in the collection in which it first appeared, as what is very sadly the last chapter in the discussions that Mark and I had on matters transcendental over many years, from which I learned so much.

4

Moral Scepticism and Agency

Kant and Korsgaard

This paper is about moral scepticism, but also about agents and their actions: in particular, can reflection on the nature of agency be used to address moral scepticism? Within the contemporary literature, Christine Korsgaard is well known for arguing that it can, while her approach is widely taken to be Kantian. At the same time, one prominent criticism of her position has been that is succumbs to difficulties famously highlighted by H. A. Prichard, that all attempts to answer the sceptic who asks why they should act morally end up undermining themselves, as they only succeed in treating moral actions as a means to non-moral ends—where this may also be taken to be a Kantian worry. After showing how Korsgaard makes herself seem vulnerable to this sort of objection by the way in which she presents her sceptical target, I want to then claim that Kant himself sees the sceptical challenge in a way that avoids Prichardian difficulties. I will then close by suggesting that if we read Korsgaard along these Kantian lines, we can understand her appeal to agency in a way that also avoids becoming a self-undermining response to moral scepticism, and thus put her debate with her critics in a different light.

4.1 Korsgaard on Moral Scepticism and Practical Agency

Korsgaard's treatment of moral scepticism may be seen as part of a broader project in meta-ethics, which is to argue for constructivism and against realism, where her claim here is that the former has the advantage of being able to respond to moral scepticism in a way that the latter cannot. This scepticism comes about, she argues, when we are faced with what she calls 'the normative question', which arises when we encounter a moral demand, and find it to be problematic:

The normative question is a first-person question that arises for the moral agent who must actually do what morality says. When you want to know what a philosopher's theory of normativity is, you must place yourself in the position of an *agent* on whom morality is making a difficult claim. You then ask the philosopher: must I really do this? Why must I do this? And his answer is his answer to the normative question.[1]

Korsgaard then goes on to complain that realism does not and cannot answer this question. It *does* not answer it, because all it says is that you must act in a certain way because it is the morally right thing to do, but the question precisely concerns what real force that consideration should have for you.[2] And realism *cannot* answer the question, because on the realist account moral norms and values obtain independently of the agent, so the agent can always question their hold on him and wonder why he must act on them.[3]

Korsgaard argues, therefore, that we must turn from realism to a more constructivist form of metaethics, which instead of starting with reasons and then trying to show the agent why he must follow them, we start with agency and its conditions, and argue that moral norms and values can be constructed out of that in some way. Korsgaard claims that by proceeding in this manner, we can give the normative question an adequate answer, insofar as following the demands of morality and acknowledging its values can be shown to be constitutive of agency itself, so that 'the right of these concepts to give laws to us'[4] will have been established.

How might this strategy work? The argument has a transcendental flavour: that is, the sceptic is shown that they cannot intelligibly reject the demand that morality makes, such as that they must act on the principle of universalizability, or must value the humanity of others, or whatever, because following that principle or acknowledging that value is a necessary condition of being an agent at all;[5] from this perspective, then, just raising the normative question successfully resolves it, as a commitment to these norms and values is already presupposed in being the kind of agent who poses it in the first place, just as a commitment to the principle of non-contradiction is necessary to the kind of mind who wonders if they should follow it.[6] This strategy, Korsgaard thinks, will successfully answer the moral sceptic in a way that the realist does not and cannot, where this is used by her as one of the central arguments in favour of her more constructivist approach.[7]

[1] Korsgaard 1996b: 16.

[2] Cf. Korsgaard 1996b: 38: '*All* [the realist] can say is that it is *true* that this is what you ought to do... But this answer appears to be off the mark. It addresses someone who has fallen into doubt about whether the action is really required by morality, not someone who has fallen into doubt about whether moral requirements really are normative.'

[3] Cf. Korsgaard 2008a: 7: 'The rationalist account... cannot explain why rational principles necessarily motivate us. So long as bindingness or normativity is conceived of as a fact external to the will, and therefore external to the person, it seems possible to conceive of a person who is indifferent to it. But this throws doubt on whether such principles can be binding after all.' Cf. also Korsgaard 2008c: 52–3.

[4] Korsgaard 1996b: 9.

[5] Cf. e.g. Korsgaard 1996b: 228–9: 'I need to will universally in order to see my action as something which *I do*'; and p. 232: 'it is the claim to universality that *gives* me a will, that makes my will distinguishable from the operations of desires and impulses in me'.

[6] Cf. Korsgaard 1996b: 235 and 2008a: 7.

[7] Although his constructivism differs from Korsgaard's, David Copp also argues that constructivism is better placed than realism to deal with sceptical issues: see Copp 2005.

4.2 Prichardian Objections to Korsgaard

This, I hope, is a reasonably faithful sketch of Korsgaard's general position and its concerns. Turning now to some assessment of it, we must therefore consider whether it succeeds in its objective of answering 'the normative question' and so dealing with the moral sceptic, and of showing that the realist fails to do so in a way that reveals a serious weakness in the realist's position. In making this assessment of Korsgaard's case, one could of course criticize the details of Korsgaard's argument; but I want to focus instead on a broader strategic challenge to her view, which (following H. A. Prichard's celebrated article 'Does Moral Philosophy Rest on a Mistake?' and related works of his)[8] might be called *the Prichardian challenge*.[9]

The challenge can be presented as follows: to take scepticism seriously in the way that Korsgaard does, is to assume that morality needs some extra-moral basis; however, to be moral is precisely to think the moral reasons one has to act are compelling in themselves, without any such basis for them being required by someone who is a genuine moral agent. So, the Prichardian thinks that all we can really do is remind the sceptic what his moral obligations are, and not get tempted into trying to offer further support for them in some way, as then the sceptic may end up acting morally, but will be doing so for the wrong reasons, so that we have ultimately failed in our efforts to deal with his scepticism.[10] Thus, the realist will claim that the higher wisdom here is not to try to answer the sceptic, but to refuse to engage with him for these Prichardian reasons; as a result, it is argued, Korsgaard's strategy of criticizing the realist for failing to answer the 'normative question' is fatally flawed.[11]

That this is indeed a difficulty for Korsgaard's approach may seem confirmed by passages such as the following:

> I believe that the answer [to the normative question] must appeal, in a deep way, to our sense of who we are, to our sense of our identity. As I have been emphasizing, morality can ask hard things of us, sometimes that we should be prepared to sacrifice our lives in its name. This places a demanding condition on a successful answer to the normative question: it must show that sometimes doing the wrong thing is as bad or worse than death. And for most human beings on most occasions, the only thing that could be as bad or worse than death is something that for us amounts to death—not being ourselves any more... If moral claims are ever worth dying

[8] See Prichard 2002a and other writings in the collection containing this paper.

[9] Korsgaard herself discusses Prichard's position in Korsgaard 1996b: cf. pp. 38–9, 42–4, 60–1.

[10] Cf. McDowell 1998a: 86: 'The question "Why should I conform to the dictates of morality?" is most naturally understood as asking for an extra-moral motivation that will be gratified by virtuous behaviour. So understood, the question has no answer. What may happen is that someone is brought to see things as a virtuous person does, and so stops feeling the need to ask it.'

[11] Cf. Gerry Cohen's response to Korsgaard, where he argues that once she allows the sceptic to characterize the problem in the way she does, any prospect of answering him is lost: see Cohen 1996: 178–83.

for, then violating them must be, in a similar way, worse than death. And this means that they must issue in a deep way from our sense of who we are.[12]

In the light of passages such as these, we might interpret Korsgaard as follows: Morality asks us to act against our immediate interests on many occasions, and thus the moral sceptic might well ask why he should be at all motivated to act as morality demands, and thus why he should consider morality as giving him any *reason* to act. In response, it seems, Korsgaard sets out to show that we cannot act immorally without undermining our agency, which the sceptic presumably wants to preserve. In the end, then, the sceptic can be brought to see that she should not 'experience moral obligation as something alien to her innermost self or her heart's desire',[13] so that a reason for the moral action can be given in terms that will convince her to be moral.

It is precisely this appeal to the apparent interest the agent has and must have in acting morally, however, that has alarmed those who follow Prichard in thinking that to link morality to our interests in this way is to distort what is required, which is that the moral agent should act morally simply because he or she sees what is asked of them. So, for example, Nagel has objected that Korsgaard's approach is in danger of 'cheapening the motive' of moral action, and comes close to being an 'egoist answer to egoism',[14] while Larmore is critical of 'Kantians [who] ... trace our moral concern for another back to what they regard as our supreme interest—namely, the affirmation of our own rational freedom. Recognizing the moral point of view for what it is really means, in contrast, learning to see the reason to do well by others as a reason that speaks for itself.'[15] Similarly, Watkins and Fitzpatrick have raised the following worry from a realist perspective:

What is wrong with enslaving someone, for example, seems to be something straightforwardly and simply about her, given what she is—the dignity that belongs to her as a rational being. To cash out the wrongness of such an action and its normative force for me in a way that requires a detour through a story about what I have to do in order to exercise my will at all seems like a move in precisely the wrong direction. It does not seem true to ordinary moral experience, which certainly does not represent other people's value and its significance for us as deriving from commitments bound up with the exercise of our own wills under certain generic constraints inherent in the nature of willing.[16]

[12] Korsgaard 1996b: 17–18. [13] Korsgaard 1996b: 240.

[14] Nagel 1996: 206. Korsgaard responds to Nagel's worry in Korsgaard 1996b: 246–51.

[15] Larmore 2008: 115. Larmore is spirited in his defence of Prichard's approach at several points in the book, and critical of what he sees as Korsgaard's failure to take Prichard's position sufficiently seriously: see e.g. pp. 90–1, p. 113.

[16] Watkins and Fitzpatrick 2002: 361. Cf. also Enoch 2006, where I think Enoch intends to strike a Pritchardian note on p. 180, where he remarks that Korsgaard will end up distorting things is she tries to use the fact that adopting certain principles and values is constitutive of agency as a way of getting the sceptic to be moral: 'However strong or weak the reasons that apply to [the sceptic] and require that he be moral, surely they do not become stronger when he realizes that unless he complies with morality his bodily movements will not be adequately described as actions'—where I take it that Enoch's point is that *if*

Thus, from this perspective, in raising the normative question Korsgaard is in fact said to play into the hands of the sceptic, and so to make precisely the mistake Prichard accused moral philosophy in general of making.

4.3 Kant and Moral Scepticism: Sections I and II of the 'Groundwork'

I now want to turn to Kant, and consider how far the issues discussed above turn out to apply to him, and if he therefore falls into the same Prichardian trap as Korsgaard seems to do. My strategy will be to argue that while Kant was indeed deeply concerned with a certain type of moral scepticism, this differs from the type discussed above, and so does not lead him to make the mistake of trying to deal with a question that is better left set aside. To keep the discussion within reasonable bounds, I will mainly focus on Kant's *Groundwork of the Metaphysics of Morals*. My claim will be that in the first two sections of the *Groundwork*, the issue of scepticism of any sort hardly arises at all, and that while an important sceptical threat is discussed and dealt with in the third section, this is a threat of a distinctively different kind.

In the Preface and first two sections of the *Groundwork*, it is perhaps scarcely surprising that Kant does not take up any serious sceptical challenge. For, in this part of the work, the main task Kant sets himself is to identify 'the supreme principle of morality', where he does so by taking our commonly shared moral conceptions for granted (for example, about the good will, duty, the imperatival nature of morality, and certain moral cases), and attempting to derive the Formula of Universal Law as the supreme moral principle from them by a process of analysis. In these sections, therefore, Kant seems more than happy to accept that we have a good grasp of morality without any need for philosophy, where he does not expect us to find the Formula of Universal Law to be revisionary of that grasp in any way—indeed, if it were, he would allow that it would be an objection to his claim that it constitutes the supreme principle that he is looking for here. Thus, Kant willingly accepts that in arriving at the Formula of Universal law, he is not teaching 'the moral cognition of common reason' anything new, but simply making it 'attentive to its own principles': 'there is, accordingly, no need of science and philosophy to know what one has to do in order to be honest and good, and even wise and virtuous'.[17] Kant therefore seems to take for granted that our moral practices are in good order and in no need of defence or justification, and that philosophy can proceed by simply reflecting on

the sceptic came to think they *were* stronger on this basis, he would then see a reason to act morally, but not in a way that would make his action genuinely moral, so that Korsgaard's strategy here is self-defeating.

[17] *GMM*: 58 [4:404]. For similar remarks, see 66 [4:412], where Kant comments that 'common moral appraisal' is 'very worthy of respect'; and *CPrR*: 153 note [5:8]: 'Who would even want to introduce a new principle of all morality and, as it were, first invent it? Just as if, before him, the world had been ignorant of what duty is or in thoroughgoing error about it.'

them, to bring out the fundamental moral principle on which they rely. Given this kind of approach, it is scarcely surprising that sceptical challenges have little place.

Now, Kant is sensitive to a worry that might seem to follow: namely, that if our ordinary moral thinking really is in such good order, and if philosophy must base itself on this thinking, what is the point in engaging with the effort of doing philosophy here at all—particularly, as he admits, when our ordinary thinking is quite adept at a pretty high level of reflection on moral matters, while philosophizing might lead it astray, and so make matters worse.[18] Kant thinks he has a response to this worry—but again, it is a response that so far gives no anti-sceptical role to his philosophical project. For, the value Kant places on philosophy here is that by arriving at the supreme principle of morality, philosophy can lead us to be better moral agents by making it harder for us succumb to the 'natural dialectic' whereby we deceive ourselves on moral matters;[19] its value does not lie in making it easier to answer those who see no reason to be moral.

It may seem, however, that Kant gets closer to addressing a genuine scepticism about morality at the start of Section II, where he raises the spectre of 'those who ridicule all morality as the mere phantom of a human imagination overstepping itself through self-conceit'.[20] The sceptic Kant is considering here makes much of the frailties Kant has already noted, and who claims that we can therefore never be sure that anyone in fact acts for anything other than self-interest; they then try to bring morality into doubt by pointing to this fact. Kant may therefore seem to getting closer here to an engagement with the moral sceptic.

However, although Kant is indeed bringing in a reference to the sceptical position here, I do not believe that he is taking it seriously in its own right, or setting out to show how it can be refuted as such; rather, he is using it as a means to criticize an empirical approach to moral philosophy, which is his main target. For, Kant holds that the evidence of human moral weakness, and the consequent difficulty of finding clear examples of action done from duty and with no regard for the 'dear self'[21] *can only* lead to scepticism about morality *if* one takes the content of morality to be something we must leave to our experience to determine, by generating this from examples of moral behaviour; for then, of course, if we are truly unable to find any such examples, we could not conduct our investigation into morality, and we might regard all moral principles as suspect. But, of course, Kant thinks anyone who is drawn to this conclusion has simply adopted a mistaken view of the nature of our

[18] Cf. *GMM*: 59 [4:404]: '[The] philosopher, though he cannot have any other principle that that of common understanding, can easily confuse his judgment by a mass of considerations foreign and irrelevant to the matter and deflect it from the straight course.'

[19] *GMM*: 59 [4:405]. For further discussion of this aspect of Kant's position, see Henrich 1994; and Guyer 2000: 207–31.

[20] *GMM*: 62 [4:407]. Cf. Copp 2001: 5, where Copp cites this passage as evidence of Kant's engagement with the moral sceptic.

[21] *GMM*: 62 [4:407].

moral principles, which are known a priori rather than being based on examples—and indeed, must be if we are to treat the moral law as valid for all rational agents, and to explain how we could come up with any moral assessment of the examples of moral action in the first place.[22] Far from taking scepticism here as a serious threat, therefore, Kant uses the possibly sceptical consequences of any empirical approach in ethics as a reductio of that position.

It would seem from the first two sections of the *Groundwork*, therefore, that there is no real evidence to suggest that Kant is seriously troubled by the sort of scepticism identified by Korsgaard. Rather than setting out to refute such scepticism, Kant merely takes the contribution of his enterprise thus far to lie in perhaps enabling us to be better moral beings, in offering us a kind of pure philosophical approach to ethics that will help us guard against sophistry and self-deception in our moral conduct, while its a priori nature can also help us argue that the lack of clear examples of moral behaviour is no threat to thinking about morality—for example, we can still see how friends are required to be sincere with one another, even if we are not certain that anyone has managed to be motivated solely by friendship and not self-interest.[23] Much like Aristotle, therefore, Kant may be read up to this point as working within a pre-existing moral framework, rather than as trying to answer someone challenging it from the outside and asking why they should adopt it,[24] where this is the sort of project that can lead to the kind of problems raised by the Prichardian.

4.4 Kant and Moral Scepticism: Section III of the 'Groundwork'

However, it could now be said, we have so far only discussed Sections I and II of the *Groundwork*, which adopt the analytical approach of starting with our common moral cognition, and so may indeed work in this 'internal' fashion; but (the objection runs) Kant's approach is very different in Section III, with very different results. Moreover, it can be argued, this division in the structure of the *Groundwork* between the first two sections and the last corresponds to the two-fold task that Kant has set himself in the Preface, of not only searching for or identifying the supreme principle of morality (which he claims to have achieved through Sections I and II), but also *establishing* it, or making it good.[25] In addition, he speaks here in terms of offering a 'deduction', which as we know from the first *Critique* is something he associates with

[22] *GMM*: 62–3 [4:408–9]. [23] Cf. *GMM*: 62 [4:408].

[24] Cf. Aristotle 1984: II, 1731 [1095b1–13]. John McDowell, in particular, has emphasized how it is a mistake to see Aristotle as attempting to offer a 'grounding' for ethics: see e.g. McDowell 1998b.

[25] Cf. *GMM*: 47 [4:392]: 'The present groundwork is, however, nothing more than the search for [*Aufsuchung*] and establishment [*Festsetzung*] of the *supreme principle of morality*.' Cf. also *CPrR*: 143 [5:8], where Kant says that the *Critique* 'presupposes, indeed, the *Groundwork of the Metaphysics of Morals*, but only insofar as this constitutes preliminary acquaintance with the principle of duty and provides and justifies a determinate formula of it [*und eine bestimmte Formel derselben angibt und rechtfertigt*]'.

justificatory issues. And, finally, it can be pointed out that there are several points in Sections I and II where Kant raises what seem like sceptical concerns about morality and its principles, explicitly saying that he will postpone such issues until he gets to Section III: so the fact that Kant has not focused on answering the sceptic in the previous parts of the *Groundwork* can hardly be taken as evidence that he did not take the sceptic seriously, or wanted to leave sceptical worries on one side.

Now, this is all indeed true. So, Kant does indeed characterize his approach in Section III as synthetic rather than analytic; he does give the *Groundwork* a two-fold task; he does speak of offering a deduction; and he does hint at deeper sceptical worries in Section I and II that he promises to return to, where for example he speaks of taking it for granted at this stage that there are practical propositions which command categorically, without having proved that there really are any such propositions.[26] My suggestion now will be, however, that Kant takes this turn in Section III *not* because he is seeking to address here the sort of sceptic who sees no reason to be moral, but rather a scepticism that has a very different basis, and which can thus be addressed without leading to the kind of Prichardian concerns raised above.

To see how Kant's engagement with moral scepticism is distinctive in this way, we must appreciate the *transcendental* character of that scepticism, where this involves a different *kind* of puzzlement about morality than any so far discussed.[27] Whereas the earlier moral sceptic may be characterized as standing 'outside' morality and as asking why they should enter into it at all, Kant's sceptic is more like someone who is already inside the moral life but who nonetheless comes to find it problematic *from within*, and so questions it as a result—where they are not looking for reasons to be moral, but ways of understanding how morality is even possible. What gives rise to this transcendental doubt, Kant thinks, is the way in which morality relates to us *as human beings*, where for us it takes the form of duties that are *obligatory* or *binding* in a particular way, where it is this obligatoriness that raises worries that can lead to deep sceptical concerns about the very possibility of morality. Thus, the issue here is whether morality can be made sense of by those already living the moral life, not whether those outside that life can be persuaded into it.

One of the crucial features of Kant's discussion of morality is the contrast he draws between us as moral beings, and the moral life of those with 'holy wills'.[28] The difference, Kant argues, is that whereas for us, morality takes the form of imperatives which tell us what we *must* do, for holy wills this is not the case: for such wills, Kant claims, there is no imperatival force to morality. And because it is an essential feature

[26] See *GMM*: 82 [4:431] and 76 [4:425].

[27] It can be hard to see what is distinctive about such puzzlement. For general accounts to make this clear that I have found helpful, see Nozick 1981: 8–11; and Conant 2004.

[28] See, for example, *GMM*: 88 [4:439].

of morality for us that it involves obligatoriness, Kant thinks that problematic issues are raised here that do not arise for holy wills.

The first, and perhaps most obvious, concerns freedom. For, taking the principle of 'ought implies can',[29] and allowing that morality is obligatory for us, then for morality to be anything more than a 'chimera',[30] we must have freedom. This means, therefore, that a metaphysical basis for moral scepticism can come from a position that denies that we have any such freedom. Indeed, Kant faced a concrete example of such scepticism in the figure of Johann Henrich Schulz, whose work *Attempt at an Introduction to the Doctrine of Morals* was reviewed by Kant in 1783, a couple of years prior to the publication of the *Groundwork*. In his book, Schulz had denied the existence of free will, and thus (as far as Kant was concerned, at least) adopted a 'general fatalism which... turns all human conduct into a mere puppet show and thereby does away altogether with the concept of obligation',[31] and thus with all morality. Here, then, is one form of scepticism about morality that has a metaphysical basis, as a threat to the very possibility of morality.

A second metaphysical issue that arises out of the obligatory nature of morality for us as humans, concerns a puzzlement about that obligatoriness *as such*, rather any doubts one might feel about the freedom that it requires as a condition. What makes that obligatoriness problematic, Kant thinks, is the peculiar kind of *necessity* that the obligations of morality claim for themselves, where this is problematic not because of issues to do with our motivation or clashes with other concerns, but because it is hard to see what makes a necessity of this kind possible. Just as in the theoretical case, where the problematic nature of the necessity claimed by metaphysicians for their principles can be shown through bringing out the synthetic a priori nature of such claims, where in turn that synthetic a priority is profoundly puzzling, so Kant thinks that the problematic nature of the necessity claimed by morality can be shown through bringing out the synthetic a priori nature of what it says we *must* do, in the form of categorical imperatives. It is this issue, therefore, that Kant flags in Section II when he first introduces these imperatives as characteristic of morality, but where he postpones any resolution of it to Section III,[32] in such a way as to put to rest any scepticism about morality based around it, from those who think that perhaps there just *are* no such imperatives of this problematic and mysterious kind, so that Kant is misguided in Section II in deriving any supreme principle of morality from reflection upon them.

In Section II, therefore, Kant sets up the transcendental or 'how possible?' question in the practical case, by contrasting moral imperatives which are categorical, and imperatives of skill or prudence, which are hypothetical. Both types involve a necessity for both tell us that there is something we *must* do; but in the former case, Kant thinks that the necessity is problematic in a way that in the latter case it is

[29] For further discussion of Kant's attitude to this principle, see Chapter 6, this volume.
[30] Cf. *GMM*: 93 [4:445]. [31] Kant *Schulz*: 9 [8:13]. [32] Cf. *GMM*: 72 [4:419–20].

not. This is not because the hypothetical imperatives asks us to do something that is in line with our interests, and the categorical imperatives do not, so it is puzzling how we can be motivated to follow the categorical imperatives of morality, or what could (therefore) make such imperatives rational.[33] The difficulty Kant is interested in, I think, is deeper than this: namely, how can it be that there is anything I *must* do, how is such prescriptivity or obligatoriness possible? As Kant puts it: 'This question does not inquire how the performance of the action that the imperative commands can be thought, but only how *the necessitation of the will*, which the imperative expresses in the problem, can be thought [or conceived, or made sense of: *gedacht*]'.[34] Kant thinks this question can be answered easily enough in the case of hypothetical imperatives, because there is an analytic relation of containment[35] here: if I want to be a pianist, I must practice, because I cannot be a pianist otherwise, so I am necessarily constrained in this way, by the end I have set myself; and while Kant thinks things are a bit more complicated when it comes to imperatives of prudence, this is not because the connection is any less analytic in theory, but just because it is harder in practice to know about what the necessary means to happiness actually are.[36] In these cases, therefore, it is easy to see how certain actions can come to be represented as necessary for me to do. The problem, however, in the case of the necessity involved in morality, is that this necessity cannot be accounted for analytically as part of the means/end relation, because this relation makes the 'must' conditional on having something as an end, whereas the moral 'must' is unconditional and inescapable and so stronger than this;[37] but then, we lose the way of accounting for the 'must' straightforwardly in analytic terms, as there is now no end in which it can be contained as the required means. If the 'must' in 'you must not tell lies' is not to be explained analytically, therefore, we are left with the question in the moral case of explaining it some other way, which seems much more challenging, and can leave us wondering how there can be any such necessity—just as in the case of metaphysical necessity, we can be left wondering how it can be the case that every event *must* have a cause.

[33] This is perhaps the standard view, expressed for example by Hill when he writes: 'Kant held the Hypothetical Imperative to be easier to follow and to justify than the Categorical Imperative. The Categorical Imperative often demands the sacrifice of self-interest whereas the Hypothetical Imperative, typically, is in the service of long-term interest. The Hypothetical Imperative rarely calls for the sort of internal struggle that the Categorical Imperative demands' (Hill 1992: 32).

[34] *GMM*: 69–70 [4:417], my emphasis.

[35] Cf. *GMM*: 70 [4:417], my emphasis: 'the imperative *extracts* the concept of actions necessary to this end merely from the concept of a volition of this end'.

[36] Cf. *GMM*: 69–71 [4:417–19].

[37] Cf. *GMM*: 72 [4:420]: 'The categorical imperative alone has the tenor of a practical *law*; all the others can indeed be called *principles* of the will but not laws, since what it is necessary to do merely for achieving a discretionary purpose can be regarded as in itself contingent and we can always be released from the precept if we give up the purpose; on the contrary, the unconditional command leaves the will no discretion with respect to the opposite, so that it alone brings with it that necessity which we require of a law'.

On this approach, therefore, there is a rather precise parallel between how Kant sees scepticism arising in the practical case, and in the theoretical one, where both hinge on the question of how necessity of a certain kind is possible. Thus, as is well known, Kant holds that Hume became a sceptic about causality because he saw on the one hand that the necessary relation between events and their causes cannot be accounted for analytically and thus thought of as akin to *logical* necessity, but on the other hand did not see how necessity could obtain otherwise, as anything other than a logical relation. Hume's scepticism is this 'consequent' rather than 'antecedent',[38] based on an apparently well-founded puzzlement concerning the necessity at issue. Likewise, I would argue, Kant saw moral scepticism arising in a similar manner, based on an inability to see how there could even be such a thing as a moral 'must', once the peculiar nature of that 'must' is made clear. And, we cannot console ourselves with the thought that we don't really need to *answer* that question in order to keep morality safe, by thinking that even if we don't know how it is possible, we know at least that in fact agents *are* so bound, because we can see in experience that people's behaviour is governed in this way by nothing but a sense of duty: for, Kant thinks, when it comes to it, this is never really clear, given the murky nature of what really motivates people.[39] Thus, while as a result of Sections I and II of the *Groundwork*, we might agree with Kant about what the supreme principle of morality is, the question still remains how the obligatory force we seem to feel in association with this principle is to be understood and explained, given that no analytic means/end account is open to us; and the worry is, that if no adequate explanation is forthcoming, we will be led to give up the notion of duty as a bad job (much as Hume came to have his sceptical doubts concerning causality), thereby bringing down the whole deontological conception of morality Kant has developed in Sections I and II, and which he thinks is the conception we all share, so that in the end, we would lose our grip on morality altogether. Thus, just as Kant raises the 'how possible?' question in relation to the problem of synthetic a priori knowledge in his theoretical philosophy, so too he raises it in relation to the problem of synthetic a priori practical propositions in his practical philosophy, where those propositions are made synthetic because they express categorical rather than hypothetical imperatives.

Finally, Kant's conception of the obligatoriness raises a transcendental question concern our moral psychology. For, even assuming that we are free, there is a question about how our psychological structure could work in the way that seems to be required by morality, as Kant conceives it. The difficulty is in seeing how it can be that on the one hand moral action consists in following duty and not inclination, while on the other hand desire and inclination seem to be fundamental to our behaviour as agents—so the question is, how is moral action so much as possible for us? The sceptic Kant is envisaging here is looking for an explanation of how moral

[38] Cf. Hume 1975: Section XII, Parts I and II, pp. 149–60.
[39] Cf. Kant *GMM*: 71–2 [4:419].

agency is possible at all, not a reason to be a moral agent. As Kant says, 'I am willing to admit that no interest *impels* me to [follow the principle of universalisability], for that would not give a categorical imperative; but I must still necessarily *take* an interest in it' if we are to understand how I come to act at all, where what we therefore need is 'insight into how this comes about'.[40]

We have seen, therefore, that for Kant there are three important and interrelated ways in which a kind of transcendental puzzlement about morality can arise, in such a way that if left unchecked, could lead one to feel that morality is a 'chimera' for us, however unproblematic it may be for 'holy wills' who are clearly free, under no peculiar moral 'oughts', and possessed of a different moral psychology.[41] And, I would claim, it is Kant's engagement with these bases for moral scepticism which form the substance of Section III of the *Groundwork*, as we can now briefly set out. In all cases, as we shall see, Kant thinks it is vital to make appeal to aspects of his transcendental idealism, as the only way to settle the puzzlement about morality as it arises in these areas.

As is well known, Kant's response to the worry about freedom is to use his transcendental idealism to distinguish between appearances and things-in-themselves, and thus between a causally ordered realm of nature and a non-causal realm, in which the freedom of the moral subject can be preserved. This allows Kant to show how the freedom required to make sense of morality might be possible, while arguing that the fact we feel under moral obligations gives us a practical ground on which to think it is actual, though this can never be established as certain in a theoretical manner as all such knowledge concerning things-in-themselves is denied us.[42]

Kant can also use the dualistic picture of the subject that comes with transcendental idealism to help him explain the peculiar obligatoriness of morality, and so resolve the question of how categorical imperatives are possible. As we have already

[40] Kant *GMM*: 96 [4:449].

[41] Jens Timmermann has also emphasized how it is the issue of *explanation* that is at the centre of Kant's engagement with scepticism, rather than the challenge raised by the sceptic who is looking for reasons to be moral. Cf. Timmermann 2007: 129–30, where Timmermann characterizes the question Kant is addressing as one raised by 'that of a morally decent person whose trust in the supreme authority of ethical commands is challenged by the elusiveness of their source as well as the obvious threat of natural determinism', rather than that raised by 'a radical moral sceptic who, say in the face of robust self-regarding interest, asks for a *normative* reason why he should take up the moral point of view at all'.

[42] Cf. Kant *GMM*: 98–100 [4:450–3]. Although I cannot go into the details here, this is one place where Kant's strategy changes somewhat between the *Groundwork* and the *Critique of Practical Reason*, where I would argue that in the former Kant uses an appeal to transcendental idealism to argue for the division between appearances and things-in-themselves on which his argument for freedom there is presented as depending, whereas in the latter Kant thinks he can place enough weight on an appeal to our moral commitments, and can argue from there to our freedom—a strategy that Kant worried in the *Groundwork* might be question begging (cf. *GMM*: 97–8 [4:450]), but which in the second *Critique* he thinks is adequate for what is required (where for our purposes, it is again notable that it would clearly *not* be adequate against a sceptic who just did not recognize any moral commitments as valid in the first place). For further discussion of Kant's strategy in the second *Critique*, see Chapter 12, this volume.

mentioned, this question only arises from a human perspective, as it is a feature of how morality presents itself to *us*, not to holy wills. Kant then uses this very fact to provide himself with a solution to the puzzle: for, just as it is *because* we have desires and inclinations that morality involves imperatives for us, so he argues that this division within the self *explains* that very obligatoriness, insofar as it is a kind of projection of the fact that the subject's desires set themselves *against* the moral course of action, and so make the latter seem to us to be something to which we are obliged, in a way that does not and cannot happen for the holy will. At the same time, transcendental idealism gives us a framework in which this dualistic picture of the self, and how it operates, in such as away as to make the moral 'ought' explicable:

> And so categorical imperatives are possible by this: that the idea of freedom makes me a member of an intelligible world and consequently, if I were only this, all my actions *would* always be in conformity with the autonomy of the will; but since at the same time I intuit myself as a member of the world of sense, they *ought* to be in conformity with it; and this *categorical* ought represents a synthetic proposition a priori, since to my will affected by sensible desires there is added the idea of the same will but belonging to the world of the understanding—a will pure and practical of itself, which contains the supreme condition, in accordance with reason, of the former will.[43]

This, then, is Kant's distinctive answer to the question of obligatoriness that has shaped the debate in the history of ethics between natural law theorists and voluntarists. Kant can be seen as steering a path between both traditions: like the natural law theorists, he treats the rightness of morality in a realist manner, but like the voluntarists he treats the *obligatoriness* of what is right as arising out of the nature of our will with its dualistic structure; and on the other hand, the will that makes morality obligatory is ours and not an external source of reward or punishment like God, while what is thereby made obligatory is fixed by what is right, so that this voluntarism is constrained and does not go all the way down to the content of the moral law itself. In a slogan, therefore, we might say that Kant combined anti-realism about obligatoriness, with realism about that which is obligatory and thus with realism about the right.[44] Once again, therefore, Kant can claim to have offered an answer to someone who questions morality because they just do not see how it can get to have its peculiarly imperatival nature.

Finally, we can also see how Kant uses the framework he has established in Section III of the *Groundwork* to resolve the third source of moral scepticism, which questions the intelligibility of the kind of psychological account that seems required for moral action to be possible. Here, Kant's strategy is to admit that there is indeed something fundamentally puzzling here, but in a way that we should not feel pushes into anything like moral scepticism: for the puzzlement is in an area where we

[43] Kant *GMM*: 100–1 [4:454].

[44] For further discussion of these issues, see Chapter 2, this volume.

have good reason to acknowledge that we can only have a limited understanding of such matters, so the fact that we find the issue hard to grasp should not be taken as any reason to doubt the possibility of the phenomenon in question. The difficulty arises, Kant thinks, because on the one hand morality requires that we act out of duty and not inclination, while on the other hand as human agents we are caused to act through our feelings, so that the thought of something as a duty or what is right for us to do must bring about such feelings of pleasure in us; but we then become puzzled about this, because the causal relation here is highly problematic and mysterious-seeming, because what brings about the feeling of pleasure is not anything empirical, so we assume that it could only come about if our action is directed at our happiness, but where this would render true moral action impossible on the account we have given of what this must involve. But, Kant argues, rather than becoming dubious about the possibility of moral action on this score, we should recognize that the problem just reflects out general lack of understanding of the relation between the phenomenal and noumenal realms, so that while no positive solution to the puzzle can be given, there is no reason to jump to a purely hedonistic model of human action, as here we have a 'blind spot' that leaves room for the account we need in order to allow for the possibility of the kind of picture of action as involving duty and not inclination that is implied by morality.[45]

However, though Kant uses one aspect of his transcendental idealism here to try to convince us that we must simply accept that the mechanisms of moral action will always remain mysterious to us in this way, he also uses another aspect of that idealism to explain why it is we feel such admiration for our capacity for moral agency, which again otherwise might seem mysterious in a way that could lead us to question the value we place upon that agency. The worry, then, is this:

> If someone asked us why the universal validity of our maxims as a law must be the limiting conditions of our actions, and on what we base the worth we assign to this way of acting—a worth so great that there can be no higher interest anywhere—and asked us how it happens that a human being believes that only through this does he feel his personal worth, in comparison with which that of an agreeable or disagreeable condition is to be held as nothing, we could give him no satisfactory answer.[46]

Here, it may seem, Kant comes closer than at any point so far in trying to answer the non-transcendental sceptic, who asks why they should ignore what is 'agreeable or disagreeable' to them in favour of acting morally, and thus questions the 'validity and practical necessity of subjecting oneself' to the moral principle.[47] However, even

[45] Cf. Kant *GMM*: 106 [4:460]. Kant continues in a similar vein in the following paragraphs, concluding that given the limitations of our intellects, 'we do not indeed comprehend the practical unconditional necessity of the moral imperative, but we nevertheless comprehend its *incomprehensibility*; and this is all that can fairly be required of a philosophy that strives in its principles to the very boundary of human reason' (108 [4:462]).

[46] Kant *GMM*: 97 [4:449–50].

[47] Kant *GMM*: 97 [4:449].

here, I would argue, the dialectic is importantly different, as Kant is considering someone who already *does* value their status as a moral being above what is 'agreeable and disagreeable' to them in this way, and who is just wondering 'how it happens' that this is the case—how can the value of being a moral agent be accounted for if *not* in the way in which it furthers my interest?

Now, Kant also uses his transcendental idealism and its dualistic conception of the self to provide an answer to this question, by arguing that the moral self is the *authentic* self, by virtue of its status as a member of the 'intelligible world'; it must thus be given higher value in our eyes, in a way that enables our respect for ourselves and others to be explained, as well as the 'contempt' and 'abhorrence' we feel for ourselves when we fall short.[48] As Kant famously argues, even the most 'hardened scoundrel' is sensitive to this distinction, and therefore wishes that he could be moral even if he can't quite manage it.[49] Kant thus offers an explanation for the admiration we feel for moral agency, and why we value it so highly, thus dispelling the apparent mystery here; but this is a value that will only be apparent to the agent who (even if a hardened scoundrel) has some sensitivity to the moral life, not to the agent who is asking to be brought into that life from the perspective of the egoist or amoralist.

It is not my purpose here to defend in detail the various answers Kant gives to the transcendental sceptic, who raises these 'how possible?' questions against morality, and to ask in particular whether Kant's appeal to the framework of his transcendental idealism actually settles these questions in the way he would like; all I have tried to argue for is the distinctive nature of such questions within Kant's philosophy. And as a result, I would also argue, Kant's position is free of the dangers highlighted by Prichard and others, where it was claimed that the attempt to supply the sceptic with reasons to act ethically has the cost of seeming to distort the very moral phenomena that we are seeking to defend, and so of feeding the sceptical flames; for, nothing in the kind of scepticism that Kant takes seriously is likely to result in his response to that scepticism becoming self-defeating in this manner.

4.5 Kant and Korsgaard

We began this paper by considering Korsgaard's constructivist criticism of realism, that it could not offer an adequate response to moral scepticism; and we also began by considering the realist's Prichardian reply, namely that no such response is needed, as to offer one is to seek to give morality a non-moral grounding, in a way that immediately leads us astray. We also saw how Korsgaard might be read as falling into this Prichardian trap.

Following our discussion of Kant, however it should be clear that this dialectic is too simple: for the example of Kant shows how sceptical problems can arise in such a way

[48] Cf. Kant *GMM*: 77 [4:426]. [49] See Kant *GMM*: 101 [4:454–5].

that do not succumb to Prichardian concerns, as these arise from *within* morality. When it comes to Korsgaard, therefore, this opens up a way of reading her 'normative question' in a *transcendental* manner—that is, concerning doubts about morality raised by the need to understand how the moral demand is *possible*, how it can be adequately *explained*, where it is in offering a response to this question that the appeal to the conditions of agency may be said to lie. Understood in this way, Korsgaard could claim to be addressing a form of moral scepticism on the one hand, while avoiding the Prichardian challenge on the other, much as (we have argued) Kant himself manages to do.

Now, there is no space to explore this possibility as an interpretation of Korsgaard in any detail here; the aim has simply been to open it up as a model, by drawing the comparison with Kant. Moreover, it also remains to be seen whether, even understood in this manner, Korsgaard is right to think that constructivism is in a better position to resolve the 'normative question' than the realist: for, of course, the constructivist's transcendental puzzlement has to be properly motivated, and it may be that the realist can claim that some of the puzzlement here is not, but can easily be set aside as spurious. This, again, cannot be considered fully here.[50] It is to be hoped, however, that by considering the interpretation we have offered of Kant, we have also shed light on a strategy Korsgaard can also adopt in answering her Prichardian critics concerning the 'normative question' and thus how her appeal to agency might come to answer it—that is, by treating it as a *transcendental* question, of the sort that might lead to moral scepticism even in the best of us, if it cannot be resolved.[51]

[50] For further discussion, see Chapter 5, this volume.

[51] I am grateful to those who commented on this paper at the *Ratio* conference at which it was first delivered, and also those who heard it as Royal Institute of Philosophy lecture at the University of York—where I am particularly grateful for discussions with Christian Piller on that occasion and subsequently. I would also like to thank Max de Gaynesford for his kind invitation to contribute to the *Ratio* conference and to the related collection.

5

Moral Scepticism, Constructivism, and the Value of Humanity

In the current debates between constructivists and realists, there a number of issues on which the constructivist claims superiority over her opponent, a superiority which of course the realist disputes. Thus, the constructivist will argue that she is better able to make ethics consistent with naturalism; better able to make ethics consistent with human autonomy; and better able to distinguish between the roles of practical and theoretical reason in our ethical deliberations.[1] In addition to these issues, the constructivist will also characteristically insist that she is better able than the realist to avoid the threat of moral scepticism—where it is this claim that I want to consider further in this paper, particularly as it figures in the work of Christine Korsgaard.

However, I want to consider this claim not in itself, but rather how it has fuelled a certain way of reading Kant, namely as a constructivist rather than a realist about the moral value of rational beings. For, it is held, we can see a constructivist and not a realist sensibility at work in the way in which Kant seeks to address sceptical concerns over such value claims, where this is said to be particularly evident in the Formula of Humanity argument in the *Groundwork*. I want to contend, by contrast, that when properly understood this text suggests the opposite: namely, that Kant's attitude to scepticism here fits better with the one that Korsgaard attributes to the realist, and that the constructivist manoeuvres that she claims to identify are not to be found. Of course, this in itself does not show that Kant should be read as a realist, as there are other issues and other texts at stake in this controversy;[2] nonetheless, I hope this discussion will at least neutralize one important part of the constructivist's interpretative argument, while shedding light on the broader debate.

I will begin (in section 5.1) by outlining the way in which Korsgaard characterizes the relative positions of realism and constructivism vis-à-vis moral scepticism, and why she thinks that the former is at a disadvantage. I will then (in section 5.2) consider the reading of the Formula of Humanity argument that emerges in Korsgaard and the work of other constructivists. I will then (in section 5.3) challenge that reading on textual grounds. Finally, I will conclude by asking what lessons

[1] For a helpful overview of some of the supposed virtues of constructivism, see Street 2010.
[2] I discuss these issues further in Stern 2012, esp. Chapters 1–3.

should be drawn from this interpretative discussion, both in relation to Kant and to the question more generally.

5.1 Korsgaard on Moral Realism and Moral Scepticism

While it is of course a complex matter, for the purposes of this discussion we can characterize the difference between the realist and the constructivist as follows. According to the realist, rational agents are taken to have a distinctive moral value which makes some ways of acting towards them right and others wrong, and which imposes duties or obligations on us to treat them in some ways and not in others. For the realist, this value is said to form part of the 'fabric of the world,' as a mind-independent property that rational agents possess, grounded in the properties that distinguish them as agents from other beings that exist. According to the constructivist, by contrast, what constrains us to treat other rational agents in a certain way is not the prior value that they exemplify, but the formal limitations of practical reason which limit how we can act, just as the formal limitations of theoretical reason (such as the laws of logic) arguably limit how we can think. On this view, therefore, what it is for rational agents to have value is for there to be certain constraints on how we must behave towards them as a result of being rational agents ourselves, rather than those constraints arising out of their antecedent possession of a special moral status, as the realist contends. To put the point schematically: for the realist, practical reason is governed by a prior order of values, whereas for the constructivist, the direction of explanation is reversed, and the order of values is constituted out of the constraints on practical reason. Thus, what it is for ourselves and others to be valuable, on this constructivist view, is for reason to be compelled to treat rational agents a certain way, and not for reason to be compelled to treat rational agents a certain way because they have value, which is the realist's picture.

Now, as we have said, one important advantage that Korsgaard attributes to the constructivist approach[3] is that it can deal better with the 'normative question' as this arises for us, and thus with moral scepticism. In order to understand this claim, it is important to be clear as to exactly which kind of scepticism Korsgaard has in mind. For, I think it is wrong to understand this as simply a 'why be moral?' scepticism, of the sort that has been dismissed by Prichard and others, or of a scepticism that simply insists on pressing for a justification for the realist's value claims without giving any grounds for doing so, where the realist may then reasonably reject this demand as empty and unmotivated.[4] Rather, my view is that Korsgaard takes the sceptical threat

[3] In *The Sources of Normativity* (Korsgaard 1996b), which will form our primary focus here, Korsgaard does not just use the terminology of constructivism and realism, but also draws a distinction between 'procedural realism' and 'substantive realism', which are clearly related notions but are perhaps not exactly equivalent to the first two. Elsewhere she just employs the terminology of constructivism and realism (e.g. Korsgaard 2008b), and it is this that has become more widely used.

[4] For further discussion related to this issue, see Chapter 4, this volume.

to arise not *just* because morality can seem to go against our interests or *just* because it can seem to rest on ungrounded claims about value, but *also* because the sceptic can suggest that morality may not be all it seems, in ways that *then* make these features of it problematic, in a way that they might not be on their own. Thus, Korsgaard points out, 'masters of suspicion' from Mandeville to Nietzsche and beyond have opened up the possibility that morality is no more than a cover for hidden exercises of power, interest and corruption, where in *these* circumstances it is not mere egoism to ask 'why should I be moral?' or mere idle and unmotivated doubt to ask 'is what we take to be right really so?' What we have here, then, is a *debunking explanation* of morality, of the sort that makes it pressing to question the point of favouring it over our interests, or accepting what it tells us about how we should act: for, as Korsgaard puts it in relation to Mandeville, 'Why give up your heart's desire, just because some politician wants to keep you in line?'[5] Korsgaard argues, therefore, that unless we can offer an explanation of morality that will vindicate it, by explaining 'why morality seems so important to us and moves us in the way that it does,'[6] but without undermining its appeal, then moral scepticism will be the result, where 'the moral sceptic is someone who thinks that the explanation of moral concepts will be one that does not support the claims that morality makes on us. He thinks that once we see what is really behind morality, we won't care about it any more.'[7]

The problem with realism, Korsgaard then claims, is that it is just not in a position to respond to this challenge, because the realist lacks the machinery needed to explain morality in this vindicatory way, because it lacks the machinery genuinely to explain morality at all. Suppose, for example, reading Mandeville has led me to wonder if our moral system exists as a creation of those in power as a way of keeping the rest of us in order, and as a result I start to question my allegiance to it. What can the realist say in response? According to Korsgaard, all she can offer as a competing explanation of this moral system is that people really *do* have a special ethical status, and that morality is a response to this normative fact (amongst others); but Mandeville has precisely put the status of such 'facts' in question by giving us grounds on which to doubt any such appeals. In the face of the debunking explanatory challenge, therefore, Korsgaard thinks that the realist is impotent, because his position lacks the necessary explanatory bite:

The realist's response [to the normative question] is to dig in his heels. The notion of normativity or authority is an irreducible one. It is a mistake to try to explain it. Obligation is simply there, part of the nature of things. We must suppose certain actions to be obligating in

[5] Korsgaard 1996b: 9. [6] Korsgaard 1996b: 12.

[7] Korsgaard 1996b: 13–14. Cf. also p. 49, where Korsgaard claims that 'we seek a philosophical foundation for ethics in the first place... because we are afraid that the true explanation of why we have moral beliefs and motives might not be one that sustains them. Morality might not survive reflection'. For further discussion of this way of taking the sceptical challenge that concerns Korsgaard, see Chapter 4, this volume.

themselves if anything is...[8] Having discovered that obligation cannot exist unless there are actions which it is necessary for us to do, the realist concludes that there are such actions, and that they are the very ones we have always thought were necessary, the traditional moral duties...But when the normative question is raised, these are the exact points that are in contention—whether there is really *anything* I must do, and if so whether it is *this*. So it is a little hard to see how realism can help.[9]

Given the way it works, therefore, Korsgaard believes that realism cannot possibly address the sceptical challenge raised by Mandeville et al. in an adequate manner.

By contrast, Korsgaard argues, a more constructivist approach is in a stronger position, because it has the resources to offer a genuinely competing and vindicatory explanation of 'why morality seems so important to us and moves us in the way that it does,' and so justify us in keeping our moral commitments in place. Very briefly, as we have already seen, that explanation takes the form of an appeal to the nature of practical reason and the constraints on us as rational agents. Thus, Korsgaard argues, she can explain why we are so unwilling to betray our fundamental humanity, because 'if we do not treat our humanity as a normative identity, none of our other identities can be normative, and then we can have no reasons to act at all'.[10] And likewise, she thinks she can explain why we respect the humanity of others, because 'to act on a reason is already, essentially, to act on a consideration whose normative force may be shared with others'.[11] With these explanations in place, Korsgaard thinks, she is then in a position to see off the debunking explanations of morality offered by Mandeville and others, in a way that the realist cannot.

5.2 Korsgaard on the Formula of Humanity

Having characterized the different stances that Korsgaard attributes to realism and constructivism in relation to scepticism, we can now turn to her reading of Kant, and in particular to her celebrated treatment of the Formula of Humanity argument in the *Groundwork*. Because she reads Kant as a constructivist, she takes him to be using constructivist resources to answer the moral sceptic, by offering a vindicatory explanation of the moral value that we attribute to ourselves and others—an explanation that she thinks he could not offer if he were a realist.

Kant's discussion of the Formula of Humanity occurs in Section II of the *Groundwork of the Metaphysics of Morals*, in which Kant produces his various formulations of the categorical imperative, or what he takes to be '*the supreme principle of morality*' for which he has been searching.[12] The first formulation Kant offers is the Formula of Universal Law: 'Act only in accordance with that maxim though which you can at the same time will that it become a universal law,' where this is followed by the closely related Formula of the Law of Nature: 'Act as if the maxim of your action were to

[8] Korsgaard 1996b: 30. [9] Korsgaard 1996b: 34. [10] Korsgaard 1996b: 129.
[11] Korsgaard 1996b: 136. [12] Cf. Kant *GMM*: 47 [4:392].

become by your will a *universal law of nature*.'[13] The Formula of Humanity is the variant that follows next: 'So act that you use humanity, whether in your own person or in the person of any other, always at the same time as an end, never merely as a means.'[14]

Now, Kant's argument for the Formula of Humanity has been the subject of much debate between realists and constructivists, for on the one hand realist readers have claimed that here Kant attributes a value to rational nature that is to be understood in realist terms, whereas constructivist readers have claimed that what he says here better fits a constructivist approach.[15] Korsgaard, of course, is in the latter camp, where she therefore sees the argument as performing an anti-sceptical function. Thus, in response to the 'normative question', Korsgaard argues that Kant does not merely insist that we do have such value, but shows how this is grounded on the conditions of rational agency, where this grounding will leave our moral commitments intact, and counteract the threat from debunking sceptics like Mandeville and others.

Korsgaard outlines her account of Kant's argument as follows:

> [Kant] started from the fact that when we make a choice we must regard its object as good. His point is the one that I have been making—that being human we must endorse our impulses before we can act on them. He asked what it is that makes these objects good, and, rejecting one form of realism, he decided that the goodness was not in the objects themselves. Were it not for our desires and inclinations—and for the various physiological, psychological, and social conditions which gave rise to those desires and inclinations—we would not find their objects good. Kant says that we take things to be important because they are important to us—and he concluded that we must therefore take ourselves to be important. In this way, the value of humanity itself is implicit in every human choice. If complete normative scepticism is to be avoided—if there is such a thing as a reason for action—then humanity, as the source of all reasons and values, must be valued for its own sake.[16]

For Korsgaard, therefore, Kant is arguing as follows: In order to act, we must make a choice to do one thing rather than another thing, where to do this we must decide that the former has some value that the other lacks. Kant rejects the realist view that value resides in things independently of our desires and inclinations; rather, they get their value because *we* value them. However, in order for us to see value in things in this manner, we must value ourselves qua human beings, as otherwise we would see the things that we desire as valueless, and thus lose any reason on which to act. Moreover, in taking ourselves to have value as individual human beings, so we must attribute a comparable value to others. In this way, we arrive at an account of the

[13] Kant *GMM*: 73 [4:421]. [14] Kant *GMM*: 80 [4:429].

[15] Aside from Korsgaard herself, constructivist readers of Kant here include Dean 2006; Sensen 2009; Formosa 2013. For more realist approaches, see Langton 2007; Guyer 2000; Hills 2008; Wood 2008: 108. For an overview of aspects of this debate, see Denis 2007.

[16] Korsgaard 1996b: 122. As Korsgaard notes, her account here is a summary of the one offered at greater length in Korsgaard 1996a: 106–33.

value of humanity, a value that requires us to treat others as ends and not merely as means.

Conceived in this Korsgaardian way, this argument for the Formula of Humanity has been much discussed and disputed, not only by realists but also by constructivists themselves, where many have questioned whether the argument can work. There have been two principal worries: first, even if things get their value through us, it does not follow that we have value; and second, even if this argument might show that we have to take ourselves to have value, it doesn't succeed in establishing that we must attribute this value to others.[17] Although both constructivists and realists have acknowledged these concerns, however, the former have of course not taken this to show that a more realist account of Kant's argument is needed. Rather, constructivists have deepened the constructivism of their account (so to speak), by downplaying the value claims that seem to create the difficulties for Korsgaard; instead, they stress the link between the Formula of Humanity and the Formula of Universal Law,[18] arguing that the latter is a constitutive principle of practical reason, from which it follows that others must be treated as ends: for, 'the formula of universal law requires that no rational being be subject to a maxim that could not arise from its own will [which] is the same as requiring that one treat another always as an end-in-itself'.[19] This reading therefore stresses Kant's claim that the two formulae are 'at bottom the same',[20] where claims about value are seen as less important in grounding the argument for the Formula of Humanity;[21] rather, the special status of rational beings as ends in themselves follows not from their value, but from the principle of universalizability, where what it is for them to *have* such value is for them to *be* such ends, where what makes them ends is the rational requirement to act only on maxims that can be universalized and so accepted by other rational agents.

Now, despite their differences, both the Korsgaardian and non-Korsgaardian constructivist interpretations of Kant share a common assumption, which is that Kant is here trying to respond to the sceptic who questions the moral value that we place on humanity in ourselves and others, and the special treatment we give and expect as a result. For, as we have seen, it is this assumption that leads Korsgaard to turn to Kant for inspiration in developing her constructivist response to such scepticism, while Korsgaard's constructivist critics offer their alternative reading because they take Korsgaard's own anti-sceptical argument to fail, which is why

[17] Korsgaard herself admits that the latter step seems weak, and instead supplements it by an appeal to the publicity of reasons mentioned above: see Korsgaard 1996b: 132–45. For other examples of these concerns, see Langton 2007; Sensen 2009; Formosa 2013.

[18] Cf. Kant *GMM*: 85–7 [4:436–8]. The question of the exact relation between Kant's various formulations is of course a topic of much dispute in its own right, and cannot be gone into here.

[19] Sensen 2009: 113. [20] Kant *GMM*: 87 [4:437].

[21] Cf. Dean 2006: 124: 'The natural conclusion of [Kant's Korsgaardian] regress argument is a point about some fundamental requirements regarding how to treat rational nature, not a point about value. Although these requirements can later be interpreted into talk about value, it is misleading to treat value as the primary concern.'

they look at Kant again to find a better one. And we have also seen how Korsgaard understands the connection between these two issues: given that Kant has a serious concern with scepticism, it follows that he must be a constructivist and not a realist, as any such concern is not possible for the realist.

At this point, however, I want to turn Korsgaard's position on its head, and suggest that in fact the best way to understand argument for the Formula of Humanity is precisely to see that it is *not* concerned with scepticism, which itself suggests (on Korsgaardian grounds) that his position is best understood in a realist rather than constructivist manner. In order to make this plausible, we must therefore look at Kant's discussion of the Formula of Humanity once again, and in greater detail.

5.3 Kant on the Formula of Humanity

There is general agreement in the interpretation of Kant, that following an interlude running from 4:425 to 4:427, the derivation of the Formula of Humanity principle begins at 4:427.19, until we arrive at the Formula itself in the middle of 4:429, before Kant goes on to illustrate the use of this formula with four examples. However, there is less agreement concerning the structure of the derivation itself. On one view, the main argument for the Formula consists in an argument from elimination for the value of rational nature in the main paragraph of 4:428;[22] on another view, this is a rather unsatisfactory hors d'oeuvre, and the real argument comes in the paragraph that runs from 4:428 to 4:429, where it is this argument that is often treated in constructivist terms.[23] Generally speaking, therefore, constructivists have discounted the argument from elimination in favour of a supposed second argument that better fits the constructivist picture; and they have discounted that prior argument, largely on the grounds that it cannot satisfy the sceptic.[24] I will argue now, by contrast, that the only argument here is the one by elimination in 4:428, and what the constructivists take to be a second argument designed to defeat the sceptic is simply not to be found. And the fact that this is so, I will suggest, is telling in what it shows us about Kant's relation to realism. Let me therefore work through the relevant passages, in order to make this case.

[22] Cf. Timmermann 2006.

[23] As well as Korsgaard herself, cf. Dean 2006: 109–30. Denis also states that the argument from elimination is one part of the argument, with the subsequent paragraph constituting a further part: see Denis 2007: 245–6. Wood also finds the argument from elimination to be unsatisfactory, and finds a further argument in the next paragraph, which resembles Korsgaard's, though taken in a more realist manner: see Wood 1999: 122–32.

[24] Cf. Dean 2006: 119: 'This argument [from elimination] is not particularly powerful... But Kant immediately follows the argument by elimination with a second argument for the claim that humanity, or rational nature, must be the end in itself ([Kant *GMM* 4:]428–9).'

5.3.1 Paragraph 1: 427.19–428.2

Kant believes himself to have already shown that the supreme principle of morality must take the form of a categorical rather than hypothetical imperative, and that it must apply to all rational beings. In this paragraph, he introduces a series of distinctions to show what kind of end is needed in order to make such an imperative possible.

Kant says that the end in question must be one that is valid for all rational beings if the imperative is going to be properly categorical, and so must be something that all rational beings have reason to act on. He therefore argues that the end cannot be given to us by desire, as such ends will not be valid for those beings who lack the relevant desire. Kant distinguishes between two ends that can be related to desires in this way. The first are *subjective* ends, where an incentive [*Triebfeder*] such as hunger produces a desire, such as the desire to eat, where satisfying the desire is then the end of the action. The second are *material* ends, where the desire gives the agent a reason to bring about a certain state of affairs as a result of his actions, but where that end is relative to the desire: so, for example, if I want to get a good job, I have reason to make doing well at school my end. Kant distinguishes ends of this sort from *objective* ends, and argues that only these can constitute the right ends for the imperative we are interested in, which is formal and categorical: for subjective ends have incentives as their basis, where no incentive can form the basis of a moral action, while relative ends would render the imperative hypothetical, as the agent only finds the end of his actions to be worthwhile because of his interests.[25]

5.3.2 Paragraph 2: 428.3–428.6

Kant therefore takes himself to have shown why the ends set by desire cannot constitute the end to be served in following the categorical imperative qua supreme principle of morality; for, such ends are too arbitrary and contingent, whereas the principles of morality are necessary and universal. What is needed instead, he argues, is something of absolute worth or value, which can then ground the necessity and universality of the categorical imperative in the right way, and hence explain how such an imperative is possible.

5.3.3 Paragraph 3: 428.7–428.33

Kant now conducts his search for what might have absolute value, and thus what might form the basis for the categorical imperative. He asserts dogmatically at the outset what he takes such a thing to be, namely rational beings including us human beings, for these are precisely what he thinks form the kind of universal and necessary

[25] Cf. also Kant *GMM*: 81 [4:431]: '[In the principle of humanity] humanity is represented not as an end of human beings (subjectively), that is, not as an object that we of ourselves actually make our end [through desiring or wanting it, for example], but as an objective end that, whatever ends we may have, ought as law to constitute the supreme limiting condition of all subjective ends.'

ends that the categorical imperative requires. He then proceeds to argue for this conclusion by elimination of other possibilities, bearing in mind that he already takes himself to have excluded other candidates.

On a standard reading, Kant is said to discuss four such possibilities: (i) the objects of the inclinations; (ii) inclinations themselves; (iii) non-rational objects produced by nature; (iv) rational objects produced by nature. My own view differs slightly from this, where I think he deals only with three candidates, namely (i), (iii) and (iv), where he discusses inclinations themselves only to give himself an argument for excluding (i). On my account, therefore, the first candidate for absolute value that Kant considers are things that satisfy our inclinations, and that we acquire for ourselves as a result, such as a house or a car.[26] Kant argues, however, that such objects cannot have absolute value, as they would have no value at all if we didn't want or need them, but where such wants and needs are clearly not themselves of absolute value, as we would rather be without them if that were possible for us. Hence, he concludes that 'the worth of any object to be acquired by our action is always conditional'.

Kant now turns to consider two further candidates: beings that are created by nature which lack reason, and those which are created with it. Regarding the former, Kant argues that such beings are obviously without absolute value, as it is clear that they can be treated as means and not ends. The only candidate left, therefore, is beings created by nature that possess reason, namely persons; these are then taken to be the objects of absolute value that can serve as the end we need if we are to explain how there can be the sort of categorical imperative that constitutes the supreme principle of morality.

5.3.4 Paragraph 4: 428.34–429.14

Kant thus reiterates what has been shown so far: if we are to take there to be a categorical imperative at all, we must allow that human beings qua rational agents have the kind of value that makes them into ends valid for themselves and other rational agents, and thus as ends in themselves. From what has already been established, Kant thinks he is entitled to assert that 'human beings necessarily represent their existence' as an end in itself, given the argument above, which has shown that it is our status as rational creatures (not merely natural ones, such as animals) in which our value resides, where this is independent of the value things get

[26] It may seem puzzling that Kant discusses this possibility here, given what he has already said about desire in Paragraph 1 (though the similarities and differences between desire [*Begehr*] and inclination [*Neigung*] for Kant are not always easy to make out). But one explanation for this discussion could be to exclude a position which he hasn't discussed in Paragraph 1, namely the thought that there may be some ends which all agents are inclined towards obtaining, and which may therefore involve the kind of necessity and universality that is required here. To this, Kant's response would appear to be: even if there were such an end, this would not show it to have absolute value, given the doubts raised about the value of the inclinations that direct us towards it, where this argument differs from anything discussed in Paragraph 1.

from our desires, and so is necessary and not contingent or relative. However, Kant acknowledges a limitation to this result, which he therefore calls a '*subjective* principle of human action'. For, not all rational creatures (such as God) are produced by nature, so that it may be that for them, their value could be held to reside in some *other* feature that differentiates them from persons (for example, in God's case, his omnipotence), where the worry for Kant is that this would make them superior to us and so open to differential treatment: they may not be required to treat us morally as we are required to treat ourselves and each other, thus endangering the necessity and universality of the moral law.[27] At this point, however, Kant admits in a footnote that he has not blocked this lacuna in his argument, and defers his answer to Section III of the *Groundwork*, where he will say more about *what it is* about rational nature that gives us our value (not merely *that* it is this nature which does so), where once this is clear, it will also be clear why it is this that gives value to other rational beings such as God.[28] For the moment, Kant can therefore only assert as a postulate to be supported later, that 'every rational being also represents his existence [as an end] on just the same rational ground [i.e. the value of rational nature] that also holds for me [qua human being]'. Granted this assumption, Kant therefore asserts that this is an *objective* principle holding for all rational beings, from which the Formula of Humanity therefore follows.

Now, having set out this account of Kant's argument in these paragraphs, we can see how it differs from the constructivist interpretation.

First of all, when it comes to arguing for the value of humanity, on my account the only argument for this conclusion is given in Paragraph 3, and it is an argument from elimination rather than any sort of Korsgaardian regress argument. Now, as we have said, constructivists have typically accepted that there *is* an argument from elimination in Paragraph 3, but have found it to be hopelessly unsatisfactory, and so have sought for a different sort of argument in Paragraph 4, of a more constructivist kind. However, if my account of Paragraph 4 is right, they have misread what is going on there, as in fact that paragraph contains no argument at all, and just a promissory

[27] Cf. the discussion in Kant *CBHH*: 167–8 [8:114–15], which parallels this part of the *Groundwork* to a considerable degree. Kant takes as his text here Genesis 3:22, which he interprets as God saying that through his ability to know good and evil, and thus his difference from the animals which this rational capacity implies, 'Man has become like us,' and so equal in moral status to God himself, no matter how superior such 'higher beings' may be in their other abilities.

[28] On this account, the crucial part of Section III concerns Kant's employment of the transcendental distinction between the 'world of sense' and the 'intelligible world', where the latter is occupied by the rational self (Kant *GMM*: 98–100 [4:450–4]), where even the 'hardened scoundrel' can see that his 'inner worth' comes from operating at this level, despite the fact that he will find it very hard to overcome his 'inclinations and impulses' in order to do so (101 [4:454–5]). It is this transcendental account of value that Kant uses to answer the question posed earlier in Section III, namely why we see so much value in moral action, even though it can involve a sacrifice of our personal pleasures and satisfactions—namely, the question 'how it happens that a human being believes that only through [moral action] does he feel his personal worth, in comparison with which that of an agreeable or disagreeable condition is to be held as nothing' (97 [4:449–50]).

note about a lacuna to be filled in Section III of the *Groundwork*. There are therefore two issues to be considered further: is there an extra argument in Paragraph 4, and does the weakness of Kant's argument in Paragraph 3 suggest there really needs to be, in order to make Kant's derivation of the Formula at all convincing?

When it comes to Paragraph 4 itself, the crucial sentences are these:

> The ground of this principle is: *rational nature exists as an end in itself*. The human being [der Mensch] necessarily represents his own existence in this way; so far it is thus a *subjective* principle of human actions. But every other rational being also represents his existence in this way consequent on just the same rational ground that also holds for me [Footnote: Here I put forward this proposition as a postulate. The grounds for it will be found in the last Section].[29]

On my account, the crucial issue here is that while we as human beings must see our rational nature as constituting our status as ends, whether *any* rational being (such as God) must see this as constituting that status for them, or whether they could reasonably take that status to be based on some other feature which they possess but which we do not. The constructivist, however, reads the second sentence as relating to individual human beings, who are said to have to take their own particular existence as an end; and then reads the third sentence as claiming that every individual human being will have to do the same concerning the existence of others, so making it an objective rather than a subjective principle. But this fudges what seems to be the crucial contrast drawn in sentences two and three, which is not between how each individual must represent themselves versus how they must represent others, but how human beings as a class must represent themselves and how rational beings more generally must so represent *themselves*. Of course, it might be said that 'me' at the end of sentence three suggests otherwise: but 'me' here can also suggest 'me' qua human being, not 'me' qua individual. It might also be said that Kant wasn't that concerned about the distinction between 'human being' and 'rational being', so could just have well have written the same term either way in both sentences. But this is to neglect the fact that Kant *was* deeply concerned about the difference, where his conception of the necessity and universality of morality depended on addressing *both* constituencies, conceived as narrower and wider classes respectively—where I have argued that it is this concern that is at the forefront here, not the desire to refute a sceptic who is wondering why, even if he must see himself as an end, he must also see other people the same way.[30]

Another difficulty with the constructivist reading of these sentences, is to see what contrast there is meant to be between them, in a way that fits the text. One way to get a contrast might to be to read the second sentence as pointing to how I represent my existence, and the third then saying that this is also how each of us sees ourselves, not

[29] Kant *GMM*: 79 [4:428–8].

[30] Cf. Kant *GMM*: 81 [4:430–1]: 'This principle of humanity . . . is not borrowed from experience . . . because of its universality, since it applies to all rational beings as such and no experience is sufficient to determine anything about them.'

just me, then trying to argue on this basis concerning how we must treat others. But the difficulty with this is that the second sentence already makes this point, by saying that this is how *human beings in general* view themselves, so that the contrast marked by 'aber' here seems to be lost. Of course, if the third sentence read 'But every other rational being also represents the existence *of others* in this way consequent on just the same rational ground that also holds for me' then there would be a contrast with the second sentence; but it doesn't. The advantage of my reading above, however, is that it explains more clearly how Kant might have thought he was drawing a contrast here, between how we represent our existence to ourselves qua human beings, and how other rational but non-human beings represent their existence to themselves.

Moreover, it is precisely because they view Kant's ambitions to be anti-sceptical that constructivists are so dismissive of the argument from elimination in Paragraph 3, while at the same time feeling the need to find a better sort of argument in Paragraph 4. A key part of that argument is supposed to be the claim that 'The human being necessarily represents his own existence in this way; so far it is thus a *subjective* principle of human actions;' but while on my account, this is meant to be a conclusion based on Paragraph 3, the constructivist cannot take the argument for this claim to come from there, as Paragraph 3 works on the assumption that human beings will accept this because they will accept the categorical nature of ethics, which can hardly be expected of the sceptic. This means, however, that not only do they render Paragraph 3 redundant, but constructivists are also obliged to see the necessity claim as following from an argument that Kant just does not give in this part of the text or indeed *anywhere* very explicitly, but which (they hold) can be 'reconstructed' from various Kantian materials, in the manner of Korsgaard's regress argument,[31] or perhaps as following from the Formula of Universal Law.[32] But surely, it is much more plausible to think that if this *was* intended to be a premise supported by anything other than the argument in Paragraph 3, Kant would have supplied the argument needed here?[33]

[31] Cf. Dean 2006: 119, who says of the text itself: 'Several things are puzzling about this argument, if it is an argument', and admits that it is 'so compressed as to be largely mysterious'. In Korsgaard 1996a, Korsgaard clearly feels some sort of need to connect Paragraph 3 to Paragraph 4 taken in her way, so valiantly suggests that it is 'possible to read' the former as 'at least suggesting a regress towards the unconditioned: moving from the objects of our inclinations, to the inclinations themselves, finally (later) back to ourselves, our rational nature' (p. 120). Apart from the fact (I have claimed) Kant gives no separate consideration to inclinations, this suggestion leaves out the case of non-rational natural beings altogether, which surely counts against it. Perhaps sensing the difficulty, Korsgaard then goes on to speak of her argument as a 'reconstruction', and gives it no further textual support from this part of the *Groundwork*.

[32] It might also be said that Kant is just asserting the claim without *any* argument, because he just takes it to be an obvious and uncontentious psychological generalization about how each of us thinks of ourselves. But Kant is rarely inclined to make necessity claims in such a psychologistic way, while taken as such a claim, it seems implausible: for example, human beings have clearly thought of themselves as means to be used by others in various sorts of situations, or been willing to sacrifice their rational nature in order to satisfy their inclinations.

[33] Dean suggests that there *must* be an argument in Paragraph 4, because Kant uses the word 'therefore' [also] prior to his statement of the Formula of Humanity at the end of the paragraph. But this use of

At the same time, by taking the sceptic to be the target, I would claim that constructivists underestimate the effectiveness of the argument in Paragraph 3. Some of the concerns commonly raised seem plainly anachronistic. Thus, much as we may feel uncomfortable with Kant's quick dismissal of the value of animals on the grounds that it is acceptable to treat them as means, this would doubtless have seemed entirely unobjectionable to Kant and his audience, and so provide an inadequate basis for thinking he therefore would have felt the need to offer a further (and better) argument in the next paragraph. Other concerns about the argument from elimination also seem to neglect the rather narrow focus of the argument, a focus that has been narrowed by other moves Kant has made elsewhere. In particular, Kant takes it that the end he is looking for is not some goal to be brought about or realized (such as maximizing happiness, or bringing about international peace), but an 'objective ground' [*ein objektive Grund*][34] qua object in the world, for the sake of which one acts (as when we say that he fought not for the sake of his family, but his country) and which therefore *sets* one's ends qua goals. Kant has excluded ends qua goals already in Section I of the *Groundwork* on the basis of his understanding of the moral worth of actions, which he thinks cannot depend on what we succeed in bringing about and thus the goals we manage to achieve.[35] Now, clearly, this already cuts down the field of candidates to be considered in Section II. Finally, of course, there may be the worry that no argument from elimination can satisfy the sceptic, as such arguments are open to the objection that we have unwittingly neglected some alternative; but this becomes less pressing if we do not take scepticism to be our target.

Lastly, if it is accepted that Kant's argument lies not in Paragraph 4 but in Paragraph 3, then we must allow that his concern is not an anti-sceptical one; for the strategy of the argument in Paragraph 3 rests on claims in the previous paragraph, that there must be an end of absolute value in order for the categorical imperative to have a proper ground, where it is taken for granted that there *is* such an imperative which serves as the supreme principle of morality. Now this, of course, is precisely what the sceptic will question, so will hardly believe that this search for such an end will take us anywhere. But, Kant is proceeding here in the manner he does throughout the first two sections of the *Groundwork*, which is to take our ordinary conception of morality for granted as the basis for his investigation.[36] When

'therefore' can of course be explained insofar as it is the culmination of the argument contained in Paragraph 3, from which (assuming Kant can make good on his claim that *all* rational beings get their value on the same basis) the Formula follows. Dean may object that Kant's use of 'therefore' suggests that the argument needs to be a *deductive* argument, which an argument from elimination is not: but the argument here is that the Formula of Humanity is the practical imperative that follows from the value of rational nature, which is why the use of 'therefore' is appropriate. See Dean 2006: 119.

[34] Cf. Kant *GMM*: 78 [4:427]. For discussion of Kant's use of this phrase, see Timmermann 2007: 91.

[35] Cf. Kant *GMM*: 55 [4:439–40].

[36] Cf. Kant *GMM*: 47 [4:392], where Kant says he is proceeding analytically here from 'common moral cognition to the determination of its supreme principle.' Cf. also Kant *GMM*: 58 [4:404] and 66 [4:412],

it comes to this discussion of the Formula of Humanity in Section II, therefore, we should not be surprised to find that it is not offered as a response to the sceptic, and that attempts by Korsgaard and others to read it in this manner have gone astray, both philosophically and interpretatively.

5.4 Concluding Remarks

If what I have said about the failure of constructivist attempts to interpret Kant's argument for the Formula of Humanity are correct, I think we can turn Korsgaard's position on its head at least as far as this text goes, when she takes it that because Kant offers a response to the sceptic, he must be operating as a constructivist and not a realist; on the contrary, I have suggested, Kant offers no such response here, so no such suggestion follows. In fact, I hope to have shown, Kant's approach is very much in line with the kind of approach that Korsgaard attributes to moral realism:

> The metaphysical view that intrinsically normative entities or properties exist must be *supported by* our confidence that we really do have obligations. It is because we are confident that obligation is real that we are prepared to believe in the existence of some sort of objective values. But for that very reason the appeal to the existence of objective values cannot be used to support our confidence. And the normative question arises when our confidence has been shaken, whether by philosophy or the exigencies of life. So realism cannot answer the normative question.[37]

Now, from what we have seen, Kant's discussion of the Formula of Humanity in fact fits this realist pattern very closely. That is, he takes it for granted that there is a categorical imperative that sets obligations of a certain kind upon us, and from this argues to the existence of a special sort of moral value which we possess, namely our value as rational agents. Far from conforming to the constructivist model, of seeking some explanation of such values that will vindicate our acceptance of them once we have fallen into some sort of doubt concerning our moral obligations, Kant rests his account on a prior acceptance of those ordinary moral beliefs and commitments, in just the way that Korsgaard takes to be typical of the realist. Far from providing us with a *contrast* to Kant's procedure, it is almost as if this paragraph from Korsgaard was written *with Kant in mind.*

Of course, even if my reading Kant's argument for the Formula of Humanity is accepted, and thus even if it is acknowledged that this part of the *Groundwork* fails to fit Korsgaard's constructivist approach, my conclusion is limited in important respects.

where Kant comments that 'common moral appraisal' is 'very worthy of respect'; and *CPrR*: 153 note [5:8]: 'Who would even want to introduce a new principle of all morality and, as it were, first invent it? Just as if, before him, the world had been ignorant of what duty is or in thoroughgoing error about it.'

[37] Korsgaard 1996b: 40.

First of all, I have not here considered *other* grounds that might be considered for taking Kant to be a constructivist, where I have focused only on the Formula of Humanity and its relation to scepticism. This is a much wider issue, which I have tried to tackle elsewhere, as have others.[38] However, I think this focus is nonetheless justified, for (as we have seen) many constructivists place great weight on this text, and give it a central role in their reading of Kant, so it is far from of merely peripheral importance if their account of this text can be overturned in the way that I have suggested.

Secondly, I have not tried to move beyond interpretative issues, and so have not showed that, even if Kant's approach to the sceptical question (at least in this part of the text) is more realist than constructivist, whether this is adequate as a philosophical position. Thus, the worry might be, if I am right to claim that Kant did not share Korsgaardian concerns over the debunking sceptic, doesn't this then show his position to be inadequate, and that there is therefore a need to adopt a more constructivist approach, perhaps using Kantian materials, in the manner of Korsgaard herself? This too is a broad question, which I will not attempt to deal with fully here, but put briefly I think the response should be as follows. First, even assuming that Korsgaard is right to say that the realist cannot provide an explanatory story that will not beg the question against the sceptic, it is not clear why this is needed as part of the dialectic: for, it could be enough to show that the debunking explanation offered by the sceptic herself to motivate her doubts is *itself* flawed as an explanation, because of the various assumptions and implausible claims it makes.[39] If this can be established, then it can be dismissed as a threat to our confidence in morality, without any alternative *positive* story needing to be told. Of course, other sceptical threats may still remain, such as the challenge posed by egoism, or the sceptic who is unhappy with taking anything for granted but always asks for further justification; but as argued previously, the realist has other strategies for dealing with these threats by dismissing them as better left unanswered, as on Prichard's response. Now, a strength of Korsgaard's challenge was that the debunking problem appeared to make this response less acceptable; but if that problem can also be undermined by the realist in this negative way, then arguably the challenge posed by scepticism can be said to have been met, without the need to appeal to anything like her positive constructivist story.

Secondly, nothing that has been said on this should be taken to imply that Kant has *no* concern with scepticism of *any* kind, or that he says nothing of value on this topic—and the same can also be claimed of the realist generally. For, of course, Section III of the *Groundwork* does offer a defense of morality of a kind, and it does concern questions of explanation. However, I would argue that the explanation issue

[38] See Stern 2012, esp. Chapter 1.

[39] As Korsgaard herself notes (Korsgaard 1996b: 9), when it comes to Mandeville, Hume and Hutcheson questioned it internally in this manner for its 'explanatory adequacy'.

here is not of the sort identified by Korsgaard, where the problem is to see off some sort of debunking account; Kant never seems to have been troubled by a spectre of this sort. Rather, the explanation issue concerns a *transcendental* question, namely 'how is morality possible?' in the face of the challenge of certain threats that would render it a 'chimera' for us,[40] such as the lack free will. In this way, Kant thinks, doubts about morality can indeed arise for us, where we no longer see how in the face of other beliefs, we can make sense of morality any more. Now, similarly, the realist may accept that the very possibility of morality can be put in doubt by other assumptions we make about the world and that such 'excluders'[41] need to be dealt with appropriately, and so an explanation for morality in this sense needs to be given. But in relation to an explanatory scepticism of *this* sort, there seems to be no reason to think that the realist is somehow prevented from giving any response to it by virtue of his realism, in the way that Korsgaard suggests he is when it comes to debunking scepticism; rather, these debates will hinge on a range of considerations, to which the realist can offer answers as well as the constructivist, without being forced to somehow beg the question at issue. It would therefore be a mistake, both in interpreting Kant and in considering the philosophical threat of scepticism itself, to confuse the problem raised by transcendental explanation, with the demand for explanation raised by the debunking sceptic who Korsgaard (I have argued) mistakenly thinks cannot be addressed by the realist.[42]

[40] Cf. Kant *GMM*: 93 [4:445]. For further discussion of the issues discussed in this paragraph, see Chapter 4, this volume.

[41] Cf. Nozick 1981: 8–11.

[42] I am grateful to various readers and audiences for comments on this paper, including particularly Carla Bagnoli, Paul Formosa, and Jens Timmermann.

6

Does 'Ought' Imply 'Can'? And Did Kant Think It Does?

My aim in this paper is twofold. First, I want to consider the plausibility of the principle that 'ought implies can', and in particular to consider how much work this principle can be made to do. I will argue that while the principle is certainly plausible in *some* form, it is tempting to misconstrue it, and that this has happened in the way it has been taken up in some of the current literature. Second, I want to consider Kant's understanding of the principle. Here I will argue that these problematic conceptions put the principle to work in a way that Kant does not, so that there is an important divergence here which can easily be overlooked.

6.1 'Weak' vs 'Strong' Readings of 'Ought Implies Can'

The principle 'ought implies can' has been employed in several different debates in ethics and related areas: for example, it has been used to address the issue of free will vs determinism; of moral dilemmas; of internalism vs externalism as accounts of moral motivation; of obligation and blame; and of excuses and wrongdoing. None of these ways of using the principle have been entirely free of controversy, in the sense that different sides have disputed the way in which the principle has been employed to argue for one position over another. In these disputes, it is rarely that the principle of 'ought implies can' has been rejected *altogether*; rather, it is usually claimed that while there are clearly some arguments in its favour, these nonetheless establish the principle in a fairly weak form, so that in fact it cannot be used to do what it is being asked to do by one side or other in the dispute. To take one example: In his well-known article 'Obligation and Motivation in Recent Moral Philosophy',[1] William Frankena takes issue with W. D. Falk's attempt to argue from 'ought implies can' to motivational internalism (the view that to have a moral obligation, an agent must have a motivation to act on that obligation). Frankena summarizes Falk's position as follows: 'Falk appeals to the familiar principle that "I morally ought" implies "I can,"

[1] Frankena 1958. Frankena is responding to the following arguments in Falk 1945: 139 and 1986: 167.

adding that "I can" implies "I want to (in the sense that I have, at least dispositionally, some motivation for doing)," and then [draws] an internalist conclusion.'[2] Frankena then responds to Falk by suggesting that 'ought implies can' may be understood more weakly than Falk's argument requires:

> ['Ought implies can'] may plausibly be understood as saying: (a) moral judgments 'presuppose,' 'contextually imply,' or 'pragmatically imply' that the agent is able to act as proposed or is believed to be, but do not assert or state that he is; or (b) the *point of uttering* moral judgments disappears if the agents involved are not able to act as proposed or at least believed to be; or (c) it would be morally wrong to insist that an agent ought to do a certain action, if he is or is thought to be unable to do it. If Kant's dictum is interpreted in one of these ways the externalist need have no fear, for then it will not serve to refute him.[3]

Frankena thus claims that to use 'ought implies can' to argue for internalism is to misunderstand the principle; in fact, the principle is too weak to establish the desired conclusion.

In general, then, disputes in these areas have arisen because 'ought implies can' has seemed to some to license a particular conclusion that others have disputed, by claiming that in fact the principle is not strong enough to warrant that conclusion. To settle that issue, of course, one must consider the arguments for the principle, which are supposed to support it: do these arguments succeed in establishing it in a (comparatively) weak or a (comparatively) strong sense? Thus, while few would reject the principle altogether, there is disagreement about how exactly it should be understood, and thus about what work it can be made to do, in the light of arguments in its favour.

Now, in this paper I want to consider a use for the 'ought implies can' principle which also raises this question, but is different from any so far mentioned. The use is this: It is argued from 'ought implies can' that what is right must be something that we as agents are capable of following or acting upon, so that the principle of 'ought implies can' is said to imply that we should focus on the capacities of agents in moral theorizing and action, and adjust our accounts of what is right and wrong accordingly. It is suggested that the arguments that support 'ought implies can' are sufficient to license a reading of the principle that warrants this conclusion, so that the principle can be employed to help us determine the extent of the normative considered in this way. Against this, I will claim that in fact these arguments are *not* sufficient to license this view of the principle, and that therefore 'ought implies can' is *not* strong enough to be used in this manner.

6.2 Strong Readings of 'Ought Implies Can'

I will begin by giving some examples of how the principle has been understood in the way that I want to criticize. The examples will come from ethics, and epistemology.

[2] Frankena 1958: 59–60. [3] Frankena 1958: 60.

The clearest example in ethics is to be found in the work of James Griffin. In a recent book and associated articles, Griffin has argued for what might be called a greater degree of *realism* in ethics, in the sense that we should begin by understanding *ourselves* and our capacities, as a necessary first step to thinking about moral issues.[4] He claims that moral theories have too often neglected facts about human nature and society, and as a result have become distorted and inadequate to our real needs: we have theorized in a vacuum, and so have failed to do so successfully.

A particular example here, Griffin thinks, is utilitarianism. Utilitarianism has a commitment to impartiality, in the sense that it tells us that the right thing to do is whatever maximizes general utility. But, Griffin says, the reality of human life is that we usually cannot either calculate or act on what this maximization demands, because of our natural partiality to family, our interests, and other commitments. Griffin therefore claims that human limitations mean that utilitarianism cannot play a genuine role in our lives, and as a result the moral norms it proposes should be rejected as spurious:

> Moral norms must be tailored to fit the human moral torso. They are nothing but what such tailoring produces. There are no moral norms outside the boundary set by our capacities. These are not some second-best norms—norms made for everyday use by agents limited in intelligence and will—and then, behind them, true or ideal norms—norms without compromises to human frailty. Moral norms regulate human action; a norm that ignores the limited nature of human agents is not an 'ideal' norm, but no norm at all.[5]

Here, then, we find the 'ought implies can' principle being used in the way I am interested in: from certain facts about human nature and capacities, Griffin sets limits to what standards a moral theory can put forward, thereby using 'ought implies can' as a fundamental determinant of what is right and wrong.

It is worth emphasizing that Griffin does indeed want to use 'ought implies can' in this strong way. This is made clear in his discussion of a possible utilitarian response to his claim that impartiality is impossible for us to achieve, both cognitively and motivationally, the response being that impartially promoting interests is not meant to be a decision procedure (how we should go about deciding how to act on a particular occasion), but a criterion (what in the end makes an act right or wrong). Griffin's reply is that this does not help, as any criterion of what is right and wrong must also be constrained by human capacities, otherwise it will become too remote from human practices, and hence will lose its standing as a criterion: 'What most promotes interests is often permanently beyond our reach. Then a would-be "criterion" like that can play no role, not even that of a criterion.'[6] Thus, for Griffin, 'ought

[4] Clearly the term 'realism' here is being used in a different sense from that employed in the debate between realism and constructivism that forms the focus of previous papers in this collection.

[5] Griffin 1992: 131. Cf. also Griffin 1996: 105.

[6] Griffin 1996: 106. Cf. Flanagan 1991: 32–8, where Flanagan claims that act utilitarianism fails his Principle of Minimal Psychological Realism as a decision procedure, because it is psychologically

implies can' in a strong sense: no act can be right if it is beyond human capacities to act in this way, or wrong if it is beyond human capacities to avoid acting in this way; therefore (he thinks) utilitarianism is mistaken as a moral theory.

Having set out Griffin's position in ethics, we may now consider a second example of the strong use of 'ought implies can', this time in epistemology. The context here is a form of naturalistic response to scepticism, of the sort proposed by P. F. Strawson. According to this response, one way to answer scepticism is to show that there are certain beliefs which we must hold and cannot give up, for example, that there is an external world. This response is not without its ambiguities: but one way of taking it is to use it in conjunction with the strong 'ought implies can' principle, so that the sceptic is defeated by arguing that because we cannot give up the belief in question, there is no violation of a cognitive norm here. Thus, as one proponent of the Strawsonian position has put it: 'Showing that we must have such a belief as a condition of experience is not the same as proving that such objects exist. One is stating what we must believe, not how things are; but since the sceptic wishes us to justify the belief, doing so—the argument goes—is enough to put an end to scepticism.'[7] So, in response to the sceptical challenge that a belief we hold is epistemically illegitimate, the naturalistic strategy is to argue that we must hold this belief, and so cannot be violating any cognitive norm in retaining it, insofar as 'ought implies can' (in a strong sense).

I have chosen to highlight these positions because they are particularly clear instances of the outlook I want to criticize. But I do not think they are the only ones. For example, within political philosophy, the criticism of a viewpoint as 'utopian' would in part seem to reflect the idea that a political philosophy cannot be valid unless the principles it proposes are within the capacities of normal human beings to adopt. Of course, this may simply reflect nothing more than a commitment to politics as 'the art of the possible', in which case such theorizing is dismissed not as invalid, but merely as pointless; but it may also reflect the stronger view, that a theory which argues for principles that are unrealizable by us must be wrong, in which case here 'ought implies can' is once again being used in a strong sense.

In what follows, I will go on to claim that if 'ought implies can' is used in this way, the principle is being used *too* strongly. I will argue that while there are plausible arguments for the principle, these arguments only support a weaker reading of it; on the other hand, I will suggest that arguments that might be used to support the

impossible to determine which action promotes the best consequences; but he accepts that this does not rule out act utilitarianism as a criterion of rightness: 'For our purposes the point is best put this way: although utilitarianism qua philosophical theory will tell us that the action is best which produces the best outcome, it need not tell us that agents should always act or be motivated to act to produce the best outcome' (p. 34). Griffin's position is significantly stronger than this, in attacking utilitarianism qua criterion of right action *as well as* qua decision procedure.

[7] Grayling 1992: 508. For further discussion of this approach to scepticism, see Stern 2000: 107–12 and 2003.

stronger reading are not plausible. I will then go on to consider whether Kant's use of the principle shows him to be committed to the weaker or the stronger reading.

6.3 Arguments for the Strong Reading of 'Ought Implies Can'

Let me begin with what is perhaps the most plausible argument for 'ought implies can', namely what I will call the *argument from blame*. The argument, put simply, is that it is wrong to blame someone for something that they cannot control. Many people find this argument plausible, and although there are complexities (for example, can a deliberately incurred incapacity negate blameworthiness?), I propose simply to accept the argument for the sake of this discussion. The issue here, however, is whether accepting the argument is sufficient to establish 'ought implies can' in the strong sense.

I do not believe it is, because there is a distinction that can be drawn between *agent* evaluation, and *act* evaluation. That is, I can say that you are not to be criticized for doing or believing *A* because you were unable to do otherwise, while still holding that what you did or believed was wrong. So, the fact that an agent cannot be blamed for doing *A* does not show that no wrong was committed, and no norm violated.[8] Thus, the argument from blame shows merely that 'blame implies can', not that 'right implies can'; the principle it establishes therefore cannot be used to argue against a moral theory that says that some acts are right that nonetheless are unachievable by human beings. My claim, therefore, is that while the argument from blame is indeed plausible, it is not sufficient to support a strong reading of the 'ought implies can' principle.

If this is accepted, it therefore appears that a proponent of the strong reading needs to find another argument to support his position. I will consider five such arguments: the argument from obligation; the argument from motivation; the argument from anti-utopianism; the argument from agents; and the argument from naturalism. I will claim that while these arguments might be sufficient enough to support the strong reading of the principle, none is plausible, so that only a weak version of the principle remains defensible, on the basis of the argument from blame.

The *argument from obligation* is an attempt to reinforce the argument from blame in order to deliver a stronger conclusion, where the problem with that argument was that it appeared that an action might be right, even if an agent could not be blamed for not performing it because of their inability to do so. But, it might be asked, is it coherent to take an action to be right, if no agent *whatsoever* could be blamed for not

[8] Cf. Sinnott-Armstrong 1984: 250: 'Another common argument is that we do not blame agents for failing to do acts which they could not do, so it is not true that the agents ought to have done the acts. No such conclusion follows. The premise is about *agents*, but the conclusion is about *acts*. It is possible that an act ought to be done even though the agent would not be blameworthy for failing to do it.'

doing it, on the grounds that *no* agent is capable of performing it? This is not coherent, it could be argued: for it would suggest that an action is right, while no agent is under any obligation to do it, because no agent can perform it; but surely to be right, the action must be a duty for *some* conceivable agent? Now, I think this point has some force: but it is still not sufficient to support the position of those who understand 'ought implies can' in a strong sense. For, their claim is that for an act to be right, *we* must be under an obligation to perform it, qua human agents, with our cognitive and motivational limitations; but then it is harder to see why to be right, an act must be a duty *for us*, something *we* are obliged to perform, any more than it must be a duty for a dog or a monkey. (Of course, this might follow if it was claimed we were morally exemplary in some way, for then it could be said that unless we (qua moral agents) had *A* as our duty, then *A* would not be good (because if *A* were good, then as exemplary moral agents we would have it as our duty); but this is not part of the position I am criticizing.) So, provided the moral theorist can show how the act they take to be right would be obligatory to *some* conceivable agent (where that agent is without our various limitations), their position would appear to meet the requirements of the argument from obligation; the theorist does not have to show it can be made obligatory *to us*, so that once again our capacities cannot be used to set limits on claims about the right.

Turning now to the next argument I will discuss, the *argument from motivation* is this: An act cannot fall under a moral rule unless an agent is capable of obeying that rule, otherwise there would be moral rules that do not engage with our motivational set. What is the basis for this argument? A first suggestion might be that it is somehow unfair that there are rules which determine what is right or wrong, where we are constitutionally incapable of obeying them. But if this is the idea behind the argument, then it really takes us back to the argument from blame, and can be handled by allowing (once again) that we would not be *blameworthy* for failing to act rightly, as this *would* be unfair, while maintaining that there is no unfairness *beyond that*, in the fact that something is right which we cannot do. A second suggestion might be that moral rules have the status of *commands*, and that it makes no sense to issue a command that cannot be obeyed. Now, this view of moral rules is not uncommon; but it is important to distinguish two ways in which it can be taken. One way is (so to speak) *phenomenologically*: we *feel* moral rules to be imperatives or orders, telling us what do to in such a way that we take ourselves to be commanded to do it, and so obliged to act in a certain manner. Taken in this way, it is then plausible to infer that we would not feel *commanded* to act unless we thought we could so act. However, this just shows that our *experience* of morality suggests that we can do what we are morally required to do, insofar as we feel moral rules to be imperatives that apply to us. But of course, this does not show that acts are right only if we are obliged to perform them in this way, and so does not show that they cannot be right unless the commands of morality are addressed to us. It therefore appears that the proponent of this arguments needs a stronger claim, namely, that moral rules are not just experienced by us as commands, but *are* commands, in the sense that they are issued as orders for us to follow, and would not be issued otherwise. How might this position be supported? One option, of course, would be to move to a theistic conception of morality, and to conceive of moral acts as commanded by God, who would not so command us unless he thought we could obey him. But the familiar response to such a conception is with a version of the Euthyphro dilemma: are such acts commanded because they are right, or are they right because they are commanded? Assuming that the first horn of the dilemma is the more attractive (otherwise God's commands become somehow arbitrary), then the rightness of an act remains prior to its status as a command of God, and the normativity of a moral rule is not to be identified with its status as a command. Another, non-theistic, option brings us to the third attempt to defend the argument from motivation, namely that moral rules, like commands, imperatives and so forth, must be action guiding otherwise they would be *pointless*. This then takes us to the third argument for the strong version of the 'ought implies can' principle, which is the argument from anti-utopianism.

The *argument from anti-utopianism* is this: if there were moral rules that we could not act on, then these rules would be pointless, and the normative realm would be utopian, full of high ideals that are unrealizable; but this cannot be the case, so these rules must be ones we can obey. Griffin has put this argument as follows:

> Why choose a standard for moral action so remotely connected to what one can do? Of course, 'strange' does not imply 'wrong'. But 'ought' implies 'can'. Action-guiding principles must fit human capacities, or they become strange in a damaging way: pointless.[9]

Now, Griffin recognizes that this argument assumes that a moral rule is supposed to be action-guiding for us, whereas it might just be taken as a criterion of right and wrong. But Griffin also thinks that a criterion that tells us what is right and wrong must respect our capacities, as otherwise it too is pointless:

> Although criterion and decision procedure can diverge, they should not, I think, get too far apart from one another. Our decision procedures must take account of our capacities, but any criterion for a human practice cannot become too remote from our capacities without losing its point even as a criterion. Health is a reasonable criterion for medical practice because doctors can, directly or indirectly, act to bring it about. In contrast with that, a very demanding moral criterion (say, Jesus's "Be ye therefore perfect") may go too far even to be a moral criterion.[10]

Now, Griffin's position here rests on two assumptions. First, if a moral rule says that what is right is something we cannot do, it is pointless; and second, if a moral rule is pointless, it cannot really be a moral rule. Against the first assumption, it might be argued that a moral rule that goes beyond our capacities is not ipso facto pointless: for example, it may serve as a source of inspiration, or awe. Many of us admire

[9] Griffin 1992: 123. Cf. Griffin 1996: 163–4.

[10] Griffin 1992: 123–4.

certain figures or acts which we know we could not follow or even try to follow because of our own incapacities, where nonetheless this admiration gives these exemplars a kind of point.[11] And against the second assumption, it could be argued that nothing has been said to support it: even if a moral rule has no practical point, why should this bear on the normative question?[12]

One possible response to this is an *argument from morality as 'indexed' to agency*: It could be argued that it is mistaken to speak of an action being right or wrong *simpliciter*, as actions are only right or wrong for particular *agents*, where the capacities of the agent then has a direct bearing on the rightness or wrongness of the action. Thus, it could be argued, we cannot just say that 'Act *A* is wrong', but only that '*A* is the wrong thing for person *S* to do', where this judgement requires us to take into account what *S* is capable of doing. To taken an analogy: Someone might argue that we cannot say that a particular pastime is worthwhile *simpliciter*, but only whether particular agents should follow it, given their capacities. So, it does not make sense to say of a child that the right thing for him to do is to read the works of Shakespeare, because whether an activity is worthwhile is 'indexed' to the capacities of the agent. Thus, on this view, someone might argue that while it would be morally right for agents capable of greater impartiality than us to act as the utilitarian says, it is not right for *us* to so act, given our capacities—so that utilitarianism cannot form *our* morality (and so must fit the 'human moral torso' in this sense).[13]

The difficulty here, however, is first of all that we still need an argument to show that right or wrong requires 'indexing' to the capacities of agents, rather than simply being properties of actions. This is plausible in the case of pastimes, of course, because the value of pastimes lies largely in the benefits they bring to the person pursuing them; so, if a child would get little or nothing from reading Shakespeare, then it is indeed the case that it would not be right for them to do so. But moral actions rarely get their value in this way. Moreover, unless one embraces relativism, then there must be some way of assessing the value of an action that is independent of the capacities of the agent, as when we judge that it would be better if the child *could* read Shakespeare rather than just Harry Potter books, or that we *could* act more impartially rather than less so: but surely this requires us to judge the value of the act as right on its own merits, regardless of the capacities of particular agents?

[11] Cf. Rescher 1987, esp. Chapters 1 and 6.

[12] Cf. Sinnott-Armstrong 1984: 251: 'Finally, saying that agents ought to do what they cannot do is often claimed to be pointless and therefore not true. This argument is not valid. The premise concerns the *point* or *purpose* of saying something, but the conclusion concerns the *truth* of what is said. What is said might be true even when saying so could not serve any purpose.'

[13] I think this position and argument is one that Griffin himself would not accept, as it still leaves open the possibility of a morality different from ours, that would apply to agents with different capacities, whereas Griffin emphasizes that morality is really only an institution that applies *to us*: 'Moral norms are shaped for us, with all our limitations. There are no moral norms outside the boundary set by our capacities' (Griffin 1996: 100).

It is likely, however, that these replies will lead to the fifth argument I want to consider, namely the *argument from naturalism*. For, some may feel that these replies show what is fundamentally right about the 'ought implies can' principle: that it prevents the separation of the moral from what is possible for us as human beings, and so stops morality becoming profoundly *unhealthy*, by being conceived of in a way that fails to take our natures into account. This is the difficulty with my positive replies, it will be argued: talk of 'exemplars', 'unrealizable ideals', 'moral perfection' and so on leads to a radical separation between how we are and what we value that can only be damaging to our self-conception. Against this, the kind of naturalism associated with Nietzsche, Dewy, and others would suggest that we should take care to construct a moral system that begins by taking into account human capacities, in order to avoid the life-denying otherworldliness of an abstract realms of 'oughts'.

Now, this clearly raises large issues that cannot be fully dealt with here.[14] A central question is how far the naturalist's concern about the damage done by a morality of this sort is plausible. For, it could be argued that while undoubtedly *blame* and *guilt* can have this corrosive effect, we have already allowed (in discussing the argument from blame) that these moral sentiments are inappropriate in these cases. So, if the moral standard is viewed as exemplary, but in a way that is free from blame and guilt, would this be damaging and harmful? In a well-known passage, Iris Murdoch has suggested a more positive picture:

> Let us consider the case of conduct. What of the command 'Be ye therefore perfect?' Would it not be more sensible to say 'Be ye therefore slightly improved?' Some psychologists warn us that if our standards are too high we shall become neurotic. It seems to me that the idea of love arises necessarily in this context. The idea of perfection moves, and possibly changes, us (as artist, worker, agent) because it inspires love in the part of us that is most worthy. One cannot feel unmixed love for a mediocre moral standard any more than one can for the work of a mediocre artist.[15]

Aside from this big issue, we can also make a narrower point in this context, namely, that if the proponents of the strong version of the 'ought implies can' principle adopts the argument from naturalism, then they are implicitly conceding that they are taking a revisionist position, and so are accepting that this is not how we currently use the principle. For, the argument from naturalism is a critique of our *current* view of morality, from the perspective of a more 'healthy' outlook, where 'can' will determine 'ought'; but if it is a critique of our current view of morality from this

[14] As Frankena observed of the related dispute between motivational internalism and externalism, where the internalist holds that the externalist fails to recognize 'morality's task of guiding human conduct autonomously', while the externalist accuses the internalist of 'having to trim obligation to the size of internal motives': 'The battle, if war there be, cannot be contained; its field is the whole human world, and a grand strategy with a total commitment of forces is demanded of each of its participants. What else could a philosopher expect?' (Frankena 1958: 80–1).

[15] Cf. Murdoch 1970: 62.

perspective, then it is admitted that we currently *do not* conceive of 'ought implies can' in this strong sense. So, one cost of using the argument from naturalism is that the proponent of the strong 'ought implies can' principle must admit that what he says goes against our current understanding of the principle; he is therefore implicitly admitting that he cannot straightforwardly appeal to the principle in attacking some moral system (as Griffin does), for our present understanding of the principle licenses no such criticism. In this sense, then, the naturalist's strategy undermines the dialectical force of the principle when used as a critique of some moral theory. Of course, it is open to the naturalist to *challenge* our present (weak) understanding of the principle and revise it in the light of some argument: but then, as I have tried to suggest in the rest of this section, none of the arguments put forward so far have been successful in this respect.

6.4 Kant and 'Ought Implies Can'

It seems, then, that the 'ought implies can' principle has been understood by some of its current proponents in a way that is too strong, because in this strong form it cannot be defended. The question I now wish to raise is a more historical one: namely, did Kant wish to use this principle in the way it has come to be used recently, and so how far do my arguments against the principle in this strong form apply to Kant himself?

It is certainly the case that the principle of 'ought implies can' is usually thought of as a Kantian principle,[16] and he is widely seen as bringing it to prominence within modern philosophy. But there is little analysis of what exactly he meant by the principle, or what he supposed it to entail.[17] Moreover, given the common association between Kant and the principle, it is perhaps surprising that there are rather few passages in which Kant actually uses it, and none where he provides any discussion of or argument for it. I will consider those passages which are usually cited as cases where Kant adopts the principle, and I will claim that they show him using it in a weak sense, which suggests that he did not have the strong understanding of the principle that has been discussed and criticized in previous sections.

I will consider the following passages:

Passage A: *Critique of Pure Reason*, A807/B835:
Pure reason thus contains—not in its speculative use, to be sure, but yet in a certain practical use—principles of the *possibility of experience*, namely of those actions in conformity with moral precepts which *could* be encountered in the *history* of humankind. For since they command that these actions ought to happen, they must also be able to happen.[18]

[16] Cf. Frankena's reference to it as 'Kant's dictum' in the passage cited above.

[17] But for a very helpful discussion, which distinguishes different ways in which Kant related 'ought' and 'can' that are overlooked in the contemporary uses of the principle, see Timmermann 2003.

[18] Kant *CPR*: 678.

Passage B: *The Metaphysics of Morals*, 6:380:
Impulses of nature, accordingly, involve *obstacles* within the human being's mind to his fulfilment of duty and (sometimes powerful) forces opposing it, which he must judge that he is capable of resisting and conquering by reason not at some time in the future but at once (the moment he thinks of duty): he must judge that he *can* do what the law tells him unconditionally that he *ought* to do.[19]

Passage C: *Religion within the Boundaries of Mere Reason*, 6:47:
But if a human being is corrupt in the very ground of his maxims, how can he possibly bring about this revolution of his own forces and become a good human being on his own? Yet duty commands that he be good, and duty commands nothing but what we can do.[20]

Passage D: *Religion within the Boundaries of Mere Reason*, 6:50:

For if the moral law commands that we *ought* to be better human beings now, it inescapably follows that we must be *capable* of being better human beings.[21]

Passage E: *Critique of Practical Reason*, 5:143, footnote:
The moral law... necessarily binds every rational being and therefore justifies him a priori in presupposing in nature the conditions befitting it and makes the latter inseparable from the complete practical use of reason. It is a duty to realize the highest good to the utmost of our capacity; therefore it must be possible; hence it is also unavoidable for every rational being in the world to assume what is necessary for its objective possibility. The assumption is as necessary as the moral law, in relation to which alone it is valid.[22]

Passage F: *Critique of Practical Reason*, 5:142:
A need *of pure practical* reason is based on a *duty*, that of making something (the highest good) the object of my will so as to promote it with all my powers; and thus I must suppose its possibility and so too the conditions for this, namely God, freedom, and immortality, because I cannot prove these by my speculative reason, although I can also not refute them.[23]

Passage G: 'On the Common Saying: That May Be Correct in Theory, but It Is of no Use in Practice', 8:276–7:
But in a theory that is based on the *concept of duty*, concern about the empty ideality of this concept quite disappears. For it would not be a duty to aim at a certain effect of our will if this effect were not also possible in experience.[24]

Passage H: 'On the Common Saying: That May Be Correct in Theory, but It Is of no Use in Practice', 8:278–9:
I explained morals provisionally as the introduction to a science that teaches, not how we are to become happy, but how we are to become worthy of happiness. In doing so, I did not fail to remark that the human being is not thereby required to *renounce* his natural end, happiness, when it is a matter of complying with his duty; for that he cannot do, just as no finite rational being whatever can.[25]

Passage I: *Religion Within the Boundaries of Mere Reason*, 6:62:
From the practical point of view this idea [of a moral exemplar] has complete reality within itself. For it resides in our morally legislative reason. We *ought* to conform to it, and therefore we must also *be able* to.[26]

[19] Kant *MM*: 513.
[20] Kant *Relig*: 92.
[21] Kant *Relig*: 94.
[22] Kant *CPrR*: 255.
[23] Kant *CPrR*: 254.
[24] Kant *CS*: 280.
[25] Kant *CS*: 281–2.
[26] Kant *Relig*: 105.

Passage J: *Religion Within the Boundaries of Mere Reason*, 6:64:
For let the nature of this human being well-pleasing to God... be thought as superhuman... inasmuch as his unchanging purity of will, not gained through effort but innate, would render any transgression on his part absolutely impossible. The consequent distance from the natural human being would then again become so infinitely great that the divine human being could no longer be held forth to the natural human being as *example*... [T]he idea of a conduct in accordance with so perfect a rule of morality could no doubt also be valid for us, as a precept to be followed. Yet he himself could *not* also be presented to us *as an example to be emulated*, hence also not as proof that so pure and exalted a moral goodness can be practised and attained *by us*.[27]

Passage K: *Critique of Pure Reason*, A548/B576:
Now of course the action must be possible under natural conditions if the ought is directed to it.[28]

Taken together, these represent the main examples where Kant uses the principle of 'ought implies can', and so can best help us gauge his views. The question, then, is not whether Kant adopted the principle, but which *version* of the principle: how strongly did he understand it? In order to consider this, I will discuss the passages in groups, beginning with Passages A, B, C, and D.

On the face of it, these passages may seem to show that Kant is indeed using the principle in a way that suggests he understands it in a strong sense, where, for example, Kant claims that 'duty commands nothing but what we can do' (Passage C). This surely is to argue that the moral law is fixed by our capacities, which is what Griffin and others would also claim. However, I would suggest that in fact, these passages are not quite so straightforward. For, what Kant is focused on here is not the moral law *as such* (so to speak), but how the moral law relates to us, as something that commands *us* (Passages A, C, and D), that tells *us* what to do unconditionally (Passage B), that has a certain *authority* over us.[29] Kant holds that the moral law is addressed to us as agents, as something we are called upon to carry out, so that (as Henry Allison has put it) for Kant 'the moral law confronts us not merely as a lofty and admirable ideal but also as a source of an unconditional, inescapable demand upon the self';[30] and the moral law could not relate to us in this way unless we were capable of acting upon it, otherwise it would appear as no more than a 'lofty and admirable ideal' rather than as an 'inescapable demand'. So, the way we experience the 'right', as something we are in fact obliged to follow, shows that we think of ourselves as capable of acting as the moral law prescribes, and that we must accept the conditions that (Kant believes) explain this possibility, such as free will and the

[27] Kant *Relig*: 106–7. [28] Kant *CPR*: 540.

[29] Cf. Kant *PP*: 338 [8:370]: 'Morals is of itself practical in the objective sense, as the sum of laws commanding unconditionally, in accordance with which we *ought* to act, and it is patently absurd, having granted this concept of duty its authority, to say that one nevertheless *cannot* do it. For in that case this concept would of itself drop out of morals (*ultra posse nemo obligatur*) [no one is obligated beyond what he can do].'

[30] Allison 1990: 68.

existence of God (cf. Passage E). But, nothing here shows that Kant is committed to the view that the moral law *as such* must be constrained by the capacity of agents to obey it, as is suggested by the strong version of the 'ought implies can' principle. Nor does his argument for the postulates (of God, freedom, and immortality) require this: the fact that we are obliged to act in accordance with the moral law is sufficient to make these postulates rational, as explaining how we can come to be obliged in this way; Kant doesn't need the stronger claim, that these postulates make it possible for us to follow the moral law, and unless we could follow it, it would lose all normative content. So, I would argue, a closer inspection of these passages shows that Kant is using the principle of 'ought implies can' in a weak sense, by arguing that the moral law only has its status of being obligatory for us because we are able to act upon it, and that we can thus only explain this obligatoriness by accepting certain claims about our capacities and their conditions ('we ought implies we can'); but this is distinct from the claim that no act can be right (rather than just obligatory for us) unless we are able to perform it, which is how the principle is understood in the strong sense.

It might be argued, however, that this way of taking Kant's position is highly problematic, as it would appear to open up a gap between what I have called 'the moral law as such', and our relation to it as moral agents: surely Kant would have denied that the moral law could obtain *without* our being commanded by it, in which case isn't the latter really constitutive of the former? My response to this objection is to dispute this strong claim as a reading of Kant. Of course, Kant certainly held that *given what we are*, the moral law is a command to us: but that is (so to speak) a fact about us, rather than a fact about the moral law, that it must be such that it can be commanded to human agents.[31] So, insofar as Kant thinks that nothing can prevent the moral law commanding us, he does so because his conception of our agency is such that he holds us to be essentially capable of acting as right requires, not because our capacities as human agents naturalistically conceived puts limits on what the moral law can comprise,[32] so that no such gap can arise based on his conception of us qua exemplary agents, and not merely on his conception of 'ought implies can'.

[31] Cf. Kant *MM*: 528 [6:399], where Kant says that every human being has the predispositions of '*moral feeling, conscience, love* of one's neighbor, and *respect* for oneself (*self-esteem*) . . . and it is by virtue of them that he can be put under obligation.—Consciousness of them is not of empirical origin; it can, instead, only follow from consciousness of a moral law, as the effect this has on the mind.'

[32] Cf. Kant *GMM*: 44 [4:389], where he suggests that he has worked out 'for once a pure moral philosophy, completely cleansed of everything that may be only empirical and that belongs to anthropology'. Cf. also *MM*: 533 [6:405–6]: 'Ethical duties must not be determined in accordance with the capacity to fulfil the law that is ascribed to human beings; on the contrary, their moral capacity must be estimated by the law, which commands categorically, and so in accordance with our rational knowledge of what they ought to be in keeping with the idea of humanity, not in accordance with the empirical knowledge we have of them as they are.' It is hard to see he could make these claim unless he understood 'ought implies can' in the weak sense suggested here; for of course, it is precisely by understanding it in the strong sense, that theorists like Griffin hope to bring such empirical and anthropological issues back in. Kant makes clear his hostility to any naturalistic arguments for doing so in his *LE*: 86 and 91–2 [27:294–5 and 301].

Let me now consider Passages E and F. Once again, there is some reason to take these passages as supporting the view that Kant had a strong reading of the 'ought implies can' principle. However, I also think appearances here are misleading. For, what Kant is focusing on here is the *content* of the moral law as it is addressed to us, namely, that it tells us that we must 'realize the highest good to the utmost of our capacity' (Passage E) and that I must 'promote [the highest good] with all my powers' (Passage F). Thus, Kant clearly thought the moral law was such as to demand of us that we use our abilities in such a way as to further the highest good, and that this demand would be incoherent unless we could so act. But again, this is a fairly weak use of the 'ought implies can' principle: it takes it that there would not be a moral rule telling *us* how we ought to use *our* capacities unless we could so use those capacities, which seems very plausible, because unless we had those capacities (in ourselves, or internally) and were able to exercise them (in the world, or externally), how could our use of them be prescribed by the moral law? Thus, on this view, the moral law engages with us (tells us what to do) because it fits with our capacities; but this is distinct from the stronger view, that *unless* it engages with our capacities, and so states what is right *for us* to do, then it cannot tell us what is right at all.[33] To take an example: It certainly seems correct to say that the moral law could only say that 'people should try as hard as possible to act benevolently' if people are capable (both internally and externally) of acting benevolently, as otherwise the injunction to try would be meaningless; but this is a moral law that concerns our capacities, and it doesn't follow from that if we lack that capacity, we can no longer say that benevolent acts are right. Thus, Kant would seem to be arguing here merely that an agent can only be under an obligation to try to bring about an end (the realization of the highest good) if he has the ability to do it; but this doesn't commit Kant to denying that the end (the realization of the highest good) is right, even if no human agent is under any such obligation to use his abilities to bring it about, because he lacks those abilities.

Similar remarks apply to Passage G and H. These occur in Kant's essay 'On the Common Saying: That May Be Correct in Theory, but It Is of no Use in Practice', which is in part a reply to Christian Garve's criticism that for Kant, we have a moral duty to give up our desire to be happy, but that this is contrary to our nature. In Passage G, Kant accepts the seriousness of this kind of worry, but in Passage H he says that Garve is wrong to claim that he saw our moral duty in this way. Now, again, these passages may appear to support a strong reading of 'ought implies can'. But, once more, I believe this is mistaken. For, it is clear on closer inspection that Kant is talking about what the moral law commands *us* to do, what *our* obligations consist in, where Kant accepts that something cannot be an obligation for *us* unless we can bring

[33] As I have observed, this might follow with the additional premise that we are morally exemplary in some way, so that what is morally right is then necessarily something we are capable of acting upon, and so necessarily engages with us in this way: but this is an additional step, rather than something that follows from 'ought implies can' on its own.

it about: but, as I have argued, this is a weak conception of 'ought implies can'. And, in Passage H, Kant says it cannot be someone's duty to do something he is incapable of doing, which again fits with the weak conception. What he does *not* say here is anything that implies the strong reading: namely, that nothing can be right that we are incapable of achieving; rather, all he seems to be accepting is that we cannot *be obliged to do what is right* unless we are capable of acting in that way, which is a weaker claim than the one made by Griffin et al.

Turning now to Passages I and J, these concern the role of a Christ-like figure as a moral example to us. Again, these passages may seem to support a position like Griffin's, which opposes the notion of moral ideals that we cannot follow, and thus the counsel of perfection 'Be ye therefore perfect'. Nonetheless, I would claim that it would be wrong to assimilate Kant to this view. For, Kant's focus is on Christ as an actual *example*, as a figure we are told we ought to imitate, where we would be to blame if we did not. Now of course, if the example of Christ is treated in this way, then we must be *able* to imitate him. But this does not show that there could not be moral ideals which were still valid, even though we could not imitate them (where in these cases the most we could do would be to *try* to imitate them, and so would not be to blame for failing to attain any real likeness to our ideal). Indeed, Kant seems to accept the 'validity' of these ideals himself, as something we might strive to copy, without being able to imitate. I do not believe, therefore, that these passages show that Kant had anything resembling the naturalist's concerns discussed earlier: he is merely suggesting that if we are to be blamed for not following a moral example, then our capacities must resemble those of the example; but as we have seen, this argument from blame can be accepted without being committed to the strong interpretation of the 'ought implies can' principle.

Finally, let me consider Passage K. This passage is in fact the one most often cited in support of the claim that Kant had a strong conception of 'ought implies can'. And certainly, taken on its own, it seems fairly compelling. Nonetheless, it is much less conclusive when set in context, as follows:

> The action to which the '*ought*' applies must indeed be possible under natural conditions. These conditions, however, do not play any part in determining the will itself, but only in determining the effect and its consequences in the [field of] appearance.

I would argue that the context alters the implication of the original sentence. For now it seems clear that Kant merely intended that sentence to say that 'natural conditions' (i.e. the phenomenal world) must play a role in determining moral actions as well as other actions, but that that role is not a determinant of the will. The passage is therefore all about Kant's view of moral action and the will, and not about 'ought implies can' at all, and is therefore of no real concern to us here.

I think the discussion of these passages suggests something more generally about the difference between Kant's outlook and the stronger use of 'ought implies can' that we have been analysing. A feature of this stronger use, is that it tries to develop an account of right and wrong by *beginning* with an account of human capacities, to set the parameters of moral theorizing. (As Griffin puts it: 'The limits of "ought" are fixed by, among other things, the limits of "can".'[34]) I think Kant's procedure is in many ways the opposite of this: that is, he first fixes his moral theory, where what matters is not what we are capable of qua human beings, but what obligations can be shown to apply to rational agents capable of acting rightly; and then, once the moral law is fixed, he uses 'ought implies can' to determine what we are capable of qua human beings, insofar as we fall under this law.[35] Thus, whereas the strong conception argues from what we can do to what we ought to do, Kant's weaker conception of 'ought implies can' argues from what we ought to do to what we can do, and so is used to provide his ethical argument for freedom and the existence of God.[36] It is therefore hardly any surprise that on close inspection, Kant's position diverges from the current one.

6.5 Conclusion

We have therefore considered how far the principle of 'ought implies can' should be used, and the extent to which Kant (as one of the proponents of this principle) wanted to use it. If my discussion has been right, some current uses of the principle go too far, and in a direction that receive little support from the comments on this principle made by Kant himself.[37]

[34] Griffin 1996: 96.

[35] Cf. Kant *CPrR*: 169 [5:36]: 'But the moral law commands compliance from everyone, and indeed the most exact compliance. Appraising what is to be done in accordance with it must, therefore, not be so difficult that the most common and unpracticed understanding should not know how to go about it, even without worldly prudence.'

[36] Griffin therefore emphasizes the 'modesty' of his moral position: 'Ethics, particularly the ethics studied in modern universities, strikes me as often too ambitious. It usually fails to operate with a realistic conception of human agency' (Griffin 1996: 100). While Griffin uses 'ought implies can' as a justification for such modesty, I would argue that Kant had no desire to use the principle in this way, but only to establish what our capacities are, in the light of the demands of morality (which in Kant's case are of course notoriously high). Cf. Kant *CPrR*: 163–4 [5:30], where Kant argues that because a person judges he ought not to give false testimony even on pain of death, he will therefore judge that he can overcome his love of life, when 'ought implies can' is used in this way: 'He judges, therefore, that he can do something because he is aware that he ought to do it and cognizes freedom within him, which, without the moral law, would have remained unknown to him.' As Timmermann argues (in 'Sollen und Können') the Kantian principle in these cases is best rendered not as 'ought implies can', but as 'you can because you ought' ('*Du kannst, denn du sollst*'), insofar as here the 'ought' is presupposed rather than being used to determine whether a duty can properly be demanded of an agent.

[37] I am grateful to Christopher Bennett, Fabian Freyenhagen, David Owens, Walter Sinnott-Armstrong, Philip Stratton-Lake, Jens Timmermann, and Leif Wenar for helpful comments on earlier versions of this paper.

7

Why Does Ought Imply Can?

While it does not go entirely undebated, the principle of 'ought implies can' (OIC) is widely taken to be highly plausible, and as such forms the cornerstone of many arguments in ethics and beyond. What is less often discussed, however, is what exactly makes it so plausible, and thus why the principle of OIC holds at all: what is it about an act being obligatory, that means this only obtains when the agent can carry out that action?[1] It is this question that I would like to consider in this paper.

In order to do so, it is necessary to bring in different accounts of moral obligation; for, as we will see, different accounts will lead to different ways of responding to this question, while some accounts may make it plausible to reject the principle of OIC altogether. Thus, while often the merits or otherwise of the principle are discussed in isolation, I will suggest that we can only really consider it properly within this wider context, so that broader issues are at stake than just the principle taken on its own.

That there is some such connection between OIC and theories of moral obligation is not really surprising: for, on the one hand, a central role for such theories is to explain what makes the moral ought distinctive from other kinds of ought (such as prudential or proper functioning oughts), while on the other hand OIC seems to be most at home in the moral case (to say I ought to keep my promise even though I can't seems problematic, in a way that it does not seem problematic to say I ought to save more for my pension, even though I can't, or ought to be able to eat more even though I can't). We might therefore expect the former project, of explaining the distinctiveness of the moral ought, to shed light on why it is only the moral ought that relates to ability in the way in which the OIC principle suggests.

I will thus consider the principle in relation to four prominent accounts of moral obligation: divine command accounts, natural law accounts, self-legislation accounts, and social command accounts. I hope to show how each gives a rather different kind of context to the question of how 'ought' relates to 'can', suggesting that while we may find the principle 'intuitive', those intuitions relate back to wider background assumptions about moral obligation in general, which need to be taken into account when considering the principle's merits. I will begin by briefly outlining the four views of moral obligation which I will be discussing, and then go on to show how

[1] By 'acts' here I intend something suitably broad: so not just individual actions, but also act types and also for example the development of dispositions or character traits: e.g. 'he ought to be more tolerant'.

each gives a rather different rationale for the principle of OIC, and how we should make sense of it. In showing how the fate of the principle is bound up with these wider theories, I will suggest that deciding for or against it is much less simple than is sometimes thought.

7.1 Theories of Moral Obligation

In her paper 'Modern Moral Philosophy', Elizabeth Anscombe famously makes the claim that the moral ought as we understand it only came on the scene with Christianity and its '*law* conception of ethics', whereby 'the ordinary (and quite indispensable) terms "should," "needs," "ought," "must,"... acquired this special sense by being equated in the relevant contexts with "is obliged," or "is bound," or "is required to," in the sense in which one can be obliged or bound by law, or something can be required by law'.[2] For Anscombe, therefore, the way the moral ought is to be understood is in terms of a divine command, which lays down a moral law in terms of which our actions are to be judged, and against which they are to be measured. This appeal to divine command, of course, is one of the classic accounts of moral obligation, and the one that Anscombe claims makes most sense in its own terms.

However, Anscombe also recognizes that there are other options, which we may want or need to explore. For, she holds that in the current secular age, we lack the belief in God that is required to make the divine command account work, so that for us 'it is as if the notion "criminal" were to remain when criminal law and criminal courts had been abolished and forgotten'.[3] She briefly considers three such options—an appeal to nature; self-legislation; and socially imposed norms—but her conclusion is that none are workable, and thus as it stands our current conception of moral obligation is broken-backed. I do not want to consider her critical arguments in any detail, but do want to follow her taxonomy of theories of obligation, as background to our subsequent discussion.

Of the appeal to nature, she says: 'The search for "norms" might lead someone to look for the laws of nature, as if the universe where a legislator; but in the present day this is not likely to lead to good results: it might lead one to eat the weaker according to the laws of nature, but would hardly lead anyone nowadays to notions of justice; the pre-Socratic feeling about justice as comparable to the balance or harmony which kept things going is very remote from us.'[4] Anscombe's reference here, I take it, is to some sort of natural law approach, with its origins in thinkers such as Anaxagoras and Heraclitus, which appeals to nature and its workings as a source of moral order. On Christian natural law theory, it is because nature has been created in a certain way by God that certain obligations hold, rather than being directly commanded; but of course, if the divine command view is in jeopardy because of doubts about God's

[2] Anscombe 1958: 5. [3] Anscombe 1958: 6. [4] Anscombe 1958: 14.

existence, so too is this form of theistic natural law theory. Alternatively, as a way to avoid these difficulties, one could just take nature itself to be ordered in such a way as to create obligations, or maintain that there are reasons with obligatory force which are inherent in the nature of things. Anscombe is clearly sceptical about this option too, as based on a conception of nature that we can no longer take seriously; but it remains a possibility for us to consider in relation to the OIC principle. It will be important to remember, therefore, that natural law theory can take these two forms—theistic and non-theistic.

Another option Anscombe also briefly considers is Kantian self-legislation, namely that obligation comes from a law that one imposes on oneself. Anscombe's central concern here is that a self-imposed law is not really sufficiently binding to constitute any genuine constraint, arguing instead that 'the concept of legislation requires superior power in the legislator'.[5] It remains a matter of dispute whether the Kantian position has to be as voluntaristic as this makes it sound, and (notwithstanding Anscombe's critique), it remains a live option in current debates.

Finally, Anscombe mentions the possibility of seeing moral obligation as coming from the society of which the individual is part, as imposed on the individual through socially enforced norms or constraints. Once belief in God is lost, such a secularized type of divine command theory may well seem a natural option, where the former is replaced by a form of *social* command instead, as we exercise authority over one another in a way that puts us under obligations. For Anscombe, the main worry here is that societies have in fact tried to enforce norms that are far from moral, so to turn to this as a source of obligation is highly problematic;[6] whilst others have argued that to move to a more hypothetical form of social command in order to escape this criticism is to deprive those commands of obligatory force.[7] Nonetheless, social command account of various kinds remain an important option which needs to be considered in relation to the principle of 'ought implies can'.

Having briefly set up these four accounts of moral obligation, I now want to investigate where they lead us in thinking about the principle.

7.2 Divine Command Accounts of Obligation and OIC

Starting with divine command accounts of obligation, an explanation and defence for the principle of OIC may not seem hard to find,[8] as it would appear to follow

[5] Anscombe 1958: 2; cf. also p. 13. [6] Cf. Anscombe 1958: 13.

[7] Cf. Adams 1999: 246.

[8] I am here focusing on divine command accounts rather narrowly; other elements of theistic ethics, such as the doctrine of original sin, may seem to count against OIC in so far as our necessary failure to meet God's commandments is not taken to undermine their authority—although my comments in this section about grace and forgiveness are also relevant to this issue.

naturally from the very idea of a command, which would arguably make no sense in a context in which the agent commanded was unable to obey, for both pragmatic and moral reasons. First of all, pragmatically it seems pointless to issue an order that cannot be followed; and secondly, if command involves some process of sanctioning for non-compliance, then it would equally seem unfair to attach such sanctions to an action that the agent cannot perform, hence again supporting the principle, as God qua commander may be expected to be sensitive to such considerations of fairness.

However, in fact things are not really that simple when it comes to divine command views. One important complicating factor is the place of grace (charis) and forgiveness (aphesis) within these accounts, which has been a traditional part of such conceptions, where grace is what empowers us to live justly after we have been forgiven for our inability to do so relying only on our own resources. Thus, while it may seem pragmatically pointless to command someone to act in a way that they cannot, this changes once grace and forgiveness come into the picture, as demonstrating such grace and forgiveness may then give a reason to make the unfulfillable command. Similarly, grace and forgiveness alter the issue of the unfairness of sanctions and blame, as the former precisely come into play (it could be agued) insofar as the unfairness of the latter are recognized.[9]

Nonetheless, it could be argued that there is still something problematic about this picture: for, it may still seem curious to issue a command *knowing in advance* that the person to whom it is issued will need to be forgiven for failing to follow it, as it might seem more rational simply not to issue the command in the first place. However, this is to assume that the sole point of commanding here is to bring about an action; but it could also be to demonstrate forgiveness and the power of grace, or indeed some other purpose, such as showing us something about our limitations as human beings.[10]

But still, it could be replied, in these circumstances where the agent cannot carry out the command, while there may be some other purpose in speaking how he does, God has still not managed to *actually* command anyone, because this presupposes an ability to act accordingly by the person who is being commanded. Of course, a command can still be issued where it turns out afterwards that it cannot be fulfilled; but it is less clear that it can be issued when this is known in advance. As Hare puts it: 'If I tell or ask someone to do something (whether by way of advice, request, instruction, order, or even prayer does not matter), I give him to understand that I think that the question to which I have given him an answer arises—i.e. that a

[9] Cf. Wittgenstein 1998: 87:

> 'God has commanded it, therefore we must be able to do it.' That means nothing. There is no '*therefore*' about it...'He has commanded it' means here roughly: He will punish anybody who does not do it. And nothing follows from that about anyone being able. And *that* is the sense of 'election by grace'.

[10] Cf. Martin 2009. As Martin makes clear, in adopting this approach, he is following in a broadly Lutheran tradition, as against Erasmus.

decision is open to him. It would not do to tell a soldier to pick up his rifle if it were fixed to the ground.'[11] 'It would not do' is a bit equivocal, but I think Hare can be read as saying that it is part of the 'logic' of telling someone to act that one assumes that there is at least some chance it can be done, otherwise one has not really told them to do anything at all, and so not issued any sort of instruction or order whatsoever.[12]

At this point, far from the divine command account helping to explain and support the principle of OIC, a divine command account of this sort could instead find itself a victim of it. For, it could be argued, if OIC holds, then in these circumstances where forgiveness and grace are known to be required in advance, God cannot generate an ought as he cannot issue a command; so either this shows that divine commands are not sufficient to create obligations as some capacity to act on them is also required, or it shows that in these circumstances these are not really commands as such capacity is known to be lacking.

Now, claims about the 'logic' of command are perhaps not as clear-cut as this, and doubtless could ultimately be resisted as begging the question.[13] Nonetheless, faced with the difficulty we have identified, the divine command theorist may choose instead to embrace OIC and drop these radical appeals to forgiveness and grace, by returning to our starting point and arguing that an advantage of her account is that it illuminates the principle for us: as moral obligations are based on commands, and commands are only intelligible as commands when issued to those who are in some position to obey them, this explains why ought implies can. I now want to turn to other accounts of moral obligation, to see if they can do any better, or conversely might persuade us more effectively than a divine command account that we should give up the principle, where the nature of command proved a sticking point in this respect.

7.3 Natural Law Account of Obligation and OIC

Taken in a theistic form, many of the same considerations will apply to natural law accounts as we saw in relation to divine command theories. Putting it very generally, according to the theistic natural law theorist what we are obliged to do is what God, through his creation, has made good for us to do, in the sense of allowing us flourish or making our lives goes well, so that our obligations arise out of God's purposes in creating the world. In this context, then, similar pragmatic and moral considerations

[11] R. M. Hare 1963: 54. Cf. also MacIntyre 2007: 164: 'The notion that we can be required to respond to a demand that is always and inevitably unfulfillable is necessarily incoherent. If I say to you "This cannot be done; do it," you will necessarily be baffled.'

[12] One complicating case may be to introduce the idea of God's *assistance*, so that God issues the command knowing full well we cannot meet it *on our own*, but that we are capable of achieving it with his help, where part of the point of the command is to make this clear to us. This, however, may be said not to pose a real challenge to OIC, as the 'can' is just understood in a broader sense than merely 'can on one's own'. For a discussion that places emphasis on God's assistance in this way, see J. E. Hare 2001b.

[13] Cf. Pigden 1990.

as we discussed in relation to divine command theory might apply here. So, at the pragmatic level, it could be argued that it would be pointless for God to make something good for us, and yet not equip us with the capacity to realize that good; we must therefore have the capacity to act in accordance with our obligations understood in these terms, so that ought will imply can. And relatedly at a moral level, it could be argued that a God who set things up in a way that made our good unattainable would have a dubious moral character, as it is hard to see what could justify him in putting what is good for us out of our reach. The theistic natural law theorist would therefore seem to have reasonable grounds within the resources of their theory to support the OIC principle.

One possible complication, however, relates to an alleged shortcoming in theistic natural law theory itself, where it is often claimed (not least by divine command theorists) that while it can accommodate 'oughts' in some sense, these are not properly speaking *moral* 'oughts', but more like proper functioning oughts, where for the former some form of constraint or necessitation is required that is lacking in the latter.[14] These are large issues that cannot be properly dealt with here: but if this objection to theistic natural law theory were upheld, then while the theory might show that 'oughts' in some general sense imply can, it may not show that *moral* oughts do so, as the latter are not properly part of this picture at all.

Turning now to non-theistic natural law theories, a similar worry could of course be expressed. But these non-theistic natural law theories also have special complications of their own in relation to OIC, that merit some further discussion. For, once God is taken out of the picture, as it were, then the pragmatic and moral reasons considered above in favour of OIC no longer seem to apply, as moral obligation is no longer being traced back to the providential order of a legislator or creator; it may be less clear, therefore, how OIC is to be explained and justified once we move to a theory of this type.

For the secular natural law theorist, it is not necessary to appeal to God to explain the normativity that results from the goods that fulfil our natures, as these goods can be understood simply in terms of the kinds of beings we are, where what we then ought or ought not to do results from whether an action does or does not conform to that good in various ways. Thus, as Mark Murphy has put it recently: 'The explanation [of the moral law] runs from the nature of the good to the inevitable badness of certain sorts of response to that good, and thus to the necessity of agents' not performing such actions'.[15] The question that then arises, therefore, is whether on this sort of account there is a way to justify OIC or not.

It may help to focus on a particular example, such as lying. On the secular natural law account, this will be said to be prohibited because it damages some good for

[14] Cf. Evans 2013: 70.

[15] Murphy 2011: 74. Note that Murphy himself is not defending this view, as he wants to argue for a theistic natural law theory.

agents, such as the possession of knowledge or even agency itself, making it the case that one ought not to lie. But suppose you have a psychological condition such that you are a pathological liar, unable to do otherwise: does anything in the secular natural law account suggest that we cannot appropriately say of you that you ought not to lie, as the OIC principle would suggest?

On the one hand, it might seem hard for the secular natural law theorist to claim that we cannot say of you that you ought not to lie. For, because the 'ought' here is not related to considerations of blame and sanction, she cannot appeal to the inappropriateness of the latter to rule the 'ought' out: by lying, one is still damaging a good, and if that is all that matters for something to be an obligation, then one's inability to do otherwise would seem to be neither here nor there.

On the other hand, the secular natural law theorist could argue that of course capacity to do otherwise is relevant, as otherwise *anything* that damaged a good would be violating a moral prohibition, which could then include a tree that kills me or a signpost that points in the wrong direction, which is obviously absurd. It is thus not just *any* damaging of the good in question that violates a moral ought, but only those performed by agents who thus, qua agents, must have the capacity to do otherwise and so conform to their obligations.

However, this response arguably brings us back to an issue mentioned earlier, namely whether the natural law theorist (of either type) is really in a position to distinguish between moral and non-moral oughts. If they *are*, then it seems right that they will need to introduce considerations evinced in the previous paragraph in order to do so. But it might also be said that the most consistent thing for the natural law theorist to do instead is just to reject the moral/non-moral distinction here, and so accept that it is intelligible on their view to say that the tree ought not to have killed me, and the signpost ought not to have led me astray, simply because both damage goods and thus it would have been better if neither had occurred. Of course, they can also agree that notions like blame and sanction do not apply to such cases; but if they don't make such notions central to their conception of oughts anyhow, that need not affect their position. If one then wants to *add* to that position by saying that *moral* oughts relate to actions that damage goods *for which the agent is blameable* and hence responsible, then one might get closer to a justification of OIC principle; but this principle does not seem to be central to the theory thus far, in the way it was for divine command accounts and theistic natural law accounts.

There is, however, another way in which the secular natural law theorist might respond to these issues, which is to bring in one of the ways in which non-secular theorists like Aquinas and Leibniz also attempt to incorporate some notion of constraint into the natural law picture in order to explain the obligatory force of moral actions: namely, by appeal to the place of *reason*. On such accounts, the imperatival or binding nature of morality is taken to come from the way in which reason instructs us to act in order to achieve the human good. Thus, Finnis argues that for Aquinas, 'law is an act of intellect; this reason has nothing to do with the will of a superior needing to be made known, but only with the fact that it is intelligence that grasps ends, and arranges means to ends, and grasps the necessity of those arranged means; and this is the source of obligation';[16] and Leibniz accuses Pufendorf of failing to see that the 'efficient cause of the law' is not a divine command, but lies in 'the nature of things and in the precepts of right reason which conform to it'.[17] For the theistic natural law theorist, as our reason is itself part of God's creation, we can be confident that we would not have it unless it were effective in leading us towards the good, and thus in prescribing means towards that good which we can follow. Taking over this idea, the secular natural law theorist might then argue that if moral obligation issues from the precepts of reason, it could not do so unless what reason were telling us to do were achievable, so that the role of reason in laying down the law ensures that ought implies can.

However, once again it may be harder for the secular natural law theorist to make their case than the theistic natural law theorist. For while the theist can appeal to God's purposes to explain why reason will in general only prescribe means that are within our capabilities, as it is the function of reason to help us to achieve our ends on this account, it is more difficult to make this connection on the secular account: just as in the prudential case, where reason might tell me I ought to eat, even when I cannot, so it could be argued that in the moral case reason might prescribe some means to a good that nonetheless I cannot adopt, like telling the truth. Thus, taken in this instrumental way, but in a secular form, it may again be unclear why a natural law theory should endorse OIC.

7.4 Kantian Accounts of Obligation and OIC

It may be, however, that another way can be found to make use of the idea of reason in the account of moral obligation that will provide a way of linking it to the OIC principle, where this approach is arguably to be found in Kant's notion of self-legislation.

One way to think about Kant's position on moral obligation, is to see him as transferring the commanding authority that binds us to the moral law from God to our own reason, where it does really serve a constraining role in holding back our desires to act otherwise. Thus, Kant argues, while the holy will does not fall under any 'oughts' because it lacks any inclination to transgress the moral law, we are necessitated to act precisely by the role that reason plays in overcoming those inclinations.[18] This means, therefore, that the Kantian can also transfer some of the arguments

[16] Finnis 1980: 54–5. Cf. also Finnis 2002: 5–6: 'the source of obligation and law [lies] in the kind of necessity which we identify when we notice that some specific means is *required* by and for the sake of some end which it would be unreasonable not to judge desirable and pursuit-worthy', where Finnis contrasts this with command views which treat 'obligation and law... as matters of superior *will*'.

[17] Leibniz 1988: 70.

[18] For further discussion, see Stern 2012, Chapter 3.

concerning OIC into this new context. Thus, just as the divine command theorist can argue that God could not intelligibly command us to act in a way that we could not, so the Kantian can say the same of reason; but because Kant puts the 'right' prior to the 'good', reason here does not merely serve the instrumental function outlined above in the natural law account, so she can disallow the suggestion that if reason is being used instrumentally, ought might not imply can after all, thus reaping the rewards of Kant's distinction between hypothetical and categorical imperatives.

However, while this model might allow the Kantian to explain the OIC principle, she is arguably in a weaker position than the divine command theorist to do so: for, while in the latter case the commander is an agent of some kind, who we can therefore think of as constrained by the 'logic' of what it is to give a command, it is less clear that we can think of reason in these terms, without anthropomorphising our faculties in an unacceptable way.[19] The Kantian might instead turn to some sort of teleological account of our faculties, in the manner of the theistic natural law theorist—but this would seem to lose anything that might be distinctive in the Kantian position, while introducing a reliance on purposiveness that Kant would presumably find unacceptable given his views on teleological explanations in general. It may still therefore not be clear what the Kantian can do to explain the plausibility of the OIC principle.

There might, however, be another way to connect Kant's position with the OIC principle, which focuses not on the parallel between the commands of God and the commands of reason, but more on the fact that unless OIC held, our reason would fail to be genuinely *practical*, where for Kant it is practical and not theoretical reason that informs us of what we ought to do, by involving practical deliberation intended to settle questions about what is to be done. Thus, for Kant practical reason does not just inform us that some act is right or wrong, good or bad, as if what practical reason tells us were on a par with telling us that some act will take a long time, or involve six people, for this would collapse the distinction between theoretical and practical reason; rather, in telling us that an act ought to be done, practical reason is *ipso facto* telling us we *can* do it,[20] otherwise it would not be a case of *practical* reason but merely theoretical reasoning instead—as when we think, when tied to a chair, not that we ought to save the kidnap victim, but that it would nonetheless be right for it to be done, if *per impossibile* we were able to do so. Thus, because a Kantian ought is a conclusion of pure practical reason, its practicability is already built into it, meaning it is something that can be done.[21]

[19] For an example of the problem, cf. Korsgaard 1996b: 107: 'The acting self concedes to the thinking self its right to govern. But the thinking self in turn must try to govern well. It is its job to make what is in any case a good idea into law.'

[20] This, of course, is one way of taking Kant's famous argument for freedom in *CPrR*: 163–4 [5:30–1]. For further discussion, see Chapter 12, this volume.

[21] For an argument along these lines, see Rödl 2013.

It might be argued, however, that there is still a possible lacuna in this Kantian attempt to link 'ought' with 'can'. For, while the argument may show that thinking in a practical way that one ought to act entails thinking that one can so act, this doesn't show that ought implies can as such—just that our capacity to think of an act *as* an 'ought' implies thinking of it as a 'can'. Thus, someone might argue, nothing Kant has said rules out the possibility of the moral law laying down what we ought to do, even though we cannot follow it; all Kant has shown is that we could not grasp these aspects of that law using our practical reason. Of course, this possibility might be ruled out on other grounds involving idealist or constructivist conceptions of the moral law, such that it could not outstrip our capacity to think it in this way and thus act on it; but this is to use controversial assumptions to defend OIC, when we might have hoped that something more neutral might be all that is required. Alternatively, the Kantian could go back to some of the earlier moves regarding the unfairness or pointlessness of a moral law that we cannot grasp, but that would be to lose the distinctiveness of her appeal to reason in arguing for the principle.

7.5 Social Command Accounts of Obligation and OIC

We turn now, finally, to the fourth account of moral obligation which I wish to discuss, which is the social command account. Here, the fundamental thought is that what puts us under an obligation is the authority of others in society over the individual agent. As Robert Adams has put the basic idea of this account (which he does not himself endorse in this secular form): 'According to social theories of the nature of obligation, having an obligation to do something consists in being required (in a certain way, under certain circumstances or conditions), by another person or a group of persons, to do it.'[22]

To someone who adopts this account, one way to make the link to OIC is along the lines we have considered previously, in relation to divine command accounts and some ways of taking Kant's view: namely, that it would be wrong and/or pointless for society to require of people things that they cannot do, so that what these socially grounded requirements will consist in will always be things that people generally (if not necessarily in individual cases) can actually perform, at least to some degree. And the pointlessness argument, in particular, may seem reinforced by the kind of naturalism that plausibly goes along with the social command view: namely, that the role or function of morality is to guide human behaviour in a way that will enable us to live together, so that there really is nothing to be said for a system of rules or social practices that completely outstrip our power to conform to them.[23]

[22] Adams 1999: 242.

[23] Cf. Griffin 1992: 123: 'Why choose a standard for moral action so remotely connected to what one can do? Of course, "strange" does not imply "wrong". But "ought" implies "can". Action-guiding principles must fit human capacities, or they become strange in a damaging way: pointless.'

There are, however, some relevant complications here. One is that while a function of morality may be to help us live together, so that rules to which we could not conform could not serve this function, morality may also serve other roles—for example, by inspiring us with models and exemplars which though completely unattainable, can still enrich our lives, so it would not be pointless in this respect for society to enact some entirely unrealizable ideals of behaviour. And while a social command theorist might recognize some callousness or unfairness in requiring a moral norm to which people find it difficult or even impossible to comply in many cases, she might still think there are sufficient benefits to doing so, or just feel committed to it sufficiently *as a norm*, to think these disadvantages can be outweighed on moral grounds.[24]

However, there is one feature of social command accounts which could provide a more compelling basis for adopting the OIC principle, which has to do with the emphasis that such accounts tend to put on *blame* as central to the idea of moral obligation, where this blame comes from others or oneself and thus has a social source. Thus, as Mill famously puts it: 'we not call anything wrong, unless we mean to imply that a person ought to be punished in some way or other for doing it; if not by law, by the opinion of his fellow-creatures; if not by opinion, by the reproaches of his own conscience'.[25] It is important to recognize, however, that there are different ways in which this idea of blame can be used in an account of moral obligation.

A first way might be to use it to account for the way in which morality is made binding, on a par with the punishment and sanctions that form part of some divine command accounts. Blame would thus become one of the central ways in which we enforce and hold people to moral norms, and turn them into requirements. On this view, therefore, the connection with OIC would come about in the ways discussed above, through considerations of pointlessness and fairness: it is both pointless to blame people for things they cannot do, and also unfair precisely because they are unable to do them. But as we have seen, while it does provide some basis for defending OIC, there are nonetheless limitations to this sort of approach, which uses blame to account for the particular directive force of morality.

There is, however, another way to think of blame in relation to moral obligation, which is not as a directive force that binds us to act, but rather as a way of *appraising* actions in a distinctive manner, which marks off the realm of the moral.[26] Thus, the thought is, there is an important difference between critically appraising (and hence

[24] Cf. Rödl 2013: 44: 'We might say it is not incoherent [to have a code to which someone cannot conform], but cruel. A code that requires someone to do something even as he cannot do it is cruel. The code should be relaxed: if someone cannot do what it requires, he should be exempt, or be required to do the best he can. This demand may be just. But there is no incoherence in rejecting it: in thinking that he who cannot live up to the code is a weakling and justly despised; that the code must never be relaxed and that relaxing it would be our downfall.'

[25] Mill 1972: Chapter V, para 14, p. 45.

[26] In drawing this distinction between the directive and the appraisive, I am following Thomas Pink: see Pink 2014 and forthcoming.

blaming) someone for being foolish, humourless, imprudent, or graceless on the one hand, and for being morally bad on the other, where the difference precisely relates to the lack of control one may have in the former cases while still being blameworthy, where this control might be said to be required in the latter case, when it is *moral* blame that is at stake. The crucial difference is that in the moral case, the fault is attributed to individuals in a way for which they can be held to account, which may not be so in the former cases—for while being foolish and so on are certainly faults, and one may think less well of a person as a result, doing so does not necessarily involve attributing the fault to *them*, as something for which they can be held responsible, which is why we do not withdraw the criticism and the negative appraisal when we find out it is just part of their character or disposition. But on this view, precisely what makes *moral* appraisal different, is that we *do* withdraw moral blame once we find the act was beyond their control, suggesting that it is the special nature of moral blameworthiness and hence moral appraisal that underlies the link with OIC.[27] Thus, the thought is, if it is the case that in our dealings with one another that moral blame operates in a fundamentally different way from other sorts of blame, and thus constitutes a distinctive form of appraisal, we cannot give up the principle of OIC, as the kind of control that this principle requires is precisely the kind of control that marks moral appraisal off from other forms of appraisal—which is why those who have been sceptical that we possess this kind of self-determination (like Hume) have been sceptical about the special character of moral blame.[28] If we want to hang on to the latter, it would then seem, we must hang on to OIC; at the same time, this explains why intuitions regarding OIC can vary, as those who do not think of moral blame as anything distinctive will assimilate it to other kinds of negative appraisal, where OIC does not have to hold.

Looking at social command accounts of obligation, therefore, and the place that they characteristically give to blame, has led us to a position where the significant place of OIC in morality has become clearer: namely, not at the directive level in relation to the constraining force of morality, but at the appraisive level, in marking off moral censure from other kinds of critical appraisal. At the directive level, it seems, while considerations of practicality and fairness may give some weight to OIC,

[27] Cf. Pink 2014: 7: 'In moral blame, the agent is not merely criticised for some fault in their action, attitude or character. Moral blame involves a further step: the fault is put down to them as their fault. This putting a fault down to someone as their fault is essential to the content of blame. And it is at this point that a power on the agent's part comes in. We are going beyond dispositions or states of the agent or occurrences in their life, and criticism of the agent just for these, such as for being selfish or unreasonable, and addressing the agent as having a further responsibility for these states and occurrences—for their selfishness or unreasonableness. And this brings in the agent not just as someone involved in these states or occurrences but as determinant of them. Why should these faults on the agent's part be their fault unless they had a power to determine their occurrence for themselves—or a power to prevent which, though possessed by the agent, they failed to exercise?'

[28] 'A blemish, a fault, a vice, a crime; these expressions seem to denote different degrees of censure and disapprobation; which are, however, all of them, at the bottom, pretty nearly of the same kind or species' (Hume 1975: appendix iv, p. 322).

these claims can also be resisted; but at the appraisive level, the relation between morality and OIC is made more constitutive and thus harder to resist, except by questioning the distinctiveness of the moral altogether. This may seem to make the link between morality and OIC more secure, and help explain why we take ought to imply can in a more satisfying manner.

However, while it was considerations of social command theories that brought us to this point, there does not seem to be anything particularly about such theories that give them a privileged position to draw the connection between morality and OIC on this basis. For, while what distinguishes the moral theories we have discussed is primarily the way they account for the *directive* force of morality (through divine command, natural law, self-legislation, or social command); but when it comes to the issue of appraisal, they are all likely to agree, in taking moral censure to be different from censure of other kinds.

Nonetheless, it could be argued, the social command theorist is in a distinctively favourable position, insofar as they can find a way to *link* the directive *with* the appraisive aspects of moral obligation on their account, while other accounts will find this more difficult. This may be illustrated in the case of Stephen Darwall's recent treatment of moral obligation, and the place of blame within it.[29] For Darwall, blame is not merely a sanction that can be applied to enforce moral norms, but is a particular form of second-personal address, whereby we demand *of others* that they act in certain ways, where then this directive force of moral blame is also what makes morality distinctive at the appraisive level, as in non-moral cases of blame we do not demand anything *of* others in the same way precisely because we do not think it is in their control to act as we require. Thus, this form of social command account is doing more that just saying that when I morally blame you for being unkind, I am not just criticizing you as the bearer of the fault, as I might when I blame you for being foolish—this is something that all accounts of moral obligation as distinctive can allow. But additionally to this, on Darwall's account, in blaming you I am also demanding of you that you follow this requirement, and not simply sanctioning you via blame, where the directive force of this demand also only arguably makes sense if you have the relevant capacity to determine yourself accordingly, as it is requiring something *of you* in a special way. Thus, while natural law and Kantian accounts may also treat morality as distinctive from the appraisive point of view, as involving a particular sort of moral blame and thus also a connection with OIC on this basis, because they do not give blame any sort of *directive* role but give that to practical reason instead, the link with OIC may seem weaker, thus putting a social command theory such as Darwall's at an advantage.

[29] For Darwall's general position, Darwall 2006; and for his view that moral blame is distinct from other kinds of blame, see Darwall 2013b.

Things are less clear, however, on a divine command account: for, it is possible to treat such accounts (as Darwall himself does)[30] as 'ancestors' of the social command view, insofar as one thinks of God as also addressing a kind of second-personal demand to us to act in various ways, and also as open to a distinctive kind of criticism if we fail, thus mirroring in this respect the structure of the social command view. Thus, while divine command theories may of course be criticized on other grounds (as Darwall himself does),[31] their ability to accommodate OIC may seem just as secure as the position adopted by the social command theorist, at least if the complications introduced by questions of forgiveness and grace we discussed earlier are set to one side.

7.6 Concluding Remarks

In this paper, I have not been trying to argue for or against OIC. Rather, I have been trying to understand why it is that the principle might hold *if* it does, and thus on what basis it could rest, where looking at how broader accounts of moral obligation differ on this issue has suggested different kinds of answers. As Kant might have said, assuming that the principle is not simply analytic, but in some sense synthetic a priori, and thus in need of some 'third thing' to connect 'ought' with 'can',[32] then it is plausible to think that this will come from the background theory of moral obligation with which one is working. Thus, one factor in distinguishing such theories and choosing them over one another may be on how far they support the principle; or, if one finds the principle objectionable in the first place, rejecting the principle may provide grounds on which to reject the theories themselves. Either way, the connection seems to warrant continued exploration.[33]

[30] Cf. Darwall 2006, Chapter 5, notably in relation to Pufendorf.

[31] Cf. Darwall 2006: 107–15.

[32] Cf. Kant *GMM*: 95 [4:447]. Cf. Martin 2009.

[33] I am grateful for comments on previous versions of this paper to Marcel van Ackeren, Sophie Grace Chappell, Michael Kühler, Tom Pink, and Sebastian Rödl.

PART II

Ethics after Kant

8

On Hegel's Critique of Kant's Ethics

Beyond the 'Empty Formalism' Objection

In the current literature on Hegel and Kant, an uneasy truce seems to have broken out in the trench warfare between Hegelians and Kantians over Kant's ethics. On the one hand, at least some commentators on Kant have started to take seriously the critical fire directed by Hegel at Kant's treatment of the Formula of Universal Law as the 'supreme principle of morality', and so to that extent have accepted the force of Hegel's so-called 'empty formalism' objection.[1] On the other hand, the Kantians' response has been to beat a tactical retreat on this issue, and to press forward on a new front, by arguing that the Formula of Universal Law (henceforth FUL) was never *meant* to stand alone as the supreme principle of morality, and that once it is put together with Kant's other formulae (particularly the Formula of Humanity (FH)), this can resolve the formalism problem, so that Hegel's point regarding the FUL can safely be conceded, while Kant's position *as a whole* can be saved. One attraction of this more concessive approach,[2] it may seem, is that both sides can then go away happy: Hegelians can be content that rather than simply being dismissed, Hegel's objections to Kant have been taken seriously and to some extent accepted as valid, while Kantians can be pleased that the damage caused by Hegel can nonetheless be shown to be limited and only narrowly focused, and that overall Kant's ethics with its several related formulae remains intact.

In this paper, I want to consider whether the questions at issue between Kant and Hegel can really be satisfactorily resolved in this manner. I will suggest that in fact Hegel's concerns go deeper than this concessive response to the 'empty formalism'

[1] See, for example, Lo 1981; Wood 1999, esp. pp. 97–110; Galvin 2009.

[2] Needless to say, not *all* commentators on Kant have adopted this concessive approach to Hegel's criticism: some remain resolute, and have stuck to the more traditional response of defending the Formula of Universal Law itself against the formalism objection. For examples of this more resolute approach, see e.g. O'Neill 1989: 81–104; Schnoor 1989; and Korsgaard 1996a: 77–105. Of course, resoluteness with respect to the FUL does not preclude these commentators from also taking the other formulae very seriously too, and relating all the formulae together in various ways.

objection allows, and that these deeper concerns have still not been dealt with by the Kantians who adopt this less resolute approach—where, put briefly, those concerns resemble those of the particularistic intuitionist, and so will extend to *any* attempt to uncover a 'supreme principle of morality', whether this is the FUL *or* the FH. However, I will also suggest that hopes for peace between the two camps should not be abandoned entirely: for, I will argue, on a certain understanding of what Kant was up to in seeking to identify the 'supreme principle of morality', his position may be made more compatible with the sort of particularistic intuitionism which I claim is favoured by Hegel, so that a truce of sorts may be viable after all—albeit one that requires further concessions on the Kantian side, but where these concessions are ones (I will argue) that Kant himself may well have been happy to make.

I will begin by briefly recapping the history of the hostilities as they have been conducted in the recent literature thus far, and say more about the strategy adopted by the more concessive Kantians (section 8.1). I will then show why Hegel would not be satisfied by their position (section 8.2), and explore whether a further re-thinking of Kant's approach might give rise to a more lasting peace (sections 8.3 and 8.4).

8.1 Hegel's Empty Formalism Objection, and the Concessive Kantian Response

In the *Groundwork of the Metaphysics of Morals*, Kant sets out to identify and establish 'the *supreme principle of morality*',[3] which he initially claims to be the following: '*act only in accordance with that maxim through which you can at the same time will that it become a universal law*'.[4] It is this that has come to be called Kant's 'Formula of Universal Law'.[5]

In picking out the FUL as the supreme principle of morality, Kant stresses that unlike other candidates for this role that have been put forward by previous philosophers,[6] the FUL is a *formal* principle, not a material one. This, Kant claims, must be

[3] Kant *GMM*: 47 [4:392]. [4] Kant *GMM*: 73 [4:421]. Cf. also *GMM*: 57 [4:402].

[5] The FUL is sometimes then immediately grouped together with the next formula Kant offers, which is known as the Formula of the Law of Nature (FLN): '*act as if the maxim of your action were to become by your will a* ***universal law of nature***' (Kant *GMM*: 73 [4:421]). The two formulae together are then sometimes called 'the Universal Law formulas'. This in itself then immediately introduces a complexity in the debate with Hegel, as on the one hand Hegel himself mainly just concentrates on FUL rather than FLN or any combination of the two, which may seem to put Kant at an immediate disadvantage in an unfair way; on the other hand, it is not clear whether Kant's move from FUL to FLN is already a concession to worries about the formalism of FUL itself and thus a stepping back from the latter, while in practice most Kantians who adopt the concessive approach to Hegel's objections are prepared to admit that they apply to *both* FUL *and* FLN, where it is only really when Kant gets to the FH that they are dealt with properly. So, in order to avoid complicating my discussion too much at this stage, I will focus mainly on the problems with FUL, and assume for the sake of this discussion that moving just to the FLN would not really be enough to help on its own, though I do not attempt to argue this here.

[6] Kant discusses those alternatives at two main places in his published writings: at *GMM*: 90–2 [4:441–4], and *CPrR*: 172–5 [5:39–41]. They are also discussed at some length in Kant's lectures on ethics,

the case if the principle is really going to reflect the categorical nature of dutiful moral action, of the sort that common sense morality takes for granted as an essential part of moral life; for, such action must not involve any expectation that performing it will help the agent to realize some non-moral end. It therefore follows, Kant argues, that what determines the will must be the formal properties of the maxim on which the agent acts, namely whether or not some sort of *contradiction* would be involved in acting in this way, where Kant locates the contradiction in the idea that if others adopted this maxim as their own too, acting on it would somehow become impossible, so that as a maxim for action it would undermine itself in this way.

Now, put at its simplest, Hegel's 'empty formalism' objection is that precisely because Kant is operating here in purely formal terms, by trying to determine what is right and wrong by testing to see whether a maxim does or does not lead to a contradiction when universalized in this way, the FUL cannot in fact plausibly be used to give any *content* to morality, and so cannot really constitute the supreme principle of morality at all.[7] In order to demonstrate the FUL's uselessness in this respect, Hegel and Hegelians have introduced a series of puzzle cases, where the FUL seems to either deliver no result at all, or one that is clearly mistaken, which Hegel and Hegelians take to show that the FUL is too flimsy to bear any normative weight, and so is in practice empty and always in need of further 'content' or supplementation. Thus, as Hegel puts it in the *Phenomenology*, 'The criterion of law which Reason possesses within itself fits every case equally well, and is thus in fact no criterion at all'.[8] In order to bring the problem out, Hegel gives various examples, where the FUL seems either to yield conflicting results and so is indeterminate, or yields so-called 'false negatives',[9] in seeming to rule out actions that we would ordinarily accept as perfectly morally legitimate.

To illustrate the indeterminacy claim, Hegel refers to Kant's own 'deposit' case, where Kant considers someone who has had someone else's money entrusted to him, and who avariciously desires to keep it, or who is also in great need.[10] Hegel argues that the FUL cannot be used to determine one's duty in this case, for it cannot

e.g. *LE*: 65–8 [*Ak* 27:274–8]; 239–46 [29:620–9]; *LE*: 280–2 [27:517–19]. For a thorough discussion of Kant's position on the issue, see Kerstein 2002: 139–59.

[7] Hegel's critique of Kant's FUL occurs in four main places: *NL* [II: 434–532]; *PS*: 256–62 [III: 316–23]; *PR*: §§133–6, pp. 161–4 [VII: 250–4]; and *LHP* III: 458–61 [XX: 366–9]. It also occurs more briefly in *EL*: §§ 53–4, 100–2 [VIII: 138–9].

[8] Hegel, *PS*: 259 [III: 319]. Cf. also *PR*: §135, p. 162 [VII: 252–3]: 'There is no criterion within that principle [of absence of contradiction] for deciding whether or not [some action] is a duty. On the contrary, it is possible to justify any wrong or immoral mode of action by this means.'

[9] Hegel himself does not give any examples of 'false positives' on their own, i.e. cases where the FUL would license what are intuitively wrong acts (although, in the context of the indeterminacy objection, the fact that the FUL might be used to justify the abolition of property would perhaps count as such a false positive for Hegel, given his views on property). However, others have offered such examples, e.g. Brentano 1969: 50, where Brentano argues that the maxim of not accepting bribes is ununiversalizable and so should be rejected by Kant. For a response to Brentano, see Patzig 1959.

[10] Cf. Kant *CPrR*: 161 [5:27]; and *OCS*: 287–8 [8:286–7].

determine whether or not property or a social system without property is a morally good thing, as the contradictoriness of both options can be argued either way.[11] And to illustrate the false negatives claim, Hegel mentions the examples of fighting for your country, and of helping the poor, neither of which (he claims) can be universalized:[12] for if everyone defended their own country, no one would attack other people's, so that there would be no defending to be done, while if everyone helped the poor, no one would be in poverty, so that again acts of benevolence would be prevented if universalized, seeming to suggest (absurdly) that maxims like 'help the poor' are immoral in so far as they would fail the FUL test.

It is perhaps not surprising, however, that the response of some readers of Kant to these Hegelian objections has been rather dismissive.[13] For, in relation to the deposit case, Hegel may seem to have simply misunderstood how the FUL is meant to function, which is in relation to the *maxim* on which a person proposes to act, and whether or not if universalized, so acting would lead to an undermining of the kind of trust required to keep the institution of property going on which they themselves rely: it therefore seems irrelevant that the FUL is indeterminate when it comes to deciding whether or not the institution of property *itself* is contradictory in some way—indeed, the Kantian may well agree with Hegel, that it is hard to know what this could even mean. Now, to this, perhaps, the Hegelian might respond that surely if I am trying to decide whether to keep some property, I need to first know whether property is a good or bad thing? However, again the Kantian might reasonably deny this, arguing that it is sufficient to know that keeping the property is wrong if I can see that in keeping it, I would be free-riding or exploiting the good will of others—so that again, the contradictoriness or otherwise of property *itself* is irrelevant here.

And, when it comes to Hegel's supposed 'false negatives', Kantians have responded by arguing that Hegel has misunderstood the maxims that would realistically be involved, and failed to show that these would genuinely fail the FUL test. For, it is pointed out, in order to count as a maxim, something like 'help the poor' must have some specified end in view, and when this is spelt out in the morally admirable case (e.g. 'help the poor in order to abolish poverty'), then there is no difficulty in the fact that by everyone helping the poor, the end of so doing would be achieved—quite the contrary, in fact.

However, notwithstanding the plausibility of these Kantian responses, and the further ingenuity that has been used to deal with related complexities, there remains a feeling to which the more concessive Kantians are also sensitive, that Hegel was still onto something in raising his concerns, however much he may be convicted of

[11] *NL*: 125–6 [II: 462–3]; *PS*: 257–9 [III: 317–18]; *PR*: §135, 162–3 [VII: 252–3]; *LHP* III: 460–1 [XX: 368–9].

[12] *NL*: 127–8 [II: 465–6]; *LHP* III: 460 [XX: 368].

[13] Typical is perhaps Marcus Singer's reaction, where he calls Hegel's objection 'almost incredibly simple-minded' (Singer 1963: 251).

somewhat misrepresenting and over-simplifying the way in which Kant presents the FUL as working. For, it can be argued on Hegel's behalf, that in an important sense, he can use these Kantian responses to his own advantage. Thus, in relation to the property case, it may indeed be right to say that the FUL is not designed by Kant to adjudicate on the question of whether or not it is right or wrong for people to possess private property:[14] but isn't this *itself* a limitation? Surely anything purporting to be a 'supreme principle of morality' *should* be able to adjudicate on such an issue, which has clear moral as well as political implications? Isn't it precisely a fault of the FUL that it is too narrow in this respect, and silent on this sort of question, which can plausibly be regarded as just one instance of many such cases concerning institutions? (e.g. is democracy more morally legitimate than any other political system? Is monogamy a better system of marriage from the moral point of view than polygamy? Is there any moral significance to marriage at all?) And secondly, in relation to the 'help the poor' case, the Kantian response may also be said to highlight a deeper difficulty for their position, which is the notoriously problematic issue of determining how exactly maxims are to be framed and determined, where an agent might find he can come up with a different outcome for the FUL test by adjusting the maxim by which he proposes to act in ways that do not really alter the moral situation—for example, by making his maxim more specific in various ways, it might then become universalizable, but where what is still fundamentally a morally wrong action is being licensed, so that the problem of false results for the test re-emerges.

In addition to these ways in which Hegel's 'empty formalism' objection may continue to be pressed, it can also be argued that there is a yet deeper worry underlying it, which is that the FUL is inadequate as the supreme principle of morality taken on its own, because something more substantive is required if we are to understand *why* there is any moral significance in acting on maxims that are universalizable—why this *matters* from a moral point of view. The problem might be put as a dilemma for the Kantian: on the one hand, he could answer this question by relating the FUL to considerations such as equality, fairness, or free-riding,[15] but then it is not clear why 'treat others fairly' is not the supreme moral principle and the FUL merely a test for whether or not in acting a certain way one would be doing so; or he could treat the FUL as somehow prior in itself, but then make its moral relevance mysterious.

[14] As David Couzens Hoy has pointed out, however, in his *Rechtslehre*, Kant does seem to claim that the absence of property is contradictory: see Hoy 1989: 218, where he refers to Kant *MM*: 404–6 [6:246–7].

[15] These considerations are the ones usually put forward by proponents of the FUL as the basis for its moral significance: see e.g. O'Neill 1989: 156: 'In restricting our maxims to those that meet the test of the Categorical Imperative we refuse to base our lives on maxims that necessarily make of our case an exception. The reason why a universalizability criterion is morally significant is that it makes of our own case no special exception'; and Korsgaard 1996a: 92: 'What the test shows to be forbidden are just those actions whose efficacy in achieving their purposes depends upon their being exceptional'. One further difficulty here is whether exceptional actions of this kind are always wrong (cf. Wood 1999: 108); another more exegetical worry is that while Kant himself mentions this as a central issue (cf. *GMM*: 75–6 [4:424]), it is hard to see how this can be made into the moral issue underlying some of his examples (e.g. suicide).

Now, while some commentators on Kant have continued the tradition of remaining unimpressed by these sorts of Hegelian considerations, others have accepted their force, and have given up the attempt to defend the FUL as a candidate for the supreme principle of morality in its own right. However, rather than then abandoning Kant's project in the *Groundwork* and elsewhere altogether, they have instead insisted that Hegel was being myopic in concentrating on *just* the FUL in the first place, and that the more significant ethical principles for Kant are given in the other moral formulae, particularly perhaps the so-called Formula of Humanity: '*So act that you use humanity, whether in your own person or in the person of any other, always at the same time as an end, never merely as a means.*'[16] The suggestion is that once the FH is made central in this way, Kant has a candidate for the supreme moral principle that can be said to overcome the difficulties faced by the FUL, in being more determinate; in recommending actions that better fit our intuitive moral judgements; and in making a clear connection to the sorts of values (such as our rational nature as agents) that make moral basis for the principle readily apparent.[17]

And, on their side, commentators on Hegel have been generally prepared to accept this kind of Kantian approach, where in exchange for Kantian concessions regarding Hegel's critique of the FUL, they have been willing to allow that this critique is indeed rather narrow, and that using his other formulae, Kant may be able to escape the charge of 'empty formalism' made against the FUL on its own.[18] In this way, therefore, a kind of stable consensus between both sides has emerged, with some ground being conceded on both sides.[19]

[16] *GMM*: 80 [4:429].

[17] Cf. Riley 1983: 38–50, where Riley speaks of the other formulae as adding 'a bit of nonheteronomous teleological flesh to the bare bones of universality' (p. 49); Wood 1990: 156: 'It is a mistake for Hegel and other critics to fasten so exclusively on the FUL in their attempts to prove that Kantian ethics is empty of content... Hegel and other critics will have not shown Kantian ethics to be empty of content until they have demonstrated the emptiness of [the] other formulas along with that of FUL'; Lo 1981: 197–8: 'Those philosophers who keep charging Kantian ethics with "*empty* formalism" only pay attention to [the FUL] and brush aside [the other formulae] as though they were unworthy of consideration. This is completely un-Kantian because [the FH] is straightforwardly formulated in the *Groundwork* and is carefully applied in *The Doctrine of Virtue*. It seems clear to me that [the FH] is a practicable criterion for determining moral rightness or wrongness, and is by no means barren.'

[18] Cf. Smith 1989: 73–4, where Smith allows that it is probably correct 'that Hegel's view of Kant derives from an undue attention to the first formulation of the Categorical Imperative, which emphasizes the universality of its form, and not enough from the second, which commands respect for persons or treating others as "ends in themselves." Had he done so, he might well have found in Kant a set of objective ends that he criticizes him for not having. Kant's moral theory may well be formal, but it need not be empty'. Cf. also O'Hagan 1987: 142: 'The radical Kantian can escape the Hegelian ['emptiness'] charge only if he moves on to the [FH] formulation of the categorical imperative'; and Geiger 2007: 11, where Geiger accepts that on the traditional view of Hegel's critique of Kant, that critique is unfair in that 'it focuses exclusively on the universal law formula of the categorical imperative and ignores its other formulations', and so he argues that battle much properly be joined elsewhere.

[19] Another approach is to accuse Hegel (and other similar critics) of overlooking not the other formulations of the supreme principle of morality, but the 'impure' aspects of Kant's ethics, and its incorporation of more empirical elements: see e.g. Louden 2000, esp. pp. 167–70. This approach, too,

I now want to argue, however, that this consensus is premature,[20] and that Hegel's concerns do not *just* apply to the FUL and its peculiarities, but to *any* attempt to propose a 'supreme principle of morality', *even* the less 'formal' FH. Once the full extent of these concerns are considered, therefore, I will argue that if we are still searching for some consensus between Kant and Hegel, it must involve more than just this move from the FUL to the FH, or any other of Kant's proposed formulae.

8.2 Hegel's Intuitionism: Against a 'Supreme Principle of Morality'

On the view of Hegel I want to put forward in this section, Hegel's objection to Kant may be compared with a form of intuitionism, where this is to be understood not primarily as an epistemological doctrine ('we know moral truths or propositions by intuition'), but as a doctrine that rejects the idea that morality has any single highest principle, and thus the view that there might be any 'supreme principle of morality' at all, whether that is the FUL, the FH, or any other principle of a Kantian or non-Kantian kind (such as the utilitarian principle of maximizing happiness or well-being).[21] As generally conceived, intuitionism of this sort stands between those theories that think there is *one* highest moral principle that underpins all others, and those theories that say there are no moral principles *at all*, not even the many prima facie principles that the intuitionist allows, where this latter position is a form of strong particularism.[22]

A broad sympathy with the ideas behind an intuitionism of this sort is reflected in many aspects of Hegel's work. At the highest and most abstract structural level, Hegel is deeply preoccupied with the categories of universality, particularity, and individuality, where he argues throughout that any position that becomes too general and

has the effect of the reducing the 'gap' between the Kantian and Hegelian positions, though in ways that cannot be fully explored here. For further discussion see Westphal 2003.

[20] Another way to challenge this consensus might be to argue that the Hegelian should not allow the Kantian to move beyond the FUL in this way, as to do so is inconsistent with the basis of Kant's position, such as his view of autonomy. Though I don't think Hegel ever says as much, I think this is perhaps why Hegel nowhere really discusses the other formulae in any detail, and only really focuses on the FUL: see e.g. *LHP* III: 260 [XX: 367–8]: 'this freedom is at first only the negative of everything else; no bonds, nothing external, lays me under an obligation. It is to this extent indeterminate; it is the identity of the will with itself, its at-homeness with itself. But what is the content of the law? Here we at once come back to the lack of content.' For a contemporary discussion of the difficulties involved in moving from the FUL to FH, given a certain understanding of what Kant means by autonomy, cf. Johnson 2007.

[21] Cf. Urmson 1975, who characterizes Prichard's brand of intuitionism as 'attacking... the view that there was some supreme moral principle from which all others could be derived' (Urmson 1975: 112); cf. Prichard 2002a: 14. Cf. also McNaughton 2002.

[22] The relations between intuitionism (of the sort favoured by W. D. Ross) and strong particularism (of the sort favoured by Jonathan Dancy) are complex, as intuitionism certainly contains some particularistic elements, while nonetheless seeing more scope for moral principles in our ethical thinking than the strong particularist will allow. For a helpful discussion of the relation between intuitionism and particularism, see Hooker 2000.

abstract will become empty, while any that focuses too much on the specificity of the individual case will lose sight of what is common between individuals, where the inadequacies of each of these sides will then cause us to oscillate to the extreme of the other. What is needed, therefore, across all philosophical positions (so for example in metaphysics, epistemology, philosophy of nature, philosophy of religion, philosophy of art as well as ethics and political philosophy) is a standpoint that enables us to move between these extremes, and thus a theory that combines elements of generality with a sensitivity to the particularities of the situation. It is therefore scarcely surprising, then, that while Hegel opposes those who reject all talk of duties and rules as too abstract and general in favour of an inarticulable moral 'feeling', he equally opposes attempts to reduce the complexity of the details of the moral situation to a simple principle to be applied to all cases, where one has thereby abstracted too much away from any differences between them. In his ethical writings, Hegel therefore makes no attempt to offer any 'supreme principle of morality', as if particular duties were to be derived from or grounded in such a principle: it is these particular duties that must be treated as fundamental, as the higher principle is too abstract to plausibly serve as their foundation or basis—only if we 'already had determinate principles concerning how to act',[23] could we know how to operate with such a principle, rendering its claims to supremacy highly dubious.

Hegel's most extended discussion of the issues raised here can be found in the *Phenomenology*, in his analysis of a rationalistic approach to ethics that forms part of the 'Reason' chapter as a whole, in the sub-sections on 'Reason as law-giver' and 'Reason as testing laws'.[24] In the first of these sub-sections, Hegel attacks a rationalism that lays down certain particular principles as *absolute* rather than as provisional, and thus tries to treat them as exceptionless and simple to apply, rather than as guidelines that require sensitivity to where they can go wrong. He thus considers the examples 'Everyone ought to speak the truth' and 'Love thy neighbour as thyself'. In the former case, Hegel argues, this principle is only plausible if we are conscious of our own fallibility in knowing the truth, so that rather than being a principle one can use straightforwardly to determine one's behaviour, it in fact requires one to take one's epistemic condition into account in a way that can be far from easy. Likewise, when it comes to the principle 'Love thy neighbour as thyself', Hegel argues that I must exercise judgement in deciding what is genuinely in the best interest of the individual I am dealing with, where simply giving him what he wants or what would make him happy is not what is required: 'I have to distinguish what is bad for him,

[23] Hegel *PR*, §135 Z, p. 163 [VII: 253–4].

[24] Hegel's position here is pre-figured in some of his earlier writings, e.g. *SC*: 246 [I: 361–2]: 'A living bond of the virtues, a living unity, is quite different from the unity of the concept; it does not set up a determinate virtue for determinate circumstances, but appears, even in the most variegated mixture of relations, untorn and unitary. Its external shape may be modified in infinite ways; it will never have the same shape twice. Its expression will never be able to afford a rule, since it never has the force of a universal opposed to a particular.'

what is the appropriate good to counter this evil, and what in general is good for him: i.e. I must love him *intelligently*. Unintelligent love will perhaps do him more harm than hatred.'[25] But, Hegel claims, this may mean that in some situations, it might be best if I did nothing to aid the individual, so that 'this acting for the good of others which is said to be *necessary*, is of such kind that it may, or may not, exist; is such that, if by chance the occasion offers, the action is perhaps a "work" and is good, but also perhaps not'.[26]

Now, for the sort of rationalism that Hegel is considering at this stage of the *Phenomenology*, this is a frustrating outcome, as it cannot see how such provisional rules that require such complex judgements to apply can really count as genuine moral laws: 'This law [of loving thy neighbour as thyself], therefore, as little has a universal content as the one we first considered [i.e. of telling the truth], and does not express, as an absolute ethical law should, something that is valid in and for itself.'[27] Frustrated by this outcome, reason then adopts another strategy of trying to find a more absolute position in ethics, by moving from particular moral principles, to some general moral principle that perhaps stands above them, on which all lower-level principles are to be grounded and against which they are to be tested: '[Consciousness] takes up their *content* simply as it is, without concerning itself, as we did, with the particularity and contingency inherent in its reality; it is concerned with the commandment simply as a commandment, and its attitude towards it is just as uncomplicated as is its being a criterion for testing it.'[28] However, Hegel argues, by attempting to base these particular principles on a single principle that is supposedly more fundamental than they are, we in fact invert the true order of priority; for, the latter is no more than an abstraction from the former. Consciousness acknowledges this by the end of the sub-section, in returning to a position that accepts (for example) that we 'hit moral bedrock'[29] by recognizing that stealing someone's

[25] Hegel *PS*: 255 [III: 314]. [26] Hegel *PS*: 256 [III: 315]. [27] Hegel *PS*: 256 [III: 315].

[28] Hegel *PS*: 257 [III: 317].

[29] I take this phrase from Philip Stratton-Lake's very helpful characterization of the intuitionist's position (Stratton-Lake 2002a: 25–6):

> If asked why we think lying is wrong, we might point to the fact that in lying we betray the trust the other person has placed in us to tell the truth, or that we harm the other person in some way. If someone then went on to ask us what is wrong with harming, or betraying the trust of others, most would find it difficult to find something further to say. To many it will seem as though we have already hit moral bedrock with considerations of fidelity and non-maleficience.
>
> It might be argued that betraying the trust of others is wrong because in doing this we are acting on a principle that could not be willed as a universal law, or because a society in which trust is respected will be a happier society than one in which it is betrayed. But such Kantian and consequentialist support will strike us as both irrelevant and unnecessary. Pre-theoretically we do not think that considerations of fidelity are morally salient for the reasons Kantians and consequentialists claim, but treat them as salient on their own account.

Cf. Kant *GMM*: 57 [4:403], where I think Stratton-Lake would want to argue that once we know that an act would involve breaking a promise, this in itself carries all the normative information we need, and that the appeal to universalizability considerations is therefore superfluous and unconvincing.

property is wrong because it belongs to them and so should not be appropriated, where seeking for some more general moral and genuinely 'absolute' principle to underlie it can only lead to a distortion in our moral attitudes.[30]

Of course, given the complex dialectical structure of the *Phenomenology*, Hegel should not be simply taken as stating his final position here, or straightforwardly expressing his *own* view at all, as he is just laying out the next phase in the development of consciousness as it moves through the stages on its 'highway of despair'; and consciousness will certainly need to move beyond the pre-modern view of the ethical that it returns to at this point, which treats morality as involving 'the unwritten and infallible law of the gods'.[31] Nonetheless, I would claim, this basis critique of abstract rationalism is preserved within Hegel's final position, and is reflected in the structure of the *Philosophy of Right*, where as I have noted, there is no attempt to offer anything equivalent to a 'supreme principle of morality'.

Moreover, Hegel's commitment to an intuitionist position of this sort is indirectly confirmed when it is seen that he is sensitive to a worry that one might therefore have about the *Philosophy of Right*, which is often said to arise for intuitionism more generally: namely, that it must end up treating the normative realm as nothing but a 'heap of unconnected duties'.[32] Now, for some philosophers this may not be a matter of concern; but Hegel, of course, is a systematic philosopher par excellence, and his conception of philosophy as a science is tied directly to the idea that it can find a rational structure in what otherwise may appear to be a random set of phenomena.[33] Indeed, in the early *Natural Law Essay* of 1802–3, this is precisely the issue that Hegel thinks drives us from an empiricist approach that is happy to treat laws and principles as a 'heap' in this manner, to an a prioristic approach like Kant's, which then tries to reduce the 'many' to a 'one'.[34] However, Hegel makes plain here that he

[30] Cf. Hegel *PS*: 262 [III: 322]: 'Ethical disposition consists just in sticking steadfastly to what is right, and abstaining from all attempts to move or shake it, or derive it. Suppose something has been entrusted to me; it *is* the property of someone else and I acknowledge this *because* it *is so*, and I keep myself unfalteringly in this relationship . . . It is not, therefore, because I find something is not self-contradictory that it is right; on the contrary, it is right because it is what is right. That something *is* the property of another, that is fundamental; I have not to argue about it, or hunt around for or entertain thoughts, connections, aspects, of various kinds; I have to think neither of making laws nor of testing them.'

[31] *PS*: 261 [III: 322].

[32] Cf. McNaughton 2002, esp. pp. 77–85. Cf. also Stratton-Lake 2002b: xxxvi–xxxviii.

[33] Cf. *PR*: 20–1 [VII: 25]: 'For what matters is to recognize in the semblance of the temporal and transient the substance which is immanent and the eternal which is present. For since the rational, which is synonymous with the Idea, becomes actual by entering into external existence [*Existenz*], it emerges in an infinite wealth of forms, appearances, and shapes and surrounds its core with a brightly coloured covering in which consciousness at first resides, but which only the concept can penetrate in order to find the inner pulse, and detect its continued beat even within the external shapes.'

[34] Cf. *NL*: 108 [II: 442]: 'But since this empirical science finds itself [immersed] in a multiplicity of such principles, laws, ends, duties, and rights, none of which is absolute, it must also have before it the image of, and need for, [both] the absolute unity of all these unconnected determinacies and an original simple necessity; and we shall consider how it will satisfy this demand, which is derived from reason, or how the absolute Idea of reason will be presented in its [different] moments [while] under the domination of the one and the many which this empirical knowledge cannot overcome.'

thinks this approach is itself distorted and cannot succeed; instead, he suggests (in a way that then points to his procedure in the *Philosophy of Right* itself) that we must achieve a systematic and structured account of our various duties and moral principles in a *different* way, that can do without any such supreme principle to guide it.[35] Thus, like other intuitionists, Hegel suggests that there are way of finding necessary interrelations between the various duties in an organic manner that makes them amenable to rational and philosophical treatment, but *without* being committed to the search for a single 'master' principle in order to do so—where this is precisely the project that is carried out (I would argue) in the *Philosophy of Right*, through Hegel's consideration of freedom and the will. Hegel thereby produces an account of the normative realm that is certainly more than a 'heap of unconnected duties', but which also avoids the need to present any single principle of morality as somehow 'absolute' or 'supreme' as the method by which this is achieved.

Thus, interpreted in this way, while in these and related discussions, it is certainly the FUL as the 'supreme moral principle' that Hegel criticizes, there is no reason to think that his criticisms apply *only* to that in particular: in fact, his critique seems general enough to apply to *all* attempts to come up with such a principle, whether that is the FUL, or the FN or some other Kantian or non-Kantian candidate.[36] And if this is right, then the move by those concessive Kantians from the FUL to the FH cannot really be taken to address Hegel's fundamental concerns; to do this properly, a more radical view of Kant's position will need to be adopted.[37] It is that which I will now attempt to offer and defend.

[35] Cf. *NL*: 175 [II: 524]: 'It is this individuality of the whole, and the specific character of a nation [*Volk*], which also enable us to recognize the whole system into which the absolute totality is organized. We can thereby recognize how all the parts of the constitution and legislation and all determinations of ethical relations are completely determined by the whole, and form a structure in which no link or ornament was a priori present in its own right [*für sich*], but all came about through the whole to which they are subject.'

[36] David Couzens Hoy has noted this aspect of Hegel's position: '[Hegel's] criticisms are intended to show the limitations of the Kantian approach to moral experience that turns it into a deduction of principles. Hegel's strategy is not to offer an alternative set of principles, and, more importantly, it is not to offer an alternative "grounding" of these principles in one meta-principle like the categorical imperative or the utility principle. In our more contemporary parlance, I am suggesting that Hegel is not offering an alternative "foundational" account to Kant's (like the utility principle)' (Hoy 2009: 167–8). I think similar considerations apply to Bradley's position, which also takes an intuitionist line in criticizing the Kantian view, stressing the priority of particular duties over any single general formula: cf. Bradley 1927: 156–9 and 193–9. A different view has been taken by Tony Burns, who sees Hegel as holding a 'natural law theory [which] incorporates a definite hierarchy of moral principles', where '[a]t the top of this hierarchy there is a primary principle of morality or justice', which 'is a version of what is probably best described as the principle of equity and reciprocity' (Burns 1996: 60). While I would agree, as mentioned above, that Hegel's position is certainly *structured*, I would dispute that it is hierarchical in this manner, and that any such 'primary principle' can be found in the textual references that Burns gives.

[37] A more moderate response might be to say that Kant himself is a pluralist rather than a monist here, in offering several principles rather than one (not *just* the FUL, but also the FN and the Formula of Autonomy, and other sub-formulae). Whilst it is of course true, however, that Kant does offer a variety of principles in this way, he is quite explicit about them all amounting to 'so many formulae of the very same law' (*GMM*: 85 [4:436]), and so always presents himself as seeking and finding *a* supreme principle of

8.3 Kant on the Supreme Principle of Morality: Socratic or Pythagorean?

In order to do so, I will now appeal to a helpful distinction drawn by J. B. Schneewind, between conceptions of moral theory that are *Socratic*, and those that are *Pythagorean*.[38]

What Schneewind means by the Socratic picture, is the idea that while people have always had moral opinions and beliefs, what is still required is for philosophers to find an undeniable foundation to those beliefs which will make them indubitable, where without this ordinary moral thinking will always remain insufficiently secure and warranted. By contrast, the Pythagorean[39] picture holds that the truths of morality have already been discovered and known as a result of divine revelation, so that ordinary moral thinking has no need of philosophy to play any such systematizing and grounding role. Rather, the task for philosophy is a different one, which is to help frail human beings keep to the moral path:

> Belief that the Noachite revelation was the origin of moral knowledge itself would make it natural to ask why we have moral philosophy anyway... The answer to [this] question lies in human sinfulness. Our nature was damaged by the Fall. It not only dimmed our faculties, lessening our ability to understand God's commands and accept them. It also unleashed the passions. Evildoers, driven by their lusts, seek to avoid the pangs of conscience, so they blind themselves to its clear dictates. They also strive to veil and confuse the moral thoughts of those whom they wish to entangle in their wicked schemes. Bad reasoning is one of their basic tools. Now reason is one of God's gifts to humanity. Among other things it enables us to hold on to at least some of the moral knowledge we need, once revelation has ceased. If reason makes moral philosophy possible, pride leads men to try to outdo one another in inventing schemes and systems of morality, and morality itself gets lost in their struggles. Since the causes of the misuse of reason and of bad philosophy are now ingrained in our nature, there will be no final triumph of good philosophy until after the last judgment. But the battle must be kept up. Moral philosophy is to be understood as one more arena for the struggle between sin and virtue.[40]

As Schneewind notes, even when God played less of a role within the Pythagorean story in the more modern period, it was still accepted by some that 'the basic truths of morality are readily accessible to human reason',[41] so that the task of philosophy was still conceived as correcting for our tendency to stray from the moral path,

morality (no matter how difficult it has then been for commentators to unite the various formulae in the way that Kant seems to require).

[38] Schneewind introduces this distinction in the final chapter of Schneewind 1998b: 533–54. Cf. also Schneewind 2010b. As Schneewind notes, a related distinction can be found in Griffin 1996: 131–2.

[39] Schneewind calls this second picture 'Pythagorean' because the early modern account of why ordinary moral thinking has already attained the truth about moral matters is that it is has been revealed to us by God; but this opens up the question of why Pythagoras, who was Greek, should have been credited by Aristotle and others as the first to think about virtue—where one ingenious solution to this problem was to claim that Pythagoras was Jewish or was at least incorporating Jewish ideas.

[40] Schneewind 1998b: 537.

[41] Schneewind 1998b: 541.

rather than to give our ordinary moral thinking a grounding it needs and would otherwise lack.

Now, within the Socratic approach, there is a clear pressure towards the view that in order for philosophy to play its role properly, it needs to come up with a 'supreme principle of morality', as this is precisely the way in which our messy and insufficiently reflective ordinary ways of thinking about moral issues can be made properly systematic and given a stable grounding. This pressure was clearly felt strongly by J. S. Mill, who puts forward his case for the principle of utility in precisely these terms:

> There ought either to be some one fundamental principle or law, at the root of all morality, or if there be several, there should be a determinate order of precedence among them; and the one principle, or the rule for deciding between the various principles when they conflict, ought to be self-evident.
>
> To inquire how far the bad effects of this deficiency [of failing to have identified this principle] have been mitigated in practice, or to what extent the moral beliefs of mankind have been vitiated or made uncertain by the absence of any distinct recognition of an ultimate standard, would imply a complete survey and criticism of past and present ethical doctrine. It would, however, be easy to show that whatever steadiness or consistency these moral beliefs have attained, has been mainly due to the tacit influence of a standard not recognised. Although the non-existence of an acknowledged first principle has made ethics not so much a guide as a consecration of men's actual sentiments, still, as men's sentiments, both of favour and of aversion, are greatly influenced by what they supposed to be the effects of things on their happiness, the principle of utility, or as Bentham latterly called it, the greatest happiness principle, has had a large share in forming the moral doctrines even of those who most scornfully reject its authority. Nor is there any school of thought which refuses to admit that the influence of actions on happiness is a most material and even predominant consideration in many of the details of morals, however unwilling to acknowledge it as the fundamental principle of morality, and the source of moral obligation.[42]

Mill then immediately goes on to mention Kant, assuming without question that Kant too was looking for the 'one fundamental principle or law' that is needed here, but criticizing the FUL for its failure to adequately serve this role, which is why something more like the principle of utility is needed.[43] By putting Kant alongside himself within the Socratic tradition, Mill therefore has no difficulty in making Kant's outlook seem as at odds with any form of intuitionism as his own self-consciously sets out to be, making any possible reconciliation with Hegel seem irredeemably bleak.[44]

[42] Mill 1972: 3.

[43] Cf. Mill 1972: 3–4. In an influential essay in which she offers a critique of moral theory, Annette Baier accepts this Millian picture of Kant's ambitions, as do many such critics: see Baier 1989, esp. p. 36.

[44] Cf. also Schneewind 2010a: 44, where Schneewind contrasts the position of the utilitarian and the intuitionist as follows: 'For the utilitarian the paradigm moral problems are those in which we do not know what we ought to do, and in which the solution comes as soon as we do know; while for the intuitionist the central sort of problem is that in which the agent knows what he ought to do but finds it difficult to bring himself to do it. His problem is one of will or feeling.'

However, as Schneewind notes, there are perhaps good grounds for criticizing Mill's assumption here, and in fact thinking of Kant not as operating with Mill's Socratic picture, but rather as working with something more like the Pythagorean one.[45] For, when Kant comes to explain why his attempt to come up with the 'supreme principle of morality' is needed, he does not express any sense that without it ordinary morality is in jeopardy, in failing otherwise to have a proper systematic structure or rationale; on the contrary, he seems to think that ordinary moral thought is in perfectly good order just as it is. Where the supreme principle is needed, rather, is in the Pythagorean fight between good and evil within the human breast, as a way of helping us avoid the kind of bad faith and self-deception that can so easily allow us to become corrupted in our actions, where at one level we know perfectly well what we should do, based on the various principles imparted to us through our ordinary moral education which come prior to any philosophizing.

Kant's position here can be seen most clearly, perhaps, in the *Groundwork*, particularly in Sections I and II, which is where Kant sets about identifying the FUL (and related formulae) as the 'supreme principle of morality'. In those sections, Kant presents himself as proceeding *analytically*, starting from our commonly shared moral conceptions. In these sections, therefore, Kant seems more than happy to accept that we have a good grasp of morality without any need for philosophy, where he does not expect us to find the Formula of Universal Law to be revisionary of that grasp in any way—indeed, if it were, he would allow that it would be an objection to his claim that it constitutes the supreme principle that he is looking for here. Kant therefore does not see himself as adding to our ordinary moral understanding, or to be offering some sort of philosophical perspective from which he can address those who lack it. Thus, Kant willingly accepts that in arriving at the Formula of Universal law, he is not teaching 'the moral cognition of common reason' anything new, but simply making it 'attentive to its own principles': 'there is, accordingly, no need of science and philosophy to know what one has to do in order to be honest and good, and even wise and virtuous'.[46] Kant therefore seems to take for granted that our moral practices are in good order and in no need of defence or justification, and that philosophy can proceed by simply reflecting on them, to bring out the fundamental moral principle on which they rely.

Nonetheless, it might be said, nothing in this shows that Kant was not proceeding in the Socratic manner.[47] For, one might consistently think that the only way to find

[45] Cf. Schneewind 1998b: 543–8; and Schneewind 2010b: 119–20. For a related discussion of Kant in terms of Schneewind's distinction, see Krasnoff 2004.

[46] Kant *GMM*: 58 [4:404]. For similar remarks, see *GMM*: 66 [4:412], where Kant comments that 'common moral appraisal' is 'very worthy of respect'; and *CPrR*: 153, note [5:8]: 'Who would even want to introduce a new principle of all morality and, as it were, first invent it? Just as if, before him, the world had been ignorant of what duty is or in thoroughgoing error about it.'

[47] Cf. Kant's own reference to Socrates at *GMM*: 58 [4:404].

the supreme principle of morality is to start from our ordinary moral beliefs and opinions, while still holding that unless and until some principle can be uncovered in this manner, those beliefs and opinions remain inadequate and limited, much as Mill claims, in arguing that 'whatever steadiness or consistency these moral beliefs have attained, has been mainly due to the tacit influence of a standard not recognised', which it is then the philosopher's role to make explicit. Thus, one might hold that as far as it goes, the philosopher should certainly take ordinary moral thinking seriously and not seek to come up with anything too revisionary of that thinking; nonetheless, that thinking requires the services of philosophy and the principle it comes up with, if it is not to struggle with conflicts between lower-level principles; difficult moral cases where our ordinary moral convictions give out; and an unanswerable sceptical challenge to articulate what the basis is for our convictions on moral matters.

Now, of course, intuitionists have been doubtful that any proposed supreme moral principle will really bring the advertised benefits promised on these issues. But what is notable about Kant in this context, is that rather than making these sorts of claims for the value of identifying a supreme principle of morality, his focus lies elsewhere. For, the value Kant emphasizes most in arriving at the supreme principle of morality, is that we can then be led to be better moral agents, as having such a principle made explicit will make it harder for us to deceive ourselves on moral matters, and so will help to keep us more securely on the moral path. Kant's approach in this respect therefore seems to be closer to the Pythagorean tradition than the Socratic one.

So, in the Preface, Kant claims that lying behind a 'metaphysics of morals' is no mere 'motive to speculation',[48] but a more pressing practical need, 'because morals themselves remain subject to all sorts of corruption as long as we are without that clue and supreme norm by which to appraise them correctly'.[49] Kant clearly hopes, therefore, that by identifying the supreme principle of morality, he will be able to prevent the 'corruption' of our moral lives by making our conformity to morality less 'contingent and precarious',[50] as we can then combat our inclinations more effectively by giving pure practical reason a clearer voice: for, without this, 'the human being is affected by so many inclinations that, though capable of the idea of a practical pure reason, he is not so easily able to make it effective *in concreto* in the conduct of his life'.[51] Similarly, in the first section of the *Groundwork*, having identified the principle of universalizability in a preliminary way as the supreme principle of morality,[52] but having admitted that this principle is already implicit in our moral thinking,[53] Kant argues that nonetheless this philosophical exercise is valuable in making it harder for our inclinations to distort our view of what is right and wrong by twisting it to fit our interests (for example, as when I convince myself that it is somehow right for me to keep the money I have been mistakenly refunded by the bank because I need it more than they do, so that this will lead to more good

[48] *GMM*: 45 [4:389]; cf. also p. 60 [4:405]. [49] *GMM*: 45 [4:389]. [50] *GMM*: 45 [4:390].
[51] *GMM*: 45 [4:389]. [52] *GMM*: 56–7 [4:402]. [53] *GMM* 58 [4:403].

overall and so is justified thereby, where the application of the Formula of the Universal Law and related formulae would make it clear to me that what I am presenting to myself as the justification for the action does not carry any moral weight, and in fact merely masks a desire to further my interests that is lurking beneath the moralistic façade):

Would it not therefore be more advisable in moral matters to leave the judgment of common reason as it is... [and] not to lead common human understanding, even in practical matters, away from its fortunate simplicity and to put it, by means of philosophy, on a new path of investigation and instruction?

There is something splendid about innocence; but what is bad about it, in turn, is that it cannot protect itself very well and is easily seduced. Because of this, even wisdom—which otherwise consists more in conduct than in knowledge—still needs science, not in order to learn from it but in order to provide access and durability to its precepts. The human being feels within himself a powerful counterweight to all the commands of duty, which reason represents to him as so deserving of the highest respect—the counterweight of his needs and inclinations, the entire satisfaction of which he sums up under the name of happiness. Now reason issues its precepts unremittingly, without thereby promising anything to the inclinations, and so, as it were, with disregard and contempt for those claims, which are so impetuous and besides so apparently equitable (and refuse to be neutralized by any command). But from this there arises a *natural dialectic*; that is, a propensity to rationalize against those strict laws of duty and to cast doubt upon their validity, or at least upon their purity and strictness, and, where possible, to make them better suited to our wishes and inclinations, that is, to corrupt them at their basis and to destroy all their dignity—something that even common practical reason cannot, in the end, call good.[54]

Thus, as Henrich puts it, Kant sees a problem for us in the fact that 'man subtly refines the moral law until it fits his inclination and his convenience, whether to free himself from it or to use the good for the justification of his own importance'.[55] Kant hopes that his identification of the supreme principle of morality as involving universalizability can play a significant role in helping us overcome this natural dialectic of practical reason,[56] where one significant criticism he has of other

[54] *GMM*: 59–60 [4:404–5]. Cf. also *CPrR*: 143, note [5:8], translation modified: 'But whoever knows what a *formula* means to a mathematician, which determines quite precisely what is to be done to solve a problem and *does not let him go astray* [my emphasis], will not take a formula that does this with respect to all duty in general as something that is insignificant and can be dispensed with.' And cf. *LE*: 136–7 [27:359].

[55] Henrich 1994: 66. For further discussion of Kant's position here, see also Guyer 2000: 207–31; and Shell 2009: 129–31, where Shell writes that 'The goal of science is not to teach common moral understanding something new, but to enhance the force and staying power of the knowledge it already possesses' (p. 131). Rawls adopts a similar perspective in Rawls 2000: 148–9, as does Geiger 2010. More generally, cf. Nussbaum 2000, where Nussbaum sets out to defend moral theory, but does so in Pythagorean terms: '*Theory,* then, *can help our good judgements by giving us additional opposition to the bad influence of corrupt desires, judgements, and passions*' (p. 252).

[56] Kant did not think that this would be enough on its own, however: the more metaphysical speculations of Section III of the *Groundwork* are also required to complete the job, in order to answer questions that may arise concerning the status of the moral law, questions that may prevent frail human beings from keeping to the moral path.

candidates for this supreme principle is that they will make this dialectic harder to resolve, by introducing hedonistic elements into morality itself, in such a way as to make moral self-deception easier for us to achieve.[57]

Thus, Kant's position seems Pythagorean, in that he clearly recognizes how our self-interested motivations can be powerful enough to lead us to view our actions in a spurious moral light, and believes his project in the *Groundwork* will make this harder. He is therefore addressing us as frail and easily corrupted moral agents, rather than dealing with the sort of Socratic questions raised by Mill. The value Kant claims for the FUL or his other formulae as candidates for the 'supreme principle of morality' is the role they can play in helping us to unmask our bad faith on this issue, and make it harder to dodge the right course of action which our ordinary moral thinking has already made clear; and the advantage he claims for the FUL and his other formulae over other candidates is that, because they are not related to the happiness of the agent or based on merely empirical considerations, his formulae will serve this role better than those other candidates, which can make it too easy for us to stray or remain undecided (for example, if keeping the cheque would make me *much* happier than the unhappiness caused by not returning it, perhaps I *ought* to keep it? or, at least, perhaps the moral considerations could be argued either way?).

Seen in this light, therefore, the real significance of the formulae Kant offers is in a sense heuristic, where deploying them will make it very difficult for a moral agent to use spurious moral considerations as a smokescreen for what are really his own interests; for, all these formulae force us to consider the situation in a more objective manner in different but complementary respects, by abstracting from those interests and so take into account the perspective of all the others affected.[58] Considered in a Pythagorean light, therefore, we can give significance to Kant's search for a supreme principle of morality, while allowing us to think of that search in a way that is free of any ambition to reduce the plurality of prima facie duties that make up ordinary

[57] Cf. *GMM*: 65 [4:411]: 'On the other hand a mixed doctrine of morals, put together from incentives of feeling and inclination and also of rational concepts, must make the mind waver between motives that cannot be brought under any principle, that can lead only contingently to what is good and can very often also lead to what is evil'; and also *MM*: 370–1 [6:215–16]: 'If the doctrine of morals were merely the doctrine of happiness... [a]ll apparently *a priori* reasoning about this [would come] down to nothing but experience raised by induction to generality, a generality... still so tenuous that everyone must be allowed countless exceptions in order to adapt his choice of a way of life to his particular inclinations and his susceptibilities to satisfaction and still, in the end, to become prudent only from his own or others' misfortunes.'

[58] Cf. *GMM*: 75–6 [4:424]: 'If we now attend to ourselves in any transgression of a duty, we find that we do not really will that our maxim should become a universal law, since that is impossible for us, but that the opposite of our maxim should instead remain a universal law, only we take the liberty of making an *exception* to it for ourselves (or just for this once) to the advantage of our inclination. Consequently, if we weighed all cases from one and the same point of view, namely that of reason, we would find a contradiction in our own will, namely that a certain principle be objectively necessary as a universal law and yet subjectively not hold universally but allow exceptions.'

moral thinking to any single, underlying, formula in a Socratic manner, and so in a way that would bring it into conflict with a more intuitionistic approach.

8.4 Kant and Hegel: A Reconciliation?

Taken in this way, therefore, Kant's preoccupation with identifying a supreme principle of morality in the *Groundwork* need not set him at odds with Hegel's apparent resistance to anything resembling the Socratic project, and thus with Hegel's underlying intuitionism. Thus, whereas the move from the FUL to the FH was perhaps not sufficient in itself to settle their differences, this more Pythagorean treatment of Kant's position might be. However, just as some Kantians have resisted the former as too concessive, and have instead sought to defend the FUL, so one might expect some Kantians to resist the latter move from a Socratic to a Pythagorean picture of Kant as being too conciliatory as well. Nonetheless, I hope to have done enough here to at least suggest that such a reading of Kant can be made plausible; and to suggest, moreover, that when viewed in this manner, the Hegelian can find more common ground with Kant's ethics than has generally been supposed. Of course, the Hegelian can (and probably will) still quarrel with Kant's Pythagorean account of how it is that we get led astray in moral matters, and what role moral philosophy and moral theory can realistically play in keeping us on track; but these disagreements, even if they persist, are not those usually associated with the Kant/Hegel debate in this area. In this way, therefore, I hope to have shed new light on an old controversy, while perhaps also bringing it to a conclusion that will be satisfying to both sides.[59]

[59] I am grateful to Tony Burns and Fabian Freyenhagen for helpful comments on a previous version of this paper.

9

Does Hegelian Ethics Rest on a Mistake?

Hegelian ethics is known for two central themes that make it distinctive. First of all, it makes the notion of self-actualization, or self-satisfaction, or self-realization central. Thus, for example, Allen Wood summarizes this aspect of Hegel's position as follows, in a way that would have been familiar also to the British Idealists: 'The rational state is an end in itself only because the highest stage of *individual* self-actualization consists in participating in the state and recognizing it as such an end. This means that Hegel's ethical theory is after all founded on a conception of individual human beings and their self-actualization.'[1] Secondly, it is known for its social holism or organicism, namely the view that individual agents must be seen as essentially tied to the social whole of which they are part. Thus, as Hegel writes: 'Since the state is objective spirit, it is only through being a member of the state that the individual himself has objectivity, truth, and ethical life',[2] while Green and Bradley put the point as follows: 'it is only in the intercourse of men... that we really live as persons... [S]ociety then... is the condition of all development of our personality';[3] 'The "individual" man, the man into whose essence his community with others does not enter, who does not include relation to others in his very being, is, we say, a fiction'.[4] The question I want to explore in this paper is: what is the connection between these two themes? How do the ideas of self-realization and social holism relate to one another, and play into each other's hands? Let me call the first the *self-realization thesis*, and the second *the social thesis*. Inevitably, what precisely they mean and amount to may be rather vague at this stage, but this will hopefully become clearer as we proceed.

My title, of course, is a reference to the famous claim by H. A. Prichard that moral philosophy rests on a mistake.[5] He believed this was so, because he thought that it tries to address the threat of the egoist who asks for some reason to be moral, by giving him *non*-moral reasons, based on his interests, desires, well-being,

[1] Wood 1990: 21 [2] Hegel *PR*: §258, p. 276 [VII: 399].

[3] Green 2003: §183, p. 210. Cf. also Green 2003, §370, p. 456: 'In thinking of ultimate good he thinks of it indeed necessarily as perfection for himself... But he cannot think of himself as satisfied in any life other than a social life.'

[4] Bradley 1927: 168. [5] Cf. Prichard 2002a and 2002b.

self-realization, and the like. But he held that to act morally is to act just because you see that it is right or what is called for, not because it will further your interests in these ways: this is still to be an egoist, not a proper moral agent. And Prichard thought that Hegelian ethics makes this mistake, because it too starts with egoistic assumptions and tries get from there to morality using the idea that individual self-realization is only possible in society, but in a way that fundamentally cannot escape the egoism from which it begins. Thus, Prichard writes of Green, in particular:[6] '[Green's] view really amounts to resolving the idea of duty into the idea of conduciveness to our advantage, or, in other words, resolving the moral "ought" into the non-moral "ought" in the sense in which it means conducive to our purpose, on the presupposition that our purpose is always our greatest good or advantage.'[7]

The plan of this paper is to look at Prichard's objection as a critique of Green, and consider possible responses that could be made to it, where in the end I will allow that it has some force. But I will then look at Bradley's position and distinguish it from Green's, arguing that Bradley's more Hegelian position has a better way to respond to Prichard's concerns, and thus show that Hegelian ethics is not ultimately founded on a mistake, despite its commitment to the two theses outlined above.[8]

9.1 Green's Ethics

One can see the force of Prichard's worry concerning Green's ethics, if one has the following simple view of the latter's position:

1. We are egoists
2. Then why be moral?
3. Social thesis: we are parts of a social whole
4. We are therefore dependent on each other for our own well-being
5. So, it is rational to act for others, as well as ourselves.

So, egoism is not at odds with altruism: we can resolve the tension between them, using the social thesis.

Given this view, Prichard's response seems very reasonable, where he argues that we have not got real morality here, as the only reason the individual acts for others is because his interests are bound up with theirs, and so he is still being fundamentally guided by his own concerns and not that of others: this is just enlightened self-interest, or 'higher egoism'.

[6] Green is Prichard's central focus: he claims not to be able to understand Hegel or Bradley: cf. Prichard 2002a: 21 and 2002e: 163.

[7] Prichard 2002b: 43. Cf. Lamont 1934: 214: 'If to give another person self-satisfaction gives you satisfaction, and if *your* self-satisfaction is *always* your ultimate motive, then you are only aiming at his self-satisfaction because his being satisfied gives you self-satisfaction.'

[8] I will focus exclusively on Green and Bradley, as the leading figures in this tradition, though some of what I have to say would also be relevant to others, such as Bernard Bosanquet and Edward Caird.

Prichard argues that we should attribute (1) to Green (the claim that we are egoists), where he quotes the following passage:

The motive in every imputable act for which the agent is conscious on reflection that he is answerable, is a desire for personal good in some form or other... It is superfluous to add good to *himself*, for anything conceived as good in such a way that the agent acts for the sake of it, must be conceived as *his own good*, though he may conceive it as his own good only on account of his interest in others, and in spite of any amount of suffering on his own part incidental to its attainment.[9]

Prichard also attributes a strong version of the social thesis to Green, claiming that Green thought that individuals are *identical*, which is why their ends converge, despite (1):

The net result is that according to Green, where a group of, say, five persons are disinterestedly interested in one another, they are not really five persons but one, a state of A being related to a state of another, B, just as it is related to another state of A—these states being states of one self.[10]

We might therefore consider Pritchard's reading of Green in the light of a question posed by Henry Sidgwick of the latter's postion: 'By what logical process can we pass from the form of unqualified egoism under which the true end of the moral agent is represented to us on one page, to the unmediated universalism which we find suddenly substituted for it on another?'[11] Pritchard's answer would be that for Green, the social thesis is the bridge whereby we get from the one to the other, thereby giving it a role in what is fundamentally still an egoistical position, and thus revealing it to be caught up in an ethics that is based on a mistake.

A first response to Prichard's concerns might be to question the claim that Green held the social identity view which is attributed to him by Prichard.[12] For, it seems more plausible to attribute to him a more moderate social holism or organicism, as suggested by the following passage:

This well-being he doubtless conceives as his own, but that he should conceive it as exclusively his own—his own in any sense in which it is not equally and coincidentally a well-being of others—would be incompatible with the fact that it is only as living in community, as sharing

[9] Green 2003: §§91–2, pp. 103–4; quoted by Prichard in 2002b: 38; cf. also 39.

[10] Prichard 2002c: 242.

[11] Sidgwick 1902: 55–6. Cf. Prichard 2002b: 43:

According to [Green], the thinking that a certain action is a duty is really the concluding that it is a duty in virtue of its being, as we think, for the good of the whole and of that good's being, as we think, our greatest good, and therefore the thinking that the action is a duty requires as its explanation the prior existence of the thoughts which form the premises of the argument. And the view really amounts to resolving the idea of duty into the idea of conduciveness to our advantage, or, in other words, resolving the moral 'ought' into the non-moral 'ought' in the sense in which it means conduciveness to our purpose, on the supposition that our purpose is always our greatest good or advantage.

[12] Cf. Nicholson 1990: 68–9. For Prichard's textual support, see Prichard 2002e: 195.

the life of others, as incorporated in the continuous being of a family or a nation, of a state or a church, that he can sustain himself in that thought of his own permanence to which the thought of permanent well-being is correlative.[13]

Green's argument here seems to be as follows: In taking his own individual good as a starting point, a person nonetheless cannot think of himself as an individual with any permanence unless he thinks of himself as a member of a community of some sort, which he must therefore act to uphold, and so act for the good of the community and the other selves it contains. As a result, Green claims to be able to collapse the distinction between egoism and altruism: 'Hence the distinction commonly supposed to exist between considerate Benevolence and reasonable Self-Love, as co-ordinate principles on which moral approbation is founded, is a fiction of philosophers.'[14]

However, of course, Prichard can respond that his fundamental objection still stands, as the individual only takes into account the well-being of others because the individual sees this as the basis of her own, as a result of the dependence of the individual on the social whole. Thus, as John Skorupski has put the point recently, Green's account of practical reason still remains egoistical in a formal sense, even if the social thesis is viewed more holistically:

[For Green] there is thus no need to posit—as an underived principle in practical reason—a principle of impartiality that says that the good of any one individual has no inherently greater reason-giving force than the good of any other. The only ultimate practical-reason-giving consideration is my own good. However, the truer my understanding, or the fuller the development, of myself and my own good, the more I grasp its identity with the common good. I achieve my true good by being and doing good. Green's idealist metaphysics underpins this ethics by denying the final separateness of individuals, seeing them instead as differentiated moments of a single subject.[15]

It is Green's apparent egoism, therefore, that now seem to be the fundamental concern, at least to a Kantian such as Prichard.[16]

It could be said, however, that even if a person acts as Green suggests, there is still nothing wrong with them from the moral point of view, as this is to confuse formal egoism with selfishness or treating others instrumentally. However, if a person sees her own good as bound up with that of others, doesn't that require them to be sympathetic, caring, and attentive in various ways, and so morally admirable? Thus, a

[13] Green 2003: §232, pp. 272–3.

[14] Green 2003: §232, p. 272.

[15] Skorupski 2011: 462.

[16] Cf. Prichard 2002b: 48–9: 'I think it is possible to sum up most of what I have been contending for by a reference to Kant. His moral philosophy is of course open to many obvious criticisms. Nevertheless he always strikes me as having, far more than any other philosopher, the root of the matter in him. More especially, he seems to me to steer completely clear of those views which I have been maintaining to be errors, and indeed to insist that they are errors. He will have nothing to do either with the idea that the rightness of action depends on its being for our own good, or with that idea that we think of it as so depending, or with the idea that desire for our own good is our only motive. And it is, I think, for this reason that in spite of his obvious mistakes he retains so close a hold on his readers.'

father may well see his well-being as dependent on that of his children and act accordingly: but precisely in order to view his relation to his children in this way, doesn't that need him to have a self-less attitude towards those children, as otherwise he wouldn't take their welfare to impact on his well-being at all, as he would only be concerned with his personal interests and have no concern for them at all? So, it would appear, egoism is not the same as selfishness, and thus perhaps Prichard was wrong to think that a position based on it is making a fundamental mistake from a moral point of view.

This response to the problem is fairly familiar, and may be traced back to Aristotle on which it is modelled, and where Aristotle may be taken as an influence on Green in this respect.[17] But ultimately, the Prichardian question can still be pressed, by asking the father why he acts to help his child, and what his reason ultimately is. The response would seem to be for Green that his child's well-being is a necessary aspect of his own well-being, whereas Prichard will argue that the answer should really be: because the child needs help.[18] It would seem, then, that a more radical response is required to the difficulty that Prichard has raised.

This could be achieved, it might seem, if it is denied that Green's starting point is egoistic at all—and some readers of Green have followed this route. Thus, for example, Peter Nicholson (in part following C. A. Campbell)[19] has adopted this approach, where he argues that what Green is fundamentally doing is drawing a contrast between acting from impulse, and acting from a conscious intention or deliberately. In the latter case, what the individual does must be seen as something that will be good for her in some way, but nonetheless achieving that good is not her *motive* or *purpose*, so the act is not really self-interested in any genuine sense. So, for example, in treating your injury, my motive or purpose is to help you and so not self-interested or egoistical, where nonetheless your well-being must be something desired by me if I am to act, and I wouldn't want that unless I saw it as contributing to my self-satisfaction in some way. On this account, Green's view may be compared to any desire or pleasure based account of action: while on this sort of account, no one acts unless they think that doing so will satisfy their desire or bring them pleasure, nonetheless satisfying that desire or getting that pleasure need not be the motive or goal of the action concerned, in

[17] Cf. Brink 2001: 44–50.

[18] A similar worry may apply to David Brink's way of presenting Green's position: he argues that for Green 'concern for my overall good requires, as a constituent part, concern for the welfare of those to whom I am appropriately psychologically related', where that concern is then for their good and so 'other-regarding' and not merely instrumental; nonetheless he also allows that for Green 'the on-balance rationality of [such] other-regarding action depends on its promoting my overall good'—which may seem to put its 'other-regardingness' in doubt? See Brink 2001: 50–1.

[19] Nicholson 1990: 70–1; and Campbell 1931: 201–11 and 1967. A similar line is taken by Mander 2011: 198: 'The claim that all conscious purposive action seeks self-satisfaction may seem like the most ruthless psychological egoism... But on closer reflection we see [Green's] view is quite otherwise. Rather the derivation flows from the very definition of conscious action itself. Whatever we want, in wanting it we necessarily want also a state in which our own wanting is satisfied. There is nothing necessarily self-directed in the content of the want.'

which case is not self-interested; the agent is not acting *in order to get* pleasure or satisfy their desire, and so not treating you as a *means* to their pleasure or desire-satisfaction, and so not behaving here in an egoistical way.

Moreover, it might be said, a Kantian like Prichard must also have an account that has a similar structure. For, the Kantian will claim, if I do something deliberately, I wouldn't do it unless I believed that it was right or was my duty. However, its being right or my duty can't be my *motive* for doing it, otherwise we would have a troubling kind of 'moral fetishism'.[20] The motive, therefore, must be that you need help, but where unless I thought your needing help was my duty, I wouldn't do it. Thus, 'being right' or 'being my duty' must function as a kind of second-order necessary condition on my action,[21] but not in a way that interferes with my being motivated by your injury, thus avoiding moral fetishism. In a similar way, then, Green could claim that 'bringing me self-satisfaction' or 'contributing to my self-realization' is a second-order necessary condition on my action, but in a way that doesn't interfere with my motive being your needs, thus avoiding egoism.

Nonetheless, Green's position may still seem more vulnerable than the Kantian one to Prichard's concerns. Firstly, the difference between Green's account (as involving self-satisfaction) and the Kantian one (as involving duty) may still make one think the former is egoistical in the way that the latter is not. Secondly, one might wonder *why* self-satisfaction is a necessary condition for action, if it is not itself the motive of it? In the Kantian case, being seen as your duty can be said to be necessary, because as a rational being one needs to check that you are doing the right thing before you do it, either actually or potentially—but why is it an appeal to self-satisfaction necessary in the same way? The answer might be, that otherwise you wouldn't see the action as *good*, and you need to see the action as good before doing it, even if doing what is good is not your motive or end. But then the Kantian can respond by claiming that it is sufficient to see that the action is *right*, where this need have nothing to do with your own self-satisfaction; and anyway, why does seeing the act as good have to bring in *your own* good? Thus, the Kantian position may in the end seem more plausible. Finally, as well as these philosophical issues, there are also textual problems in attributing this sort of position to Green, because there are several places where he does seem to talk about self-satisfaction as the *motive* for actions, as in the following passage: 'in all conduct to which moral predicates are applicable a man is an object to himself; [and] such conduct, equally whether virtuous or vicious, *expresses a motive* consisting in the ideal of a personal good, which the man seeks to realise by action'.[22] There are therefore some difficulties in rejecting premise 1, and adopting a non-egoistical approach to Green.

[20] Of course, some have accused Kant himself of precisely this sort of fetishism: cf. Williams 1981b: 18.

[21] For readings of Kant along these lines, cf. Herman 1993: 24–5; Baron 1995: 12; Stratton-Lake 2000, esp. Chapters 1 and 4. For further discussion of some of the issues raised here, see Chapter 13 this volume.

[22] Green 2003: §115, p. 130 (my emphasis).

Moreover, even supposing that it were right to reject egoistic readings of Green, it might also be said that the consequences would be structurally unfortunate for his way of thinking. For, the result would seem to be that the social thesis would then have no role to play in Green's *ethics*, even if might still be something he holds on metaphysical grounds, and gives some weight to in his political philosophy. For then, it actually wouldn't be needed to provide any sort of 'bridge' from egoism to altruism, as altruism or impartiality would be assumed at the outset, and thus the dialectical role and significance of the thesis would be lost. There thus seems to be a dilemma in understanding Green's position: We can either take it that he holds that we are egoists, but then he faces Prichard's challenge; or we can take it that he thinks we are not egoists, but then render the social thesis ethically redundant. The latter price may not seem an insuperable one to pay, but I take it that it would still be of interest to see if we can avoid this second horn altogether—that is, can we say that Hegelian ethics is not egoistic in its starting point, and *also* still give a fundamental role to the social thesis? To see how this might be possible, I turn now from Green to Bradley.

9.2 Bradley's Ethics

While certain differences between Green and Bradley are noted, they are often said to be broadly similar in their approaches, so that while the latter is hardly mentioned by Prichard, it might be assumed that Bradley too falls under his critique—while this perceived similarity may explain *why* he is not given any separate treatment. In particular, then, it may also be held that because Bradley talks about self-realization a good deal in *Ethical Studies* as well as the social thesis, he also starts with egoistic assumptions and tries to handle them in Green's way.

However, as with Green, the position is more complicated than it may first appear. On the one hand, Bradley too seems to talk about self-realization as the end of our actions, as when he writes: 'What remains is to point out the most general expression for the end in itself, the ultimate practical "why"; and that we find in the word *self-realization*.'[23] On the other hand, Bradley also seems sensitive to Prichardian concerns. For example, like Prichard, Bradley thinks that the question 'why be moral?' requires very careful handling, and for similar reasons:

> Morality... teaches us that, if we look on her only as good for something else, we never in that case have seen her at all. She says that she is an end to be desired for her own sake, and not as a means to something beyond. Degrade her, and she disappears; and, to keep her, we must love and not merely use her. And so at the question Why [should I be moral]? we are in trouble, for that does assume, and does take for granted, that virtue in this sense is unreal, and what we believe is false.[24]

[23] Bradley 1927: 64. [24] Bradley 1927: 58.

Like Prichard, Bradley therefore holds that we must avoid the temptation to address the moral sceptic directly. On the other hand, he thinks we can still do something else instead, which is to ask if there may nonetheless be some relation between acting morally and achieving our good, even if the latter is not taken to be the motivation or justifying reason for the former. Thus, as it were, in a 'cool hour', an individual may reasonably wonder if their moral actions have made their life go well or not, even if at no point did this concern play a role in grounding those actions. Thus, as Bradley puts the question one might ask in this spirit: 'Is morality the same as the end for man, so that the two are convertible; or is morality one side, or aspect, or element of some end which is larger than itself? Is it the whole end from all points of view, or is it one view of the whole?'[25] Moreover, in Chapter VII (or 'essay', as he calls it) of *Ethical Studies*, Bradley offers an account of selfishness which is sensitive to the motive/necessary condition distinction outlined above, and also there accepts the idea that moral action should not be instrumental. Thus, notwithstanding his emphasis on self-realization, Bradley seems to have an awareness of the Prichardian concerns we have raised, in a way that arguably makes his account of human action and motivation non-egoistic.

But then, if we deny that Bradley is an egoist, along the same lines as it is denied that Green is an egoist outlined above, wouldn't we have the same structural worry as well, namely that the social thesis could then drop out of Bradley's ethics? If it is not required to play its 'bridging' role, why is it really needed, and couldn't it be set aside? Once again, then, the concern is that the structural centrality of the social thesis seems to be lost if we try to handle Prichard's concerns by abandoning any commitment to egoism as a starting point.

I now want to suggest, however, that when it comes to this issue, Bradley's position is importantly and interestingly different from Green's. For, to put the point rather schematically, my claim will be that the social thesis does not drop out of Bradley's position because *he* is using the thesis to solve the problem of *altruism* not of egoism, where in this he is following Hegel. So then even *if* the egoist premise is dropped, the

[25] Bradley 1927: 64. I think Bradley's position may therefore be usefully compared to one proposed by David Schmidtz, in Schmidtz 2007: 70–1:

> Even if we grant that being moral involves following a categorical imperative, we may coherently ask whether we would be better off following a categorical imperative. And, one way or another, the question has an answer. Whether or not moral imperatives are categorical, there remains a fact of the matter concerning whether following moral imperatives is to our advantage. To try to show that being moral turns out to be prudent is not to mistakenly treat moral imperatives as prudential imperatives... The point is that even agents committed to doing what is right *because it's right* might nevertheless wonder whether they would have done anything differently had they been more self-consciously prudent. Moral agents might care about this issue not because they, like Glaucon, sometimes wonder whether they have prudential reasons to *regret* being moral, that is, whether their being moral is contrary to their self-interest.

social thesis can still be given a crucial role in his thinking, in a way that is less clear in Green's case insofar as his framework is less Hegelian in its construction.

Here, in outline, is the way in which Bradley's position might be sketched:

1. As rational agents, we are able to set aside our particular interests and adopt a more universal standpoint
2. But in doing so, we face the problem of agency
3. This problem can only be resolved if we accept the social thesis, and see that we are parts of a social whole
4. So ethics requires the social thesis.

Let me now consider each of these points in a little more detail.

Regarding 1, Bradley accepts what might be thought of as the Kantian point, that as part of what it is to be free agents, we are capable of stepping back from all our particular interests and desires, and thus of moving from the 'particular' to the 'universal' standpoint. As Bradley puts it: 'In short, we do not simply feel ourselves in [desires] A and B, but have distinguished ourselves from both, as what is above both. This is one factor in volition, and it hard to find any name better for it than that of the universal factor, or side, or moment.'[26] But then (regarding 2), Bradley argues that *action* requires that we will something particular, some specific and concrete act: 'In order to will, we must will something; the universal side by itself is not will at all. To will we must identify ourselves with this, that, or the other; and here we have the particular side, and the second factor in volition.'[27] However, as such whatever we do always seems to fall short of what is universal, where the problem then is that when we step back, the 'this, that, or the other' that we do will seem inadequate and empty, because by so acting we will seem to ourselves to fail to properly realize what universality requires. For Bradley, therefore, there is a prima facie tension between these two 'factors' in action, which together yield the problem of agency.[28]

As an illustration of the kind of difficulty that I think Bradley has in mind, it is instructive to look at the following passage from Richard Rorty's autobiographical essay 'Trotsky and the Wild Orchids':

At [the age of] 12, I knew that the point of being human was to spend one's life fighting social injustice... But I also had private, weird, snobbish, incommunicable interests. In earlier years these had been in Tibet... A few years later... these interests switched to orchids... I was uneasily aware, however, that there was something a bit dubious about this esotericism—this

[26] Bradley 1927: 72. [27] Bradley 1927: 72.

[28] Cf. also Bradley 1927: 72, note: 'As we saw in our last Essay, there are two dangers to avoid here, in the shape of two one-sided views, Scylla and Charybdis. The first is the ignoring of the universal side altogether, even as an element; the second is the assertion of it as more than an element, as by itself the will. Against this second it is necessary to insist that the will is what it wills, that to will you must will something, and that you can not will the mere form of the will.'

interest in socially useless flowers... I was afraid that Trotsky... would not have approved of my interest in orchids.[29]

Brought up by his politically committed parents, Rorty was early on inculcated with the significance of the wider social good, and why this mattered more than any particular interest, so that the point of life was to follow Trotsky and other radicals in fighting injustice. This, he may have come to feel, is true willing, as it takes us beyond any of our particular concerns. On the other hand, at the same time he found himself with particular interests of his own (Tibet, orchids), but which he felt from this more universal perspective were of little value or significance, where the pull of that universal perspective made it hard for him to identify with such things. However, one difficulty with giving the first standpoint priority over the second, is then knowing how one is to act *at all*, because then in seeking for a universality that takes us beyond particularity, *any* action can look 'private, weird, snobbish' simply because it must involve some particularity to be an action of any sort, insofar as one always does what is merely 'this, that, or the other'. Indeed, as Derrida has suggested, this is apparently true even if the action is not related to the individual's interests, but done for others, as the 'others' in question will still be an arbitrarily selected subset of those who could be helped, where the action will thus fall short of all the good that could be done.[30] But then, a kind of paralysis may set in, as it may appear that nothing one can do is adequate to express the universal standpoint, so one must refrain from acting altogether.

Having set up the difficulty, Bradley then suggests a way in which it might be solved, which he thinks requires putting both 'factors' in the will together, such that in acting in a determinate way, the individual nonetheless contributes to the general good as part of a social whole. Thus, he argues the two one-sided positions of 'pleasure for pleasure's sake' (which constitutes mere particularity or hedonism) and 'duty for duty's sake' (which constitutes mere universality or Kantianism) lead in the structure of *Ethical Studies* to the position of 'my station and its duties' (which offers a balance of both).[31] In this way, one can act in a manner that is particular (as a father, teacher, doctor, politician, whatever), but which can also be seen from the perspective of the universal as having significance and value, in the contribution it makes to the social whole:

I am to be perfectly homogeneous [cf. universal]; but that I can not be unless fully specified [cf. particularized], and the question is, How can I be extended so as to take in my external

[29] Rorty 1999: 6–7.

[30] Cf. Jacques Derrida: 'I am sacrificing and betraying at every moment all my other obligations: my obligations to the other others whom I know or don't know... each of whom is the only son I sacrifice to the other, every one being sacrificed to every one else' (Derrida 1995: 69).

[31] It is important to note, however, that 'my station and its duties' is not the final resolution, as further aporias emerge within it that move *Ethical Studies* into subsequent developments: but we cannot follow that full story here.

relations? Goethe has said, 'Be a whole *or* join a whole', but to that we must answer, 'You can not be a whole, *unless* you join a whole'.

The difficulty is: being limited and so not a whole, how extend myself so as to be a whole? The answer is, be a member of a whole. Here your private self, your finitude, ceases as such to exist; it becomes the function of an organism. You must be, not a mere piece of, but a member in, a whole; and as this must know and will yourself.[32]

In this way, Bradley argued, we manage to achieve proper self-realization, as without it the self will be ruinously divided between these universal and particular 'factors', whereas what is required is to 'realize yourself as whole',[33] for which being part of social whole is then necessary, as his adaptation of Goethe's slogan suggests.

In this way, then, for Bradley the self-realization thesis and the social thesis come together, but in a way that is importantly different from what we saw before. For, on the account we gave of Green, they come together insofar as the latter forms a bridge from egoism to altruism, whereas here they come together because it is the universality of the will that creates difficulties for the agent, which the social thesis is then required to resolve. It would seem, then, that Bradley's position is immune from the Prichardian concerns that troubled Green's. Thus, while Green arguably sees the social thesis as an important adjunct to egoism, Bradley uses it as an important adjunct to Kant's own impartialism, and so incorporates it *within* Kantian ethics, rather than setting it at odds with it, as Green appears to do. For, Bradley argues not that the flourishing we find in social life is a crucial counterweight to our egoism, but that the fact that flourishing takes place in society is precisely because Kant is right, and that we are altruists who can step back from all our individual concerns and interests—but where Kant does not see this role for the social thesis, because he does not see the difficulties that 'the universal factor' in the will poses for us when it comes to action, for which some particularity is also required.

9.3 From Hegel to Bradley

Now, the crucial inspiration for this Bradleyian approach, I would argue, is Hegel, and in particular Hegel's account of the will in the Introduction to the *Philosophy of Right*. I will therefore say something briefly about Hegel's position, before showing how it relates to Bradley's strategy as outlined above, and thus how he came to adopt his particular treatment of the social thesis. The focus will be on §§5–7 of the *Philosophy of Right*, where Hegel offers his famous account of freedom of the will in terms of his three fundamental categories: universal, particular, and individual.

The universal aspect of the will consists in our ability to abstract from all content and determination, as a pure 'I'.[34] The second aspect of particularization consists in

[32] Bradley 1927: 79. [33] Bradley 1927: 73.

[34] Hegel *PR*: §5, p. 37 [VII: 49]: 'The will contains (*α*) the element of *pure indeterminacy* or of the 'I''s pure reflection of itself into itself, in which every limitation, every content, whether present immediately

the determination or limiting of the will to specific goals or projects.[35] On their own, Hegel argues, each of these moments is unsatisfactory: the purely universal moment leads to an empty indeterminacy, as the will cannot act unless it resolves on something particular;[36] but the merely particular can equally seem empty and arbitrary, as the will can step back and abandon all its goals by taking up the more universal standpoint. What we need to resolve this impasse, Hegel suggests, is some kind of particularity to the self, but one which (from a more universal standpoint) can also be endorsed or seen as fundamentally meaningful, rather than as empty and arbitrary. This, then, is the third moment of the will, as a satisfactory unity of the other two: namely, individuality, as the coming together of universality and particularity.[37]

But how is this unity to be achieved? For example, could it be achieved by the individual through satisfying whatever desires they just happen to have? Clearly not, Hegel thinks, as this is where Kant is right, that the individual can always step back from such desires and question their value. On the other hand, could the individual achieve this unity by just abandoning all particular interests and goals, by just try acting for the general good or by engaging in some form of pure willing, in a universal manner? Clearly not, Hegel also thinks, as here we would have universality but not enough particularity, where as a result this universality will lack content—as Hegel thinks was demonstrated in the French Revolution, for example, where no concrete action was deemed adequate to express the universal will, and so nothing could be done without being undone.[38] Thus Hegel, like Bradley, quotes Goethe in support of his view: 'A will which resolves on nothing is not an actual will; the characterless man can never resolve on anything... "Whoever aspires to great things", says Goethe, "must be able to limit himself".'[39] So, how can we achieve freedom, and thus the right balance between universality and particularity?

Hegel's answer, of course, is that this is only possible within the rational state, where through fulfilling their own particular ends, the individual can also contribute

through nature, through needs, desires, and drives, or given and determined in some other way, is dissolved; this is the limitless infinity of *absolute abstraction* or *universality*, the pure thinking of oneself.'

[35] Hegel *PR*: §6, p. 39 [VII: 52]: '(β) In the same way, '*I*' is the transition from undifferentiated indeterminacy to *differentiation, determination*, and the *positing* of a determinacy as a content and object.'

[36] Cf. also Hegel's discussion of the 'beautiful soul' in the *Phenomenology of Spirit.*

[37] Hegel *PR*: §7, p. 41 [VII: 54]: '(γ) The will is the unity of both these moments—*particularity* reflected *into itself* and thereby restored to *universality*.'

[38] Hegel *PR*: §5Z, p. 39 [VII: 52]:

> This form [of freedom] appears more concretely in the active fanaticism of both political and religious life. An example of this was the Reign of Terror in the French Revolution, during which all differences of talents and authority were supposed to be cancelled out. This was a time of trembling and quaking and of intolerance towards everything particular. For fanaticism wills only what is abstract, not what is articulated, so that whenever differences emerge, it finds them incompatible with its own indeterminacy and cancels them.

[39] Hegel, *PR*: §13Z, p. 47 [VII: 65].

to the good of all, and vice versa. Thus, it is only through the social world that it is possible for the tensions within the will to be resolved, and empty universality transmuted into a genuinely coherent account of action. So, going back to the example of Rorty, he can see his life as particularized in various ways (a lecturer, a father, a husband, an orchid lover etc. etc.), but if that life has a place within a wider whole with a more universal value, then he can also see these particular elements as not arbitrary restrictions and limitations but instead can come to reflectively endorse this particularity, by seeing it as related to the universal social good of which lives of this sort are part. In this way, Hegel thinks, a kind of abstract universalism can be avoided, where each of has a determinate part to play that in the light of their abilities and interests, but where those abilities and interests are not *just* 'private, weird, snobbish', given their contribution to the social whole.

9.4 Conclusion

This paper has concerned itself with the worry that Hegelian ethics rests on a mistake, because of the way in which it connects the self-realization of the individual to their life within the social whole—where the mistake is to offer this self-realization to egoistical individuals as a reason for moral action, in a way that then turns morality into a matter of self-interest. While we have seen how this suspicion can and has been raised concerning the ethics of the British Idealists, by Prichard and others, some ways of presenting Hegel's own views might raise the same concerns. For example, Frederick Neuhouser has written about Hegel as follows:

> Hegel's point... is that members of a rational social world—one in which social freedom is realized—are subjectively constituted so as to be willing to subordinate their private interests to universal ends and to be able to do so not out of selflessness but because they regard their activity on behalf of those universal ends as intrinsic to their own (particular) good.[40]

And Allen Wood also writes:

> Hegelian ethical life involves a harmony between individual well-being and the needs of the rational social order... We identify with ethical duties because they fulfill us; they alone give us a meaningful life.[41]

On the face of it, these ways of reading Hegel would seem to raise precisely the concerns that troubled Prichard: namely that while we may 'subordinate [our] interests to universal ends', we do not do so 'out of selflessness', but because we see that acting for those ends is part of our own good, so that 'we identify with ethical duties because they fulfill us', and thereby 'give us a meaningful life'. This, it would appear, connects the social thesis to the self-realization thesis in exactly the way that Prichard fears.

[40] Neuhouser 2000: 92. [41] Wood 1990: 210.

But we have now seen that for Hegel, and also for Bradley, a rather different account can be offered, where it is not that we struggle to behave selflessly insofar as we are only concerned about our own good, but it is precisely *because* we are capable of such selflessness that the social thesis has such significance: for, if we did not see ourselves as fundamentally tied to some social whole, we could not satisfy the universal element in the will in a coherent manner that leaves room for the fact that all action requires particularity. Of course, Hegel and Bradley also think that only in this way can the self be properly realized, in the sense of overcoming the tension that will otherwise tear it apart, so that living in society is still tied to the self-realization thesis in their story, but not in a way (I have argued) that need raise any Prichardian concerns; for like Prichard they allow that we are capable of aiming to act in a way that abstracts from all our interests—indeed, it is precisely this (I have claimed) that for them brings the social thesis to the fore, rather than any problem posed by egoism. In this way, I hope to have shown, we can dispel the suspicion that Hegelian ethics, at least in all its forms, rests on a fundamental mistake.[42]

[42] I am grateful for comments to the audience at the Venice conference at which this paper was first presented, and also to an audience at the University of Tübingen. I am also grateful to John Skorupski and Fabian Freyenhagen for their help.

10

'My Station and its Duties'

Social Role Accounts of Obligation in Green and Bradley

Different elements in the reception history of German Idealism have had different impacts—such as the Young Hegelians on the philosophy of religion, Neo-Kantianism on the philosophy of science, Kojève on accounts of recognition, Croce on theories of art, and so on. When it comes to the British Idealists, arguably the most obvious candidate for such impact is in the idea of 'my station and its duties'; for while the British Idealists engaged with many aspects of the thought of both Kant and Hegel (and to a lesser degree also of Fichte and Schelling), it seems that it is their notion of 'my station and its duties' that has the greatest resonance today, while their accounts of the Absolute, of relations, of the concrete universal, and other aspects of their idealist metaphysics, epistemology, and philosophy of mind have been largely forgotten.[1]

In this paper, I want to look again at this idea of 'my station and its duties', particularly as it figures in the work of T. H. Green and F. H. Bradley, who pioneered its significance.[2] For, while it is widely used as a slogan to represent both their ethical and political philosophy and that of idealism more generally, and while it is of continuing influence within certain strands of contemporary ethical and political thinking as an alternative to other approaches,[3] it is rarely given any detailed treatment in historical terms.[4] In particular, I would like to ask precisely what theory

[1] I have discussed some of these topics in essays in Stern 2009.

[2] While most closely associated with Bradley, the expression is also used by Green: see Green §183, p. 209, and cf. §313, p. 379 and §338, p. 409. Because of the close interconnection between them, it is not clear which author employed the phrase first. Though Hegel does not quite adopt the expression, he comes close to something like it in §150 of the *Philosophy of Right*, in a way that may have impressed Bradley and Green, when he writes that 'In an ethical community... in order to be virtuous [a person] must simply do what is presented, expressly stated, and known to him within his situation' (*PR*: §50, p. 193 [VII: 298]). The phrase seems to have been familiar enough in the early/mid nineteenth century ranging from the religious ('it will conduce to restore the quiet of the mind, to attend to the humble ordinary duties of our station', Newman 1907: sermon 18, volume 1, p. 240) to the popular (Cheap 1836) (with thanks to Bill Mander for these references).

[3] Cf. Norman 1983: 145–72; Horton 1992; Hardimon 1994; Horton 2006; Sciaraffa 2011: 107–28.

[4] But cf. Candlish 1978.

of duty or obligation this position is meant to embody: that is, how an appeal to this notion is meant to answer a fundamental question in ethical theory, namely how moral obligation is to be accounted for and best understood. It is most usually assumed, I think, that in tying obligations to social roles, the British Idealists were offering what I will call an *identificatory* account of obligation: that is, acting in a certain way has an obligatory force because it relates to a role which constitutes your identity. I will contrast this sort of theory with two other accounts, which I will call *hybrid* accounts and *social command* accounts—and suggest that in fact Green held the former and Bradley the latter; and I will also argue that this puts Green's account of obligation close to Kant's, while Bradley may be seen to be following Hegel (who therefore, like Bradley, should also not be seen as offering an identificatory account, which is often mistakenly what happens when his position comes to be viewed in Bradleyean terms).

As British Idealism is not a terribly well-known development in the history of idealistic thinking, I will begin by saying a little about this distinctive period in British philosophy, and particularly about Bradley and Green. I will then outline the problem of obligation that I think underlies their doctrine of 'my station and its duties', and how their approaches fits into the taxonomy of different theories, where I will defend the reading outlined above against the identificatory account.

10.1 Green, Bradley, and British Idealism

After an initial wave of early pioneers (such as Coleridge and J. F. Ferrier), Green forms part of a first generation of thinkers influenced by German idealism in Britain, alongside others such as J. H. Stirling and the Caird brothers, while Bradley forms part of a slightly later wave, including also J. M. E. McTaggart, Andrew Seth (aka Pringle-Pattison) and Bernard Bosanquet, while later generations include R. G. Collingwood and G. R. G. Mure. In a movement that stretched from the 1860s through to the 1930s or 1940s, Green and especially Bradley were significant figures at what is probably its high watermark, which is from roughly the 1880s to the 1920s.

Green, however, was somewhat older than Bradley, being born ten years earlier in 1836; but he died young at forty-six, while Bradley lived until his late seventies, and so outlived Green by forty-two years. Both had highly successful academic careers based in Oxford, with Green also having an impact in politics. Green published little in his lifetime, where his main contributions were a study of Aristotle and a powerful critique of Hume;[5] but he had several works published posthumously, including *Prolegomena to Ethics*, 'Lectures on the Principles of Political Obligation', and 'Lectures on the Philosophy of Kant',[6] while the lectures on which these publications were based also had considerable influence. Bradley published considerably more,

[5] Green 1866, 1874–5. [6] Green 1885–8a, 1885–8b, 2003.

including *Ethical Studies*, *Appearance and Reality*, and *Principles of Logic*.[7] As this suggests, Bradley's work ranged more widely than Green's, although the latter's ethics included a substantial metaphysical background, while Bradley's *Ethical Studies* was considered a fundamental treatise in idealist ethics, to put alongside Green's own *Prolegomena*.

Despite being frequently grouped together, and despite sharing many ideas and concerns, there are also significant differences between Green and Bradley. This is sometimes characterized by the suggestion that while Green was fundamentally Kantian, Bradley was more Hegelian.[8] While there is some truth in this (reflected, as we shall see, in their different accounts of obligation), neither followed their respective predecessors in any very orthodox way, nor conceived themselves as doing so—Green insisting that he was at best offering a 'friendly amendment' to Kant's approach in order to save him from himself,[9] while Bradley openly criticized Hegel despite nonetheless acknowledging his great significance.[10] And both, of course, came under other important influences, some arguably close to Hegel (such as Aristotle and Spinoza), but others arguably not (such as the British Empiricists). At the same time, as is common, neither liked to feel themselves pigeonholed into a movement or reduced to any form of discipleship—Bradley famously warning in the Preface to the first edition of his *Principles of Logic* that 'As for the "Hegelian School" which exists in our reviews, I know of no one who has met it anywhere else'.[11] Certainly, unlike some of the British Idealists (such as McTaggart), Green and Bradley published no scholarly works on the German Idealists, but clearly the latter helped to provide some of the key materials and ideas that they shaped after their own fashion, in response to their own concerns and against the background of their own assumptions—where one common point of focus was on the question of moral obligation.

10.2 Theories of Moral Obligation

How moral duty and obligation is to be understood has of course been a matter of long-standing debate within philosophy. In the medieval period, and into much of the early modern period too, there were fundamentally three major options in accounting for moral obligation. According to *radically voluntarist divine command*

[7] Bradley 1927; Bradley 1930; Bradley 1928.

[8] Cf. Brink 2003a: xciv.

[9] Cf. Green 1885–8a: §105, p. 124: 'As it is, though his doctrine [of the a priori in ethics] is essentially true, [Kant's] way of putting it excites the same opposition as his way of putting the corresponding doctrine in regard to the a priori element in knowledge.'

[10] Cf. Bradley 1928: I, x: 'I fear that to avoid worse misunderstandings, I must say something as to what is called "Hegelianism." For Hegel himself, assuredly I think him a great philosopher; but I never could have called myself an Hegelian, partly because I can not say that I have mastered his system, and partly because I could not accept what seems his main principle, or at least part of that principle. I have no wish to conceal how much I owe to his writings; but I will leave it to those who can judge better than myself, to fix the limits within which I have followed him.'

[11] Bradley 1928: I, x.

accounts, the obligatoriness of morality depends on the authority of some divine sovereign or commander, who has the freedom and power to make *any* act obligatory by so commanding. On *natural law* accounts, by contrast, the idea is that morality constitutes a natural law in which God plays a more indirect role, where an act is made right and hence something we are obliged to do because it conforms to the nature of things, where God is the source of that nature as creator, but not the source of obligatoriness as commander; moreover, his role as benevolent creator places constraints on what within this creation can turn out to be right or wrong. And there were also what have been called *intermediate divine command* positions, that held that what is right only becomes an actual obligation through God's willing that it be done (hence opposing the natural law tradition, which gave God's will a less direct role), but that rightness itself is prior to and independent of obligatoriness and hence of God's will (hence opposing any radical voluntarism, as what God can command is now constrained by what is right independent of that command).

Theories of obligation as they arise in more modern philosophy may be seen to grow out from, but also to break with, these more classical positions in different ways—where it is then these more modern theories that will concern us in considering Green and Bradley and their accounts of duty.

The first such theory can be found in Kant, and I will call it the *hybrid* theory because, like the intermediate divine command theory (of which I think it is a descendent), it combines a theory of the right with a separate theory of obligation. (Of course, like everything in Kant's philosophy in general and ethics in particular, what I say here is hardly uncontentious, and I will do little to defend the reading in any detail, though I try to do so elsewhere.[12] And even if my reading of Kant is deemed unacceptable, at least perhaps it will prove a useful background to my account of Green.) As is well known, Kant raises the question of how to explain the peculiar force that morality has for us, which takes the form of duties and obligations—that is, of commands and imperatives, telling is that there are actions which we *must* or *must not* perform. Kant calls this feature of morality 'necessitation' or 'constraint' (*Nötigung*), and he explains it not by recourse to divine command (in the manner of a voluntarist like Crusius), or to the inherent obligatoriness of the natural order of things (in the manner of a rationalist like Wolff), but in terms of the distinction between the holy will and our own, arguing that it is because we have dispositions to do things other than what is right, that the right for us involves a moral 'must'; but for a holy will, which has no inclination to do anything other than what is right, no such 'must' applies. A typical statement of Kant's view is the following from the *Groundwork of the Metaphysics of Morals*:

A perfectly good will would, therefore, equally stand under objective laws (of the good), but it could not on this account be represented as *necessitated* to actions in conformity with law since

[12] See Stern 2012; and Chapter 1 in this volume.

of itself, by its subjective constitution, it can be determined only through the representation of the good. Hence no imperatives hold for the *divine* will and in general for a *holy* will: the 'ought' is out of place here, because volition is of itself necessarily in accord with the law. Therefore imperatives are only formulae expressing the relation of objective laws of volition in general to the subjective imperfection of the will of this or that rational being, for example, of the human will.[13]

Thus, the principles that determine what it is good and bad to do apply to the holy will, where these principles are laws because they hold of all agents universally, and of such agents independently of the contingencies of their desires and goals, and thus necessarily. However, because the holy will is morally perfect, these laws lack any necessitating force for wills of this sort, whereas our lack of moral perfection means that they possess such force for us.

It can therefore be seen how Kant's distinction between the holy will and ours is designed to resolve the problem of obligation, by appeal to the fact that our will is divided between reason and inclination in a way that the will of the divine being is not. Kant characterizes this division in the terms of his transcendental idealism as mapping onto the distinction between the noumenal and phenomenal realms (or the 'intelligible world' and 'the world of sense'). Kant's distinction between the holy will and ours therefore forms a crucial part of his answer to the problem of accounting for the moral 'must', in a way that explains its possibility (unlike a view that simply treats the 'must' as a feature of the world), but without recourse to the problematic notion of a divine legislator as the source of that 'must' (thus avoiding any need to adopt a divine command theory).

Notwithstanding the ingenious nature of Kant's account of moral obligation, it seemed to Kant's successors, and particularly to Schiller and Hegel, that it involved paying an unacceptable price: namely, that moral duty is seen as a function of our imperfection as moral agents, and our status as creatures who must struggle against ourselves in order to act rightly. It thus appeared that if the Kantian account were correct, the most the dutiful agent could achieve was continence, not virtue—that is, a successful overcoming of her non-moral inclinations, rather than an alignment between those inclinations and what it is right to do, of the sort that Schiller identified with grace. While Schiller himself perhaps held back from breaking entirely with Kant on this issue, he nonetheless raised two fundamental objections that led Hegel to go further: The first is that it incorporates what appears to be a demeaning picture of human nature, as essentially 'fallen' and unable to follow what morality asks of us without some sort of resistance; the second is that ultimately, Kant's dualistic picture did not itself allow for full autonomy, even though the intention of his ethics was to avoid the heteronomy of other moral theories.

[13] Kant *GMM*: 67 [4:414].

I would argue, then, that Hegel came to be dissatisfied with Kant's hybrid approach, and as a result adopted a different kind of position, which might be called a *social command theory*. Like Kant's account, this too may be seen as a descendant of the intermediate divine command view, where what is independently right comes to be made obligatory—but not from the dualism within the human will, but from the authority of society over the individual agent. As Robert Adams has put the basic idea of this theory (which he does not himself endorse): 'According to social theories of the nature of obligation, having an obligation to do something consists in being required (in a certain way, under certain circumstances or conditions), by another person or a group of persons, to do it.'[14]

Having criticized the Kantian theory of duty and obligation in the 'Morality' section of the *Philosophy of Right*, Hegel provides this social command account in the concluding 'Ethical Life' section. The latter takes into consideration not only the individual will, but also the *'laws and institutions which have being in and for themselves'*.[15] As a result, the individual can be seen to be part of an 'ethical substance [*die sittliche Substanz*]' that consists of 'laws and powers [*Gesetze und Gewalten*]',[16] where 'these substantial determinations are *duties* which are binding on the will of the individual'.[17] Because of the authority of these duties over the lives of individuals, and of the relative unimportance of individuals within the social order, it can appear to them that the moral law has a divine origin, as it did in pre-modern societies. But this is to neglect the social basis of these obligations, and that while the social order is a substance to which individuals relate as 'accidents', nonetheless these accidents are required by the substance in order to be actual. Hegel makes clear, therefore, that he sees divine command accounts of obligation as based on a picture of our relation to the world that has been surpassed, where these obligations are now better accounted for as an aspect of our existence within the social environment of ethical life.

As a result of the 'laws and powers' of the community, therefore, the individual will find duties that are 'prescribed, expressly stated, and known to him within his situation'.[18] These ethical laws may then appear to have 'an absolute authority and power, infinitely more firmly based than the being of nature'.[19] At the same time, however, Hegel argues that insofar as they stem from the ethical community, such laws are 'not something *alien* to the subject' but something to which 'the subject bears *spiritual witness*...as to its own essence'.[20] We should not think, therefore, that just because something is an obligation because it is required by the social group, that the motivating reason the individual has for complying with it comes from these external ends: rather, it can be based on the recognized authority of the ethical community over the individual, where at the same time the individual is part of this group, and so not subordinated to it as by an alien will.

[14] Adams 1999: 242.
[15] Hegel *PR*: §144, p. 189 [VII: 294].
[16] Hegel *PR*: §146, p. 190 [VII: 295].
[17] Hegel *PR*: §148, p. 191 [VII: 296–7].
[18] Hegel *PR*: §150, p. 193 [VII: 298].
[19] Hegel *PR*: §146, p. 190 [VII: 294–5].
[20] Hegel *PR*: §147, p. 191 [VII: 295].

Now, if a social command account of this kind is going to be plausible, it can only treat what is required by society as a necessary condition for creating a moral obligation; for, if it were to also treat it as a sufficient condition, then the worry would arise that on this account, *anything* required by society would amount to an obligation. It is therefore important that Hegel considers these requirements as laid down by the *rational state*, which is seeking to uphold the freedom of its individual citizens: without this constraint, it is clear that it would not have the legitimacy to create genuine duties for people to obey.

We have seen, then, that Hegel's account of duty as this arises for the individual within ethical life can plausibly be considered to be a form of social command account, where what renders something a duty or obligation for an individual is the 'absolute authority and power' of the ethical community. And we have also seen how Hegel came to develop this account, as an alternative to both a divine command theory (which is seen as a kind of primitive forerunner of the social command account), and to Kant's hybrid theory (with its dualistic conception of the will).

It should therefore be clear how the hybrid theory of Kant and the social command theory of Hegel are to be distinguished. But we must now also distinguish both from a third position, which is the *identificatory* account of obligation. On this account, the obligatoriness of certain actions is to be explained by appeal to what constitutes the identity of the agent, where obligatoriness is said to rest on what, given their sense of their identity, they may or may not do without giving this up. Now, in a way that is ironic given her close association with Kant, the person who has most developed this sort of account of obligation within contemporary ethics is Christine Korsgaard. This is reflected in her conception of *practical identity*, which is 'a description under which you find your life to be worth living and your actions to be worth undertaking'.[21] Some of these identities can be, and for most will be, tied in with an individual's social roles, whist others (such as 'being a human being') may not:

> Practical identity is a complex matter and for the average person there will be a jumble of such conceptions. You are a human being, a woman or a man, an adherent of a certain religion, a member of an ethnic group, a member of a certain profession, someone's lover or friend, and so on. And all of these identities give rise to reasons and obligations. Your reasons express your identity, your nature; your obligations spring from what that identity forbids.[22]

Korsgaard's claim, then, is that 'an obligation always takes the form of a reaction against a threat of a loss of identity',[23] in a way that is signalled in such 'astonishing but familiar' remarks such as 'I couldn't live with myself if I did that'.[24]

[21] Korsgaard 1996b: 101. [22] Korsgaard 1996b: 101.

[23] Korsgaard 1996b: 102. Cf. also p. 18: '[Moral claims on us] must issue in a deep way from our sense of who we are.'

[24] Korsgaard 1996b: 101. Cf. also pp. 239–40: 'You may be tempted to do something but find that it is inconsistent with your identity as a teacher or a mother or a friend, and the thought that it is inconsistent may give rise to a new incentive, an incentive not to do this thing. As Luther's "here I stand, I cannot do

Now, if one starts with an identificatory account of obligation, and also takes on board the idea that our identity can be grounded in such things as our social roles, then it may seem natural to assume that any focus on the latter will lead one on to the former: and many social role theorists do indeed take this route. Thus, while Korsgaard herself takes it that our identity as humans is more fundamental than any mere social role, nonetheless she accepts the latter would give rise to obligations were we to identify with them (as she admits can happen to the Mafioso raised as an example against her by G. A. Cohen).[25] A similar outlook can also be found in other social role theorists, such as John Horton, who writes: 'Both the family and the political community figure prominently in our sense of who we are; our self-identity and our understanding of our place in the world... It should not be surprising, therefore, that some institutional obligations, through their deep-rooted connections with our sense of who we are and our place in the world, have a particularly fundamental role in our moral being. That these kind of institutional involvement generate moral obligations, and these obligations rather than standing in need of justification may themselves be justificatory, is only to be expected.'[26]

Now, one important source of this sort of identificatory account is taken to be the British Idealists, and particularly Green and Bradley with their talk of social roles. So, for example, in criticizing the identificatory position, A. John Simmons cites the following remarks from Bradley as 'the classic statement of the position': 'We have found ourselves when we have found our station and its duties, our function as an organ in the social organism... If we suppose the world of relations, in which [an Englishman] was born and bred, never to have been, then we suppose the very essence of him not to be; if we take that away, we have taken him away... The state... gives him the life that he does and ought to live.'[27] But I now want to argue that this identificatory account of Green and Bradley is mistaken, and that the former is much more plausibly read as following Kant's hybrid approach, and the latter as following Hegel's social command theory. I will begin by discussing Green.

10.3 Green on Duty

In order to understand Green's account of duty, it is necessary to say something first about his general position in ethics.

otherwise" reminds us, the human heart, being human, discovers itself not only in spontaneous desire, but in imperatives.'

[25] Cf. Korsgaard 1996b: 183–4 and 255–8. Cf. Simmons 2001: 81–2.

[26] Horton 1992: 150 and 157. Cf. also Hardimon 1994: 358–63.

[27] Bradley 1927: 163, 166, 174. Simmons cites these remarks (from a different edition) in Simmons 2001: 80–1, note 38. Hegel himself has also been interpreted as an identificatory theorist: see e.g. Neuhouser 2000: 97–8, where Neuhouser explicitly draws the parallel with Korsgaard. As briefly outlined above, however, I also think this is a mis-reading of Hegel's position, where I take his account of moral obligation to be that of a social command theorist. For further discussion, see Stern 2012: 148–61.

Green begins with an account of action, where he argues that what guides the will it not some specific want or desire, but a conception of the agent's own greatest good—hence, he claims, the agent in acting aims at 'self-satisfaction'.[28] Thus, taking Esau selling his birthright for a mess of pottage as an example, Green argues that his motive for action was not mere hunger, for otherwise he would have been acting like an unreflective animal; rather, what led him to act was 'the presentation of an idea of himself as enjoying the pleasure of eating the pottage', where 'it is not the hunger as a natural force, but his own conception of himself, as finding for the time his greatest good in the satisfaction of hunger, that determines the act'.[29] As a result of this, Green argues, Esau 'recognises himself as the author of the act', and hence praise or blame are appropriate.[30] For Green, therefore, when it comes to making a choice, there is no selection between competing desires made by the will; rather, the choice is made in determining which of the desires, if satisfied, would constitute the agent's greatest good, and on the basis of this decision the will then comes to act, with the other desires having been silenced.[31]

As a consequence of this picture, Green resists any strict division between the roles of desire and intellect in action (for example, he rejects the Humean view that reason is the slave of the passions, simply engaged in finding the means for the satisfaction of the latter).[32] For intellect plays a role in forming the conception of our good within which a desire can then play a part—as when Esau takes it that his desire for food, if satisfied, would realize that good. On the other hand, if an agent did not believe that desire satisfaction of any kind formed part of his good, then that agent would be inert. Green therefore argues that the will is not a faculty somehow separable from desire and intellect, but rather contains aspects of both, where this must be so in an agent that is seeking to bring about its self-satisfaction.[33]

Green recognizes, however, that this picture (which is articulated in Book II of the *Prolegomena*) leaves an important question unanswered when it comes to ethics: namely, what is it that distinguishes a morally good will from a morally bad one? Of course, on some accounts, this difference is marked by a distinction between the good agent who has no concern for their own well-being, and a bad one who is so concerned: but Green cannot take this option, given his account of action outlined above where such self-concern is present in *all* agents—so where does the difference lie? Green's answer is that the difference comes from the different conceptions of self-satisfaction that agents can have, and thus in 'the character of that in which

[28] Cf. Green 2003: §95, p. 106: 'We say that to every action morally imputable, or of which a man can recognise himself as the author, the motive is always some idea of the man's personal good—an idea absolutely different from animal want, even in cases where it is from the anticipation of the satisfaction of some animal want that the idea of personal good is derived.'

[29] Green 2003: §96, p. 107. [30] Green 2003: §96, p. 108.

[31] Cf. Green 2003: §104, p. 166–7 and §§145–6, pp. 163–5.

[32] Cf. Green 2003: §116, pp. 130–2 and 1885–8a: §97, pp. 111–13.

[33] Cf. Green 2003: §153, pp. 172–3.

self-satisfaction is sought, ranging from sensual pleasure to the fulfilment of a vocation conceived as given by God'. He goes on: 'It is on the specific difference of the objects willed under the general form of self-satisfaction that the [moral] quality of the will must depend. It is here therefore that we must seek for the basis for a distinction between goodness and badness of will.'[34] Green's position depends, therefore, on making out some grounds on which to distinguish good and bad conceptions of self-satisfaction that might be held by different agents, where this explains the basis on which we might make a moral distinction between them. In order to pursue this strategy, Green therefore rejects other accounts, such as hedonistic utilitarianism, which holds that *all* agents have the *same* conception of self-satisfaction, namely the gaining of pleasure, and which therefore distinguishes good and bad agents extrinsically rather than intrinsically, on the basis only of the consequences of their actions.[35]

For Green, then, the difference between the virtuous and vicious person lies in their different conceptions of where and in what manner they can attain self-satisfaction, and what this consists in—where, like the Greeks, Green is confident that this vicious person is in error about where that self-satisfaction really lies, which is not in the life of the non-moral agent, but in the life of a social being who acts in an ethical manner towards others, where as a result their capacities are properly realized. It is this conception of their good which the virtuous agent holds, as opposed to the conception adopted by the vicious agent, that leads the former into virtue and the latter into vice.[36] What makes an agent good for Green, therefore, is not how much he actually achieves, but whether he is looking for his self-satisfaction in the right place.

Though, of course, there is much more to be said, and many possible objections to be answered, this completes all that is needed as the background for Green's account of duty, to which we now turn. This is given primarily at the end of Chapter II and the start of Chapter III of Book III of the *Prolegomena*.

As we have seen, Green holds that the good agent aims at the realization of his capacities, where he now argues that this 'will keep before him an object, which he presents to himself as absolutely desirable, but which is other than any particular object of desire'.[37] In the case of such particular objects, he will take these to have value only in so far as they satisfy some desire of his; but in the case of his self-realization, 'it will be an interest as in an object conceived to be of unconditional value; one of which the value does not depend on any desire that the individual may at any time feel for it or for anything else, or on any pleasure that, either in its pursuit or in its attainment or as its result, he may experience'.[38] In other words, Green claims that while the agent may see the value of everything else in terms of his wants

[34] Green 2003: §154, pp. 174–5.
[35] Green 2003: §§156–70, pp. 177–94.
[36] Green 2003: §176, pp. 199–201.
[37] Green 2003: §193, pp. 221–3.
[38] Green 2003: §193, pp. 221–3.

and their attendant pleasures, he does not see the realization of his capacities in this way, as these constitute the end against which such wants and pleasures are measured, where 'the desire for the object will be founded in a conception of its desirableness as a fulfilment of the capabilities of which a man is conscious in being conscious of himself'.[39]

Given this picture, then, Green argues that agents can be in the position of seeing their self-realization as of unconditioned value, which is not valuable as a means to the satisfaction of some prior desire, but on the contrary can overrule any desire that does not tend to the attainment of this end:

> In such men [as are conscious of the value of self-realization] and at such times as a desire for it does actually arise... it will express itself in their imposition on themselves of rules requiring something to be done irrespectively of any inclination to do it, irrespectively of any desired end to which it is a means, *other than this end, which is desired because conceived as absolutely desirable.* With the men in whom, and at the times when, there is no such desire, the consciousness of there being something absolutely desirable will still be a qualifying element in life. It will yield a recognition of those unconditional rules of conduct to which, from the prevalence of unconformable passions, it fails to produce actual obedience. It will give meaning to the demand, without which there is no morality and in which all morality is virtually involved, that 'something be done merely for the sake of its being done', because it is a consciousness of the possibility of an action in which no desire shall be gratified but the desire excited by the idea of the act itself, as of something absolutely desirable in the sense that in it the man does the best that he has in him to do.[40]

Green thus claims to have found here a version of a Kantian categorical imperative, but one which Kant himself wrongly overlooked:[41] for, the agent can find in self-realization something that has value irrespective of what his desires or ends happen to be, where in identifying them reason has much more than an instrumental role, as here it determines the content of our desires themselves by establishing the proper object of our self-satisfaction; so in recognizing this value as lying behind the requirements on us of the moral, we will see the latter in the necessary, universal, and non-instrumental manner that characterizes morality for Kant, but which (Green thinks) is inadequately captured in Kant's more formalistic approach.[42]

However, if this gives Green some way to characterize what the content of morality might be and how it might take on a non-contingent and non-instrumental character, it does not yet quite explain its *imperatival* force, or the kind of 'necessitation' that Kant also took to be characteristic of morality for us; but when it comes to explaining this, Green adopts precisely the kind of hybrid approach that I have

[39] Green 2003: §193, pp. 221–3. [40] Green 2003: §193, pp. 221–3.

[41] Cf. Green 1885–8a: §§119–24, pp. 139–45. For further discussion of this important aspect of Green's position, see Irwin 1984 and Irwin 2009: 581–624; and Brink 2003b: 92–106.

[42] Like others who try to find in Kant resources for a less formalistic position, Green takes consolation in the Formula of Humanity, which he uses as a 'bridge' to his own position: cf. Green 1885–8a: §111, pp. 131–2.

identified previously with Kant himself. For, as Green sees it, while self-realization may constitute the objectively valuable end towards which we would align our desires if fully rational, we are *not* in fact fully rational in this manner, and therefore are subject to other desires, where the tension that this gives rise to accounts for the felt necessity and imperatival force that morality seems to exert over us:

> Such an ideal [of humanity], not yet realized but operating as a motive, already constitutes in man an inchoate form of that life, that perfect development of himself, of which the completion would be the realised ideal of himself. *Now in relation to a nature such as ours, having other impulses than those which draw to the ideal, this ideal becomes, in Kant's language, an imperative, and a categorical imperative.* It will command something to be done universally and unconditionally, irrespectively of whether there is in any one, at any time, an inclination to do it.[43]

Green's position would therefore appear to offer a variant on Kant's hybrid model, where what underlies morality is some unconditional value, but where that morality appears to us in the form of commands insofar as we are subject to desires that lead us to want to act differently, in pursuit of other ends.

Moreover, in Chapter III, Green goes on to explain why he takes the hybrid model to be more fundamental than any divine command or social command account. He begins by underlining that, because self-realization is a social matter, ethics will involve social relations. To the individual, therefore, a life of this sort will 'express itself in the form of social requirement', insofar as his 'better reason' will be 'in antagonism to the inclination of the moment',[44] where as a result the individual will feel himself to be under some sort of moral law governing his relations with others. Thus, Green argues, while it may seem natural to associate law with the idea of some sort of authoritative commander (as on the divine command and social command models), this natural picture should be resisted, where the hybrid account reveals why in fact it is unnecessary, as it shows how the imperative of 'Thou shalt' and 'Thou must' can be explained in a different way.[45] Green suggests, therefore, that rather than arising in a legalistic manner, out of the authority over us of some superior commander, the moral ought arises out of a prior awareness of the good, but where that good stands opposed to some of the agent's desires and inclinations and thus puts constraints on them, in a way that comes to assume the form of an imperative, even though the agent need not yet have any conception of a law or a sovereign law-giver.

Moreover, Green argues, it is this model that must truly be the fundamental one. For, he holds, any law-giver account must explain the authority of the law-giver, which cannot come from fear of their power as such fear does make this authority legitimate in any way; instead, Green claims, it can only arise if we see the law-giver

[43] Green 2003: §196, p. 225, my emphasis. [44] Green 2003: §202, p. 232.
[45] Green 2003: §202, p. 233.

as following the good—but then the appeal to the law-giver is made redundant, as on the hybrid model this already has its own imperatival force, as explained above.[46] Rather than being constrained by an external law-giver, therefore, for Green (as for Kant) moral obligatoriness is to be explained by appeal to the structure of the agent's own will, as her conception of the good limits her desires, in a way that makes it appropriate to talk of *self*-legislation.[47]

We have seen, then, that while Green's position is by no means that of the fully orthodox (or literal) Kantian, insofar as he treats self-satisfaction as a basis for the moral will, nonetheless his account of the moral 'must' still takes a Kantian form, in following the hybrid model we found in Kant, rather than any sort of divine command, social command, or identificatory position. Turning now to Bradley, we will see that he too eschews any identificatory account, but that he also rejects a Kantian one, opting instead for a social command theory which puts him closer to Hegel.

10.4 Bradley on Duty

Whilst the *Prolegomena to Ethics* and Bradley's *Ethical Studies* stand as the twin peaks of Idealist ethics in Britain, and while they share important similarities of outlook, the relation between the texts is not straightforward, while they are also significantly different in the approaches they adopt. *Ethical Studies* appeared nearly a decade before the *Prolegomena*; but Bradley attended Green's lectures on ethics and related matters in Oxford, as did most of the other British Idealists who were therefore fully versed in the position developed by Green, so that *Ethical Studies* cannot be said to have had an independent influence on them despite its earlier publication. Moreover, Bradley here acknowledges the significance of Green, particularly when it comes to his treatment of hedonism in Essay III[48]—although Bradley is not mentioned in the *Prolegomena*.[49]

Ethical Studies, unlike the *Prolegomena*, is a work with a dialectical structure in the Hegelian sense; that is, positions are advanced but then '*aufgehoben*' or sublated once their limitations are revealed, so that in this way the search for a more complete and less one-sided position is carried out. The book comprises seven main chapters (or

[46] Cf. Green 2003: §202, pp. 232–3.

[47] Cf. Green 2003: §203, pp. 233–4: 'It is in this sense that the old language is justified, which speaks of Reason as the parent of Law. Reason is the self-objectifying consciousness. It constitutes, as we have seen, the capability in man of seeking an absolute good and of conceiving this good as common to others with himself: and it is this capability which alone renders him a possible author and a self-submitting subject of law.'

[48] See Bradley 1927: 96 note 1—where Bradley writes that 'on the whole subject of this Essay let me recommend the student to consult him'—referring in particular to Green's Introduction to Hume's *Treatise*.

[49] For some discussion on the relation between Green and Bradley during this period, see Nicholson 1990: 50–1.

'Essays' as they are headed). In the first, Bradley defends the idea of moral responsibility against the twin threats of philosophical determinism and indeterminism, while in the second he turns to the question of 'why should I be moral?' Anticipating Prichard,[50] Bradley suggests that taken as a demand by a sceptic who want to know 'what's in it for me?' the question should be avoided, as the attempt to answer it will only reduce morality to self-interest—while the moral person will feel no need to ask it. On the other hand, Bradley allows that there can be some genuine and legitimate point to the question, which is how far morality coincides with self-realization, and in what form. How best to answer this question then becomes the main focus of the rest of the book.

Bradley begins his inquiry by considering hedonistic utilitarianism as an answer, which is then rejected for reasons we will come back to, where he then considers the opposite view, which is that morality is all about 'duty for duty's sake'. In the fifth chapter, which is the one entitled 'My Station and Its Duties', a position is adopted that Bradley represents as a kind of 'sublation' of hedonistic utilitarianism and 'duty for duty's sake'. However, in the next chapter he faces up to certain difficulties with this position, which revolve around the idea that there is more to morality and self-realization than the social world encompasses—such as the obligations of the artist to create works of beauty—which Bradley puts within an 'ideal morality'. Finally, the last chapter considers 'Selfishness and Self-Sacrifice' and how the former relates to the bad self and the latter to the good, while the 'Concluding Remarks' consider how far 'reflection on morality leads beyond it',[51] and takes us to a religious perspective.

While as this shows, the outlook of 'my station and its duties' does not represent Bradley's final position, it is here that the core of his account of ethical duties lies and it is therefore on this chapter that the identificatory accounts of his position have focused—so this will also form the centrepiece of our discussion, but where, in accordance with the structure of the book, this cannot properly be understood without taking into account the dialectic that has preceded it.[52]

As part of that dialectic, in the chapter on 'Duty for Duty's Sake', Bradley has already introduced but rejected the Kantian account of duty, emphasizing its inherent dualism in a way that echoes the critique offered by Hegel.[53] Having presented this hybrid account of duty as an essential part of the outlook he is considering,[54] Bradley then goes on to explain why 'stated as we have stated it above, the theory of duty for duty's sake carries with it little or no plausibility'.[55] Acknowledging his debt

[50] Cf. Prichard 2002a.

[51] Bradley 1927: 314.

[52] Bradley emphasizes the importance of the structure of the work, when he writes that 'These Essays are a critical discussion of some fundamental questions in Ethics, and are so far connected that, for the most part, they must be read in the order in which they stand' (Bradley 1927: viii).

[53] Bradley 1927: 146–7.

[54] In a note on 'duty for duty's sake', Bradley emphasizes 'as I have said before, this is not a statement of Kant's view'—but where with characteristic archness, he adds 'that view is far wider, and at the same time more confused' (Bradley 1927: 148, note 1).

[55] Bradley 1927: 148.

to Hegel, Bradley considers various difficulties with other elements of the theory (particularly its 'empty formalism'), but also focuses on its dualism, which he thinks creates problems both for the account of action (which, like Green, he takes to involve both the sensuous self as well as the non-sensuous self), but also for the very account it offers of the imperatival nature of morality, which (contra Green) he takes to involve some notion of a commander, where on the hybrid model this idea makes no real sense:

> We may remark in passing a contradiction involved in the doctrine of the imperative [that comes from this 'dualistic moral theory']. A command is addressed by one will to another, and must be obeyed, if at all, by the second will. But here the will that is commanded is not the will that executes; hence the imperative is never obeyed; and, as it is not to produce action in that to which it is addressed, it is a mere sham-imperative.[56]

There is no explicit mention of Green here, so we therefore cannot say for sure that Bradley took him to be a target; but as we have seen, despite their important differences, when it comes to the imperatival nature of duty Green has a position of a broadly Kantian sort, so one might expect Bradley's critique to apply also to him.

Having seen that Bradley rejects the Kantian hybrid model, the question now is what is he seeking to replace it with in moving to a discussion of 'my station and its duties'? As has been discussed, a standard approach is to take it that Bradley moves instead to an identificatory model; but I now want to suggest that this approach is mistaken, and that underlying this position is a social command account instead.

That this is so can be made plain once one recalls the structure of the dialectic in *Ethical Studies*, and the place of the chapter (or 'essay') on 'My Station and its Duties' within it. Up to this point, Bradley has considered two contrasting approaches, both of which are said to have some merit, but neither of which is wholly satisfactory as things stand. The first is 'pleasure for pleasure's sake', which has the merit of thinking about how morality might relate to the individual's 'self-realization', but does so in way that has a narrow and mistaken view of what this amounts to, namely pleasure. The second is 'duty for duty's sake', which rightly scorns the latter idea as simplistic, and instead conceives of the self to be realized as the pure will, and so conceives of morality in terms that are purely formal. Again, according to Bradley, there is some merit to thinking of morality in terms of duty, but as we have seen for familiar Hegelian reasons (including the dualism we have discussed above), it is deemed unsatisfactory.

What is needed, therefore, is some sort of synthesis or '*Aufhebung*' of these views, which Bradley tries to offer in 'My Station in Its Duties': namely, a position that has a conception of duty that overcomes the problems with the Kantian outlook, and which also relates it to a notion of self-realization that is less crude than the one

[56] Bradley 1927: 151 note 1. Cf. also p. 207: 'Command is the simple proposal of an action (or abstinence) to me by another will, as the content of that will'.

offered by the perspective of 'pleasure for pleasure's sake'. What we require, then, is a view that allows for self-realization on the one hand, and duty on the other, without treating the former as mere pleasure or hedonistic well-being, and the latter as something empty, formal and dualistic—where it is precisely in a view that tries to *achieve* both, that these respective limitations will be overcome. Bradley's positive suggestion, therefore, is that if we think of the individual as following duties that relate to a good that is *more* than his individual good, then at the same time self-realization will be achieved, and these duties will be given a content and context, in a manner that will enable a satisfactory 'middle way' to be found.

And then, Bradley claims, this is just what one will get within a state, in which the individual is both part of the general good of the community, *and* also able to find itself fully realized by participating in that community as a result. Thus, Bradley declares, in a passage of considerable rhetorical force, by living within a 'social organism' of this sort, where the individual has a 'station and its duties' through which they contribute to this goal, and therefore also has contentful and objective requirements laid upon them, by a society in which they also flourish, then a notable advance towards dialectical stability will have been achieved:

> Here, and here first, are the contradictions which have beset us solved—here is a universal which can confront our wandering desires with a fixed and stern imperative, but which yet is no unreal form of the mind, but a living soul that penetrates and stands fast in the detail of actual existence. It is real, and real for me. It is in its affirmation that I affirm myself, for I am but as a 'heart-beat in its system'. And I am real in it; for when I give myself to it, it gives me the fruition of my own personal activity, the accomplished ideal of my life which is happiness. In the realized idea which, superior to me, and yet here and now in and by me, affirms itself in a continuous process, we have found the end, we have found self-realization, duty, and happiness in one—yes, we have found ourselves, when we have found our station and its duties, our function as an organ in the social organism.[57]

My claim is, then, that up to this point, Bradley is offering a social command account, whereby on the one hand the state is such as to 'confront our wandering desires with a strict and firm imperative' because of its authority over us, but where on the other hand 'when I give myself up to it', the state 'gives me the fruition of my own personal activity, the accomplished ideal of my life which is happiness'. Bradley makes the nature of his position fully clear when he writes: '[The state] speaks the word of command and gives the field of accomplishment, and in the activity of obedience it has and bestows individual life and satisfaction and happiness'.[58]

Likewise, I would argue, from what we saw before in the earlier section, Bradley is in effect paraphrasing Hegel here (as he would no doubt happily grant), and Hegel's claim that 'in the state everything depends on the unity of universal and particular'.[59] It is precisely this, as we have seen, that allows Hegel to also strike the balance that

[57] Bradley 1927: 163. [58] Bradley 1927: 184–5. [59] Hegel *PR*: §261Z, p. 285 [VII: 410].

Bradley is after, between duty as imposed by the state on the one hand and the interests of the individual on the other, so that by having the source of those duties in the command of the rational state, the individual has obligations, has their 'particularity' taken into account, and is lifted above the narrow and egoistic concerns of the pre-social individual. By thinking of duty in these terms, as imposed by society on the individual who has a place and role within it, the dialectical harmony that both Hegel and Bradley are looking for can be achieved, but only because obligations are seen to arise from the social community of which they are part, and which has the self-realization or freedom of its citizens (which for Bradley and Hegel are in effect the same thing) at its heart.

However, if this shows him to be a social command theorist, what of the passages in which Bradley seems to make so much of the way in which an individual's identity is bound up with their role, and which have led so many to interpret him as a social role theorist concerning obligation?

When it comes to Bradley, I think the simple answer is as follows: These 'identificatory' passages are there *not* to support a social role theory, but to answer three very significant objections to any social command theory, namely:

1. that the state which Bradley claims has the authority to give individuals their duties does not really exist and is a myth, because it can always be reduced to a mere collection of individuals, with nothing but the authority of individuals over one another
2. that self-realization does not require social membership, so that there is no essential connection (as Bradley claims there is) between a morality of social duties and self-realization
3. that individuals must always see the authority of the state as taking away their freedom.

All three objections can be urged by the 'individualist', who does not think Bradley's vision of the 'social organism' is at all plausible, where it is the position of this individualist that Bradley outlines immediately after the passage that we just cited, with its high-flown talk of the 'social organism'.[60] Now, it is also clear that it is in order to refute just this view that Bradley turns to his claim about the dependence of individuals for their identity on society and their place within it.[61] After a long

[60] Bradley 1927: 163. Bradley does not identify precisely whom he was thinking of as holding this individualist position; but Peter Nicholson plausibly suggests that he 'perhaps had in mind such writers as Bentham, J. S. Mill, and Herbert Spencer' (Nicholson 1990: 24). For the problem this position raises for the social command theorist, see Wolf 2009: 345, where she notes that for 'the question of society's existence is...a legitimate and serious question...To be sure, we live among other people—in a neighborhood, a state, a world. But is any collection of them sufficiently organized and unified to constitute a group that can be seen to issue commands in the requisite sense?'

[61] Bradley 1927: 166.

disquisition in support of this view, which hinges on how much an individual's identity depends on his place within a social framework, Bradley concludes:

In short, man is a social being; he is real only because he is social, and can realize himself only because it is as social that he realized himself. The mere individual is a delusion of theory; and the attempt to realize it in practice is the starvation and mutilation of human nature, with total sterility or the production of monstrosities.[62]

Bradley's response to the reductionist objection that there cannot be any social commands, because 'in fact' there is no social organism, is that the reduction cannot work, as without the social organism there is 'in fact' no individual. What we see in this talk of identity and one's place in society, therefore, is *not* a defence of an identificatory theory of obligation, but a defence of the idea of society that is needed by the kind of social command theory that Bradley has put forward earlier in the chapter. It is also needed to substantiate his crucial link between duty and self-realization, which on the individualist position does not require the person to have any place within a social whole, while it also shows that this social will is not alien to the agent's own will.

Bradley thus uses his 'identificatory' claims as a way of supporting his anti-individualism and his account of the social organism, which he needs in order to defend his social command theory:

1. there *is* such a thing as the state or society, that can issue commands
2. the individual can realize themselves by following these social duties
3. the individual need not feel 'alienated' from these duties as external impositions, in so far as they are essentially bound up with this social whole.

It can be argued, then, that Bradley's focus on the social identity of the individual does not show that his account of duty based on roles is intended to be identificatory, but rather forms part of an approach that fits better with a social command model.

This is not quite the end of the story, however; for, as we have noted above, *Ethical Studies* is a dialectically structured work. Thus, while 'My Station and Its Duties' may defend a social command theory of the moral duties that attach to social roles, not an identificatory one, this does not mean that Bradley takes this to be the complete account of duties; on the contrary, he frankly acknowledges its limitations—where he argues, for example, that individuals who have a capacity for art or science may have a duty to take up these activities, but where that duty cannot rightfully be imposed on them by the social will, as it is a private matter that does not relate to the good of others,[63] but forms part of what Bradley calls 'ideal morality'. Within this sphere, Bradley suggests, something more like a hybrid model may be appropriate, where the 'ought' arises out of the sense that we fall

[62] Bradley 1927: 174. [63] Bradley 1927: 222–4.

short of being fully good selves because of the presence in us of what is bad[64]—a tension that points beyond morality, to religion. It is not necessary for us to follow Bradley's discussion to this level, however, because our concern has been to assess the account of obligation underlying Bradley's conception of 'my station and its duties', and not that of other aspects of his position.

[64] Cf. Bradley 1927: 232–5 and 293–312. Bradley writes on p. 234: 'Morality does involve a contradiction; it does tell you to realize that which never can be realized, and which, if realized, does efface itself as such. No one ever was or could be perfectly moral; and if he were, he would be moral no longer. Where there is no imperfection there is no ought, where there is no ought there is no morality, where there is no self-contradiction there is no ought. The ought is a self-contradiction.'

11

The Ethics of the British Idealists

Perfectionism after Kant

In his recent magnum opus on the history of ethics, Terence Irwin gives the thought of the British Idealists, and particularly T. H. Green and F. H. Bradley, an unusually prominent role, as in many ways representing the high point of moral philosophy in modern times. This is surprising, because most contemporary ethicists have probably never read their work, and would certainly hesitate to rank them above figures such as J. S. Mill, Henry Sidgwick, G. E. Moore, and John Rawls, for example. However, when one realizes where Irwin's own concerns lie, then this is less surprising. For, Irwin is interested in the Aristotelian tradition within ethics, and its subsequent development, and thus how it has fared in relation to its critics, of which perhaps none is more prominent than Kant. Irwin believes, however, that much of this Kantian critique is misplaced, and that in fact when properly developed, Kant's own thinking turns out to need some appeal to Aristotelian insights, and thus that these apparently divergent traditions can be brought together, to the mutual benefit of each.[1]

However, if Irwin's approach does the British Idealists the great favour of rescuing them from historical obscurity, it also immediately highlights what may be seen as problematic with their views: namely, that by attempting to combine Aristotelianism with Kantianism, they end up with an incoherent position that can only be dialectically unstable. Clearly, then, even if Irwin is right about what the British Idealists were trying to achieve, their impact can only prove to be lasting if they managed to succeed, and so create some sort of genuine synthesis rather than an inconsistent ethical system.

In this chapter, therefore, I want to use Irwin's suggestion as the background to my account of the British Idealists, and to explore it further. I will claim that Irwin's way of locating them within the history of ethics is indeed helpful, while also allowing us to bring out the difficulties in their position. Broadly speaking, I will argue, this position can be understood as a form of 'post-Kantian perfectionism':[2] that is, an

[1] Cf. Irwin 2007: 5. The main discussion of Green and Bradley can be found in Irwin 2009, in chapters 85 and 84, respectively.

[2] I borrow this helpful phrase from Douglas Moggach: see e.g. Moggach 2011.

ethics that is based on claims about how the moral life relates to human self-realization, but while at the same time taking into account Kant's well-known critique of any such view. After Kant, it may have appeared that such perfectionism was a 'dead duck'; but the interest of Green and Bradley, however, is that they self-consciously attempt to show how this response was premature, while nonetheless taking such Kantian concerns seriously. The result, therefore, is a new take on this traditional ethical position, which in their hands is reshaped in unexpected ways.

I will begin by sketching the Kantian critique of perfectionism, before examining how Green and Bradley[3] responded in different ways to that critique, in their attempts to revive what they took to be valuable in the approach that Kant had attempted to surpass.

11.1 The Kantian Critique of Perfectionism

The core ideas behind the approach that Kant took himself to be attacking are helpfully captured in Irwin's summary of Aristotle's position:

[Aristotle] defends an account of the human good as happiness (*eudaimonia*), consisting in the fulfilment of human nature, expressed in the various human virtues. His position is teleological, in so far as it seeks the best guide for action in an ultimate end, eudaimonist, in so far as it identifies the ultimate end with happiness, and naturalist, in so far as it identifies virtue and happiness in a life that fulfils the nature and capacities of rational human nature.[4]

While a position of this sort can be called eudaimonist, it can also be called perfectionist, because it takes such happiness to consist in the development of our distinctive capacities, rather than simply pleasure or desire-satisfaction. On the other hand, it may be distinguished from a more narrow form of perfectionism, which takes this development to be a good in itself, rather than as an aspect of the well-being of the individual.

Within the ethical thinking of his time, and when combined with certain theological themes concerning the purposes of God's creation, this outlook may be taken to be the dominant viewpoint of Kant's contemporaries, where its most influential spokesperson was Christian Wolff. Thus, when Kant came to propose that the much sought-after 'supreme principle of morality' should be 'to never proceed except in such a way *that I could also will that my maxim should become a universal law*',[5] one prominent alternative candidate amongst others that he sought to discredit was the perfectionist principle: 'Seek perfection as much as you can.' Consequently, when Kant sets out to distinguish his account of the supreme principle of morality from all those so far put forward, perfectionism is one of the options he rejects, for several

[3] In what follows, I will be focusing just on Green and Bradley, as these are by common consent the most significant ethicists in the British Idealist tradition. For discussion of other figures such as Edward Caird and Henry Jones, see Mander 2011.

[4] Irwin 2007: 4. [5] Kant *GMM*: 57 [4:402].

related reasons: it is heteronomous; it collapses morality into a system of merely hypothetical imperatives; it makes morality empirical rather than a priori; it puts the good prior to the right; and it is unable to provide any contentful guidance on how we should act. Let us briefly consider each of these points in turn.

According to Kant, all prior attempts to arrive at a supreme principle of morality, including those made by the perfectionist, are misguided because they are based on a heteronomous conception of the will: namely, that the ends of the will are set by desire or inclination, to which reason then determines the means. The consequence, however, is that 'the will in that case does not give itself the law; instead the object, by means of its relation to the will, gives the law to it',[6] and thus autonomy is undermined as reason becomes the slave of the passions. Thus, in the case of perfectionism, Kant argues that the link between perfection and well-being is foundational, where it is then the desire for the latter that is seen to motivate agents in following the principle of perfecting themselves, given the satisfactions that acting in accordance with it will bring. The result, however, is to make practical reason subservient to desire, in a heteronomous manner. Moreover, as a consequence of this connection between perfectionism and well-being, Kant argues, the perfectionist can only treat the imperatives of morality as hypothetical and not categorical: that is, they hold only because we have a sufficiently strong inclination towards the end of happiness to which perfecting ourselves and our capacities is the means. Furthermore, the position is a consequentialist and hence empirical one, for the rightness of an act is determined by how far it increases perfection, and this can be determined only on the basis of experience, whereas for Kant moral judgements should be possible a priori.[7]

As well as these mistakes, Kant also accuses perfectionism of making a fundamental but tempting methodological error in conducting its inquiry into the supreme principle of morality: namely, of starting from a conception of what is good, and from that trying to arrive at an account of the moral law, whereas for Kant we must proceed the other way round if we are not to be led into confusion. For, Kant argues, if we try to conceive of the good unconstrained by some prior conception of the moral law, we will inevitably think of the good in terms of happiness and pleasure, and thus end up with the sort of heteronomous and hypothetical view of morality that one finds in perfectionism, amongst other moral systems.[8] Kant allows that perhaps the perfectionist might respond to a worry of this sort by accepting Kant's point and so holding that attributes are not perfections because they make us happy, but because they make us morally good; but then, Kant argues, the perfectionist principle is an empty one, because we now need to know what it is to be morally good before we can assess

[6] Kant *GMM*: 89 [4:441].

[7] For helpful further discussion of some of these themes, see Guyer 2011.

[8] Kant *CPrR*: 186–7 [5:58]; cf. also 191–3 [5:64–5].

which attributes to cultivate and which capacities to realize, so the position is hopelessly circular, and cannot help us decide how to act.[9]

We have therefore seen the problems that Kant raised for the perfectionist tradition, which may seem to leave it fatally damaged. Nonetheless, of course, Kant's own position is far from unproblematic, so that once this became apparent, it was perhaps inevitable that the attempt would be made to see if in fact these two approaches can be brought together somehow to the mutual advantage of both, rather than beings set at odds with one another. As Irwin has argued, the British Idealists may be seen as adopting this strategy, and thus as developing perfectionism in a post-Kantian form, which takes aspects of Kant's critique on board, and modifies the position accordingly, thereby giving it a new lease of life.

11.2 Two Forms of Perfectionism: Capacity-based and Holistic

Before we turn to the discussion of the work of Green and Bradley, however, it is useful to draw out a distinction within the perfectionist approach which (I will claim) underlies an important difference in their respective approaches, and thus in the way that each tries to deal with the Kantian challenge. This is the distinction between a perfectionism which sees the ideal self as one that has fully developed its capacities or capabilities, and a perfectionism which sees the ideal self as a unified or harmonious whole.

This difference may be traced back to the origins of this tradition in Plato and in Aristotle. Thus, for Plato, goodness is taken to be a proper balance or order among parts in a holistic manner,[10] whilst for Aristotle the focus is more on how far certain potentialities or capacities are realized and successfully developed. In general, it might be argued, Aristotle's approach is the predominant one, and can be found for example in Aquinas when he contrasts the imperfection of potentiality with the perfection of actuality.[11] However, Plato's outlook also remains embedded in the perfectionist tradition. Thus, for example, while his position also contains Aristotelian elements, Wolff argues that 'The harmony [*Zusammenstimmung*] of the manifold constitutes the perfection of things',[12] so that the perfection of the will consists in 'the harmony of all and every volition with one another, none running contrary to the rest'.[13]

[9] Cf. Kant *GMM*: 91 [4:443]: '[Perfectionism] has an unavoidable propensity to get involved in a circle and cannot avoid covertly presupposing the morality it is supposed to explain.'

[10] Cf. Kraut 1992: 322: 'The goodness of Forms consists in the fact that they possess a kind of harmony, balance, or proportion; and their superiority to all other things consists in the fact that the kind of order they possess gives them a higher degree of harmony than any other type of object.' In support of this reading, Kraut cites *Philebus* 23c–d and 64d–e.

[11] Aquinas 1920: 1–2 question 3, article 2.

[12] Wolff 1751: §152. Cf. Baumgarten 1779: §94.

[13] Wolff 1751: §907.

Now of course, both forms of perfectionism can easily be put together, in the thought that in order to realize our capacities, we must do so in a harmonious manner, without each being at odds with the others; or, it could be argued that some capacities can only themselves be properly actualized in a unified and coherent way. This convergence between the two views explains why they are often run together and the difference is not usually highlighted or held to be significant. Nonetheless, they are still conceptually distinct; and, I will now suggest, when it comes to Green and Bradley, they do indeed come apart, under the pressure of finding an adequate perfectionist response to Kant's critique.

11.3 Green's Capacity-based Perfectionism

In his *Prolegomena to Ethics*, Green prefaces his theory of morality with an important discussion of the will in Book II. He starts by offering an account of action, where he argues that what guides the will is not some specific want or desire, but a conception of the agent's own greatest good—hence, he claims, the agent in acting aims at 'self-satisfaction'.[14] For Green, therefore, when it comes to making a choice, there is no selection between competing desires made by the will; rather, the choice is made in determining which of the desires, if satisfied, would constitute the agent's greatest good, and on the basis of this decision the will then comes to act, with the other desires having been silenced.[15]

Green recognizes, however, that this picture leaves an important question unanswered when it comes to ethics: namely, what is it that distinguishes a morally good will from a morally bad one? Of course, on some accounts, this difference is marked by a distinction between the good agent who has no concern for their own well-being, and a bad one who is so concerned: but Green cannot take this option, given his account of action outlined above where such self-concern is present in *all* agents—so where does the difference lie? Green's answer is that the difference comes from the different conceptions of self-satisfaction that agents can have, and thus in 'the character of that in which self-satisfaction is sought, ranging from sensual pleasure to the fulfilment of a vocation conceived as given by God'.[16] Green's position depends, therefore, on making out some grounds on which to distinguish good and bad conceptions of self-satisfaction that might be held by different agents, where this explains the basis on which we might make a moral distinction between them.

For Green, then, the difference between the good and the bad person lies in their different conceptions of where and in what manner they can find self-satisfaction, and what this consists in.[17] But Green recognizes a difficulty: namely, that there is a circle here, as we seem to have to already know what moral goodness consists in

[14] Cf. Green 2003: §95, p. 106.
[15] Cf. Green 2003: §104, pp. 116–17, and §§145–6, pp. 163–5.
[16] Green 2003: §154, p. 175.
[17] Cf. Green 2003: §171, pp. 194–6.

before we can characterize an agent as moral and thus what the self-satisfaction of such an agent will involve; and on the other hand, if we do already know what such moral goodness amounts to, we wouldn't have to characterize it as what brings satisfaction to the moral agent, but must be able to grasp it independently in a prior manner, or not at all.[18] Faced with this difficulty, Green refers back to the metaphysical theorizing that he had developed in Book I of the *Prolegomena*, before he turned to the will and ethics as such, which argued that the world is the realization of a self-developing eternal mind;[19] and from this, he thinks we are entitled to infer that what leads to the fulfilling of our capacities and thus our self-satisfaction is also what is morally good, and vice versa.[20]

We have seen, then, that Green holds that the good agent aims at the realization of his or her capacities, where he now argues that this 'will keep before him an object, which he presents to himself as absolutely desirable, but which is other than any particular object of desire'.[21] In the case of such particular objects, he will take these to have value only in so far as they satisfy some desire of his; but in the case of his self-realization, '[i]t will be an interest as in an object conceived to be of unconditional value; one of which the value does not depend on any desire that the individual may at any time feel for it or for anything else, or on any pleasure that, either in its pursuit or in its attainment or as its result, he may experience'.[22] In other words, Green claims that while the agent may see the value of everything else in terms of his wants and their attendant pleasures, he does not see the realization of his capacities in this way, as these constitute the end against which such wants and pleasures are themselves measured.[23]

However, we still have the problem of specifying what this unconditional good of self-realization consists in, where if we say that it is what the good will is directed towards, we will just be 'moving in a circle', because we have no independent conception of the good will, while the complete realization of human capacities has not yet been achieved.[24] Nonetheless, Green thinks, we can turn to the history of ethics to provide us with an important clue, where the key here (he argues) has been the central 'moral ideal' of the common good, in which individuals find their good to be bound up with that of others. At an earlier stage, in Greek ethics, these 'others' just comprised one's immediate community or polis; but in Christian ethics, this is widened to include all individuals. As a result of this conception of self-realization, Green argues that the distinction between 'benevolence' and 'self-love', and thus Sidgwick's famous 'dualism of practical reason', collapses and is shown to be a 'fiction',[25] insofar as no clear distinction can be drawn between the good of the individual and that of the society of which he or she is part, as the former good

[18] Cf. Green 2003: §172, pp. 196–7.
[19] Cf. Green 2003: §67, pp. 77–8.
[20] Cf. Green 2003: §181, pp. 207–8.
[21] Green 2003: §193, p. 221.
[22] Green 2003: §193, p. 222.
[23] Cf. Green 2003: §193, pp. 222–3.
[24] Cf. Green 2003: §194, pp. 223–4.
[25] Green 2003: §232, p. 272.

depends on the latter. Green therefore writes that '[t]he opposition of self and others does not enter into the consideration of a well-being so constituted'.[26] Thus, Green argues, the agent will come to treat others not merely as means, but also as ends, in so far as he will be 'living for an object common to himself and all rational beings and consisting in the perfection of the rational nature', not just in himself but also in others.[27]

Finally, in Book IV, Green considers how far his account can help in providing us with guidance for conduct. Here he admits that superficially, at least, a theory like utilitarianism may appear to be in a better position, in seeming to give us a more concrete criterion of right action. On the other hand, he argues, in practice the calculation of consequences in utilitarian terms is in fact virtually impossible, while the very search for a simple solution to cases of moral perplexity is itself wrong-headed. Thus, Green argues, while it may not be easy to use perfection to tell us how to act, it is perhaps no worse off than any other moral theory is or should be.

Taken as whole, therefore, it is easy to see why Green's student D. G. Ritchie should have characterized his view as having 'corrected Kant by Aristotle and Aristotle by Kant';[28] for, while returning to something like Aristotle's eudaimonism, this also takes a 'post-Kantian' form, and is importantly shaped by Kant's critique of the perfectionist tradition. So, in response to the charge of heteronomy, Green argues that our conception of the good is not merely set for us by desires and their satisfaction in a subjectivist manner, but involves the use of reason to determine where our proper self-satisfaction lies.[29] Thus, he argues, moral requirements can be based on the good of self-realization but still be categorical imperatives, as this goodness is independent of contingent inclinations and interests.[30] Green also shows himself to be sensitive to Kantian concerns regarding the priority of the moral law over the good, where the claim is that we must use the former to determine the latter; Green responds to this concern by using the history of ethics as a guide to the nature of self-realization, and so does not first try to offer an account of the good that does not take the principles of morality into account. Moreover, Green tries to deal with Kant's objection that the criterion of perfection is circular or morally empty—or at least, is no more so that Kant's own criterion of universalizability, or the utilitarian criterion of the greatest happiness of the greatest number. At the same time, Green may claim to have 'corrected Kant by Aristotle', in offering a theory of action and motivation that gives a more central and plausible role to the conative side of the self, and hence shows how some of Kant's notorious dichotomies can be overcome, for example between duty and

[26] Green 2003: §235, p. 276. Cf. also §232, p. 273: 'His own permanent well-being he thus necessarily presents for himself as a social well-being.'

[27] Green 1885–8a: §118, p. 139. [28] Ritchie 1891: 139. [29] But cf. Skorupski 2006: 57–8.

[30] Cf. Green 2003: §193, pp. 221–3.

inclination, reason and desire. Finally, the sense in which Green is a 'post-Kantian perfectionist' may be underlined by the way in which he connects self-realization not only with flourishing but also with freedom as a form of autonomy, in a way that gives a distinctively Kantian slant to his perfectionism.

At the same time, however, Green's way of trying to accommodate Kant's concerns may seem to reveal the weakness of his capacity-based view of perfectionism. For example, he is required to appeal to a 'divine principle' to justify his claim that we will find proper self-realization in a morally good end and vice versa, which then allows him to use the history of ethics as a guide to what human self-realization involves. This enables him to avoid the essentialist or biologistic claims of the Aristotelian regarding what our capacities consist in that then need to be exercised in order to attain flourishing; but he does so at the price of having to rely on his idealist metaphysics. Moreover, the Kantian may object to Green's attempt to show how, by starting off with a concern for our own self-realization, we will end up with a concern for that of others, based on his claim that an individual's good requires him or her to promote a common good, that is, a good in which others also share. There are two worries here. First, the bridge Green tries to build from the individual's good to the common good may seem shaky, for it seems plausible to argue (as Sidgwick does, for example)[31] that my self-realization, conceived of as the development of my capacities, will not always mean that it is best served through contributing to the good of others; or at least, Green's account of what self-realization involves seems too vague to assert this connection with any great confidence,[32] where it could plausibly be argued that some aspects of my good requires not co-operation with others, but competition against them. Second, even if this connection could be assumed, the Kantian may still argue that while on Green's picture there is a categorical imperative to realize in me a certain kind of character, and while that character may be one that takes an interest in the good of others as well as myself, nonetheless ultimately this interest is still not properly impartial, as my reason to have this attitude is that I will then have the right conception of my own good, in a way that is ultimately concerns the benefits it brings to me in terms of self-satisfaction, and so is egoistic and not properly ethical.[33] In this way, Kant may think, his claims about morality as involving an impartial concern with the significance of others are still not properly accommodated within Green's perfectionism, and that his attempts to revive Aristotelianism in this post-Kantian form have failed.

We will now consider Bradley's approach, which involves a rather different view of the perfectionist position, in a way that may allow us to see how some of these concerns might be addressed.

[31] Cf. Sidgwick 1902: 47–8 and 64. [32] Sidgwick 1902: 55–6.

[33] Cf. Dewey 1873: 51. Cf. also Prichard 2002b: 43.

11.4 Bradley's Holistic Perfectionism

In the second 'essay' or chapter of *Ethical Studies*, Bradley appears to show himself to be sensitive to the some of the concerns that have been raised in this paper so far regarding Green's position, and to echo Kantian worries over the attempt to offer a perfectionist answer to the question of 'why should I be moral?' For, Bradley observes (in ways that came to be associated with H. A. Prichard some decades later),[34] unless this is itself a moral question (in which case the answer is obvious), it will make being moral into the means to a non-moral end, as concerning the interests of the individual, where 'to take virtue as a mere means to an ulterior end is in direct antagonism to the voice of the moral consciousness'.[35] Bradley may thus seem to be more alert than Green to the dangers of approaching morality in a perfectionist spirit, and hoping to find in it a response to the question of 'why be moral?'

However, despite this, Bradley still thinks that the question can be given *some* meaning that will not lead us astray: for instead of asking if some prior end gives us a sufficient reason or motive to be moral, we can still ask what the *relation* is between acting morally and achieving our ultimate end qua human being and thus our good, even when we do not think of the former as the means to the latter, where the question then becomes: 'Is morality the same as the end for man, so that the two are convertible; or is morality one side, or aspect, or element of some end which is larger than itself? Is it the whole end from all points of view, or is it one view of the whole?'[36] Now, to answer *this* question, of course, requires us to specify what 'the end for man' is, which Bradley says is *self-realization*. He admits at once, however, that it is hard for him to prove this claim, as to do so would require 'something like a system of metaphysics',[37] which he cannot hope to provide here; nonetheless, he thinks it can be made plausible if we think about the nature of action, where again like Green he emphasizes that on a variety of different accounts, actions only occur if and when we 'feel ourselves asserted or affirmed in them',[38] and so take ourselves to realize ourselves in so acting.

At this point, therefore, Bradley thinks he is entitled to ask about the relation between morality and self-realization;[39] but now of course he needs to tell us something about self-realization and what this amounts to. It is here that his holistic perfectionism begins to emerge, where he argues that what the individual is trying to realize cannot be a 'mere one' or a 'mere many', but rather a 'one in many, or a many in one'—namely, 'the self as a whole, which is not merely the sum of its parts, nor yet some other particular beside them'. Thus Bradley asks rhetorically, 'must we not say that to realize self is always to realize a whole, and that the question in morals is to find the true whole, realizing which will practically realize the true self?'[40] This, then,

[34] Prichard 2002a.
[35] Bradley 1927: 61.
[36] Bradley 1927: 64.
[37] Bradley 1927: 65.
[38] Bradley 1927: 68.
[39] Cf. Bradley 1927: 214 and 228.
[40] Bradley 1927: 68–9.

gives the focus for the rest of *Ethical Studies*, as we can now ask, of various ethical systems, whether on their accounts morality as they conceive it would coincide with self-realization taken in this way, and thus how it would relate to 'the end for man'.

On this basis, therefore, Bradley argues that a morality of 'pleasure for pleasure's sake' or of 'duty for duty's sake' (which roughly correspond to utilitarianism and Kantianism respectively) cannot be satisfactory, as in neither can the self realize itself as a whole, as each position takes a one-sided view of this totality: the former views the self as a collection of particular interests, while the latter views it as a pure will operating at an abstractly universal level standing above all such differentiation.[41] Moving in a dialectical manner, Bradley then introduces a third option of 'my station and its duties', that seems to resolve the one-sided opposition between these earlier alternatives, and thus arrive at a moral outlook that can do justice to the unity-in-difference of the self, by balancing the plurality of particularity with the oneness of universality.

What this requires, Bradley argues, is that morality comes from the ethical life of the community, in which there is room for both particularity and universality, as the individual carries out the specific and concrete social role that they occupy, while that role fits into a wider and more universal totality of which the individual is a part.[42] Earlier in *Ethical Studies*, Bradley had adapted a saying of Goethe's to write: 'You can not be a whole, *unless* you join a whole',[43] where it is thus in the unity of the community with its ethics of 'my station and its duties' that the self can be realized in this holistic sense.

However, despite arguing with considerable rhetorical force for this position,[44] Bradley also recognizes its limitations, including the worry that the individual may live within an imperfect state and so find no self-realization in ethical life, or may find such self-realization elsewhere, outside the moral life of the community altogether, for example in scientific inquiry or aesthetic production. Thus, in his search for a view of morality that coincides more fully with self-realization, Bradley moves to what he calls 'ideal morality', where the moral is seen as including more than the social relations of 'my station and its duties', and so as involving both demands that may be made on us beyond those required by any actual society, and also the kinds of duties to oneself that make the life of the artist or theorist moral in this broader sense.[45] Once broadened in this way, Bradley observes, it may be tempting to answer his original question in the affirmative.[46]

[41] Bradley 1927: 142.

[42] The influence of the Hegelian notion of *Sittlichkeit* is clearly very strong at this point in the text.

[43] Bradley 1927: 79.

[44] Bradley admits on p. 202 that 'perhaps we have heated ourselves a little' in presenting the outlook of 'my station and its duties'.

[45] Cf. Bradley 1927: 222–3. Green also raises this kind of case as a concern for his social ethics, but did not develop a response to it: see Green 2003: §§289–90, pp. 343–5.

[46] Cf. Bradley 1927: 228.

However, despite this seemingly optimistic result of his inquiries so far, Bradley still raises a difficulty: for morality, he thinks, involves what *ought* to be, not what *is*, and this always incorporates a gap between our actual existence and our full and final self-realization, so that for morality to make sense at all, the two can never coincide completely.[47] It is this tension, Bradley holds, that in thinking about self-realization takes us beyond morality altogether, and into religion, where *Ethical Studies* closes.

Before it does so, however, Bradley interposes a chapter on 'Selfishness and Self-Sacrifice', in which inter alia he considers how far a theory like his might be accused of doing away with morality and reducing it to self-interest, in so far as he holds that 'there is self-realization in all action; witness the feeling of pleasure'.[48] He argues, however, that while pleasure does indeed come from self-realization, this does not make pleasure the motive for the action, or our reason for it, and the same is true of self-realization itself; he therefore rejects the charge of selfishness that might be raised against his perfectionist ethics.[49]

We can again see, therefore, how far Bradley's form of perfectionism attempts to offer a 'post-Kantian' variant on this tradition, by attempting to respond to or avoid Kant's criticisms of this position in ethics. Bradley in a sense concedes a good deal of ground to those criticisms, for example by allowing that perfectionism cannot and should not provide an answer to the moral sceptic, or set itself up as offering guidance as a 'supreme principle of morality'. On the other hand, he argues that the former goal is inappropriate, while we can still intelligibly ask questions regarding the relation between morality and self-realization, and whether in acting morally we *do* realize ourselves, even while allowing that we do not act morally *in order to do so* in an instrumental fashion; and as regards the latter, Bradley argues that this is also not the business of moral theory, and that Kant himself is no more successful than other moralists in providing us with such a 'supreme principle'.[50] In this sense, his strategy is more sophisticated than Green's, who is generally not so self-conscious about the limitations of his project, and the justifications for such limitations.

Equally, perhaps, Bradley's holistic perfectionism helps him avoid the difficulties that Green had in having to employ his metaphysics to show why the capacities we have can best be realized in the moral life. Bradley's answer, by contrast, depends on his account of the structure of the will and its possible harmony,[51] rather than appealing to the 'divine principle' in man to ensure that self-realization and morality will coincide. While of course not without its problems, this would seem to give perfectionism a basis that is likeliest to be persuasive to the contemporary mind, and

[47] Bradley 1927: 234–5. [48] Bradley 1927: 84.
[49] Cf. Bradley 1927: 62 note. Green makes a similar point: see Green 2003: §158, pp. 179–80.
[50] Cf. Bradley 1927: 193. [51] Cf. Bradley 1927: 71–3.

thus of the two idealist thinkers, to offer us the more powerful insight into a perfectionism that takes this post-Kantian form. At the very least, it should now perhaps be clear that as a result of the Kantian critique, perfectionism came to take two rather different forms in the hands of its idealist proponents, so what had formerly been inseparable aspects of this tradition—the capacity view and the holistic view—here come apart, with Green emphasizing one aspect, and Bradley the other.

12

Round Kant or through Him?

On James's Arguments for Freedom, and their Relation to Kant's

My title is a reference to a famous remark that James makes about Kant:

> I believe that Kant bequeathes to us not one single conception which is both indispensable to philosophy and which philosophy either did not possess before him, or was not destined inevitably to acquire after him through the growth of men's reflection upon the hypotheses by which science interprets nature. The true line of philosophic progress lies, in short, it seems to me, not so much *through* Kant as *round* him to the point where now we stand.

This comes at the end of his 1904 essay 'The Pragmatic Method', where he is arguing that Kant's critical philosophy is not really much of an advance on the approach of the 'English-speaking philosophers', who he sees as the ancestors of pragmatism insofar as they 'introduced the custom of interpreting the meaning of conceptions by asking what difference they make for life'. 'Thus', James claims, 'when all is said and done, it was they, not Kant, who introduced "the critical method" into philosophy, the one method fitted to make philosophy a study worthy of serious men. For what seriousness can possibly remain in debating philosophic propositions that will never make an appreciable difference to us in action? And what matters it, when all propositions are practically meaningless, which of them be called true or false?'

Given this situation, James concludes that 'Philosophy can perfectly well outflank [Kant], and build herself up into adequate fullness by prolonging more directly the older English lines'—although he allows that 'connoisseurs' will always be drawn back to exploring the 'wondrous and racy contents' that make up the 'antique bric-a-brac museum' that is Kant's mind.[1]

But does this present a fair picture of James's attitude to Kant, and of his indebtedness to him? Is it right to see James (and on James's view, pragmatism itself) as nothing but an extension of the 'older English lines' of thought, to which Kant is at best nothing more than an optional and perhaps diverting detour? These are large

[1] 'The Pragmatic Method', 5:138–9. References to James's works are to James 1975–88, by volume and page number.

questions, which have already received a fair amount of discussion.[2] But here I want to take a somewhat narrower focus, and consider in particular James's arguments for freedom,[3] particularly those offered in his essay 'The Dilemma of Determinism' (1897).

While on some readings of both Kant's idealism and James's pragmatism which will be discussed below, it may indeed seem that each must be committed to radically different arguments for freedom, I will argue that this essay shows their approaches to be very close, which perhaps suggests that their fundamental philosophical views are not so far apart after all—and that without some influence on him of a Kantian outlook, James could not have got to his final destination, suggesting that Kant is perhaps no mere detour after all.

My strategy will be to present two rather contrasting ways of understanding the way in which James as a pragmatist and Kant as an idealist seem to approach the problem of freedom, and then to argue that as we refine their respective positions, James and Kant can be brought closer and closer together, and in a manner that shows there to be a fundamental Kantian aspect to James's thinking on this issue, in a way that I hope does credit to them both.

12.1 Pragmatism and Idealism on Freedom: A First Pass

One way to approach James's account of freedom in 'The Dilemma of Determinism' is in the light of 'The Will to Believe', which was published in the same year, where that latter essay has been seen as defending a characteristically Jamesian attitude to matters of belief, justification, and evidence.

The interpretation of that paper is of course disputed, but on one account James can be read as claiming 'that it is foolish not to believe, or try to believe, if one is

[2] For one helpful contribution, see Carlson 1997. See also Evans 1982.

[3] In speaking about 'freedom' in this context, two cautionary remarks are needed. First, as James makes clear at the start of the article in question, he takes himself not to be arguing for freedom, but rather indeterminism—because he thinks the term freedom has been co-opted by the kind of 'soft determinism' that he takes to be incoherent and so abhors, and he therefore says he will eschew the term: 'The word "chance" I wish to keep, but I wish to get rid of the word "freedom." Its eulogistic associations have so far overshadowed all the rest of its meaning that both parties claim sole right to use it, and determinists to-day insist that they alone are freedom's champions... Now all this is a quagmire of evasion under which the real issue of fact has been entirely smothered... [The issue of fact] is the question of determinism, about which we are to talk to-night' (6:117). At the risk of some confusion, however, I will talk about freedom as much as indeterminism, so it should be borne in mind that when it comes to James, it is freedom in this latter sense that is at issue. The second point to note here is that of course this does not necessarily correspond exactly to what *Kant* means in speaking about freedom and (especially) autonomy, so that the conclusions of the two thinkers using the arguments we will consider are not necessarily to be equated. But since my main aim is to focus on the *strategy* they both employ, not the validity of these arguments as such, I will also largely set this complication to one side.

happier for believing',[4] or slightly more moderately that 'one has a *right* to believe ahead of the evidence, if one is happier for believing'.[5] This way of understanding James's view seems to have been the one that Peirce adopted when he characterizes a religious believer as saying: 'Oh, I could not believe so-and-so, because I would be wretched if I did'; and then rejected it with the scornful remark: 'When an ostrich buries its head in the sand as danger approaches, it very likely takes the happiest course'.[6] So, as Cheryl Misak summarizes this approach (which she seems to favour as the correct reading of James): 'James wants to expand the concept of evidence . . . to include as evidence the satisfaction of the believer' (Misak 2013: 63)—where to most evidentialists (including Misak, it appears),[7] this 'expansion' is enough to take James out of the evidentialist camp altogether, where this is then said to be James's aim, and so to lie at the heart of his dispute with Clifford, amongst others.[8]

If this is seen as James's approach in 'The Will to Believe', this then might suggest the following underlying argument for freedom in 'The Dilemma of Determinism': In this essay, James argues that unless we reject determinism, we will be left with a thoroughly pessimistic view of reality, as we cannot intelligibly regret the bad features of the world, and think they may not be intrinsic to it, as 'other things being what they are, *it* could not be different'.[9] James might therefore be read as taking the gloomy implications of determinism as sufficient grounds on which to reject it, in line with this interpretation of 'The Will to Believe'. This, if it were the correct way to make sense of him, would then give us a distinctively pragmatist defence of freedom, which would seem to have little corresponding to it on the idealist side.

Likewise, one could understand Kant's defence of freedom in an idealist manner that would have little echo in pragmatism. On this approach, Kant could be read as claiming on transcendental grounds that we have no option but to believe that we are free, perhaps because it cannot be doubted from the perspective of an agent, where

[4] Letter from Chauncey Wright; cited Misak 2013: 63.

[5] Misak 2011: 262.

[6] Peirce 1992b: 116; cited Misak 2011: 64. This cannot be taken as Peirce's response to 'The Will to Believe' itself, as it appears almost two decades before James gave his lecture in 1896, in 1877; but James espouses similar views in earlier publications, while as Misak makes clear, Wright and James had been disputing the issue from 1875, where the dispute was well known to people in their circle, including Peirce.

[7] Cf. Misak 2011: 67: 'We have seen that one way of thinking of James's view has it being compatible with evidentialism—with the view that one should believe in accord with one's evidence. But he has a view of evidence that is anathema to the evidentialist.' Cf. also p. 63: 'One of the ways in which James wants to expand the concept of evidence is to include as evidence the satisfaction of the believer. This is something the evidentialist will be loathe to accept. He will argue that the evidence for the truth of a belief cannot come in the form of the belief making me happy, or you comfortable.' Cf. *Principles of Psychology*, volume I, 8:322: 'The reader who finds any comfort in the idea of the Soul is, however, perfectly free to continue to believe in it; for our reasonings have not established the non-existence of the Soul; they have only proved its superfluity for scientific purposes.'

[8] Cf. 'The Sentiment of Rationality', 6:80: 'Our reasons are ludicrously incommensurate with the volume of our feeling, yet on the latter we unhesitatingly act . . . [B]elief (as measured by action) not only does and must continually outstrip scientific evidence.'

[9] James 6:126.

this then brings in considerations in support of freedom that have nothing to do with the effects of this belief on our happiness or well-being. Here, then, we would have an idealist argument for freedom, which in turn would seem to have little resemblance to a pragmatist approach as outlined above.

If these readings of James and Kant respectively are accepted, therefore, it would seem that there is little common ground between the two of them on this issue. However, it seems to me that both these readings would fail to capture properly their respective positions, where with further refinements they can be brought closer together.

12.2 Pragmatism and Idealism on Freedom: Further Refinements

A first refinement we can make to James's view is to question whether he really thought the best defence of freedom was that believing in it would increase our satisfaction by making pessimism less likely. For, even when it comes to 'The Will to Believe' itself, it is by no means clear that this is his *general* account of justification for belief. For, of course, James places significant limits to the kinds of cases to which he thinks his approach should be applied:[10] namely when the options in question are *living*, *forced*, and *momentous*, and where the question cannot be decided on 'intellectual grounds'.[11] In such circumstances, James can be read as arguing, we are not required to sit and wait for conclusive evidence to come in, as we do not have this luxury, while such proof is rarely if ever available anyway; instead he thinks we are entitled to adopt the belief in question, where if we did not, we would be sure to lose the 'goods' that accepting it would bring.

Thus, in the religious case, he holds that we cannot ever get into a position of knowing for sure if God exists or does not; and on this basis, James can be taken to argue that it is therefore not necessary for us to wait for such evidence to be available, but instead we can believe in God based on the benefits to us that accepting such belief will entail:

When I look at the religious question as it really puts itself to concrete men, and when I think of all the possibilities which both practically and theoretically it involves, then this command that we shall put a stopper on our heart, instincts and courage, and *wait*—acting of course meanwhile more or less as if religion were *not* true—till doomsday, or till such time as our intellect and sense working together may have raked in evidence enough—this command, I say, seems to me the queerest idol ever manufactured in the philosophic cave.[12]

[10] Cf. James 1992–2004: 10:449: 'I hedged my license to indulge in private faith with so many restrictions and signboards of danger that the outlet was narrow enough.'

[11] 'The Will to Believe', 6:20.

[12] James 6:117.

Like the earlier view, this is still a form of anti-evidentialism, but a more moderate kind than previously, as it is allowing that we can believe *p* on non-epistemic grounds only in cases where conclusive evidence is hard or not possible to attain—but where James's fallibilism concerning human knowledge means that in practice this will be most of the time. James's justification for the view seems to be that on many occasions we must act if we are not to lose the good in question altogether,[13] where then waiting for further evidence in our epistemic condition is not a rational option to pursue, even at the risk of possible error.

We may then think of this more moderate anti-evidentialism in relation to an argument for freedom, where we could take James to be arguing in the following way: There is no compelling evidence for or against determinism, and it is unlikely that there can even be any, while belief in freedom also meets the conditions of being live, forced, and momentous, and where rejecting this belief would lead to a pessimistic and life-sapping world view:

> [The principle of causality] is as much an altar to an unknown god as the one that Saint Paul found at Athens. All our scientific and philosophic ideals are altars to unknown gods. Uniformity is as much so as is free-will. If this be admitted, we can debate on even terms.[14]

> Now, evidence of an external kind to decide between determinism and indeterminism is, as I intimated a while back, strictly impossible to find.[15]

This way of taking James's position may then take us closer to a widespread way of reading Kant, and his emphasis on 'the primacy of practical reason', which can be understood in the following terms: Theoretical reason must leave certain questions undecided, because of the limitations of human understanding, where at this point we are entitled to believe claims about the world on practical grounds instead, that is, on the grounds that these beliefs are required if we are to act in certain ways and not others, where we take it that such actions bring with them certain 'goods', such as more knowledge of the world (as in the case of regulative ideas) or the greater likelihood of moral action (as in the postulates).[16]

[13] Cf. 'Bain and Renouvier' [1876] in James 1975–88, 17:326: 'This brings us back to our theoretical dilemma about freedom, concerning which we must now bow to the necessity of making a choice; for suspense itself would be a choice, and a most practical one, since by it we should forfeit the possible benefits of boldly espousing a possible truth. If this *be* a moral world, there are cases in which any indecision about its being so must be death to the soul. Now, if our choice is predetermined, there is an end of the matter; whether predetermined to the truth of fatality or the delusion of liberty, is all one for us. But if our choice is truly free, then the only possible way of getting at that truth is by the exercise of the freedom which it implies.' In the same essay, James also follows Renouvier in insisting that 'The "assumption" of a fixed law in natural science' and 'the assumption of an ultimate law of indetermination' are positions between which 'no man can decide empirically' (17:325).

[14] James 6:116. [15] James 6:117.

[16] Cf. James 1992–2004: 8:275: '*Adopt your hypothesis*, and see how it agrees with life—That is faith. As Kant says I have swept away knowledge in order to make room for Faith; and that seems to me the absolutely sound and healthy position.'

So we now appear to have brought James and Kant closer together: On the first way of taking the positions of James and Kant, as based on extreme non-evidentialism and on a transcendental claim respectively, they looked very different. But now they look more convergent, as two forms of what has been called 'practical non-evidentialism'.[17]

Of course, this doesn't mean they are exactly the same: In particular, their arguments for the claim regarding the impotence of theoretical reason are different: For James in 'The Will to Believe' it is mainly a general appeal to fallibilism and the role of hypotheses in inquiry,[18] while in 'The Dilemma of Determinism' it is more like a claim about theoretical underdetermination: at the highest level, when we are dealing with fundamental world-views, there just cannot be any 'objective' or 'external' evidence to settle the choice between them:

> Facts practically have hardly anything to do with making us either determinists or indeterminists. Sure enough, we make a flourish of quoting facts this way or that... But who does not see the wretched insufficiency of this so-called objective testimony on both sides? What fills up the gaps in our minds is something not objective, not external. What divides us into possibility men and anti-possibility men is different faiths or postulates—postulates of rationality. To this man the world seems more rational with possibilities in it—to that man more rational with possibilities excluded; and talk as we will about having to yield to evidence, what makes us monists or pluralists, determinists or indeterminists, is at bottom always some sentiment like this.[19]

For James, when it comes to these fundamental philosophical choices, 'hard evidence' will never settle the issue, which then opens up the space for a different approach.[20] But for Kant, it is the structure of transcendental idealism that opens up this space, with his claims about the limits of our capacity to fully grasp the nature of 'things as they are in themselves'—given which theoretical reason has inevitable limits.

Nonetheless, notwithstanding this significant difference, it still may now seem that James and Kant are broadly similar in the strategy they adopt for the defence of our belief in freedom.

12.3 Pragmatism and Idealism on Freedom: Another Step

However, I now want to suggest that this approach to Kant's position on freedom, while pretty widespread and familiar,[21] is mistaken, and that Kant is much closer to

[17] Chignell 2013: §6.1. Cf. also Chignell 2007: 354–7 and 335, where Chignell comments that the 'antievidentialist flavor [of Kant's project] anticipates strands of later pragmatism'.

[18] On the latter, cf. Klein 2015.

[19] James 6:119.

[20] Cf. also 'The Sentiment of Rationality', 6:66.

[21] For a recent defence of a non-evidentialist reading of Kant, see Willaschek 2010, e.g. pp. 168–9: 'In several places in his work, most prominently in the Dialectic of his *Critique of Practical Reason*, Kant has

an evidentialist position on this matter than this assumes—where then (if I am right in my account of Kant) the question arises whether James is an evidentialist concerning freedom too, or whether in the end they remain apart on this issue because he takes the non-evidentialist option where Kant does not. Let me begin by giving my reasons for thinking that Kant is a particular kind of evidentialist in his argument for freedom. I will here focus on Kant's discussion in the *Critique of Practical Reason*: as will be considered in §12.4, problems with my reading may make it necessary to bring in other discussions, which will therefore be dealt with there.

Kant's argument in the *Critique of Practical Reason* centres on the example of a man who is asked to give false testimony, on pain of immediate execution. Kant argues that the man will be conscious that he ought to overcome his love of life, and refuse to give false witness; but because ought implies can, he must also hold that he is free to act in this way, even if in fact he might not do so because he could be tempted to do other than he ought to do:

> He would perhaps not venture to assert whether he would do it or not, but he must admit without hesitation that it would be possible for him. He judges, therefore, that he can do something because he is aware [bewußt] that he ought to do it and cognizes freedom within him, which, without the moral law, would have remained unknown to him.[22]

Kant takes this example to confirm that 'morality first discloses to us the concept of freedom',[23] rather than the other way round, and so is the '*ratio cognoscendi* of freedom': 'For, had not the moral law *already* been distinctly thought in our reason, we should never consider ourselves justified in *assuming* such as thing as freedom (even though it is not self-contradictory). But were there no freedom, the moral law would *not be encountered* at all in ourselves.'[24] This then gives the moral law the status of a 'fact of reason' for Kant:

> Consciousness of this fundamental law may be called a fact of reason because one cannot reason it out from antecedent data of reason, for example, from consciousness of freedom (since this is not antecedently given to us) and because it instead forces itself upon us of itself as a synthetic a priori proposition that is not based on any intuition.[25]

The question I want to raise, then, is how far this argument should be seen as offering a non-evidentialist argument for freedom?

My claim is that it is in fact perfectly evidentialist; all that may make it seem otherwise is that the evidence in question comes not from what theoretical reason tells, but rather from what practical reason tells us instead. In *this* sense, then, practical reason has priority over theoretical reason: namely, that the evidence we

denied the unrestricted validity of the principle that rational belief requires evidence in favour of its truth. Rather, we can be rationally warranted in a belief even in the complete absence of evidence for it.' Willaschek draws a parallel between Kant and James on these issues on pp. 194–6.

[22] Kant *CPrR*: 163–4 [5:30].
[23] Kant *CPrR*: 163 [5:30].
[24] Kant *CPrR*: 140 [5:4 note].
[25] Kant *CPrR*: 164 [5:31].

need comes from the former and not the latter—but *not* in the sense that we are moving from evidential theoretical reason to non-evidential practical reason, as on the approach outlined previously.

The basis for this claim is the role that the awareness of the moral 'ought' plays in Kant's argument, either in the individual case ('I ought to overcome my love of life and not give false witness') or more generally ('I ought to follow the moral law in universalizing my maxims'): Here, I would suggest, Kant is using such awareness to ground the claim that we are free, insofar as *ultra posse nemo obligatur* (no one is obliged to do what it is impossible for them to do, or (in this sense) 'ought implies can'), so that the former is then adequate evidence for the latter. This would therefore seem to fit an evidentialist approach, except that the evidence does not come from what theoretical reason tells us about the workings of the empirical world, but from what practical reason tells us about how we should act.

It could be argued, however, that while this 'fact of reason' discussion might be understood in an evidentialist manner, Kant's later treatment of freedom as a postulate in the *Critique* suggests a less evidentialist approach, particularly when Kant says of such postulates that 'this is the only case in which my interest, because I *may* not give up anything of it, unavoidably determines my judgment'.[26] Indeed, it might seem that it exactly such non-evidentialism that prompts Kant to deal with the worry raised by Thomas Wizenmann, that the need for *p* entitles one to postulate the existence of *p*, where this is also the sort of worry that was frequently raised against James.

Now, much could be said on this topic, but just to mention some relevant points. First, in response to Wizenmann's objection, Kant in fact argues in an evidentialist manner, again appealing to the principle of 'ought implies can': 'It is a duty to realize the highest good to the utmost of our capacity; therefore it must be possible; hence it is also unavoidable for every rational being in the world to assume what is necessary for its objective possibility.'[27] Kant would appear to be arguing that to make sense of this duty, one must grant its necessary conditions, such that the former provides ground for belief in the latter, in contrast to the Wizenmann case of an inclination, where one can of course have a need based on an inclination, without the latter providing any basis for thinking that what makes the inclination satisfiable in fact obtains, as it is not the case that 'want implies can'. It might be replied, however, that even if this is so, what the evidence supports here is still not a belief, but something

[26] Kant *CPrR*: 255 [5:143]. Cf. Willaschek 2010: 180: 'I think it is a major insight on Kant's part that there can be theoretical propositions that follow from (or, at least, are 'inseparably connected' to) practical attitudes—ontological commitments we undertake not by accepting a theory, but rather by wanting or willing something and by accepting practical commands and imperatives as binding... For instance, if Kant is correct to claim that we are obligated to realize the highest good, and that this is possible only if God exists, then we are rationally committed to believing that God exists.'

[27] Kant *CPrR*: 255 [5:143 note].

more like a hope, or supposition, or assumption.[28] However, my response to this challenge would be to say that this is not grounds for doubting Kant's earlier evidentialist argument, but more reflects the fact that here the discussion has shifted to freedom as a postulate in relation to the highest good, rather than in relation to the fact of reason. For, the highest good is an object or goal we are obliged to aim to bring about, where what we are assuming are the conditions that make this object or goal rational to aim for, where something weaker than a belief might suffice; but in the 'fact of reason' case, we are deriving the conditions that explain or make possible the moral law as such, as it is actually applicable to us, where something stronger would seem to be required.[29] This then also explains the clear priority Kant gives to freedom over the other postulates, and why he gives it a more substantial epistemic status, which then (I would suggest) calls for a more evidentialist approach than for the postulates of God and immortality.[30]

Nonetheless, Kant's argument as I understand it does still share an important similarity with the non-evidential approach outlined previously, which is that he needs to 'neutralize' the claim of theoretical reason to be able to prove conclusively that we in fact lack freedom—for if this could be established, the argument above could be turned on its head, to show that as we are unfree, we are unable to act morally and so do not fall under the jurisdiction of the moral law. But, the machinery of transcendental idealism ensures for Kant that no such claim of theoretical reason can ever be plausibly established: From the perspective of theoretical reason on its own, it must always remain an open question about whether we are free or not, where then the evidence from practical reason can then be used to tip the epistemic balance in favour of this belief.

It is perhaps also worth noting, that while it may be right to claim that the *Groundwork* differs from the second *Critique* on these issues, so that it might be said that there is a 'great reversal' between the two texts,[31] it is nonetheless the case that in the *Groundwork* there are also suggestions of the kind of argument he will offer in the later work. I would claim that an argument of this sort can be found towards the end of the third section, for example in the following passage:

[28] But not a hypothesis: see Kant *CPrR*: 255 [5:143], where a 'postulate from a practical point of view' is distinguished from a 'permitted hypothesis'.

[29] Cf. Beck 1960: 208: 'There is a difference in the meaning of freedom as a condition of the moral law and as a condition of the *summum bonum*. Freedom in the latter sense is an object of faith, not a *scibile*; it is the faith (*Vertrauen*) in the achievability of the *summum bonum*, i.e., the belief in virtue (*Glaube an die Tugend*) as adequate to achieve the highest good.'

[30] Cf. Kant *CPrR*: 139 [5:3–4]: 'Now, the concept of freedom, insofar as its *reality is proved by an apodictic law of practical reason* [my emphasis], constitutes the *keystone* of the whole structure of a system of pure reason, even of speculative reason; and all other concepts (those of God and immortality), which as mere ideas remain without support in the latter, now attach themselves to this concept and with it and by means of it get stability and objective reality, that is, their *possibility* is *proved* by this: that freedom is real, for this idea reveals itself through the moral law.'

[31] Cf. Kant *CPrR*: 176–8 [5:46–8].

All human beings think of themselves as having a will that is free. From this stems all judgments about actions such that they *ought* to have been done even if they *were not done*... [R]eason for *speculative purposes* finds the route of natural necessity much more even and useful than that of freedom: yet for *practical purposes* the footpath of freedom is the only one on which it is possible to make use of one's reason in our behaviour; which is why it is just as impossible for the subtlest philosophy as for the commonest human reason to rationalize freedom away.[32]

Kant's position here can be understood as follows: While theoretical reason finds it compelling to view the world in terms of natural necessity, we also possess *practical* reason, which tells us how we ought to act in various ways. But we could not take this practical reason seriously unless we took ourselves to be free, as it is only insofar as we are free that the 'ought' could apply to us.[33] Thus, given the practical as well as theoretical nature of our reason, in telling us that there are things we ought to do, we are entitled to believe that we possess the freedom that such oughts require.[34] And this argument, far from being at odds with Kant's approach in the *Critique of Practical Reason*, is entirely consistent with it: for of course one of the things practical reason tells us according to Kant, is what we ought to do as moral agents, so that this then becomes the *ratio cognoscendi* of our freedom.

We have seen, therefore, how it is possible to read Kant's final position as involving an evidentialism concerning our freedom, but where that evidentialism takes a practical form, based on the way in which practical reason tells us that there are ways in which we *ought* to act. Kant allows, of course, that if theoretical reason could establish that we lack freedom, then we should reject the 'ought' as it applies to us as illusory or a 'chimera';[35] but given that this is not possible, because of the limitations imposed on theoretical reason by the very structure of transcendental idealism, we are entitled to take that evidence at face value, and so come to accept that we are free. Thus, the 'primacy of practical reason' here does not mean that it becomes some sui generis source of belief that is not properly epistemic, but rather that it extends the possibility of our rational beliefs (if not certainty) beyond the boundaries of theoretical reason, while at the same time respecting the jurisdiction of the latter.

[32] Kant *GMM*: 101–2 [4:455–6].

[33] This way of putting the argument of the passage above may seem to reverse the order in which Kant places things, where he might appear to be saying that our judgement concerning our freedom is prior, and from this arises judgements concerning what we ought to do. But of course, if Kant's fundamental point is about the presuppositions we must make before we could be capable of making ought judgements, there is a sense in which thinking that we are free must come first, as a condition of possessing practical reason in the first place. Based on this argument, and the fact that we do face ought claims, we can then infer that we are free.

[34] Cf. also Kant *GMM*: 104 [4:458]: 'The concept of a world of understanding is this only a *standpoint* that reason sees itself necessitated to take outside appearances, *in order to think of itself as practical*, and this would not be possible if the influences of sensibility were determining for a human being.' For an earlier passage that also seems to resemble the approach of the second *Critique*, cf. also *GMM*: 64 [4:410–11]: 'For the pure representation of duty, and in general of the moral law, mixed with no alien addition of empirical stimuli [is the way in which reason]... first becomes aware that by itself it can also be practical.'

[35] Cf. *GMM*: 93 [4:445].

However, if this is the right approach to take with respect to Kant, does this then put him at odds with James? Does James's pragmatism commit him to a more thoroughgoing anti-evidentialism which is now no longer apparent in Kant's strategy as interpreted above? I don't see why this should follow, for it seems to me that James's strategy could also be taken along evidentialist lines, without stretching the concept of evidence to breaking-point, as Misak fears. To see why, it may be worth saying a little bit more about the actual structure of 'The Dilemma of Determinism' essay than we have done up to now.

James starts by making clear the limits of what he is trying to do, which is that he cannot offer any conclusive proof of our freedom, but that he can give grounds for taking it to be true, and acting on that basis:

> I thus disclaim openly on the threshold all pretension to prove to you that the freedom of the will is true. The most I hope is to induce some of you to follow my example in assuming it true, and acting as if it were true.[36]

And James famously remarks that this is how it ought to be: we don't want to be compelled into believing freedom with a 'coercive demonstration', but to freely make our choice based on the evidence.[37]

He also makes a further important preliminary point: That in general, we make and are entitled to make theory choices based on which gives us the greater 'subjective satisfaction', but where this means 'makes the world appear more rational':

> The arguments I am about to urge all proceed on two suppositions: first, when we make theories about the world and discuss them with one another, we do so in order to attain a conception of things which will give us subjective satisfaction; and, second, if there be two conceptions, and the one seems to us, on the whole, more rational than the other, we are entitled to suppose that the more rational one is the truer of the two.[38]

What is the justification for this approach? It seems to have worked, as a way of finding out about the world:

> I cannot stop to argue the point; but I myself believe that all the magnificent achievements of mathematical and physical science—our doctrines of evolution, of uniformity of law, and the rest—proceed from our indomitable desire to cast the world into a more rational shape in our minds than the shape into which it is thrown there by the crude order of our experience. The

[36] James 6:115.

[37] James 6:115. The fact that James talks here of 'assuming' freedom to be true, and 'acting as if it were true' might suggest that James is arguing for a weaker cognitive status for freedom, by treating it as an assumption, a postulate, a regulative idea or a Peircean 'hope', as against belief as such—where then to attain this weaker status, various sorts of non-evidentialism may become more plausible. However, unlike Peirce and Kant, James seems to have been less keen to draw this kind of contrast, where of course it is belief that forms the focus of 'The Will to Believe', so it is not so clear that this kind of non-evidentialist route is an option for James here, even if it might have made his position less controversial, like Peirce's.

[38] James 6:115.

world has shown itself, to a great extent, plastic to this demand of ours for rationality. How much farther it will show itself plastic no one can say. Our only means of finding out is to try.[39]

This passage can already be said to have a clear Kantian aspect, in claiming that we must go beyond the data of raw experience to bring an order to it and thus our encounter with the world.

But the passage also has a less Kantian aspect: (a) there is no suggestion that this somehow imposes on the world an order it doesn't possess in itself, even though that structure may not be immediately apparent in 'the crude order of our experience',[40] (b) there is no guarantee that the ordering cannot meet with resistance from the world at some point, but no reason to think it has done so up to now (so no call for scepticism), and so no reason to hold back in our inquiries. In fact, James's position here is perhaps most reminiscent of Hegel's famous claim that: 'To him who looks at the world rationally the world looks rationally back; the two exist in a reciprocal relationship'[41]—but of course James thinks Hegel's conception of reason ultimately takes him in a monistic direction, which he deplores.[42]

James makes clear at the outset that he includes moral issues within the material that we need to taken into account when we 'cast the world into a more rational shape':

Our only means of finding out is to try; and I, for one, feel as free to try conceptions of moral as of mechanical or of logical rationality. If a certain formula for expressing the nature of the

[39] James 6:115. Cf. James's remark in the Preface to the collection in which this essay appears: 'Postulating more unity than the first experiences yield, we also discover more' (6:6).

[40] Cf. also *Pragmatism*, 1:117: 'All our truths are beliefs about 'Reality'; and in any particular belief the reality acts as something independent, as a thing *found*, not manufactured'. But for a different contemporary view of 'the pragmatic method of explanation' and thus perhaps of someone like James, cf. Kemp Smith 1920: 10–11: 'Even science, it was contended, is not a form of theoretical insight; it is merely a means to power. Science, rightly understood, never seeks to explain, but only to simplify. By scrupulously careful observation we verify the ultimate coexistences and sequences among our sensations, and under the guidance of elaborate hypotheses, which have a merely subjective value in directing inquiry, we define the coexistences and sequences in exact qualitative terms. Acquaintance with these relations, when thus precisely defined, enables us to predict the future, to construct machines, and so progressively to gain control over our physical environment; but they yield no insight, it is maintained, into the independently real. What is alone truly characteristic of science is not the obtaining of insight, but the acquisition of power. Thought is an instrument developed through natural processes for the practical purposes of adaptation. Its criteria and values are exclusively determined by the instinctive equipment of the species in its adjustment to environment. They have no independent validity of any kind. The human mind, the argument proceeds, is limited to appearances; to attain knowledge in the absolute sense, that is to say through distinguishing between the true and the false, is impossible.' Cf. also p. 14, where Kemp Smith contrasts 'present-day naturalism' (where he mentions J. S. Mill and Huxley) which aims to be more realist, with 'the skeptical, subjectivist, pragmatic view of knowledge'.

[41] Hegel *ILHP*: 29 [XII: 23]; translation modified.

[42] Cf. James, *A Pluralistic Universe*, where James writes approvingly that '"The aim of knowledge", says Hegel, "is to divest the objective world of its strangeness, and to make us more at home in it"' (4:10), but argues that ultimately Hegel's monistic tendencies makes this impossible, at least as evidenced by the British idealists: 'Albeit the absolute is defined as being necessarily an embodiment of objectively perfect rationality, it is fair to its english advocates to say that those who have espoused the hypothesis most concretely and seriously have usually avowed the irrationality to their own minds of certain elements of it' (4:55).

world violates my moral demand, I shall free to throw it overboard, or at least to doubt it, as if it disappointed my demand for uniformity of sequence, for example; the one demand being, so far as I can see, quite as subjective and emotional as the other is.[43]

Now, this may be taken as a form of coherentist evidentialism:[44] We should try to generate as coherent a system of beliefs as we can, where a test for belief is whether rejecting it would undermine that system—and where it may turn out that rejecting a moral demand may cause as much damage as anything else, which can then be grounds on which to keep it, *ceteris paribus*.[45]

James then goes on to draw his well-know distinction between 'hard' and 'soft' determinism, where he rejects the latter as a 'quagmire of evasion', so that the choice for him comes down to hard determinism and indeterminism, where he reminds us that 'evidence of an external kind to decide between determinism and indeterminism is, as I intimated a while back, strictly impossible to find'.[46] He characterizes the difference between the two positions as follows:

[Determinism] professes that those parts of the universe already laid down absolutely appoint and decree what the other parts shall be... Indeterminism, on the contrary, says that the parts have a certain amount of loose play on one another, so that the laying down of one of them does not necessarily determine what the others shall be. Indeterminism thus allows for real possibilities, while determinism does not.[47]

James also insists that (in the terms of 'The Will to Believe') the issue between them is 'forced':

The issue, it will be seen, is a perfectly sharp one, which no eulogistic terminology can smear over or wipe out [cf. 'soft determinism']. The truth *must* lie with one side or the other, and its lying with one side makes the other false.[48]

[43] James 6:115–16. Cf. 'The Sentiment of Rationality', 6:76: 'That nature will follow to-morrow the same laws that she follows to-day is, they [i.e. 'the scientific philosophers of the present day'] all admit, a truth which no man can *know*; but in the interests of cognition as well as of action we must postulate or assume it.'

[44] Reading James this way gives him a response to the criticism of J. B. Pratt (cited by Misak 2013: 264), that James confuses 'the "good", harmonious, and logically confirmatory consequences of religious concepts as such' with the 'good and pleasant consequences which come from believing these concepts', where Pratt argues that 'it is one thing to say a belief is true because the logical consequences that flow from it fit in harmoniously with our otherwise grounded knowledge; and quite another to call it true because it is pleasant to believe'. On the reading of James offered here, James can agree with Pratt's distinction, and opt for the same side.

[45] For a flavour of the sort of coherentist view I have in mind, cf. Blanshard 1939: vol. 2, p. 227: 'What really tests [a] judgement is the extent of our accepted world that is implicated with it and would be carried down with it if it fell.' One difference between this approach and Willaschek's, is that for the coherentist this test does provide a form of evidence in favour of a belief, whereas Willaschek does not seem to see evidence in this way; for example, while recognizing that to come to believe that 'I am a brain in a vat' would lead me to give up so many of my other beliefs as to reduce me to insanity, he still thinks the belief lacks any evidential basis—which is precisely what the coherentist would deny. See Willaschek 2010: 196. For further discussion of coherentism in this form, see my 'Coherentism as a Test for Truth' in Stern 2009: 177–208.

[46] James 6:117. [47] James 6:117–18. [48] James 6:118.

And he also emphasizes that the empirical sciences cannot settle this dispute one way or the other:

Now, can science be called in to tell us which of these two point-blank contradicters of each other is right? Science professes to draw no conclusions but such as are based on matters of fact, things that have actually happened; but how can any amount of assurance that something actually happened give us the least grain of information as to whether another thing might or might not have happened in its place? Only facts can be proved by other facts. With things that are possibilities and not facts, facts have no concern. If we have no other evidence than the evidence of existing facts, the possibility-question must remain a mystery never to be cleared up.[49]

Ultimately, James argues, what should and will push us one way or the other will be broader considerations concerning which view makes the world a more rationally ordered place:

What divides us into possibility and anti-possibility men is different faiths or postulates—postulates of rationality. To this man the world seems more rational with possibilities in it—to that man more rational with possibilities excluded; and talk as we will about having to yield to evidence, what makes us monists or pluralists, determinists or indeterminists, is at bottom always some sentiment like this.

James argues that what makes the indeterminist position look rationally problematic is a concern about *chance*, which people can think introduces an element of chaos into our picture of the world that will reduce it to a muddled and incoherent heap:

Many persons talk as if the minutest dose of disconnectedness of one part with another, the smallest modicum of independence, the faintest tremor of ambiguity about the future, for example, would ruin everything, and turn this godly universe into a sort of insane sand-heap or nulliverse, no universe at all.[50]

James argues against this view, holding that chance can be admitted without any such direful consequences—so he doesn't take there to be any rational grounds to rule it out, in coherentist terms. Nonetheless, he allows that while this may undercut an important argument *against* indeterminism, it doesn't yet give us any argument in *support* of it:

But although, in discussing the word 'chance', I may at moments have seemed to be arguing for its real existence, I have not meant to do so yet. We have not ascertained whether this be a world of chance or no; at most, we have agreed that it seems so. And I now repeat what I have said at the outset, that, from any strict theoretical point of view, the question is insoluble.[51]

Thus, 'after all our tedious clearing of the way', James moves to his non-theoretical argument for indeterminism and the reality of chance.

[49] James 6:119. [50] James 6:121. [51] James 6:124.

He begins by emphasizing the importance to us of the notion of *judgements of regret*, or the 'wish that something might be otherwise',[52] such as 'acts of wanton cruelty or treachery, for example, whether performed by others or by ourselves',[53] where James gives as an example a particularly callous murder that took place at Brockton, saying of it: 'We feel that, although a perfect mechanical fit to the rest of the universe, it is a bad moral fit, and that something else would really have been better in its place.'[54]

James then claims that the determinist cannot make sense of this feeling of regret:

> But for the deterministic philosophy the murder, the sentence, and the prisoner's optimism were all necessary from eternity; and nothing else for a moment had a ghost of a chance of being put in their place. To admit such a chance, the determinists tell us, would be to make a suicide of reason; so we must steel our hearts against the thought.[55]

The consequence of this outlook, James argues, is that the determinist must be committed to a *pessimistic* view of the universe as a whole: for while they cannot intelligibly regret any particular event (as this could not have been otherwise), they can only feel regret for the 'whole frame of things of which the murder is one member': 'I can see no escape whatever from this pessimistic conclusion if, being determinists, our judgment of regret is to be allowed to stand at all.'[56]

James then considers various ways in which the determinist might try to allay this pessimism by extinguishing all judgements of regret—for example, by adopting a Panglossian optimism, or a form of gnostic subjectivism which sees value in what we are taught by the experience of the bad; but James rejects all such options as jeopardizing too much in our system of beliefs:

> We have thus clearly revealed to our view what may be called the dilemma of determinism, so far as determinism pretends to think things out at all. A merely mechanical determinism, it is true, rather rejoices in not thinking them out. It is very sure that the universe must satisfy its postulate of a physical continuity and coherence, but smiles at anyone who comes forward with a postulate of moral coherence as well.[57]

James's ultimate defence of his indeterministic approach, therefore, turns on his claim that only this is consistent with our feelings of regret, so that on this basis a rejection of determinism is legitimate:

> But this brings us right back, after such a long detour, to the question of indeterminism and to the conclusion of all I came here to say tonight. For the only consistent way of representing a pluralism and a world whose parts may affect one another through their conduct being either good or bad is the indeterministic way. What interest, zest, or excitement can there be in achieving the right way, unless we are enabled to feel that the wrong way is also a possible and a natural way—nay, more, a menacing and immanent way? And what sense can there be in

[52] James 6:124. [53] James 6:125. [54] James 6:125.
[55] James 6:125. [56] James 6:126. [57] James 6:128–9.

condemning ourselves for taking the wrong way, unless we need have done nothing of the sort, unless the right way was open to us as well? I cannot understand the willingness to act, no matter how we feel, without the belief that acts are really good and bad. I cannot understand the belief that an act is bad, without regret at its happening. I cannot understand regret without the admission of real, genuine possibilities in the world. Only *then* is it other than a mockery to feel, after we have failed to do our best, than an irreparable opportunity is gone from the universe, the loss of which it must forever mourn.

If you insist that this is all superstition, that possibility is in the eye of science and reason impossibility, and that if I act badly 'tis that the universe was foredoomed to suffer this defect, you fall right back into the dilemma, the labyrinth, of pessimism and subjectivism, from out of whose toils we have just found our way.[58]

As James notes, nothing in this argument proves that we have free will, where he reminds us that 'I expressly repudiated awhile ago the pretension to offer any arguments which could be coercive in a so-called scientific fashion in this matter'.[59]

Nonetheless, he clearly holds that his argument from regret is sufficient to make his indeterministic position a plausible one, with greater support than the deterministic alternative—thus adopting what is still an evidentialist strategy based on practical grounds,[60] much like Kant's.

12.4 Pragmatism and Idealism on Freedom: A Step too far?

I have argued, then, that contrary to various prominent readings of both Kant and James respectively, there is reason to see a convergence between their two positions concerning free will, but not around some form of non-evidentialism, but rather around a form of evidentialism which nonetheless gives priority to practical reason in a real sense. In this last section, I want to look at some challenges to my position here, where these can be brought out by considering an argument that there are some weaknesses to James's position that do not apply to Kant's, thereby suggesting that the two are not to be equated after all.

One potential difficulty with James's argument as I have presented it, it could be said, is that it hinges on regret, and the claim that this 'moral belief' only makes sense if things could have been otherwise. A first worry might be to deny that regret actually does require this possibility: might I not intelligibly regret the fact that at

[58] James 6:135. [59] James 6:135.

[60] Cf. James's summary of this part of 'The Dilemma of Determinism' which is included in the contents page of the collection in which it appears: 'A world with chance in it is morally the less irrational alternative' (6:11). Cf. 6:137, where James denies that accepting the reality of chance involves 'the suicide of reason'. Cf. also his comment in a letter to Renouvier: 'I believe more and more that free will, if accepted at all, must be accepted as a postulate in justification of our moral judgment that certain things already done might have been better done. This implies that something different was possible in their place' (James 1992–2004: 5:260).

some point I will die, for example, while (regretfully) recognizing that this cannot be otherwise? However, in response to this it can be said that James here is focusing on something more like 'agent regret',[61] that is, regret for things that are seemingly tied to the work of individuals (such as the Brockton murder with which James starts), where this would not apply to my own mortality (hopefully).

However, a second and rather deeper worry might be pressed at this point: namely that it seems conceivable on James's approach that we *could* come to give up regrets of this sort, even though we might find it difficult to do, given the conceptual interconnections that James traces between this belief and many others. But still, difficulty is not impossibility, and 'one man's modus ponens is another man's modus tollens', so James's can't really claim to have shown that we might not find ourselves rationally obliged to switch sides on this matter, and so become determinists. In fact, this seems to be an implication of his approach that James is prepared to concede.[62]

It is then debatable, of course, how much damage this causes to the Jamesian strategy as I have outlined it. One might take the line (which is James's own) that no greater certainty is possible on such matters, and that at the end of the day an individual can only take up the position which seems correct to him or her given their personal starting points and convictions; indeed, as we have mentioned previously, given that this matter concerns our freedom, James thinks it could not be otherwise, as something more conclusive would take that very freedom away.[63]

It might be useful to very briefly compare James's position as I understand it here to Strawson's in his famous essay on 'Freedom and Resentment'. Like James, Strawson points to an attitude which we have to each other, namely resentment, and then brings out the close connection between the intelligibility of this attitude and the attribution to others of free will. Strawson then considers the question whether this is decisive, or whether the argument could be reversed, so that one might argue from determinism to the need to drop our reactive attitudes, such that we would then treat *everyone* as we currently treat those who we deem to lack responsibility for their actions. Strawson's response is to allow that this could happen in some sense; but he emphasizes the great difficulty we would have in doing so given the framework of beliefs, attitudes, and commitments which we currently have, in such a way as to render this possibility an essentially empty one from where we stand: 'This commitment is part of the general framework of human life, not something that can come up for review as particular cases can come up for review within this general framework.'[64] Strawson's approach would also broadly seem to be a coherentist one, along lines rather similar to those I have outlined for James, where both therefore seem to accept that as a result, the grounds on which they support our belief in freedom does not leave that belief wholly

[61] This terminological originates with Williams 1981a: 27. But Williams uses it to cover regret by the agent for actions they have performed themselves, while I am using it to cover regret for things done by agents in general, but not necessarily by oneself.

[62] James 6:135–6. [63] Cf. again James 6:135–6. [64] P. F. Strawson 1982: 70.

invulnerable on the one hand,[65] while they think any challenge to it is highly resistible on the other, given where we currently stand.[66]

However, it might now be argued that this way of putting things brings out an important difference between Kant on the one hand, and James and Strawson on the other, where this difference gives Kant another (and perhaps better) way of handling the problem we have been discussing.

Essentially, this difference may be said to arise because on my account at least, James (and Strawson) still give too great a place to theoretical reasoning in this dispute, by seeing the link between regret (or resentment) and freedom in evidential terms, where this means the reversal in the direction of argument still remains for them as a possibility (however remote and unlikely they think it is that we would ever commit ourselves to that reversal), by using the truth of determinism to cast doubt on our feelings of regret or attitudes of resentment. It could be said, however, that in Kant's case the position is very different, because for him 'the priority of practical reason' precisely means that our beliefs are *impervious* to anything theoretical reason can offer as grounds for change, so that the possibilities for belief revision which James and Strawson seem to allow are closed off to us in this manner.

To see how this might be so, it is useful to move back from the *Critique of Practical Reason*, and to consider the *Groundwork*, and an influential account of the so-called 'prefatory argument' given in the second sub-section of part III of that work which has been offered by Korsgaard and others. The key claim in this argument is generally taken to be that 'every being that cannot act otherwise than *under the idea of freedom* is actually free, in a practical respect, precisely because of that'.[67] On Korsgaard's reading, Kant is arguing here that the truth of determinism can make no difference to our deliberations as practical agents, because we must still proceed as if we are free when it comes to making our decisions, so that practical reason has priority over theoretical reason in this more radical sense:

The point is not that you must *believe* you are free, but that you must choose *as if* you were free. It is important to see that this is quite consistent with believing yourself to be fully

[65] Cf. P. F. Strawson 1982: 68: 'And our question reduces to this: could, or should, the acceptance of the determinist thesis lead us always to look on everyone exclusively this way [i.e. the way we currently look on those who we deem incapable of free will and thus as inappropriate targets for reactive attitudes like resentment]? For this is the only condition worth considering under which acceptance of determinism could lead to the decay or repudiation of participant reactive attitudes. It does not seem self-contradictory that this might happen. So I suppose we must say that it is not absolutely inconceivable that it should happen.'

[66] So the passage above continues: 'But I am strongly inclined to think that it is, for us as we are, practically inconceivable. The human commitment to participation in ordinary inter-personal relationships is, I think, too thoroughgoing and deeply rooted for us to take seriously the thought that a general theoretical conviction might so change our world that, in it, there were no longer any such thing as inter-personal relationships as we normally understand them; and being involved in inter-personal relationships as we normally understand them precisely is being exposed to the range of reactive attitudes and feelings that is in question.'

[67] Kant *GMM*: 95 [4:448].

determined. To make it vivid, imagine that you are participating in a scientific experiment, and you know that today your every move is programmed by an electronic device implanted in your brain... [But] In order to *do* anything, you must simply ignore the fact that you are programmed, and decide what to do—just as if you were free. You will believe that your decision is a sham, but it makes no difference. Kant's point, then, is not about the theoretical assumption necessary to decision, but about a fundamental feature of the standpoint from which decisions are made. It follows from this feature that we must regard our decisions as springing ultimately from principles that we have chosen, and justifiable by those principles. We must regard ourselves as having free will.[68]

On this account of Kant's position, then, practical reason is concerned with determining the will to action, and as such it is entitled to ignore what theoretical reason tells us, even if the latter tells us that in fact a necessary condition for such action does not hold. If a position of this sort could be made cogent, it might seem to put freedom in a less assailable position for Kant than for James and Strawson, and show that his approach to this issue is ultimately distinct from theirs.

There are, however, important difficulties in reading Kant this way, both interpretatively and philosophically.

First, it would leave it hard to see how Kant could be committed to the unity of reason, as it would appear to leave theoretical and practical reason at odds with one another. Second, Kant himself seems more worried by the challenge of theoretical reason than this approach would suggest. So, for example, Kant writes in the *Groundwork* that 'If even the thought of freedom contradicts itself, or nature, which is equally necessary, it would have to be given up altogether in favour of natural necessity'.[69] As Sergio Tenenbaum has observed: 'This is very far from the claim that we can act under the idea of freedom independently of what we actually

[68] Korsgaard 1996a: 162–3. Henry Allison also presents the argument in similar terms:

> But while Kant does not preclude such a state of affairs [that our belief in freedom is illusory] on theoretical grounds, he does deny the *practical* possibility of accepting any such thesis on the grounds that it is not a thought on which one can deliberate or act. To take oneself as a rational agent *is* to assume that one's reason has a practical application or, equivalently, that one has a will. Moreover, one cannot assume this without already presupposing the idea of freedom, which is why one can act, or take oneself to act, only under this idea. It constitutes, as it were, the form of thought of oneself as a rational agent. (Allison 2012: 92)

Cf. also Wood 2008: 130–2; and Darwall 2013b: 222: '[In *Groundwork* III Kant] goes on to argue that an assumption of autonomy is essential to the deliberative standpoint and that assuming autonomy commits one to the Categorical Imperative and thus to morality. If that is so, then autonomy and morality really hold, or at least, any rational agent must assume they hold when deliberating about what to do.' Darwall thinks this strategy is more promising than the one pursued in the second *Critique*, for reasons outlined above: 'It is only through taking ourselves to be morally obligated that we are forced to conclude that we can act for a reason that is independent of any property of the objects of our desire... But this leaves open the possibility that both morality and autonomy are mere figments. Even if morality and autonomy are a stable reciprocal pair, with each entailing the other, both may be illusions nonetheless' (Darwall 2013b: 223).

[69] Kant *GMM*: 102 [4:456].

believe about freedom and determinism.'[70] Thirdly, it might be asked, how does proving that we must assume we are free, or act as if we were free, or regard ourselves as free, even though we have grounds to think we are not, help settle our worries on this issue?[71] In fact, might it not seem to make them worse, as we now seem to have to assume, and so on, things about ourselves when we come to act that we otherwise know to be false? And isn't this the worst kind of sceptical nightmare, locking us into views of ourselves that we cannot escape even when they are in error?[72] One response might be that this doesn't actually matter so much, as what is in question here is not a *belief* that might be false, but some other kind of attitude;[73] but nonetheless, it could be replied, unless we are free that attitude would seem misplaced. Finally, given the claim it makes about our freedom, this would seem to leave a gap in the rest of Kant's argument in the *Groundwork*, at least as this is understood on this approach, which is meant to go as follows:[74]

1. A rational will must be regarded as a free will
2. A free will is a will under moral law
3. Therefore, a rational will is a will under moral law.

For this argument to work, it would seem that (1) requires the rational will to *be* free, where 'must be regarded as' doesn't look like it is strong enough to render the argument valid—unless the conclusion is also modified to the correspondingly weak claim that 'a rational will is a will that must regard itself as under a moral law', which itself doesn't look strong enough to dispel the threat that morality is in fact a chimera, whatever we may be compelled to think about it.

But if the preparatory argument is not an argument for our freedom of this sort, what *is* its role in the *Groundwork*? My claim is that what Kant is trying to establish here is not that we are free, but that the moral law applies to *all rational beings*, where this is a class that is obviously much wider than the merely human. The concern is therefore whether someone could hold that there might be rational beings who could be said not to stand under the moral law—where if so, Kant's basic commitment to the universality of that law (which he thinks we all share) would be put in jeopardy. This is a fundamental preoccupation of Kant's, and one that he frequently claims in

[70] Tenenbaum 2012: 559.

[71] Karl Ameriks presses this point strongly in Ameriks 2003a: esp. pp. 247–8, where he uses these problems to argue that they led Kant to change his approach in the second *Critique*.

[72] Cf. Stern 2000: 85–6. Cf. also G. Strawson 2010: 64: 'The idea that a certain view may be inescapable and therefore somehow permissible or even correct, despite the fact that we are able to get into a position in which we can see it to be false—or so we think—is very problematic. Surely "irresistibility does not entail truth"—even species-wide irresistibility?'

[73] Cf. Darwall 2013a: 229: 'The idea need not be that one must *believe* that one is free in these respects or that one must disbelieve hard determinism. The point is that deliberation is intelligible only on these *assumptions*'. Cf. also the quote given from Korsgaard above: 'The point is not that you must *believe* that you are free.'

[74] See Korsgaard 1996a: 24.

the *Groundwork* and elsewhere that he is in a better position to deal with than other moral theorists—and hence it needs to be resolved.[75]

Kant's way out of this problem is to argue that we do not have to establish that a rational being *really is* free for the moral law to apply to them, as it is sufficient that they have to *think they are free*, where every rational agent (i.e. every rational being endowed with a will) must think that of themselves:

> Now I say: every being that cannot act otherwise than *under the idea of freedom* is actually free, in a practical respect, precisely because of that; i.e. all laws that are inseparably bound up with freedom hold for it just as if its will had also been declared free in itself, and in a way that is valid in theoretical philosophy... For even if this latter [theoretical] point is left unsettled, the same laws that would bind a being that was actually free yet hold for a being that cannot act otherwise than under the idea of its own freedom. Here we can thus liberate ourselves from the burden that weighs upon theory.[76]

So, Kant thinks, the reciprocity thesis can be extended to cover not only beings that are shown *to be* free on theoretical grounds (grounds that we would find it very hard to supply given our limitations and lack of knowledge concerning such beings), but also to beings that must *think* that they are free, which includes *all rational beings which have a will*, and so the universality of the moral law is secured—as of course the moral law would not be expected to apply to rational beings without such a will. How is it that we can extend the reciprocity thesis in this way? I think the answer is that a rational being with a will must take itself to be free, and even if a being merely *takes itself to be free*, then it must take itself to be under the moral law, where this is sufficient to show that it can't repudiate the law, because (given Kant's earlier arguments for the reciprocity thesis) there is no other way this rational being can see its actions as being guided—so it is impossible for any rational agent to be a refusenik when it comes to the moral law, without at the same time repudiating its claim to agency. The universality problem has thus been solved.

It can be argued, therefore, that the *Groundwork*'s preparatory argument does not provide an argument for our freedom, and thus a strategy that is somehow different and more radical than the one that we have attributed to Kant in the second *Critique*. If this is right, therefore, we are entitled to continue to read Kant's approach to the

[75] See for example: *GMM*: 44–5 [4:389]: 'the command: thou shalt not lie, does not just hold for human beings only, as if other rational beings did not have to heed it; and so with all remaining actual moral laws'; 65 [4:412]: 'moral laws are to hold for every rational being as such'; 77 [4:426]: 'The question is therefore this: is it a necessary law *for all rational beings* always to appraise their actions in accordance with such maxims as they themselves could will to serve as universal laws?'; 81 [4:430–1]: 'This principle of humanity... is not borrowed from experience... because of its universality, since it applies to all rational beings as such and no experience is sufficient to determine anything about them.' I have also argued that this issue plays a central role in Kant's account of the Formula of Humanity in section II of the *Groundwork*: see Chapter 5, this volume.

[76] Kant *GMM*: 95–6 and note [4:448].

'primacy of practical reason' concerning freedom as operating along the same evidentialist lines that we also attributed to James.

12.5 Conclusion

We have therefore seen that when it comes to the problem of free will, that notwithstanding certain differences, James and Kant can be viewed as adopting broadly similar strategies—where that similarity suggests that when it comes to this question, at least, James chose not to merely go round Kant, but through him, while taking an route that can be understood more evidentially than has generally been supposed.[77]

[77] I am grateful for several people for very helpful comments on previous drafts, including the audience at the conference on idealism and pragmatism at which this was presented (Frankfurt 2014), and Gabriele Gava, Alexander Klein, Cheryl Misak, Joe Saunders, and Marcus Willaschek.

13

'Duty and Virtue Are Moral Introversions'

On Løgstrup's Critique of Morality

A central feature of post-Kantian ethical thought, since at least Hegel onwards, has been the critique of *moralistic* conceptions of ethical life, as involving duties, obligations, principles, rules, laws, and so on. This feature is now an important part of the contemporary landscape in ethical theory, reflected for example in Bernard Williams's critiques of morality as a 'peculiar institution', and as involving 'one thought too many'; in the renewed interest in virtue theory and Hegelian notions of *Sittlichkeit*; in the championing of various forms of particularism; and in the rise within feminist thought of an 'ethics of care'.

One significant reason to be interested in Løgstrup's work, and one significant reason why it has indeed attracted growing attention, is that his approach would appear to chime in with this turn away from an ethics of morality, while also having distinctive features of its own. In fact, it seems to me, in a central respect Løgstrup's outlook on this matter is considerably more radical than that of the other 'morality critics'—to the extent that I fear it is rather *too* radical to be made acceptable as it stands. However, I will suggest that his position also incorporates a more modest critique of morality to which he could have restricted himself, and which is in fact a critique that he shares with Kant, making them allies rather than opponents. I will therefore propose, in a spirit of friendly criticism and amendment, that this is the position he should have confined himself to instead.

I will start by outlining Løgstrup's objections to morality as I understand them, and discuss why they seem to go too far (section 13.1). I will then offer the alternative position which I think he could have adopted instead, and explain why it seems more acceptable (section 13.2), and suggest how this position can do most of the work that Løgstrup's requires such a critique of morality achieve (section 13.3).

13.1 Løgstrup's View of Morality as a 'Substitute'

In his book *Controverting Kierkegaard*, Løgstrup uses the story of the Good Samaritan to highlight what he takes to be wrong with morality as an ethical perspective.

Løgstrup first presents the parable 'as [it] comes down to us',[1] wherein the Samaritan is portrayed as responding to the needs of the injured Jewish traveller and what he requires; he thus acts, Løgstrup suggests, in a way that *exemplifies* mercy, but not because he is *setting out* to behave in a merciful manner as such, as all he is focused on is the victim—so 'it was not a question of the Good Samaritan engaging with his own mercifulness in his exercise of it as his duty; rather, in his mercifulness, he took charge of the man who has been set upon and wounded by the roadside'.[2] Løgstrup then contrasts this Good Samaritan with what he provocatively calls a *Kantian* Samaritan, who finds himself in the same situation, but who is tempted not to help, and who therefore needs to overcome this temptation. At this point, Løgstrup suggests, considerations of duty and virtue may arise for the Samaritan, and play an important role, as these can then motivate him to assist the victim and overcome his inclination to walk away: by telling himself he has a duty to act, or that he would be displaying the virtue of mercy if he did so, the Kantian Samaritan can conquer his temptations, and look after the traveller in the way that morality requires.[3]

Now, while Løgstrup allows that to behave in the manner of the Kantian Samaritan is 'better than brutality or indifference', he claims that it is nonetheless less good than the behaviour of the true Good Samaritan, being 'inferior to the immediate realization of mercy's sovereign expression of life'.[4] For, he argues, moral considerations like duty and virtue have become involved because the spontaneous expression of mercy has failed and the suffering of the victim has lost its grip on the agent, who has instead become prey to other concerns. Løgstrup therefore thinks that the difference between these two cases shows that 'duty only enters when I am trying to wriggle out of the situation', and that insofar as duty is central to morality, morality is a 'substitute' for the higher form of ethical existence exemplified by the Good Samaritan himself.[5] Likewise, as he makes clear a little later, he thinks the same is true of virtue, where what matters to us is the rightness of what we are doing, which again is a 'substitute' for a more direct response to the suffering of the victim and what this involves.[6] Moreover, not only can ideas of duty and virtue be seen as symptoms of an ethical failing in the agent; such ideas can threaten to *corrupt* an agent, as instead of being driven by the needs of the other person, she focuses on what duty or virtue requires, thus becoming preoccupied with her own moral standing and righteousness, and so acting in order to be merciful rather than acting in order to help the victim in what is in fact a merciful manner. Løgstrup's position is therefore

[1] Løgstrup 2007: 76. [2] Løgstrup 2007: 76.

[3] In his account of the Good Samaritan example, Løgstrup's position and concerns resemble Schiller's telling of the same story in his 'Kallias Letters': see Schiller 2003, especially pp. 157–9. For further discussion of Schiller's position, see Stern 2012: 104–26.

[4] Løgstrup 2007: 76. [5] Løgstrup 2007: 76.

[6] Cf. Løgstrup 2007: 78. Cf. also Løgstrup 2007: 105: 'If the motivating reason for my returning the book to John at the promised time is not one of consideration for John but my resolve to live in accordance with the general principle that promises should be kept, my act is not moral but moralistic.'

encapsulated in the claim that 'just as duty is a substitute motive, virtue is a substitute disposition', where both replace the kind of other-directed and immediate focus on the injured traveller that is displayed by the Good Samaritan.

Now, there is little doubt that taken as a critique of morality, Løgstrup's position is extremely radical. For while other 'morality critics' have focused on duty, they have nonetheless mostly exonerated virtue, and indeed have often championed the latter against the former—but as we have seen, Løgstrup condemns them both. Likewise, whilst others have criticized duty as involving 'one thought too many' in some situations, they have generally not rejected it in all. And while for some critics the problem with morality is that it does not leave enough room for a concern with oneself and one's own goals and projects, Løgstrup's complaint is the opposite one—that in fact it is not other-regarding enough. As a critic of morality, therefore, Løgstrup would appear to put those holding similar views in the shade.

The question is, however, whether in this radicalism, Løgstrup in fact goes too far. Several commentators have argued that he does, and that as a result his position is problematic. So, for example, Kees van Kooten Niekerk has asked: 'Is it not unambiguously positive when people do things that are right for the sake of their rightness, or when they act out of virtue?'[7] Likewise, Alasdair MacIntyre and Stephen Darwall have accused Løgstrup of being mistaken here, in failing to identify anything ethically inferior or second-rate in acting in a dutiful or virtuous manner, at least in certain circumstances.[8] It is this issue which I wish to consider further in this section, where I will argue that while Løgstrup has more to say against his critics than may at first sight appear, in the end those critics are correct and that Løgstrup has failed to identify anything inherently problematic and anti-ethical in morality.

My central claim will be that, sympathetically viewed, both Løgstrup's Good Samaritan and Kant's dutiful Samaritan will end up being characterized in much the same manner, so that Løgstrup has failed to show that there is some ethical element missing in the latter that is present only in the former. I will start by characterizing ways of being a dutiful agent, where the difference between such an agent and Løgstrup's Good Samaritan is clear, but then argue that Kant did not conceive of the dutiful agent in these terms; in fact, I will suggest, when we take Kant's conception into account, it is hard to see how Løgstrup's Good Samaritan could be anything other than such an agent, so that the contrast Løgstrup has tried to set up collapses, and with it his critique of Kant's position.

The first model of the dutiful agent we can consider, where Løgstrup's objections would appear to have some force, is of an agent whose end in acting is to do her duty, and so where behaving dutifully is the aim or object of what she does. Here, for example, one might think of a soldier whose goal is to have done everything that has been required of him, or a conscientious child who wishes to have carried out all that

[7] Niekerk 2007: 57. [8] Cf. MacIntyre 2007; and Darwall 2010.

has been asked of her—where the former might rescue a colleague not in order to save them, but in order to have performed his duty, while the latter might visit a sick relative for the same purpose, and not in order to cheer them up. This, then, is an agent whose primary concern is to do her duty—as opposed to Løgstrup's Good Samaritan, whose concern is to help the wounded traveller, and who thus acts *out of mercy*, rather than with the aim of *being* merciful. Clearly, if the 'Kantian Samaritan' contrasts with the Good Samaritan in this way, Løgstrup would be right to be suspicious of the former, precisely because this agent would not act with the end of helping others, but of being a dutiful person and thus with a view to her own righteousness.

However, Kantians have argued that Kant did not think of the dutiful agent in this manner, as someone who acts for the sake of duty rather than to help the other, or to treat her fairly, or whatever. To confuse the two, they have argued, is to confuse the *end* of an action with its *motivating reason*, where the crucial issue is the latter and not the former: namely, that the dutiful agent is motivated by duty, not that doing her duty is her end in acting. Thus, just as a merciful person does not act to help in order to be merciful as her aim, but because she is motivated by mercifulness, so it can be said of the dutiful person that he does not act in order to be dutiful, but because he is motivated by duty.[9]

Nonetheless, while this second model of the dutiful agent differs from the first, it may not be considered wholly satisfactory either. One difficulty concerns the idea of being motivated by duty: for surely, it can be said, this is also problematic for the sorts of reasons that Løgstrup gives, namely that the Samaritan should be motivated to act by the suffering of the traveller, not because he believes he has a duty to act in this way? The Kantian might think that the perceived suffering of the traveller cannot be enough to motivate, so the Samaritan must *either* be motivated by the distress he feels

[9] Cf. Allison 1990: 190–1: 'This puts us in a position to deal with the claim that the Kantian requirement to act from duty alone is equivalent to the (absurd) requirement to make the performance of duty itself, rather than the attainment of any determinate end, the goal of one's action... Given the distinction between the end or purpose intended by an action and the ground or reason for adopting such an intention, it becomes clear that it simply does not follow that someone who is ostensibly interested in helping others because of the recognition of a moral obligation to do so is not really interested in helping others but merely in the doing of duty for duty's sake. On the contrary, such a person is genuinely concerned to help others, just as much as another might be who behaves in a similar way from inclination. The difference between them is not the genuineness of the concern but rather its rational ground.' Cf. also Herman 1993: 24–5; and Baron 1995: 12: 'one's goal, in acting from duty, need not be to do one's duty. Duty should be our motivating conception and need not be our end. The aim or end can be to save the child who has just darted into the street, or to show concern respectfully without seeming condescending or meddlesome, or to speak both truthfully and sensitively.' As Baron and Herman note, the picture of Kant they reject is unfortunately encouraged by H. J. Paton's tendency to sometimes translate '*aus Pflicht*' as 'for the sake of duty' instead of 'from duty' or 'out of duty'. In Hegel's *Philosophy of Right*, §133, he uses the phrase '*um der Pflicht*' to characterize the Kantian position, which is correctly translated in Paton's way as 'for the sake of duty'; and in F. H. Bradley's *Ethical Studies*, this becomes the basis of the slogan of 'duty for duty's sake' which is used to describe the Kantian position discussed in chapter (or essay) IV. For a criticism of this Hegelian way of understanding Kant's position as confusing motive and end, see Allison 1990: 184–91.

at the suffering as a result of his sympathetic temperament, *or* by the thought he has a duty to relieve it; but Løgstrup's point may precisely be that this dichotomy is not exhaustive, where the Good Samaritan case shows that the suffering itself can motivate, but without any sense that there is a duty here, and without feelings of distress in the agent playing a role either.[10] A second difficulty, moreover, concerns the very idea of being motivated by duty: for, as some have argued, how *can* duty be a reason to act, simply as such? The thought here is this: if an action is a person's duty and hence ought to be done, then the motivating reasons for doing it should surely be the reasons that *make it a duty*, not the fact that it *is* a duty?[11] It thus looks as if, even when treated as a motive and not as an end, duty is still suspect and need not be present as a motivating force in the Good Samaritan, for whom the motivating ground for action could be said to be provided by the distress of the traveller and nothing more, much as Løgstrup suggests.

Now, again, Kantians have been sensitive to these concerns, but have denied that taking them seriously means that we must lose all grip on Kant's conception of the dutiful agent: for, they argue, duty can be a *secondary* motive, not just a primary one, where it is the presence of duty as a motive at *this* level that can be said to distinguish the dutiful agent from others. Authors who have appealed to this distinction include Herman, Baron, and Stratton-Lake, though they all use the idea in slightly different ways.[12] But the basic idea is that at the primary level, the dutiful agent need not act from duty as a motive, perhaps because they are motivated to act by some feeling such as mercifulness (Herman, Baron), or because they are simply motivated by the suffering of the victim (Stratton-Lake); nonetheless, they only treat this feeling or state of affairs as reason giving insofar as they take it to be in line with duty or what it is right for them to do, where therefore duty functions as a secondary motive, regulating the primary one. This approach may be said to answer Williams's well-known 'one thought too many' objection,[13] because it allows the husband to be motivated by love for his wife at the primary level, while if he does not also concern himself with the moral status of such affective states at the secondary level, he may be said to have 'one thought too few'. And it may also be said to answer Løgstrup's worry that what makes the Good Samaritan good is that he simply sees the traveller's suffering as a reason to help, where this can now be said to correctly characterize his *primary* motivation—but where also a further reflective level is required, where the Samaritan must see this need as making the action right.

Using this distinction between primary and secondary motivation, therefore, the reply to Løgstrup is essentially that he has mischaracterized the supposed contrast

[10] Cf. Løgstrup 2007: 77: 'With a phenomenon such as mercy . . . the relevant disposition is triggered by the other's misfortune and consists simply in an effort to transform his situation. Kant could only arrive at his ethics of duty by disparaging all ethically descriptive phenomena as inclinations.'

[11] Cf. Stratton-Lake 2000: esp. Chapters 1 and 4.

[12] Cf. Herman 1993: 13–17 and 33–7; Baron 1995: 129–33; Stratton-Lake 2000: 53–7 and 60–7.

[13] Cf. Williams 1981b: 18.

between the Good Samaritan and the 'Kantian' Samaritan, where he has assumed that the latter must replace treating the suffering of the other as a reason to act with treating the rightness of helping others as reason; but, the Kantian can now respond, both forms of Samaritan can be the same at the primary level and so take the suffering of the other as providing the agent with a motivating reason to act, where the only difference is what happens at the secondary level, when one asks why the agent takes this suffering to be a reason, and whether they do so because they take themselves to have a duty to help others or because so helping is right, or rather on some other grounds—for example, that it will give them satisfaction, or serve their ends, or show them to be righteous. This then suggests that Løgstrup is wrong to think that in the dutiful agent, duty comes in as a 'substitute' at the primary level; rather, it operates in a different way, instead of entering as a 'replacement' source of motivation when some other primary motivation (such as mercy) has failed.

There are, however, possible critical responses that Løgstrup might make to this third Kantian model of the dutiful agent.

The first might be that the Good Samaritan acts *without* this second reflective level, but more immediately and spontaneously—where Løgstrup always seems keen to stress this element of spontaneity in relation to 'the sovereign expressions of life', and to be concerned when it breaks down. But the Kantian can respond in a number of ways. First, if such immediacy is made too 'automatic', then there is some danger that the Good Samaritan should not be treated as an autonomous agent but more as a responsive automaton. Second, while such spontaneity is perhaps plausible in certain cases where the ethical need is obvious, there will be many other cases where this is not so, and reflective consideration will be called for, so making space for duty as a secondary motive. And thirdly, the kind of secondary motivation that the Kantian envisages here is a commitment to do what is right, which need not require constant monitoring of whether an action really *is* right on all occasions, particularly where that is clear, as it is in the Good Samaritan example.[14]

Now, in fact, despite his emphasis on immediacy and spontaneity, Løgstrup himself also still allows for the need for reflection in our ethical lives. For example, in his discussion of Joseph Conrad's *The Nigger of the Narcissus* in his paper 'Ethics and Ontology' (printed as an appendix to the English translation of *The Ethical Demand*), Løgstrup distinguishes this immediacy and spontaneity from the more reflective position that is also sometimes required. Thus, he claims that when caught up in the drama of saving Jimmy, the sailors just act in response to the demands of the situation they are in, while more generally they just get on with their lives without much thinking about the principles that might underlie their actions: 'They follow

[14] Cf. Baron 1988: 29: 'What is important... is duty as a secondary motive. The agent's conduct is governed by a commitment to acting as she should. (This does not mean that she is always thinking about morality; but she is, perhaps without being conscious of it, on the alert for indications that the circumstances call for reconsideration, for reflection on whatever it is she is up to.)'

the moral law of the sea ['do not abandon anyone in order to save oneself!'] without reflecting on it. They do not give it the remotest thought. They are too preoccupied with the task at hand to do so. Presumably, during the entire time that they were at sea that did not give a single thought to the morality that commands them just as little as human beings pay attention to logic when they reason—even when they reason properly.'[15] However, Løgstrup then asks: 'But when do we reflect on morals then? What situation has arisen when we make ourselves aware of morals? At any rate, there are two possibilities: 1) when we are in doubt in a certain situation about what is correct and what is incorrect; in an extreme situation we can run into a conflict of duties; 2) when we are lured by temptation.'[16] Løgstrup then goes on to claim that for Kant, only 2) applies, as for him 'there is... little doubt about what is right and what is wrong and... there are no conflicts of duty... there are only temptations'.[17] Now, while of course Kant did worry greatly about the problem of temptations, Løgstrup's position is surely an exaggeration. For, although Kant may indeed have thought that there are ultimately no moral dilemmas,[18] in the sense of conflicts of obligations that could not be resolved, this doesn't mean he did not think that we could *seem* to be faced with such conflicts which then need resolving, for which reflection is therefore required. Likewise, while Kant appears to have thought that our 'common human understanding' can operate pretty well without 'science [*Wissenschaft*] and philosophy', which is then only really needed in order to give us clear principles that can aid us in resisting temptation, nonetheless there is no suggestion in Kant that this 'common human understanding' involves no reflection *at all*, even if on its own it doesn't quite get to the dizzying heights of the categorical imperative.[19] It therefore seems simplistic of Løgstrup to think only 2) and not also 1) will generate a reflective turn to considerations of duty for the Kantian; and given that he is prepared to allow for 1), it is then hard to see how his position differs much from Kant's on this interpretation.[20]

[15] Løgstrup 1997: 275. [16] Løgstrup 1997: 276. [17] Løgstrup 1997: 277.

[18] For the passage that famously suggests this, see Kant *MM*: 378–9 [6:224]. As ever, however, Kant's position may not be as simple as this makes it appear, but we cannot go into the issue further here.

[19] Cf. Kant *GMM*: 58–9 [4:404–5], where on the one hand Kant writes that 'there is, accordingly, no need of science and philosophy to know what one has to do in order to be honest and good, and even wise and virtuous'; but on the other hand, he makes clear that this is only because 'common human reason' has a 'compass in hand', and so 'knows very well how to distinguish in every case that comes up what is good and what is evil, what is in conformity with duty or contrary to duty', suggesting that Kant believed that some sort of reflective process involving considerations of duty is still involved.

[20] A further point could also be made against Løgstrup here: namely that his 1) and 2) are not exhaustive, so that other grounds for reflection can also be appealed to by the Kantian. For example, one may have reason to doubt the reliability of one's immediate and spontaneous responses (for example, I know myself to be a rather soft-hearted individual), so that some questioning of those responses may be required (for example, I may feel great concern not to hurt this student's feelings by telling him his essay is not up to standard, but perhaps it would be right if I were to do so, where it seems I then need to be governed by a concern to act as I should, not just as I am being drawn to by the situation in which I find myself, faced by an eager student).

A second response that Løgstrup might make to the Kantian model proposed above, is to say that there is some awkwardness and unclarity in this talk of levels of motivation. For, one might wonder which level is the *real* motivator here, and how exactly these levels interact and relate to one another. In response to this sort of concern, however, Baron has argued that it only arises if one has an empiricist view of motivation, which is itself alien to the Kantian picture, of motivation consisting in some sort of 'impulse'—where it might then seem that only one motivating force can be in play, or be what is truly effective, either one's sense of duty, or one's concern for the other person.[21] For Kant, however, to be a dutiful agent is not to come under a different sort of 'force' distinct from that which impels the non-dutiful agent, but to be someone who interrogates what appear to her to be reasons for action, and asks of them whether acting on them would make the action right, where this is needed before the putative reasons are allowed to exercise motivating force over her. Thus, the sympathetic, the prudent, and the dutiful agent may all be led to act by the suffering of the victim, where this is what motivates them—but the sympathetic agent and the prudent agent allow this to happen for very different reasons from the dutiful one, which is why for the latter it is duty and not sympathy or prudence that operates as their secondary motive. In the end, then, for the Samaritan on Kant's model it is still the suffering of the victim which motivates him to act, but it is only permitted to do so once he has assured himself of the rightness of so acting, so that considerations of duty play a crucial role in the motivational story.

A third response Løgstrup could make, is to accept that there is indeed some distinction in motivational levels that can be intelligibly drawn, but to argue that for the Good Samaritan, this second level is not about duty, so that when he takes the suffering of the traveller to be a reason to act, it is not because he judges that he will thereby be doing what is right, but simply because he judges that he will have thereby served the interests of the traveller—so the focus is not on his success in meeting his obligations, but on whether the good of the other has been enhanced.[22]

In fact, however, there might be two different worries behind this sort of point. The first could be that the Good Samaritan is someone who does not think about the right, but only the good—namely the consequences of his acts for the well-being of others; where by contrast, the 'Kantian Samaritan' thinks about the right, because Kant puts the right prior to the good. Now, of course, it is a complex issue in Kant's ethics how these notions should be related; but even if Løgstrup were correct to characterize a difference between the two Samaritans in this way, I am not sure it

[21] Cf. Baron 1995: 188–93.

[22] Cf. Løgstrup 2007: 77: 'Mercifulness is elicited by the perception of another person being hampered in the realization of his life. It appeals to as elemental a hope as that of seeing every life realized. The other person's lot is at odds with that hope, and from the dissonance inherent in that circumstance is born the mercifulness that seeks, through action, to vindicate the hope and remove what stands in the way of its fulfillment—whether the obstacles be poverty, need, oppression, or exploitation'.

would show what he wants—namely, that the Kantian Samaritan is therefore someone who is trying to 'wiggle out of the situation' and acting out of a concern for their own righteousness. It would seem, rather, that the two Samaritans just disagree about what really matters in ethics—the right or the good—much as a consequentialist or a Kantian might, where there is no reason simply on that basis to suspect the moral motives of the latter as against the former.

There could, however, be a second worry here, which is that when it come to the second level of motivation, the motivation of the Kantian Samaritan is 'if I act in this way, I will have done what is right and thereby have acted in a righteous manner', while that of the Good Samaritan is 'if I act in this way, I will have realized the well-being of the person in need'. Thus, the thought might be, all that the Kantian has done is to transfer the concern with one's own righteousness from the primary to the secondary level, and so no real advance has been made. But, of course, the Kantian can equally reply that this objection merely repeats at the secondary level the confusion that was rejected at the primary level: namely, the confusion between duty as an end and duty as a motivating ground. Thus, the Kantian can claim, the dutiful agent is motivated by the thought that helping the traveller is the right thing to do and that at the secondary level they are committed to doing what is right, but not because by so acting they will achieve their aim of being a dutiful agent.

A fourth and final criticism from Løgstrup might be as follows: Whether duty operates at the primary or secondary levels, the fact remains that when Kant himself comes to consider the 'interest' that we take in acting morally, he treats concern with our own worth as what is fundamental, in a way that confirms the critique of Kant that he is offering. Thus, Løgstrup writes:

> Why should I do my duty? Kant answers somewhere: in order not to come to despise myself in my own eyes... in order not to come to be ashamed about myself... in order not to be unworthy in my own eyes... in order not to sink in personal worth. 'In my own eyes' shows that duty sets a magic circle around human beings and traps them hopelessly in themselves.[23]

In this way, Løgstrup could say, although he might want to avoid it, the Kantian in the end is compelled to admit that action from duty is far from the kind of selfless action that Kant himself would so like it to be.

Now, an obvious line of response open to Løgstrup's opponent at this point is to insist that for Kant, motivation to do one's duty is supposed to involve respect or reverence for the moral law, rather than concern for one's personal worth, and that Løgstrup's interpretation of Kant that has him saying otherwise is misconceived. However, this is perhaps too quick, as Løgstrup is in fact willing to acknowledge that Kant in fact hoped to offer an account of this kind; he doubts, nonetheless, whether he succeeded in doing so:

[23] Løgstrup 1938: 213, quotation translated by Niekerk.

> But what, then, is the sentiment evoked by the thought of the rightness of the act? It is easy to imagine that it would be one of rapture at one's own righteousness. The question is whether it can be anything else. It can indeed, say Kant and Kierkegaard. Couched in Kantian terms, the relation to the noumenal world cancels out what is here referred to as moral introversion, and reverence for the law precludes self-righteousness from acting as the motivating sentiment. Couched in Kierkegaardian terms, the relation to infinity and eternity represents not introversion but interiorization, and duty and virtue are replaced by decision. To put it perspicuously, albeit crudely: once motivation has been decoupled from the intended outcomes of the action, Kant and Kierkegaard deem it susceptible of a religious determination, with the result that the will, to speak with Kant, or obedience, to speak with Kierkegaard, becomes the only thing that is good in itself.
>
> But then Kant and Kierkegaard have forgotten that it is of the nature of morality to be a substitute. Their respective ethics amounts to a religious sublimation of the thinking that cleaves to the moral substitute.[24]

The difficulty with Løgstrup's position here, however, is that it simply seems to beg the question against his Kantian opponent, by *assuming* that because morality must be a substitute, then the official Kantian view must fail. And again, he seems to have made this mistake because he has taken it for granted that the Kantian must have 'decoupled [motivation] from the intended outcomes of the action', such as relieving the suffering of the traveller; but as we have seen, the Kantian can keep this in place at the primary level, while at the secondary level, our motivation to do what is right or our duty can then be said to come for Kant from the reverence we feel for the moral law—that is, for what it is that is right or our duty.

Nonetheless, it could be said that there is more force to Løgstrup's critique than this: for Kant himself poses the question of the 'interest' that we take in morality, and arguably seems to answer it in the way that so discomforts Løgstrup. Thus, on the one hand, it is true that Kant states clearly that the only correct motive for moral action is 'esteem for one's duty, [where] it is just this respect for the law that straightaway has the greatest force on a spectator, and not, say, any pretension to inner magnanimity and a noble cast of mind'.[25] On the other hand, in the passages Løgstrup is presumably referring to in the quotation above,[26] Kant repeatedly points to the self-esteem that can be generated by doing one's duty and the deeply rooted fear of being unworthy in the eyes of others when one does not[27]—where in the context of this discussion, which is moral education, such considerations are given much weight. Løgstrup might therefore seem entirely justified in seeing here a covert motive for doing one's duty, where it precisely operates as a 'substitute', to overcome the temptations we feel to act otherwise.

[24] Løgstrup 2007: 79. [25] Kant *CPrR*: 265 [5:157].

[26] Thanks to Niekerk and Svend Andersen for confirming this with me; Løgstrup himself doesn't provide any citation.

[27] Cf. Kant *CPrR*: 261 [5: 152 lines 11–12 and 27–32], 264 [155 lines 4 to 6], 269 [161 lines 16–24].

However, Kant himself is of course sensitive to this worry, and offers his own way out of the difficulty, which is to allow that we do indeed take a great interest in acting morally insofar as we see great value in being moral agents—but at the same time he treats this as completely consistent with denying that we act morally *as a result of*, or *out of*, this interest, as what motivates us to act at the secondary level is nothing more than 'esteem for our duty'. Thus, just as the virtue theorist can claim that the moral agent can gain greatly in well-being from acting morally, and thus take a great interest in so acting, without thinking that it is this interest that motivates her to be virtuous, similarly Kant can allow that the moral agent can recognize great value in having his 'higher' self realized through moral action, and so take great interest in it, without that interest being what motivates the dutiful agent to act—and thus without serving as a 'substitute' in the manner that Løgstrup suggests, and which he wrongly infers from the passage in Kant that he finds so striking.

13.2 Kant's Critique of Morality

We have seen, then, how there are problems with Løgstrup's view of morality as a 'substitute', as providing an alternative and less selfless set of motivations when the direct concern with others fails us; rather, as Niekerk and others have suggested, it appears that an agent can be motivated by duty and virtue without this necessarily being a sign that anything has gone awry for them in this way, and thus when 'the motive is no longer drawn from the consequences that the action will have for the lives of others and for society', it must then be 'sought in the individual himself'.[28] A dutiful agent acting out of a motive of duty, it seems, may no more be doing so in order to look good in his eyes and that of others, than an agent whose act is a 'sovereign expressions of life', where both may be equally self-forgetful.

However, at this point, it may be helpful to Løgstrup if we turn for assistance to an unexpected quarter: namely Kant himself. For, it will now be argued, while Kant's position on these questions is somewhat different from Løgstrup's in certain respects, there is also a surprising amount of common ground—perhaps attributable to the common Lutheran inheritance on such matters that they both share.[29]

This turn to Kant may be unexpected, not only because Løgstrup himself makes him a target, but also because it can appear that Kant himself is an unequivocal supporter of the ethics of duty as the highest form of morality[30]—which is, of course,

[28] Løgstrup 2007: 78.

[29] For discussions of Løgstrup's relations to Luther, see Niekerk 2007: 57–9; and Andersen 2007.

[30] See, for example, Kant's famous hymn in praise of duty in *CPrR*: 209 [5:86]:

> *Duty*! Sublime and mighty name that embraces nothing charming or insinuating but requires submission... what origin is there worthy of you, where is to be found the root of your noble descent which proudly rejects all kinship with the inclinations, descent from which is the indispensable condition of that worth which human beings alone can give themselves?

why Løgstrup's targeting of him seems to make perfect sense. Thus, at the start of the *Groundwork of the Metaphysics of Morals*, where Kant famously argues that only the good will can be considered 'good without limitation', he then suggests that such a will is demonstrated in acting out of duty rather than inclination, thus seeming to make dutiful action paramount. Moreover, as we have seen, unlike Løgstrup, Kant held that what makes action in accordance with duty admirable is precisely that it is not self-directed or motivated by self-regarding concerns; rather, '*duty is the necessity of an action from respect for the law*', whereby 'there is left for the will nothing that could determine it except objectively the *law* and subjectively *pure respect* for this practical law'.[31] Far from being a 'substitute' for some higher form of more selfless engagement, it is clear that for Kant acting out of a sense of duty and of the authority of the moral law is the best way in which we can exemplify a good will and display moral excellence, where (as we have seen Løgstrup recognizes) Kant would deny that the person who acts from duty must do so from a rapturous admiration for their own righteousness, or because some other more direct ethical motivation that he might have felt initially has failed him so that duty as a motive 'has to leap into the breach and ensure that the act is still performed'.[32] To this extent, therefore, Kant can deny that there is anything ethically inferior about the 'Kantian Samaritan', for though he might act out of duty, he may do so for Kant out of respect for the moral law rather than out of concern for his righteousness; and also without the motivation from duty 'substituting' for a different ethical motive he might have had instead had he been a better person, where for Kant the only alternative open to him might be an inclination (of the sort displayed by the good-hearted philanthropist)[33] that is without the moral worth that is required to put his acting from duty in a bad light.

Nonetheless, despite not sharing these aspects of Løgstrup's view, it is still the case that Kant has his own grounds for treating the dutiful agent as less than ethically ideal in certain crucial respects: for, the fact that duty and obligation figure so centrally in our moral lives is for Kant the result of our ethical limitations and the ethical inadequacy of our natures, much as it is for Løgstrup. To this extent, therefore, both may be said to share in the Lutheran view that the law exists not for the righteous, but only for the unrighteous.[34]

Kant's position here can be seen most clearly in the distinction that he draws between the human will on the one hand and the holy will on the other. The actual

[31] Kant *GMM*: 55 [4:400]. [32] Løgstrup 2007: 78. [33] Kant *GMM*: 53–4 [4:398].

[34] Cf. Luther 1930: Part 1, §3: 'By the Spirit and by faith all Christians are throughout inclined to do well and keep the law, much more than any one can teach them with all the laws, and need so far as they are concerned no commandments not laws. You [then] ask, Why then did God give to all men so many commandments, and why did Christ teach in the Gospel so many things to be done?... Paul says that the law is given for the sake of the unrighteous, that is, those who are not Christians may through the law be externally restrained from evil deeds, as we hear later [I Timothy 1:9: 'The law is not given for the righteous, but for the unrighteous']. Since, however, no one is by nature Christian or pious, but every one sinful and evil, God places the restraints of the law upon them all, so that they may not dare to give free rein to their desires and commit outward, wicked deeds.'

difference he points to is in essence a simple one, and obviously relates to standard theological conceptions of our 'fallen' state: whereas a divine will acts only in line with the good, and has no inclinations to do otherwise, we have immoral desires and inclinations, that mean we find ourselves drawn to adopt immoral courses of action. As Kant puts it: 'The dispositions of the deity are morally good, and those of man are not. The dispositions or subjective morality of the divine are therefore coincident with objective morality',[35] but ours are not.

While the contrast Kant draws is itself perhaps not unusual, the way he uses it is nonetheless considerably more distinctive. For, he deploys it in order to explain the way in which duty and obligation arise in ethics, which had been a long-standing matter of debate within philosophy and theology, and had played a central role in disputes between natural law theorists, divine command theorists, and others. The issue, put simply, was how to explain the peculiar force morality has for us, which takes the form of duties and obligations—that is, of *commands* or *imperatives*, telling us that there are actions we *must* or *must not* perform. Kant calls this feature of morality 'necessitation' or 'constraint' (*Nötigung*), and he explains it not by recourse to a divine command, or to a kind of 'fitness' in things, but in terms of the distinction between the holy will and our own, arguing that it is because we have dispositions to do things other than what is right, that the right for us involves a moral 'must'; but for a holy will, which has no inclination to do anything other than what is right, no such 'must' applies. A typical statement of Kant's view is the following from the *Groundwork of the Metaphysics of Morals*:

A perfectly good will would, therefore, equally stand under objective laws (of the good), but it could not on this account be represented as *necessitated* to actions in conformity with law since of itself, by its subjective constitution, it can be determined only through the representation of the good. Hence no imperatives hold for the *divine* will and in general for a *holy* will: the 'ought' is out of place here, because volition is of itself necessarily in accord with the law. Therefore imperatives are only formulae expressing the relation of objective laws of volition in general to the subjective imperfection of the will of this or that rational being, for example, of the human will.[36]

[35] Kant *LE*: 56 [27:263]. Cf. also *LE*: 68 [27:1425]: 'The divine will is in accordance with the moral law, and that is why His will is holiest and most perfect... God wills everything that is morally good and appropriate, and that is why His will is holy and most perfect'; and *LE*: 229 [29:604]: 'In the Gospel we also find an ideal, namely that of holiness. It is that state of mind from which an evil desire never arises. God alone is holy, and man can never become so, but the ideal is good. The understanding often has to contend with the inclinations. We cannot prevent them, but we can prevent them from determining the will'; and *LR*: 409 [28:1075]: 'A holy being must not be affected by the least inclination contrary to morality. It must be *impossible* for it to will something that is contrary to the moral law. So understood, no being but God is holy. For every creature always has some needs, and if it wills to satisfy them, it also has inclinations which do not always agree with morality. Thus the human being can *never* be *holy, but of course* [he can be] *virtuous*. For virtue consists precisely in *self-overcoming*.'

[36] Kant *GMM*: 67 [4:414].

Thus, the principles that determine what it is good and bad to do apply to the holy will, where these principles are laws because they hold of all agents universally, and of such agents independently of the contingencies of their desires and goals, and thus necessarily.[37] However, because the holy will is morally perfect, these laws lack any necessitating force, whereas our lack of moral perfection means that they possess such force for us.[38]

It can therefore be seen how Kant's distinction between the holy will and ours is designed to resolve the problem of obligation, by appeal to the fact that our will is divided between reason and inclination in a way that the will of the divine being is not. Kant characterizes this division in the terms of his transcendental idealism as mapping onto the distinction between the noumenal and phenomenal realms (or the 'intelligible world' and 'the world of sense'):

> And so categorical imperatives are possible by this: that the idea of freedom makes me a member of an intelligible world and consequently, if I were only this, all my actions *would* always be in conformity with the autonomy of the will; but since at the same time I intuit myself as a member of the world of sense, they *ought* to be in conformity with it; and this *categorical* ought represents a synthetic proposition a priori, since to my will affected by sensible desires there is added the idea of the same will but belonging to the world of the understanding—a will pure and practical of itself, which contains the supreme condition, in accordance with reason, of the former will.[39]

Kant thus uses his transcendental idealism, and his dualistic picture of the will, to offer a solution to the transcendental question he raises concerning the imperatival nature of morality, of 'how the necessitation of the will, which the imperative expresses... can be thought'.[40] Kant's distinction between the holy will and ours therefore forms a crucial part of his answer to the problem of accounting for the moral 'must', in a way that explains its possibility (unlike a view that simply treats the 'must' as a feature of the world), but without recourse to the problematic notion of a divine legislator as the source of that 'must' (thus avoiding any need to adopt a divine command theory).

[37] On universality, see: *GMM*: 65 [4:412]: 'moral laws are to hold for every rational being as such'. On necessity, cf. Kant's distinction between *principles* and *laws*, where the former are what govern 'what it is necessary to do merely for achieving a discretionary purpose', and so can be 'regard as in [themselves] contingent and we can always be released from the precept if we give up the purpose', whereas a moral law 'leaves the will no discretion with respect to the opposite, so that it alone brings with it that necessity which we require of a law' (*GMM*: 72 [4:420]). Cf. also *GMM*: 44–5 [4:389].

[38] Cf. *GMM*: 377 [6:222]: 'An imperative is a practical rule by which an action in itself contingent is *made* necessary. An imperative differs from a practical law in that a law indeed represents an action as necessary but takes no account of whether this action already inheres by *inner* necessity in the acting subject (as in a holy being) or whether it is contingent (as in a human being); for where the former is the case there is no imperative. Hence an imperative is a rule the representation of which *makes* necessary an action that is subjectively contingent and this represents the subject as one that must be *constrained* (necessitated) to conform with the rule.'

[39] Kant *GMM*: 100–1 [4:454].

[40] Kant *GMM*: 70 [4:417].

Now, leaving aside various complexities which Kant's view involves,[41] it can, I think, be seen how far Kant's position may in fact be said to resemble Løgstrup's: for Kant takes a morality of duty to be ethically inferior in important respects to that of the holy will, to whom no such moral 'must' applies. In fact, Kant's perspective on this is made evident at the very outset of the *Groundwork*, where he first introduces the idea of duty after his discussion of the good will: for, he makes clear there that duty pertains not to the good will *as such*, but to 'that of a good will though under *certain subjective limitations and hindrances*',[42] which is clearly a reference to the non-moral aspects of our nature that turn goodness into a matter of duty for us. Kant allows that these aspects do not entirely obscure the goodness in us, and in acting from duty this goodness is revealed in a way that in some respects makes it 'shine forth all the more brightly'[43] because of the contrast with what it has overcome—but nonetheless, the fact remains that the holy will represents a form of ethical life that is higher than the ethics of duty which is our lot.

To this important extent, therefore, Kant can be counted as a critic of morality alongside Løgstrup, where for both, acting from duty is to be seen as a kind of 'second best' and a departure from the ideal. At the same time, however, the differences of detail between them may enable Kant to make this critique more convincing than (we argued) Løgstrup was able to do. Let me explore this in further detail.

At the heart of Løgstrup's objections to morality, it seemed, was the following basic idea:

> When we treat *A* as a duty, we are trying to make *A* in our interests and thus provide a fresh motive to do it, as by conceiving it as a duty, we are then able to take self-righteous pleasure in doing *A*.

Now, this idea was said to be problematic in two related central respects: first, agents can take it that they have duties to act, where it seems implausible to suppose that they are thinking in this way in order to give themselves an interest in doing these actions; and secondly, in doing an act because it is a duty, an agent may not be reflecting on how doing it makes them look, and so may not get self-righteous satisfaction from it at all.

However, an advantage of Kant's position from this perspective is that he does not have to characterize things in quite this way, while still reflecting the spirit of Løgstrup's view. For, on the one hand, Kant does not treat duty as providing us with a 'substitute motive'; on the other hand, he does treat the imperatival force of duty as a sign that the agent is not a holy will, but rather plagued with desires that are not in alignment with what it is good or right to do. To this extent, therefore, Kant's position has echoes of the 'backsliding objection'. Likewise, Kant holds that we can be motivated to act from duty out of respect, and not from the sense of self-

[41] For further discussion, see my Stern 2012: Chapter 3.

[42] Kant *GMM*: 52 [4:397] (my emphasis).

[43] Kant *GMM*: 52 [4:397].

righteousness that so acting give us; on the other hand, this respect comes about only because we are fallen creatures, forced to look up to the moral law. Thus again, to this extent Kant's position has echoes of the 'self-righteousness objection'.

Rather surprisingly, perhaps, a case can therefore be made that instead of being at odds with one another here, to a large degree Kant and Løgstrup share a common outlook on the relative merits of morality.

13.3 'Our Life Is, Ethically Speaking, a Contradiction': Duty and the Unfulfillability of the Ethical Demand

Having shown how Løgstrup's critique of morality might be developed along Kantian lines, I now finally want to suggest that this need not prevent Løgstrup holding on to a central claim that he wants to make concerning the radical nature of the ethical demand that we care for the other, and particularly its unfulfillability.

Løgstrup's insistence that the ethical demand is unfulfillable has not surprisingly caused a degree of consternation, where the basis for this is often some sort of appeal to the principle that 'ought implies can'. While this principle is not without its ambiguities and complexities, and is not as obviously true as is sometimes supposed,[44] to many it will appear to cast doubt on the coherence of Løgstrup's position here. So, for example, MacIntyre writes:

> Løgstrup's account is flawed. The notion that we can be required to respond to a demand that is always and inevitably unfulfillable is incoherent. If I say to you 'This cannot be done; do it,' you will necessarily be baffled.[45]

MacIntyre is clearly appealing here to the oddity of someone ordering someone else to act in a way that is also said by them to be unachievable, where he is assuming that a command of this sort forms the basis for the demand. In raising this objection, MacIntyre is obviously interpreting the demand in what might be called a 'straight' manner, as something that we are told to do, while at the same time it is held that doing it is impossible. Although even taken in this manner MacIntyre's concerns may not be insuperable,[46] they are certainly understandable and will doubtless appear plausible to many.

However, it is questionable whether MacIntyre is correct to understand Løgstrup's position in the way that he does, as if what makes the demand into a demand is a commander telling you that something must be done, even while he thinks you are incapable of doing it. For, if we take the Kantian perspective outlined in the previous section into account, I think we can see Løgstrup's position differently, and as offering instead what might be called a 'self-effacing' conception of the unfulfillability of the ethical demand, based on the following idea: Care for the other will only

[44] For further discussion, see my paper Stern 2004; reprinted as Chapter 6, this volume.
[45] MacIntyre 2007: 164. [46] Cf. Martin 2009.

appears *as* a demand or as something *required* of them to agents who lack a holy will, and who thus to some degree *resist* caring for others by virtue of their inclinations to do otherwise. As a result, such an agent cannot fulfill the demand to care for the other, because if this demand were properly met, then they would become like holy wills, in which case it would not seem to the agent to *be* a demand at all, as the inclinations that make it so would be lacking—so qua demand it is unfulfillable. Thus, if the demand arises at all, it is already too late, as the truly good individual would not experience or be conscious of any such demand in the first place, and nor could the idea be applied to them; on the other hand, if we did in fact manage to achieve the right relation to the other, as a holy will could, we would not be under any demand, so it could not be met this way either.[47] So, it appears, the ethical demand is unfulfillable, because if it comes into play at all we are already lost, whereas if we are not lost, it does not come into play, so that either way it is radically unfulfillable in the way Løgstrup suggests:

> Every attempt to obey the demand turns out to be an attempt at obedience *within the framework* of a more fundamental disobedience... what is demanded is that the demand should not have been necessary. That is the demand's radical character.[48]

Or, as Løgstrup puts it elsewhere: 'The demand demands that it be itself superfluous.'[49] Thus, Kant's conception of the human will/holy will distinction, and how this explains the moral imperative or demand as it applies to us, can be used to show how Løgstrup's claim concerning the unfulfillability of the ethical demand can be made coherent, when this is treated not as a command from a commander who knows you cannot do what he says, but as a felt 'must' that arises for a will that has already gone wrong from the moment it has experienced it.[50]

[47] Cf. Løgstrup 1997: 145:

> The relationship to the demand varies with the relevant motives. The demand is present and asserting itself whenever a person who is without love does nevertheless, out of a sense of responsibility or out of fear, what he believes love would do. Through the sense of responsibility we are aware of its authority, and the fear is the fear of authority.

Cf. Wolf 2007: 213: '[Løgstrup points] to the fact that the ethical demand is unfulfillable in the sense that it demands to be superfluous. Once we hear the demand as a demand, it is too late. The demand tells us what we ought to have done but did not do spontaneously.'

[48] Løgstrup 1997: 146. [49] Løgstrup 2007: 69.

[50] While I think this is an important part of the 'contradiction' that Løgstrup speaks of here, there is another aspect that is more distinctive of his position rather than Kant's, which (as he puts it) 'sharpens' the contradiction yet further: namely that 'This demand comes to us because we want to be sovereign over our own lives' (Løgstrup 1997: 146), by which he means the following: We treat the ethical relation as one of *demand* because in fact (ironically) this gives us greater control over it as something we can then manage by obeying or not obeying in what we take to be appropriate ways; but in reality, according to Løgstrup, what underlies the demand is the fact that our life is something given to us over which we *do* not have control, and over which we are *not* sovereign, but rather 'receive', so that in attempting to obey the demand we are at the same time violating it. Thus, as Løgstrup puts it: 'In a sense, our attempt at obedience actually works against the demand, for every attempt at obedience is an expression of that which the demand opposes, namely, the will to be sovereign over my own life', rather than to receive it as a gift, which is why

This approach may also help resolve something else which puzzles MacIntyre about Løgstrup's position. Thinking that Løgstrup is troubled by the idea of a command that cannot be met,[51] MacIntyre notes that Løgstrup says that it is *also* fulfillable, but in a way that MacIntyre regards as hopelessly contradictory.[52] Again, puzzlement here is understandable, but in a way that can now perhaps be resolved. For, on the reading I have suggested, while the demand qua demand cannot be fulfilled, what the demand asks us to *do* can still be done, so it can be fulfilled in this sense: that is, at least on many occasions, I can do what is demanded, namely 'care for the other person in a way that best serves his or her interest'.[53] And this would seem to meet Løgstrup's central concern in this discussion of the contradictory nature of our moral lives, which is that on the one hand we should not fool ourselves into thinking we are better than is the case (where the sense in which the demand is unfulfillable will always remind us that we are not holy wills),[54] while on the other hand we need to avoid letting ourselves off the hook with the idea that we are unable to do what is required[55] (where the sense in which it is fulfillable reminds us that we can at least do the action that is demanded of us, even if this cannot ever be sufficient for us to claim that we are wholly good, as the action would not then *be* a demand at all).

Finally, if I am right to claim a shared perspective between Løgstrup and Kant here, this can be made less surprising despite their apparent disagreements, given their common Lutheran heritage. One important aspect of that heritage is Luther's focus on the Pauline claim that 'The law is not given for the righteous, but for the unrighteous' (I Timothy 1.9). One way to understand Luther's view of this claim, is that the law belongs to those who are not completely good; for those who are, there is no such law, so for such beings the law is not so much fulfilled as effaced:

> To fulfill the law, we must meet its requirements gladly and lovingly; live virtuous and upright lives without the constraint of the law, as if neither the law nor its penalties existed.[56]

'every attempt to obey the demand turns out to be an attempt at obedience *within the framework* of a more fundamental disobedience' (Løgstrup 1997: 146). To explain Løgstrup's position here fully, and particularly the conception of 'life as a gift' that this would require, must be matters for another occasion.

[51] Cf. Løgstrup 1997: 165:

> But is not the demand canceled by the fact of its impossibility? Can the demand abide its own impossibility? The assumption is that every demand, whatever its content, presupposes that it is fulfillable; otherwise it is not a demand but a meaningless pretense.

[52] See MacIntyre 2007: 164. [53] Løgstrup 1997: 55.

[54] Cf. Løgstrup 1997: 166: 'But it must be added that we cannot concede life's claim that the demand can be fulfilled by giving up our own claim that it cannot. Why not? Because this would be the same as to entertain illusions about ourselves. To give up our claim that the demand is impossible of fulfillment is to become entangled in the pious fraud that self-assertion and will to aggrandizement are not products of our nature, and that we would therefore be able to overcome them without dying. The result would be a life of pretense and a feigned unselfishness.'

[55] Cf. Løgstrup 1997: 166: 'On the other hand, the impossibility of fulfillment of the demand... is the impossibility of fulfillment for which we refuse to accept blame. We refuse to accept blame by maintaining that we cannot help it if we do not obey the demand.'

[56] Luther 1961: 21.

13.4 Conclusion

My aim in this paper has been to consider Løgstrup's critique of the Kantian conception of morality as involving duty. While I have argued that as it stands that critique fails, I have also argued that some of Løgstrup's central points in making that critique can be saved—ironically by turning to Kant himself, and seeing how his account of duty also sees it as a 'substitute' for the very different ethical life of the holy will.

14

Divine Commands and Secular Demands

On Darwall on Anscombe on 'Modern Moral Philosophy'

Elizabeth Anscombe's 1958 paper 'Modern Moral Philosophy' remains a provocation to ethical theorists, and rightly so: for such theorists characteristically take themselves to be trying to establish what moral obligations there are, what it takes to properly abide by them, how we can know what they require, and so on. But Anscombe thinks that in the present age this enterprise is a waste of time, as the whole idea of moral obligations being deployed here makes no real sense in the absence of a belief in a divine law-giver, a belief which nowadays is lacking. Thus, she argues, we should abandon the moralistic conception of the good person as one who abides by such laws and the bad person as one who violates them, and instead relate goodness and badness to an account of the virtues, which can provide an alternative conception to what we must or must not do, where this has nothing to do with the imposition on us of a law.[1]

Now, clearly, one strategy in responding to Anscombe is to accept that morality does indeed involve obligations imposed on us through demands, commands, sanctions, and the like, but to argue that these constraints do not need to be seen as imposed on us by God, but instead can come from ourselves and one another, thus rendering the legalistic moral outlook coherent in a secular manner. Stephen Darwall has recently offered us a version of this strategy, but he has also added to it. For, rather than merely juxtaposing the theistic and secular accounts or rejecting the former on external grounds, he has related the former to the latter in the style of an internal critique: that is, he has argued that if looked at closely, the theistic model is unstable and that when its difficulties are thought through, it must resolve itself into

[1] Cf. Anscombe 1981: 19: 'All this, it may be said, does not prove the *necessity* of acting justly in the manner of contracts; it only shows that a man will not act well—do what is good—if he does not do so. *That* necessity which is the first one to have the awful character of *obligation*, is a tabu or sacredness which is annexed to this sort of instrument of the human good.'

the more secularized account which overcomes those difficulties, and so is to be preferred. In this way, he suggests, Anscombe's position in 'Modern Moral Philosophy' can be 'turned on its head': far from the move from the theistic to the secular view of moral obligation leading us into incoherence, it is rather the only way to save the former from more fundamental problems of its own, where resolving them will show why the secular position deserves our allegiance instead.[2] This may be taken to highlight a limitation in Anscombe's approach: whereas she holds that the divine command view is closed off to us simply because we live in a secular culture, Darwall holds it is closed off because it is inherently unstable, but that once the grounds of this instability are understood, we can also see how it needs to be transposed into a more stable secular form, and thus how we can retain the strong notion of moral obligation even when we have given up our belief in a divine law-giver. As such, clearly, Darwall's argument has great interest and significance, for if it were successful, it would in effect demonstrate that the logic of divine command morality itself shows that it must give way to the social command position instead, where as individuals we can impose moral obligations on each other, rather than such obligations having to come from God alone.

In what follows, I will examine whether the negative aspect of this internal critique proposed by Darwall really works, of showing that the divine command account of ethics has internal pressures that require it to be transformed into a secular social command view; I will not consider in any detail the positive aspect of this critique, and thus Darwall's claim that this secular social command view is itself fully defensible, where we might expect Anscombe herself to dispute both of these suggestions.[3] The question is, then, whether the difficulties Darwall raises for the divine command view can be resisted, or if they cannot be, whether they are just as much difficulties for his own view as well.

I will begin by saying more about Anscombe's position, and Darwall's critique of it, in Section 14.1. In Section 14.2, I will then explore the adequacy of that critique, as a response to Anscombe's view that moral obligation must involve law-giving by God, and cannot come from another source such as man or the world. I will suggest that Darwall's attempt to overturn Anscombe's position here in an internal manner encounters serious problems in two central respects: first, that while the legitimacy of God's commands shows we must be able to blame ourselves and others for failing to obey them, this does not entail that we can also act as moral legislators alongside

[2] Darwall 2006: 115, n. 45: 'This will turn Anscombe's famous claims in "Modern Moral Philosophy" (1958) on their head. Although I agree with Anscombe that morality is inconceivable without the idea of addressable demands, I maintain that her claim that they require divinely addressed demands ultimately overturns itself in the way I have indicated.' Gary Watson also remarks on the relation between Darwall's project and Anscombe's: see Watson 2007: 37–8, where he then worries about the adequacy of Darwall's response on pp. 40–6. For Darwall's reply to Watson on this score, see Darwall 2007: 65–9.

[3] For some questioning of the secular social command view, with which I think Anscombe might well be sympathetic, see Adams 1999: 241–8.

God; and second that the divine command position is not problematically circular in the way that Darwall suggests. As a result, therefore, it will be argued that Darwall's critique of Anscombe, despite its undoubted interest and significance, in the end must be seen as a failure.

14.1 Darwall contra Anscombe

In 'Modern Moral Philosophy' Anscombe argues that while the ethics found in Aristotle was based on the virtues, Judeo-Christian ethics came to be based on laws, with God acting as the law-giver; so, whereas for Aristotle a bad person was one who failed to live virtuously, for the religious ethicist the bad person was one who broke the rules laid down by God.[4] Anscombe argues that this new picture of ethics as involving moral duties rather than the virtues makes sense as long as one is thinking in theistic terms, with God as the law-giver who makes the laws the breaking of which means a person is bad or wicked or sinful.[5] However, once this idea of God has been lost (as she thinks it predominantly has in modern culture) then it does not make sense any longer, as such laws need legislating, and only God has the characteristics necessary to operate as the legislator of the *moral* law: for only he has the requisite power, knowledge, authority, and so on, which neither we nor the world itself can claim, making it impossible to replace him with another kind of law-making—and if we were to try to do so, we would run the serious risk of ending up with a distorted form of moral thinking.

Anscombe makes these concerns clear when she runs through various attempts that modern moral theorists have made to substitute some other law-giver for God, where she comments: 'Those who recognize the origins of the notions of "obligation" and of the emphatic, "moral", *ought*, in the divine law conception of ethics, but who reject the notion of a divine legislator, sometimes look about for the possibility of retaining a law conception without a divine legislator. This search, I think, has some interest in it' (Anscombe 1958: 5–6). As the last remark suggests, Anscombe did not believe that there is anything *obviously* misguided in attempting to hold onto a legalistic conception of morality without God, or that to do so is clearly crazy or absurd; it is just that on past history, it turns out that attempts to do so have misfired, in ways that suggest that it is more problematic than it first appears.

The options she considers are as follows, in the order she considers them, together with her objections, where the whole discussion (in line with the style of 'Modern

[4] It is of course a large question, which cannot be gone into here, how far Anscombe's historical claims can in fact be substantiated—or indeed whether insofar as she is providing a 'genealogy' they even have to be. As the focus here is on Darwall's critique of Anscombe, where he makes no play with such issues, I will therefore leave them aside.

[5] Cf. Anscombe 2008: 117: 'We may say that there are two definitions of sin: 1. They are behaviours against [right] reason. 2. They are behaviours against divine law.'

Moral Philosophy' as a whole) is notably brief, programmatic, and also pugnacious (see Anscombe 1958: 13–15):

> *The laws come from society, and its 'norms'*: but society can have and has had norms that tell people to do things that are clearly objectionable, so this is not a very trustworthy ground for morality.
>
> *Individuals can make laws for themselves as individuals, in a process of 'self-legislation'*: but this is 'absurd', as one cannot impose laws on oneself, any more than in making a decision, a person can be said to have authorized that action in a democratic manner by counting this as a majority vote in its favour.[6]
>
> *The laws come not from actual social norms, but ones that we set out to find*: Anscombe praises the element of self-criticism in this option as opposed to the first one, but argues that it is still not clear where one is going to look to identify such norms.
>
> *Laws come from the natural world, 'as if the universe were a legislator'*: but nature is not nowadays seen in a moral light, but as governed by, for example, evolutionary laws, which do not seem very likely to offer us a guide to the moral norms we are after.
>
> *Laws come from a social contract, as a constraint that we have put ourselves under in living together*: but Anscombe raises various difficulties. One difficulty is to make sense of the contracting involved: When did we sign up to it, and if we did not how can we be held to it? And if the contract is somehow treated as implicit, for example in the very use of language, Anscombe is concerned about the kind of moral law that would come from this model, where she writes that 'I suspect that it would be largely formal; it might be possible to construct a system embodying the law (whose status might be compared to the "laws" of logic): "what's sauce for the goose is sauce for the gander," but hardly one descending to such particularities as the prohibition of murder or sodomy'.
>
> *Laws come from proper functioning, so the content of the moral law relates to how the individual should best live in order to flourish*: but this is to take us back to the virtue model rather than the law model, so we haven't really got anywhere with the project of making sense of 'law—without bringing God in'.

It is worth noting two things about this list. First, Anscombe does not proceed very systematically through the options, and I do not think she would claim to have shown that they are exhaustive. Second, she applies two tests to the options proposed: are they coherent as sources of law, and if we took them to be such sources, would we end up with a form of morality that is objectionable? So, for example, self-legislation and contract are seen to be problematic as sources of law, whilst on the other hand the difficulty with nature or the norms of society is that it would be morally dangerous to treat them as guides in ethical matters, even if we could coherently conceive of them as embodying law-like structures.

[6] Cf. Anscombe 1958: 2: 'Kant introduces the idea of "legislating for oneself", which is as absurd as if in these days, when majority votes command great respect, one were to call each reflective decision a man made a *vote* resulting in a majority, which as a matter of proportion is overwhelming, for it is always 1–0. The concept of legislation requires superior power in the legislator.' Cf. also p. 13: 'That legislation can be "for oneself" I reject as absurd; whatever you do "for yourself" may be admirable; but it is not legislating.'

We can now turn to Darwall's challenge to Anscombe's position here, as expressed in his recent book *The Second-Person Standpoint* and related articles.[7] As mentioned previously, Darwall's challenge is particularly interesting for its 'internal' nature: that is, while many reject divine command ethics and then defend a more secularized alternative instead, Darwall argues that the problems he identifies with the former then *lead* to a cogent version of the latter, so that when properly thought through, Anscombe's model of God as the law-giver can and must resolve itself into just the kind of *non*-theistic law conception which she says cannot make sense, hence turning her position upside down.

Darwall begins by agreeing with Anscombe that the moral ought differs fundamentally from other 'oughts', where this difference does not just lie in their universal, categorical, and conclusive nature—that is, that they apply to all rational agents, that they give agents to whom they apply reasons to act regardless of their aims or desires, and that they override or silence countervailing reasons. For, Darwall argues, much the same might be said of the 'oughts' of logic or reasoning more generally,[8] where these 'oughts' still differ from those of morality. However, these 'oughts' of logic and reasoning hold independently of anyone being in a position to demand or require that one think in these ways: it is not down to anyone's authority over you that you ought to believe in climate change given the evidence, or ought to draw a particular conclusion from these premisses. But when it comes to the moral 'ought', Darwall holds, things are different: here you are accountable to yourself or others, involving a demand or requirement or claim or command that can be made in a second-personal manner, from addresser to addressee, where the latter is accountable to the former. Darwall thus agrees with Anscombe that a command model fits morality in a way that does not apply to other oughts, and gives moral oughts their distinctive nature.[9]

Nonetheless, despite this common ground, Darwall thinks he can avoid Anscombe's claim that this model must be a *hierarchical* one, with God and God alone being seen as capable of issuing moral commands and hence legislating the moral law. To argue for this, he looks in some detail at the positions of Francisco Suarez and Samuel Pufendorf, to try to show that insofar as they adopt divine command positions, they accordingly face certain fundamental difficulties, which require a more secular and non-hierarchical position if these are to be resolved. The key issue here concerns what gives God his unique role as commander or legislator. If this is said to come simply from his power over us, then the moral 'ought' becomes

[7] As well as Darwall 2006, see also 2004 and 2007. Related issues are also dealt with in Darwall 2012.

[8] Actually, I think that this could be questioned: if believing *p* would ruin your life, but *p* clearly follows from all the evidence before you, is it clear that the reasons you have to believe *p* override your reasons to reject it? But let this pass.

[9] See Darwall 2004: 110–11; 2006: 5–15, 26–8; and Darwall 2013b, where he explicitly sides with Anscombe and against Hume in claiming that 'What makes morality distinctive among normative notions is its network of juridical ideas' (p. 19).

purely prudential and hence loses its categorial nature, as we seek to avoid his punishments or to attract his rewards; if, on the other hand, it is said to come from his legitimate authority and not merely his power, then the question arises how this authority is to be explained or grounded, if the moral ought *depends* on this authority in the first place. For Suarez, this question was less pressing, because he allowed that there was right and wrong prior to God's making any actions obligatory through his commands, so that this prior normative framework could then be used to account for God's legitimacy.[10] But for Pufendorf, there was no such prior framework, as moral properties only came about at all through God's willing and hence 'imposing' them on the natural order of things[11]—where it is this picture that then gives rise to the problem identified by Leibniz and others, and sometimes referred to as 'Pufendorf's circle'. The problem is this: if God's authority is to be legitimate and not merely coercive, it must be right to obey it; but then this rightness cannot come from that commanding authority itself, as it is presupposed in order to render that authority legitimate and hence a source of moral commands; but if instead it is said that the rightness of obeying God is just basic or rests on the fact that he orders us to do right things, then rightness is made prior to God's commands and the latter is rendered redundant. Pufendorf thus seems caught in a circle from which he cannot escape.[12]

Darwall's next move is to argue that the only way to get out of this circle, and to show that God's power is exercised over us legitimately, is to show that we would

[10] Cf. Suarez 1612: Bk. II, Ch. VI, §17, p. 202: 'Therefore, my own [view] is that in any human act there dwells some goodness or evil, in view of its object, considered separately insofar as that object is in harmony or disharmony with right reason . . . In addition to this [objective goodness or wickedness], human actions possess a special good or wicked character in their relation to God, in cases which further involve a divine law, whether prohibitory or preceptive.' For some further discussion of Suarez's 'intermediate' view, see Irwin 2008: 1–69.

[11] Cf. Pufendorf 1688: Bk. I, Ch. I, §4, pp. 5–6: 'For [moral entities] do not arise out of the intrinsic nature of the physical properties of things, but they are superadded, at the will of intelligent entities, to things already existent and physically complete, and to their natural effects, and, indeed, come into existence only by the determination of their authors.'

[12] Cf. Leibniz 1706: §V, pp. 73–4:

> Nor do I see how the author [Pufendorf], acute as he is, could easily be absolved of the contradiction into which he falls, when he makes all juridical obligations derivative from the command of a superior . . . while . . . he [also] states that in order that one have a superior it is necessary that they [superiors] possess not only the force [necessary] to exercise coercion, but also that they have a just cause to justify their power over my person. Consequently the justice of the cause is antecedent to this same superior, contrary to what had been asserted. Well, then, if the source of law is the will of a superior and, inversely, a justifying cause of law is necessary in order to have a superior, a circle is created, than which none was ever more manifest. From what will the justice of the cause derive, if there is not yet a superior, from whom, supposedly, the law may emanate?

Cf. also Ralph Cudworth's related argument against Hobbes: 'And if it should be imagined, that any one should make a positive law to require that others should be obliged or bound to obey him, everyone would think such a law ridiculous and absurd. For if they were obliged before, then this law would be in vain, and to no purpose. And if they were not before obliged, then they could not be obliged by any positive law, because they were not previously bound to obey such a person's commands' (Cudworth 1781: Bk. I, Ch. II, §3, pp. 18–19).

blame ourselves for not acting as he requires us to act, so that in legislating over us God must take it that we have this capacity for holding *ourselves* responsible for our actions, and criticizing ourselves when we fail. But, Darwall then claims, to blame oneself in this way involves having moral standing in one's own right, as it is to exercise authority over oneself; so again, in commanding us, God must also presuppose that we have this standing. But then, if we have standing that enables us to exercise authority over ourselves, this then gives *us* the authority to make demands of ourselves and others, rather than that authority belonging merely to God.[13] So, Darwall claims, it turns out that in starting with a conception of morality as involving commands, one must end up with a secularized view of moral obligations, where we are all capable qua rational agents of making demands of ourselves and others, and so making it morally right and wrong to act in certain ways through a system of *mutual* accountability, and not a hierarchical one.[14]

Darwall thus claims that there is a dynamic internal to a divine command conception of morality that, when played out, pushes it towards a system of mutual accountability between persons, of the sort favoured by more secular moral theorists such as Kant and his modern-day contractualist successors. In this way, therefore, a divine command theory becomes transformed into a form of social command theory, where the normative structure which must not be violated in order to be good comes

[13] In this context, Darwall is fond of quoting Kant's remark from *The Metaphysics of Morals*: 'I can recognize that I am under obligation to others only insofar as I at the same time put myself under obligation' (Kant *MM*: 543 [6:417]). See Darwall 2006: 23, n. 47, and 218, n. 7. In general, this is what Darwall refers to as 'Pufendorf's Point'.

[14] Cf. Darwall 2006: 114:

> We should view voluntarists like Pufendorf as putting forward but one *conception* of a more general *concept* of morality as accountability. Any interpretation of this general concept must see morality as grounded in the possibility of a second-personal community. What characterizes a voluntarist conception is that it takes a moral hierarchy for granted and then derives the rest of morality (by fiat) from that. As we have seen, however, tendencies within the general idea of morality as accountability put heavy pressure on a voluntarist interpretation of that idea. To distinguish between moral obligation and coercion, Pufendorf required an account of moral agents' distinctive capacity for self-censure from a shared second-person standpoint and its role in free rational deliberation. But this effectively assumes that to be accountable to God, moral agents must also be accountable to themselves.

Cf. also p. 105:

> Pufendorf believed that morality essentially involves accountability to a superior authority, namely God. But, he also believed that being thus accountable is only possible for free rational agents who are able to hold themselves responsible—who can determine themselves by their acceptance of the validity of the demands, thereby imposing them on themselves. I argue that this idea exerted a pressure on his thought in the direction of morality as equal accountability, although the latter is not, of course, a conception he accepted or likely would have accepted on reflection.

Cf. also Darwall 2012: 231: '[For Pufendorf] Someone can be accountable only by *holding himself* accountable. If, consequently, moral obligations are that for which we are appropriately held answerable by God, it follows that God must be able to expect us to accept his authority to issue legitimate demands and to judge ourselves censurable for failing to obey.'

not from God, but from us. As a result, Darwall claims, Anscombe's position has been turned upside down.

14.2 Anscombe contra Darwall

I now want to consider two responses that I think Anscombe can make to Darwall's argument against her; the first to Darwall's claim that our capacity to blame gives us the standing necessary to generate moral obligations, and the second to Darwall's use of Pufendorf's circle to show that the divine command view is inherently problematic.

14.2.1 Response to the argument from blame

As we have seen, Darwall's argument against the divine command theorist moves from God's command, to questions concerning the legitimacy of that command, to an appeal to self-blame as a way of responding to those questions, to the capacity to make mutual demands, to a social command theory in which we (and not God) hold each other to account. Our capacity to blame ourselves therefore plays a crucial role in the argument. A central question, then, is whether this notion can carry the weight that is required to move the internal critique forwards, or whether a gap in the dialectic opens up at this point. It is this issue which I now wish to explore.

I think Anscombe would do well to accept one important aspect of Darwall's position, namely that there is a constitutive link between taking an authority to be legitimate, and viewing oneself as being blameworthy if one fails to obey it; thus, it seems correct for Darwall to argue that in taking God's authority over us to be legitimate and not merely coercive, the divine command theorist must allow that this is to see ourselves as blameworthy if we do not do as he requires of us. If we did *not* see ourselves as blameworthy in this way, we would therefore be rejecting the commander's authority, so that some aspect of self-blame does seem to follow from seeing that authority as legitimate.

The question is, however, whether in granting this much, Anscombe has to be committed to granting that this then gives us any *legislative* capacity, on a par with God's, where for the divine command theorist as Anscombe sees her, it is this capacity which creates obligations. Does it follow from our capacity for self-blame that we have the standing necessary to legislate over ourselves and others, or is this something that could still intelligibly be granted just to God by the divine command theorist, even though we must be able to blame ourselves for failing to obey his laws? The question still arises, therefore, whether this self-blame can amount to law-giving or legislating: for if it cannot, then it does not follow that our capacity for the former is sufficient to mean we have a capacity for the latter. So, how might blaming oneself be said by Anscombe to differ from legislating the moral law?

A first difference, she could argue, is that law involves sanctions, and that unless the legislator has superior power over those on whom the law is imposed, the legislator cannot exercise these sanctions; but it is absurd to think one has superior power over oneself, so while one can blame oneself, one cannot meaningfully be said to legislate over oneself in this manner. A second difference is that, in the case of law, sanctions are used as punishment for violations that the law-giver decides to apply, whereas in the case of self-blame, even though blame may resemble punishment in being painful or unpleasant in certain ways, it is not imposed *as* a punishment that one thereby decides to inflict on oneself; I may feel guilt or self-blame at telling a lie, for example, but if I do this is not because I have decided to cause myself to suffer as an appropriate form of self-inflicted punishment—self-blame is not like self-harm, which is intentional in this way.[15] Thirdly, even if a law does not directly involve sanctions, it still involves the taking away of a person's freedom, as it involves the prevention of the person acting in a way that the law prohibits.[16] Again, however, it can be said that this does not make sense in the case of self-blame: for while self-blame may in part involve a resolution not to act some way in the future, how can I deprive myself of the freedom to act in this respect, any more than I can take away my freedom by forming an intention or plan? So, in general Anscombe's argument here would be this: even if Darwall is right that to impose a law on us God must presuppose that we would blame ourselves for violating it, this does not make us law-givers over ourselves, as self-blaming is not the same as legislating, for much the same reason that self-legislating is not either, as it has the wrong relation to issues like sanctions, loss of freedom, power, and the like. The essential difficulty, it seems, is that legislating involves enforcement between subjects, where it is not clear that

[15] For similar observations relating to these two points, see Teichmann 2008: 109:

> For there to be a law, (a) it must be promulgated, (b) it must be enforced or enforceable. Enforcing a law means wielding sanctions against those who knowingly break it, i.e. punishing them—something that in general requires that the legislating authority have adequate physical power to do that, power superior to that of law-breakers. A law is not a request, nor yet a cooperative agreement. In fact, one cannot make requests of oneself, or make agreements with oneself, any more than one can legislate for oneself; but in the case of legislation, as Anscombe indicates, the main problem for Kant's view is that one cannot punish oneself for breaking one's own 'laws'. Of course, one can feel guilty at breaking one's own resolutions, but guilt is not something one decides to impose on oneself, in the way that sanctions must by definition be deliberately imposed (so that they can also be threatened). To call guilt a sanction can only be to speak metaphorically.

Interestingly, Kant would appear to agree, where he distinguishes between *repentance* and *penance*, and accuses 'monkish ascetics' of confusing the two, by failing to see that self-punishment does not make sense: 'Instead of morally *repenting* sins (with a view to improving), [the monk] wants to do *penance* by punishments chosen and inflicted by oneself. But such punishment is a contradiction (because punishment must always be imposed by another)' (Kant *MM*: 597 [6:485]).

[16] This aspect of law can be made constitutive, even by those who do not think that the manner in which this freedom is taken away is through force or sanctions, such as Aquinas or more recently Joseph Raz. Cf. Aquinas 1920: I–II q90 a1: 'Law is some sort of rule and measure of acts, in accordance with which someone is led towards acting or is restrained from acting; for law [lex] is derived from binding [ligare], because it binds one to acting.' And cf. Raz, who denies that law requires sanctions, but accepts that law must claim authority, and authority is understood as a matter of binding (that is, preemptive) directives, and thus limits to freedom. See Raz 1975: 154–62.

self-blame can incorporate this in the right way; thus, even if Anscombe were to accept that we have the standing necessary for the latter, it would not follow that she need be committed to allowing that we have the capacity and hence standing for the former. At this point, therefore, Darwall's argument seems to rest on a non sequitur.

Darwall might offer various responses to these worries, however. First, he could try to get round the problem that self-blame differs from legislation insofar as it involves no relation between subjects, and hence no superior power, no sanctions, and no taking away of freedom, by a strategy of dividing the self into parts or aspects, and then treating self-blame as a legislative relation between these parts or aspects. So, for example, he might claim in a Kantian manner that the rational self has power over the sensuous self, and so can impose sanctions on it and limit its freedom, and thus legislate over it, where this is then done through some process of blame or censure whereby the former controls the latter. Or, he might claim that as self-blame involves an intention not to act some way in the future, this involves my present self restraining my self in the future. However, I suspect Anscombe would reject this response as resting on little more than metaphor: whilst the self can be divided into faculties or temporal parts, the results of these divisions are not actual selves with wills, and so cannot be thought of as replicating the relation between subjects that the legislative picture requires. Indeed, it could be argued, it is clear that no genuine loss of freedom occurs here, as none of the ethical issues that normally come with any such loss make sense in these contexts—no one worries, for example, over whether my present self is really entitled to infringe the liberty of my future self in this way. Moreover, as many divine command theorists have argued, since this position involves nothing but a relation within the same self, it cannot count as genuine law-giving, for it is then too easy for the self to annul it, meaning that it lacks any real binding force—it would be more like a new year's resolution than a law.[17]

However, to get over this difficulty over enforcement and the apparently problematic nature of self-legislation, Darwall might move from self-blame to blame by other selves, but who are human rather than divine. Here, then, we really do have

[17] This sort of worry was commonplace among divine command theorists, such as Pufendorf himself and also Jean Barbeyrac, who set out to defend Pufendorf from Leibniz's critique. See for example Pufendorf 1688: Bk. I, Ch. VI, §7, p. 94 and Bk. II, Ch. III, §20, p. 217, as well as 1672: Axiom II, §2, p. 218; and Barbeyrac 1735: 293–4: 'Now no one can impose on himself an unavoidable necessity to act or not to act in such or such a manner. For if necessity is truly to apply, there must be absolutely no possibility of it being suspended at the wish of him who is subjected to it. Otherwise it reduces to nothing. If, then, he upon whom necessity is imposed is the same as he who imposes it, he will be able to avoid it each and every time he chooses; in other words, there will be no true obligation, just as when a debtor comes into the property and rights of his creditor, there is no longer a debt. In a word, as Seneca long ago put it, no one owes something to oneself, strictly speaking. The verb "to owe" can only apply between two different persons.' John Selden applied the same worry not only to self-legislation, but also to legislation within a social context: 'I cannot bind myself, for I may untie myself again; nor an equal cannot bind me: we may untie one another. It must be a superior, even God Almighty' (Selden 1892: Ch. LXXVII, p. 101). Cf. also Aquinas 1920, I–II q93 a5: 'law directs the actions of those who are subject to the government of someone; wherefore, properly speaking, none imposes a law on his own actions'.

other people, who can operate blame as something more like a sanction or punishment, and who can thus more plausibly be said to act as law-givers than can one part of the self over another. A difficulty with this response, however, is that the internal critique may seem to break down at this point: for, while it may be plausible to think that to recognize an authority as legitimate, I must be inclined to blame myself for failing to obey it, it may seem possible to recognize an authority as legitimate without thinking that *other people* are in a position to blame me for failing to obey it. For example, suppose I am ordered by my sergeant to perform fifty press-ups and do not do so, where I am the only one in the platoon who is fit enough to actually do them at all. I might therefore think none of the platoon members can blame me for failing to accomplish this task as none of them could have done it themselves, but without feeling the sergeant's authority to demand this of me is jeopardized.

However, Darwall could respond to this worry by saying that at least my action must be counted as *blameworthy* by others, even if some or maybe even all people are not really entitled to actually blame me, given that they could do no better, where this still involves holding me to account for my actions in a significant way. Thus, he might maintain, the enforcement of my action by others must still apply if God's authority is to be legitimate, where this still gives us a legislative power. This response may be further reinforced if we allow Darwall another point he insists on:[18] namely that when one individual holds another to account (including themselves), they do so not qua individuals, but as a member of the 'moral community', so that it is never just the individual exercising authority over themselves, but must involve others as well, hence moving us from *self*-blame to blame by others and so avoiding the problematic features of merely self-legislation outlined above. It may seem, then, that the bridge from our capacity for self-blame to our capacity for legislation is reasonably robust after all, at least when it comes to understanding the aspect of law-giving that involves the application of sanctions and constraints through the practice of blame: Darwall has arguably done enough to show that God does not have a monopoly over such blaming, and that the divine command theorist must allow that we can also go in for it too.

A further significant issue remains, however: namely that even if this is granted, it arguably does not show that we possess any law-giving capacity alongside God's. For, as well as sanctions being needed, the laying down of law also essentially involves the creation of *new reasons* based on the exercise of authority involved in law making. So, for example, when the sergeant makes it compulsory for his platoon to do twenty push-ups every morning, or the state makes it a law for us to pay certain taxes, by using their authority there is now a new reason to do these things that was not there

[18] Cf., from a passage already cited above: 'To distinguish between moral obligation and coercion, Pufendorf required an account of moral agents' distinctive capacity for self-censure from a *shared second-person* standpoint and its role in free rational deliberation' (Darwall 2006: 114, my emphasis). It is this 'shared second-person standpoint' that Darwall conceives of as constituting the moral community.

before, a reason derived from that authority.[19] By contrast, however, blame does not create reasons for a person to act, but rather is a response to a failure to act on reasons that the agent *already has*. Thus, no matter how much I might blame myself or be blamed by others for failing to act as God commands, this does not show that in so doing an act of legislating is going on, in the sense of giving myself new reasons to act; rather, in taking myself as blameworthy, all this shows is that I am capable of responding to reasons I take myself to have already, and so it has not been shown that I have the kind of legislative capacity needed if we are to replace God as a law-giver.[20] Thus, even if Darwall's argument concerning God's legitimacy can show that this entails we have the capacity to hold ourselves to blame for not acting in certain ways, this further worry still remains: namely, that any such exercise of blame does not show we have the authority to give other agents new reasons to act based on that authority, in a way that legislation requires.

In fact, Darwall himself seems to be aware of the essential point here, but without apparently recognizing the damage it does to his argument against Anscombe and the divine command theorist:

> [Bernard] Williams evidently assumes that it is a conceptual truth that violations of moral obligations are appropriately blamed and that blaming implies the existence of good and sufficient reasons to do what someone is blamed for not doing. The idea is not, of course, that normative reasons follow from the fact of someone's being blamed. Rather, in blaming one implies or presupposes that there are such reasons.[21]

This seems exactly right: blame does not itself create normative reasons to act, but reflects those that are there. But this then allows the divine command theorist to open up a gap between Darwall's argument concerning our capacity to blame and his claims about our standing in relation to God, because this theorist can grant us the capacity to blame without granting us the capacity for legislation, insofar as fresh normative reasons *do* follow from that. This is why, as we have said, I can think you are blameworthy by me and the rest of us for not doing what the sergeant says, and can think that we would not see her authority over us as legitimate unless you were so blameworthy, while still not thinking that anyone other than the sergeant is in a position to make the commands that we blame you for not following, where a

[19] This is a point that Darwall himself seems happy to allow: see e.g. Darwall 2006: 12: 'When a sergeant orders her platoon to fall in, her charges normally take it that the reason she thereby gives them derives entirely from her authority to address demands to them and their responsibility to comply... The sergeant's order addresses a reason that would not exist but for her authority to address it through her command'.

[20] It might be said, perhaps, that in blaming myself for not ϕ-ing, I *am* giving myself a reason to ϕ, namely a prudential reason to avoid this felt discomfort. But this would not be the sort of reason created by authority, which gives one a reason to act not merely to escape the sanctions that such authority can wield—rather, the reason one has to act is that ϕ is now obligatory, otherwise the reason such authority creates would no longer be moral but merely prudential.

[21] Darwall 2006: 94.

normative hierarchy between us and the sergeant therefore still remains: only *she* can issue the orders, while we can all blame you for failing to obey them. It is precisely a hierarchy of this sort that the divine command theorist will insist upon in the case of God's relation to us as well, so that the internal critique seems to have broken down at this point.

Finally, however, it might be said on Darwall's behalf that this is to underestimate what his argument from blame has succeeded in establishing, for it has shown that the divine command theorist must allow that we have a certain sort of moral standing which puts us on a par with God, which Darwall's picture of 'morality as equal accountability' requires (cf. Darwall 2006: 101). This might be brought out in two ways. First, it could be said that the argument shows that we must at least have the standing needed to legitimately impose sanctions such as blame on ourselves and others, which is not a negligible moral fact about us, but shows that we can hold ourselves and others accountable and make demands of ourselves and others, which is something we share with God and other creatures do not. Thus, the fact that I can hold you blameworthy shows that you must respond to me in certain ways, for example you must explain to me why you failed, or apologize, where my capacity to hold you blameworthy is creating reasons for you to do at least these things, even if it is not creating the reasons that make me blameworthy in the first place if I fail to follow them. In this way, Darwall could argue, the fact that we can make these demands shows precisely that Rawls was correct to say that we are 'the self-originating sources of claims',[22] where then it is not God alone who is the source of such claims and thus of obligations. Secondly, it could also be argued, from the very fact that the distinction between merely coercive power and legitimate authority applies to God's relation to us, it follows that we must have some kind of moral standing—or otherwise, how could this distinction between coercion and legitimate authority even make sense in the human case? Unless we had some such standing, how could there be any intelligible difference between the two—there would just be a being with power over us, where the question concerning the legitimacy of exercising that power would not arise, as it does not when applied to things without that standing, such as my desk, a plant, or (some) animals. So, if the question of legitimacy is even going to come up, and so make it the case that God must not use merely coercive force over us, it might seem that we must be granted some moral status by the divine command theorist, in a way that apparently constrains how God can act towards us.

It seems, then, that in either or both these ways, the divine command theorist must be committed to giving us some position in the moral universe, and one that God cannot ignore. But then, it could be argued, if this is so, does not this mean we can in effect make moral demands of God, by requiring him to act some ways and not

[22] Cf. Darwall 2006: 21, 121, 316. This phrase is taken from Rawls 1980: 546.

others; and moreover, if we can make demands of him in this way, why can we not do the same of other people, regarding how they too exercise their powers over us? So, finally, it looks like we must have the kind of authority required to impose obligations on others, not to simply coerce us but to respect us—with the result that not only God can claim to be the source of such demands, but so too can we in relation to our fellow human beings. It thus seems, then, that we could use the notion of blame, and unpack this idea to arrive at something like Darwall's social command theory, in which we are shown to be in a position to impose moral obligations on others, through establishing that we have the sort of moral status which this capacity requires.

However, I believe this approach also fails to achieve what Darwall is looking for in criticizing the divine command theorist. The problem, I think, is that the divine command theorist can accommodate these suggestions that we have some moral standing on the one hand, without on the other granting us an authority to impose obligations on God or others, on a par with God's authority.

When it comes to the first point, the divine command theorist could allow that the fact that I can legitimately wield sanctions over myself and others through processes of blame, and so make demands that hold myself and others to account, shows that I indeed have some status in the moral universe, without it following from that fact that I have the kind of *legislative* capacity which God possesses, where as we have seen this requires more than the applying of such sanctions and the making of such demands. For, the divine command theorist could argue, it is quite possible for him to allow that we are beings who can make demands, while also holding that what we demand is compliance with a law legislated by God, not ourselves, where my ability to make these demands thus depends on the moral law that God has laid down, as it is *this* that I am able to hold myself and others to, rather than *myself* being the source of valid claims in a way that is 'self-originating'. Of course, if Darwall's internal critique had shown that we possess this legislative capacity alongside God, then he could claim that the demand is to comply with a law of our own making; but he has not done so, I have argued, and an appeal to this capacity to make demands does not in itself then add anything to his case. And it would not be enough for Darwall to say that just being able to make this demand of oneself and others is sufficient to show that we can create obligations in Darwall's sense, because the authority is still parasitic on God's, where it is on this basis that we can blame others for their failures and hold them to account, not our own authority or that of the secularized moral community. This means, then, that the fact that we can blame people for not acting in certain ways does not mean that they owe any explanation or apology to *us*—this is all owed to God, as the being who ordered them to act in those ways in the first place. The divine command theorist can thus allow this claim about our capacity to treat certain actions as blameworthy and hence make demands in this sense, while still insisting that the second-personal authority relation fundamentally only holds between us and God, not between ourselves. Darwall, of course, is inclined to put blame together with reactive attitudes such as resentment, which is a reactive attitude in response to a failure to abide by what is owed *to you* rather than to others and so is more clearly second-personal;[23] but blame, it seems, does not have to take this form. The divine command theorist can therefore legitimately grant us the capacity to blame without also thinking that the restitution needed to respond to the blame is something that ties us to the transgressor in a second-personal way, and thus assumes we have this kind of moral authority over them—God alone could still have that.

When it comes to the second point, I think the divine command theorist can again claim that Darwall's position falls short, even while allowing that the coercion/legitimate authority distinction as it applies to us shows that we have some moral status. For, as Darwall himself recognizes, something can have a status such that there is good reason to treat it in certain ways and not others, without that treatment being something the being in question can *require*, or demand in a second-personal manner.[24] So, for example, insofar as coercing me would harm me, belittle me, or fail to respect me, where such considerations do not arise for my desk or car or tree in my garden, we could speak of God using his power over me legitimately or illegitimately insofar as he respects these facts about me or not, thereby accommodating the relevant distinction between mere coercion and legitimacy, and explaining how it applies to his treatment of me; but the divine command theorist can admit this much, without also granting that we can *demand* this treatment from God, on the basis of our second-personal authority over him.[25] Rather, these could be treated as third-personal normative facts about me, which seem sufficient to ground the legitimate/illegitimate distinction, but without granting us any second-personal authority alongside God. It would seem, then, that once again the divine command theorist can grant Darwall his starting point, but resist being pushed down the dialectical path that would force him to adopt Darwall's stopping point, namely a form of social command theory.[26]

[23] Darwall thus introduces blame as part of what he calls 'Strawson's point' concerning the reactive attitudes: see e.g. 2006: 17.

[24] Cf. Darwall's key distinction between second-personal reasons and other reasons in 2006: 5–10.

[25] We might get closer to this idea of demand, of course, if the only way to make sense of talk of God's legitimacy or illegitimacy is in terms of how far he respects or violates the rights of those over whom such power is exercised, where having such rights would arguably give us the authority to make claims on God as well as others; this is a line of argument Darwall seems to offer in 2012: 232. But as I have suggested above, provided the divine command theorist can make sense of the legitimacy/illegitimacy distinction in other terms, which it seems she can, then there is no need for them to accept this assumption, so once again the immanent critique breaks down.

[26] In his 2012, Darwall raises another interesting internal critique, but one which seems too directed at Pufendorf specifically to merit more general discussion here: namely, that there is a tension between Pufendorf's insistence that what God commands is that we have a sociable attitude on the one hand, and on the other hand the fact that our reason to adopt this attitude is said to come from that command, where this would seem to undermine the very attitude in question: 'Despite the fact that Pufendorf holds that the mutual obligations entailed within sociability themselves derive from God's command to take a sociable attitude (the "fundamental law of nature"), it simply seems impossible to come to have a sociable attitude of esteem for someone *for the reason that God commands it*. One could, of course, desire to acquire the

14.2.2 Response to the argument from Pufendorf's circle

Even if I am right so far, however, it could still be said that Darwall has a good case against the theist, in so far as she faces the problems raised by Pufendorf's circle: Surely, if Anscombe cannot successfully resolve that, her position is in trouble, and will need to be replaced by some other view?

As will be recalled, Darwall argues that the circle arises when Pufendorf moves from thinking of God's commands as more than just an exercise of coercive power over us, but as also the exercise of a legitimate authority with some normative basis. However, it is then difficult for Pufendorf to explain what this normative basis could be, as he thinks that all moral properties come about through 'imposition' and thus through God's command, so there then appears to be no prior normative order on which his legitimacy can be grounded. Likewise, it could be argued, the same problem arises for Anscombe: for, if God is a law-giver whose laws make actions right or wrong, then how can it be right to do what God legislates; and if it is not, how can he have legitimate authority over us, and not merely coercive power? Then, Darwall argues, the way out of this problem for both Pufendorf and Anscombe must be to answer questions about God's authority by relating this to self-blame: for, if we hereby call ourselves to account for acting in certain ways, then this will also mean we accept the legitimacy of God commanding us to act in those ways as well, hence seeing his power over us as not merely coercive, just as a criminal who blames himself for his crimes can be said to accept the legitimacy of the outlawing of those actions rather than seeing it as a case of mere force.

Now, one obvious worry about Darwall's position here is how this move to internal or self-blame can really help give us a way out of Pufendorf's circle, and so act as a transition point in the dialectic journey from a theistic to a secular outlook. For, consider the position of someone who takes Pufendorf's circle seriously, and who therefore sees no grounds on which God can be anything other than a coercive power over us, as there is no prior normative framework through which to make the exercise of his power legitimate. Darwall's response is to argue that escape lies in self-blame, for if you would blame yourself for the action, this is to accept that God and then others are right to prevent you from so acting, thereby rendering their constraints justified and not mere exercises in arbitrary power. However, the worry is that this position is in fact no less problematic and circular than Pufendorf's: for if blame is the exercise of power over oneself, the question still seems to arise what makes *this* a case of legitimately exercised authority rather than mere coercive force, such as neurotic self-repression; or if blame is not such a legitimate exercise of power, how can self-blame then legitimate the power used by others?

attitude for this reason, or undertake steps to try to inculcate it for this reason. But trying to see someone as intrinsically worthy of esteem or respect for this reason would be like trying to form an intrinsic desire for a saucer of mud for some external reason having nothing to do with any features of mud that one might be able to see as making it desirable' (pp. 229–30).

Now, I think Darwall would be ill-advised to opt for the second horn of this dilemma and so suggest that blame is not really an exercise of power: because if he did so, he would make it even easier for Anscombe to then insist, as we have already seen she will do, that self-blame is unlike the kind of imposition or binding involved in genuine law and command. But there are also problems if he opts for the first horn. For it seems that the natural way to try to deal with the first horn is to say that self-blame is legitimate because you have done something wrong, so you are fully entitled to blame yourself for your action and to try to commit yourself to not so acting in the future. But then it turns out that the way of escaping from Pufendorf's circle relies not so much on an appeal to self-blame, as to an appeal to the fact that there is a prior normative order of right and wrong that does not come about through blame, command, law-giving, or anything else—much as Leibniz and other normative realists argued against Pufendorf.[27] However, if it therefore turns out that the only effective way to get out of Pufendorf's circle is to be a realist in this manner, then the argument from here does not really go through self-blame, which Darwall needs if he is to get from a divine command to a social command theory; rather, the dialectic will take him to a view that legitimate commands and legitimate self-blame *both* depend on what is commanded or blamed already being right, so that the fundamental normative structure is not really derived from *anyone's* authority to demand actions of us and so is not genuinely second personal at all. Thus, while Darwall's worries about Pufendorf may mean that Pufendorf's position is problematic, it transpires that when taken seriously, they mean that Darwall's is too, as it seems that the lesson to be learned from Pufendorf's difficulties is that what is right and wrong is not dependent on the claims we can make on each other; rather, the claims we can make on each other depend on what is already right and wrong.

Perhaps, however, Darwall might choose to respond to this challenge by distinguishing between moral rightness and wrongness on the one hand, and moral obligation on the other, and arguing that the latter involves a further normative dimension not present in the former—just as it can be right to give to the poor, but not obligatory to do so. Using this distinction, Darwall could then claim that while we cannot make legitimate demands on ourselves and others unless what we are demanding is the right thing to do, nonetheless *by* so demanding we make the act morally obligatory in a way that it was not before—and whereas the divine command theorist thinks that only God can do this demanding, a secular theorist thinks that we

[27] Cf. Leibniz 1706: §IV, p. 71: 'Neither the norm of conduct itself, nor the essence of the just, depends on his [i.e. God's] free decision, but rather on eternal truths, objects of the divine intellect, which constitute, so to speak, the essence of divinity itself; and it is right that our author is reproached by theologians when he maintains the contrary; because, I believe, he had not seen the wicked consequences which arise from it. Justice, indeed, would not be an essential attribute of God, if he himself established justice and law by his free will. And, indeed, justice follows certain rules of equality and of proportion [which are] no less founded in the immutable nature of things, and in the divine ideas, than are the principles of arithmetic and of geometry.'

can do so instead. Taking this option, therefore, Darwall could claim to escape Pufendorf's circle in Leibniz's manner, but still leave room for the demands we make on each other as explaining what turns moral rightness into moral *obligatoriness*.

Nonetheless, there is still a dialectical cost here: for now both sides of the debate between the theist and the secularist accept that some demander is needed to make what is right into something that it is obligatory to do, where the question is then whether God or we are best placed to be this demander, concerning which there are points to be made by each party to the dispute. What the dialectic has lost, however, is the suggestion that the divine command position faces a special problem concerning how to conceive of God as a legitimate authority, resolving which was meant to *lead to* the more secular view: now, it turns out, all the theist is required to give up is the extreme voluntarism of Pufendorf's position, which many theists do not accept anyway, and once he has done this, there is then no particular internal pressure towards the more secular option. Thus Suarez, for example, held the view that certain acts are intrinsically right prior to God commanding them, but God's so doing then makes them obligatory; and Suarez would hold that God is better placed than us to be seen as the ground of obligatoriness in this way, for obvious reasons: he is more knowledgeable, more powerful, wiser, possesses absolute goodness, and so on, in areas where we fall short, making us problematic sources for the moral law—even before we rehearse the considerations that were raised earlier against the idea of legislating for ourselves. Now, such theistic arguments can of course be challenged; but in challenging them, there does not seem to be the sort of charge of internal incoherence that Darwall originally started with, and which appeared to make his argument so compelling.

Turning now to Anscombe, where does she stand on all this? At first sight, at one point in 'Modern Moral Philosophy' she may seem to reject the problem of Pufendorf's circle altogether by suggesting that the issue of legitimacy that gives rise to it can be straightforwardly brushed aside, as really the legitimacy question is an empty one when it comes to God:

> And such is the force of the term ['morally wrong'] that philosophers actually suppose that the divine law notion can be dismissed as making no essential difference even if it is held—*because* they think that a 'practical principle' running 'I *ought* (i.e. am morally obliged) to obey divine laws' is required for the man who believes in divine laws. But actually this notion of obligation is a notion which only operates in the context of law.[28]

It may appear, then, that Anscombe holds that the legitimacy problem that gets Pufendorf into difficulties is really a pseudo-problem, as questions about this only make sense subsequent to God's laying down the law, and cannot intelligibly be asked beforehand—just as one cannot ask 'when did time begin?' And this approach may be

[28] Anscombe 1958: 18.

said to fit into a broadly Wittgensteinian way of trying to dissolve certain questions in terms of the 'language-games' of which they are part, rather than answering them, where Wittgenstein's influence on Anscombe is of course well known.[29]

However, I think there is also another way of taking Anscombe's position here, a way that connects instead to the case for virtue theory that she makes in the rest of the paper and allows her then not only to take the question seriously but also to address it. On this approach, her remark here is not an attempt to dismiss the question of legitimacy when it comes to God, but rather a challenge to the assumption that it can only be answered in moral terms based on a normative system of right and wrong. If Anscombe were making this assumption, she would agree that either this is derived from God's law-giving in a way that must lead to Pufendorf's circle, or that this is to be resolved in a way that makes right and wrong prior to God's law-giving, and so renders God redundant. What this assumption misses, however, is that instead of the normative framework that makes God's power legitimate being one of right and wrong, it could instead equally well be based on a consideration of the *virtues*, which (Anscombe thinks) both make sense prior to God's law-giving (contra Pufendorf),[30] and can also justify his authority without leading us into Pufendorf's circle. Of course, she thinks, such is the 'force of the term' *morally wrong*, and thus the decline in our appreciation of the virtues, that we may be blind to this possibility and think that it is only if we can be shown to be morally wrong to disobey God, that his law-giving can be made legitimate—where on this reading, it is the naturalness to us of this assumption that Anscombe is pointing out in the passage above. But her challenge is precisely that this assumption is false: in fact, by considering God's relation to us in virtue-theoretic ways, we can understand why God exercises his legislative power over us in a justified manner, a justification that comes not from a problematic appeal to notions of right and wrong (which indeed she thinks only make sense when that legislation has occurred), but from an appeal to the virtues that we would display in obeying it, and the vices we would display if we did not.

The distinctive character of Anscombe's position can be seen more clearly, I think, when one considers the role of *gratitude* in the theistic story. As Darwall notes in his discussion of Pufendorf, the latter made use of this notion when he raised the legitimacy issue, seeming to argue that it is because God has done so much for us in creating us and the world in which we live, that he merits our gratitude and is thus entitled to take away our liberty through his laws in a way that makes this more than just a case of coercive force (cf. Pufendorf 1688: Bk. I, Ch. VI, §12, p. 101). But, Darwall responds, this appeal to gratitude cannot help, as it depends on there being

[29] See, for example, the relevant essays collected in Anscombe 2011.

[30] Cf. Pufendorf 1688: Bk. I, Ch. II, §6, p. 29: 'Nay, these very terms [for vice] do not signify simple physical motions or acts, but only such as are contrary to laws, and for that reason complete moral acts. For why should [*Schadenfreude*] and envy be considered evil affections, unless it is that by a law of nature every man should be touched by another's fortune? while this rule is broken when one takes pleasure in the misfortune of others, and grieves at the sight of their success.'

some obligation to repay one's debts or to obey those who have done one considerable good, or some such moral constraint; however, this then grounds God's authority in a prior moral framework once more, and if this framework contains obligations like gratitude, it is hard to see why the rest of the actions we take to be obligatory should not also be included, hence rendering God's position here redundant.[31]

But of course, Anscombe herself predicts this very result, and accepts that it follows given Darwall's assumption—that only if ingratitude is morally wrong can it be bad, where it can then only be wrong in this way if it violates some obligation. However, her point precisely is to question why our failure in being grateful to God has to be seen in *moral* terms, and hence as the violation of some obligation he has imposed on us, and not rather as a failure to be virtuous and so bad in *this* sense—that is, given all he has done for us, if we responded to his commands by ignoring them and rebelling against him, we would show ourselves to be ungrateful, churlish, haughty, disrespectful, and so on, where it is *this* feature of our relation to him that makes his exercise of power over us more than mere coercion.[32] The idea here, then, is that all these can be seen as vices, but in a way that does not require appeal to some prior framework of moral obligations or moral wrongs: I have shown myself to be bad in failing to display the requisite virtues in relation to God and so gone astray ethically, but not because I have broken a prior moral law or gone wrong in a *moral* sense at all, which can only happen subsequent to his commands being in place.[33] Thus, it is precisely by her appeal to the virtues in this manner, and her idea that they differ from the framework of morality, that Anscombe is able to escape from Pufendorf's circle in a way that Darwall does not recognize, because he is only operating within that moral framework and its terms.

[31] Cf. Darwall 2006: 110:

> Pufendorf tries to fix this problem [of the circle] by arguing that we are obligated to obey God out of gratitude, since we are indebted to him for our 'very being' (101). But this creates problems of its own. If we are permitted to help ourselves to an independently standing obligation of gratitude in order to give authority to the structure of command, then why suppose that all obligations require command for their moral force? What is special about gratitude? Once a voluntarist makes a concession on this obligation, why should he not make it also on others?

For related worries, cf. also Schneewind 1998b: 136.

[32] Of course, God will also need to possess virtues himself in order for this gratitude to warrant his authority over us: as others have noted, we may have cause to be grateful to a villain, without this licensing him to command us to act. See e.g. Hutcheson 1755: Vol. 1, Bk. ii, Ch. 3, §7, p. 266: 'But benefits alone, are not a proper foundation of right, as they will not prove that the power assumed tends to the universal good or is consistent with it, however they suggest an amiable motive to obedience.' Cf. Irwin 2008: 425.

[33] For a response to the problem of Pufendorf's circle that I think can be related to Anscombe's as I conceive it, see Adams 1999: 252–3:

> Gratitude is instanced by Pufendorf as a source of reasons for regarding the command of another as giving rise to obligation... On my views, the appropriateness of gratitude is an excellence, a form of the excellence of prizing excellent relationships and of acknowledging the good deeds of others; and like excellence in general, it does not depend on God's commands.

The suggestion here, then, is that the source of God's authority does not rest on him telling us to do right things and thereby making us more likely to do them (as on a 'service conception'),[34] or on there being some prior requirement to do what he says which gives him that authority (as there would be if we were under an obligation to obey him out of gratitude). Rather, the idea is, he has his authority over us because not to do what he says would be to fail to be virtuous and thus good, where as a result of that authority, he is then in a position to make other virtuous actions obligatory or required.[35] Thus, to use a rather hackneyed analogy: given all that some parents have done for their children, one might think that in failing to do what they are told to do by those parents, the children show a lack of gratitude towards them, where it is precisely in this that the authority of those parents, and thus their ability to oblige their children, consists. Of course, this gratitude and thus this authority has limits, given how much the parents are responsible for in the lives of their children; but when it comes to God, the range of gratitude is much wider, and thus the range of that authority is correspondingly expanded as well. Therefore, the fundamental normative notion here is *virtue*, out of which notions of obligation can then arise in a way that enables us to escape from Pufendorf's circle. There is thus no moral obligation that precedes God's directives: there is only the reason we have to be virtuous (which is not an obligation owed to anyone); but to conform to this reason, and so be virtuous, we must show appropriate gratitude to God, where this then involves treating his directives as authoritative. And, if his directives *are* authoritative in this way, and he directs us to Φ, then we have a genuine moral obligation to Φ. If, however, we *start* with deontological notions and treat them as primary (in the way that Anscombe suggests modern moral philosophy characteristically will do), *then* the problem will appear insuperable, and Darwall's concerns will seem legitimate. If we bear in mind the place that virtues can have in ethical theory, however, this is not a mistake that we need to make. Once again, therefore, there seems no reason for the divine command theorist to feel pushed down the dialectical path that Darwall sets out, and thus no reason to feel compelled to accept the kind of secularized and humanistic ethics which he thinks it must in the end give rise to; his immanent critique, it appears, has failed.[36]

[34] Cf. Raz 1986: 53.

[35] This means, of course, that Anscombe would not accept a divine command theory of a radically voluntaristic kind, where there is no normative framework of *any* sort prior to God's command; to that extent, she would be closer to a more moderate position like Suarez's and Aquinas's. Cf. also Teichmann 2008: 107–8, who notes that for her, 'God requires what is good because it is good—a thing is not good because God requires it'.

[36] I have presented drafts of this paper at several conferences and seminars, and I am grateful to the audiences (which have included Stephen Darwall) for their helpful comments. I am also grateful to the anonymous referees of *Mind*, and to its editor, for their very useful suggestions. Particular thanks are due to my colleague Daniel Viehoff, who has been very generous with his time in discussing this topic with me, in ways that greatly improved the paper.

Bibliography

Acton, H. B. (1970), *Kant's Moral Philosophy*. London: Macmillan.

Adams, Robert Merrihew (1999), *Finite and Infinite Goods: A Framework for Ethics*. Oxford: Oxford University Press.

Allison, Henry E. (1990), *Kant's Theory of Freedom*. Cambridge: Cambridge University Press.

Allison, Henry E. (2012), 'We Can Act only under the Idea of Freedom', reprinted in his *Essays on Kant*. Oxford: Oxford University Press, pp. 87–98.

Ameriks, Karl (2003a), 'Kant's *Groundwork* III Argument Reconsidered', reprinted in his *Interpreting Kant's 'Critiques'*. Oxford: Oxford University Press, pp. 226–48.

Ameriks, Karl (2003b), 'On Two Non-Realist Interpretations of Kant's Ethics', reprinted in his *Interpreting Kant's 'Critiques'*. Oxford: Oxford University Press, pp. 263–82.

Ameriks, Karl, and Otfried Höffe (eds) (2009), *Kant's Moral and Legal Philosophy*. Cambridge: Cambridge University Press.

Andersen, Svend (2007), 'In the Eyes of a Lutheran Philosopher: How Løgstrup Treated Moral Thinkers', in Andersen and Niekerk (eds) 2007: 29–54.

Andersen, Svend, and Kees van Kooten Niekerk (eds) (2007), *Concern for the Other: Perspectives on the Ethics of K. E. Løgstrup*. Notre Dame: University of Notre Dame Press.

Anscombe, G. E. M. (1958), 'Modern Moral Philosophy', *Philosophy* 33: 1–19.

Anscombe, G. E. M. (1981), 'On Promising and its Justice, and Whether it Need Be Respected *in Foro Interno*', reprinted in *The Collected Philosophical Papers of G. E. M. Anscombe III: Ethics, Religion and Politics*. Oxford: Blackwell, pp. 10–21.

Anscombe, G. E. M. (2008), 'Sin', in *Faith in a Hard Ground: Essays on Religion, Philosophy and Ethics by G. E. M. Anscombe*, edited by Mary Geach and Luke Gormally. Exeter: Imprint Academic, pp. 117–56.

Anscombe, G. E. M. (2011), *From Plato to Wittgenstein: Essays by G. E. M. Anscombe*, ed. Mary Geach and Luke Gormally. Exeter: Imprint Academic.

Aquinas, Thomas (1920), *Summa Theologica*, second edition, revised, tr. the Fathers of the English Dominican Province. London: Burns Oates and Washbourne.

Aristotle (1984), *Nicomachean Ethics*, in *The Complete Works of Aristotle*, the revised Oxford translation edited by Jonathan Barnes, 2 volumes. Oxford: Oxford University Press, II, pp. 1729–867.

Bagnoli, Carla (ed.) (2013), *Constructivism in Ethics*. Cambridge: Cambridge University Press.

Baier, Annette (1989), 'Doing Without Moral Theory?' reprinted in Stanley G. Clarke and Evan Simpson (eds) 1989: 29–48.

Barbeyrac, Jean (1735), 'The Judgment of an Anonymous Writer on the Original of the Abridgement', translated by David Saunders in Pufendorf 2003: 267–305.

Baron, Marcia (1988), 'Morality as a Back-up System: Hume's View?' *Hume Studies* 14: 25–52.

Baron, Marcia (1995), *Kantian Ethics Almost without Apology*. Ithaca and London: Cornell University Press.

Baumgarten, Alexander (1779), *Metaphysica*, 7th edition, reprinted Hildesheim: Olms, 1962.

Beck, L. W. (1960), *A Commentary on Kant's 'Critique of Practical Reason'*. Chicago: Chicago University Press.

Bittner, Rudiger (1989), *What Reason Demands*. Cambridge: Cambridge University Press.

Black, Sam, and Evan Tiffany (eds) (2007), *Reasons to Be Moral Revisited*. Calgary: University of Calgary Press.

Blanshard, Brand (1939), *The Nature of Thought*, 2 volumes. London: George Allen & Unwin.

Bradley, F. H. (1927), *Ethical Studies*, 2nd edition. Oxford: Oxford University Press.

Bradley, F. H. (1928), *Principles of Logic*, 2 volumes, second edition, corrected. Oxford: Oxford University Press.

Bradley, F. H. (1930), *Appearance and Reality*, ninth impression (corrected). Oxford: Oxford University Press.

Brandom, Robert B. (ed.) (2000), *Rorty and his Critics*. Oxford: Blackwell.

Brender, Natalie, and Larry Krasnoff (eds) (2004), *New Essays on the History of Autonomy: A Collection Honouring J. B. Schneewind*. Cambridge: Cambridge University Press.

Brentano, Franz (1969), *The Origin of Our Knowledge of Right and Wrong*, edited by Oskar Kraus and Roderick M. Chisholm, translated by Roderick M. Chisholm and Elizabeth H. Schneewind. London: Routledge and Kegan Paul.

Brink, David O. (1989), *Moral Realism and the Foundations of Ethics*. Cambridge: Cambridge University Press.

Brink, David O. (2003a), 'Editor's Introduction', in Green 2003: xiii–cx.

Brink, David O. (2003b), *Perfectionism and the Common Good: Themes in the Philosophy of T. H. Green*. Oxford: Oxford University Press.

Burns, Tony (1996), *Natural Law and Political Ideology in the Philosophy of Hegel*. Aldershot: Avebury.

Campbell, C. A. (1931), *Scepticism and Construction: Bradley's Sceptical Principle*. London: George Allen & Unwin.

Campbell, C. A. (1967), 'Moral Intuition and the Principle of Self-Realization', in his *In Defence of Free Will and Other Philosophical Essays*. London: George Allen & Unwin, pp. 107–44.

Candlish, Stewart (1978), 'Bradley on My Station and Its Duties', *Australasian Journal of Philosophy* 56: 155–70.

Carlson, Thomas (1997), 'James and the Kantian Tradition', in Ruth Anna Putnam (ed.) 1997: 363–86.

Cheap, Eliza (1836), *My Station and Its Duties: A Narrative for Girls Going to Service*. London: R. B. Seeley and W. Burnside.

Chignell, Andrew (2007), 'Belief in Kant', *Philosophical Review* 116: 323–60.

Chignell, Andrew (2013), 'The Ethics of Belief', *The Stanford Encyclopedia of Philosophy* (Spring 2013 Edition), Edward N. Zalta (ed.), <http://plato.stanford.edu/archives/spr2013/entries/ethics-belief/> accessed April 2015.

Clarke, Samuel (2003), *A Discourse Concerning the Unchangeable Obligations of Natural Religion, and the Truth and Certainty of Christian Revelation*, partially reprinted in Schneewind (ed.) 2003: 295–311.

Clarke, Stanley G., and Evan Simpson (eds) (1989), *Anti-Theory in Ethics and Moral Conservativism*. Albany: SUNY Press.

Cohen, G. A. (1996), 'Reason, Humanity, and the Moral Law', in Korsgaard 1996b: 167–88.

Coleman, Jules, and Scott Shapiro (eds) (2002), *The Oxford Handbook of Jurisprudence and Philosophy of Law*. Oxford: Oxford University Press.

Conant, James (2004), 'Varieties of Skepticism', in Denis McManus (ed.) 2004: 97–136.

Copp, David (2001), *Morality, Normativity, and Society*. Oxford: Oxford University Press.

Copp, David (2005), 'A Skeptical Challenge to Moral Non-Naturalism and a Defense of Constructivist Naturalism', *Philosophical Studies* 126: 269–83.

Crisp, Roger (2004), 'Does Modern Moral Philosophy Rest on a Mistake?' in Anthony O'Hear (ed.) 2004: 75–94.

Crisp, Roger (2006), *Reasons and the Good*. Oxford: Oxford University Press.

Cudworth, Ralph (1781), *A Treatise Concerning Eternal and Immutable Morality, with a Treatise of Freewill*, edited by Sarah Hutton. Cambridge: Cambridge University Press, 1996.

Cullity, Garrett, and Berys Gaut (eds) (1997a), *Ethics and Practical Reason*. Oxford: Oxford University Press.

Cullity, Garrett, and Berys Gaut (eds) (1997b), 'Introduction', in Cullity and Gaut (eds) 1997a: 1–28.

Dancy, Jonathan, and Ernest Sosa (eds) (1992), *A Companion to Epistemology*. Oxford: Oxford University Press.

Darwall, Stephen (1992), 'Internalism and Agency', *Philosophical Perspectives* 6: 155–74.

Darwall, Stephen (1997), 'Reasons, Motives, and the Demands of Morality: An Introduction', in Darwall, Gibbard, and Railton (eds) 1997: 305–12.

Darwall, Stephen (2004), 'Autonomy in Modern Natural Law', in Brender and Krasnoff (eds) 2004: 110–29.

Darwall, Stephen (2006), *The Second-Person Standpoint: Morality, Respect, and Accountability*. Cambridge, MA: Harvard University Press.

Darwall, Stephen (2007), 'Reply to Korsgaard, Wallace, and Watson', *Ethics* 118: 52–69.

Darwall, Stephen (2010), 'Review of *Beyond the Ethical Demand* and *Concern for the Other*', *Notre Dame Philosophical Reviews* (03/05/2010), <https://ndpr.nd.edu/news/24307-beyond-the-ethical-demand-book-1-and-concern-for-the-other-perspectives-on-the-ethics-of-k-e-l-248-gstrup-book-2/> accessed April 2015.

Darwall, Stephen (2012), 'Pufendorf on Morality, Sociability, and Moral Powers', *The Journal of the History of Philosophy* 50: 213–38.

Darwall, Stephen (2013a), 'Fichte and the Second-Person Standpoint', reprinted in his *Honor, History, and Relationship: Essays in Second-Personal Ethics II*. Oxford: Oxford University Press, pp. 222–46.

Darwall, Stephen (2013b), 'Morality's Distinctiveness', in his *Morality, Authority, and Law: Essays in Second-Personal Ethics I*. Oxford: Oxford University Press, pp. 3–19.

Darwall, Stephen, Allan Gibbard, and Peter Railton (eds) (1997), *Moral Discourse and Practice*. Oxford: Oxford University Press.

Dean, Richard (2006), *The Value of Humanity in Kant's Moral Theory*. Oxford: Oxford University Press.

Denis, Lara (2007), 'Kant's Formula of the End in Itself: Some Recent Debates', *Philosophy Compass* 2: 244–57.

Derrida, Jacques (1995), *The Gift of Death*, translated by David Wills. Chicago: University of Chicago Press.

Dewey, John (1873), 'Self-Realization as the Moral Ideal', reprinted in *The Early Works of John Dewey, 1882–1898*, IV: *1893–1894, Early Essays and The Study of Ethics*, edited by Jo Ann Boydston. Carbondale, IL: Southern Illinois University Press, 2008.

Dimova-Cookson, Maria, and W. J. Mander (eds) (2006), *T. H. Green: Ethics, Metaphysics, and Political Philosophy*. Oxford: Oxford University Press.

Enoch, David (2006), 'Agency, Shmagency: Why Normativity Won't Come from What is Constitutive of Action', *Philosophical Review* 115: 169–98.

Evans, C. Stephen (1982), *Subjectivity and Religious Belief: An Historical, Critical Study*. Washington: University Press of America.

Evans, C. Stephen (2013), *God and Moral Obligation*. Oxford: Oxford University Press.

Falk, W. D. (1945), 'Obligation and Rightness', *Philosophy* 20: 129–47.

Falk, W. D. (1986), *Ought, Reasons, and Morality: The Collected Papers of W. D. Falk*. Ithaca and London: Cornell University Press.

Finnis, John (1980), *Natural Law and Natural Rights*. Oxford: Oxford University Press.

Finnis, John (2002), 'Natural Law: The Classical Tradition', in Coleman and Shapiro (eds) 2002: 1–60.

Fitzpatrick, William J. (2006), 'The Practical Turn in Ethical Theory: Korsgaard's Constructivism, Realism, and the Nature of Normativity', *Ethics* 115: 651–91.

Flanagan, Owen (1991), *Varieties of Moral Personality: Ethics and Psychological Realism*. Cambridge, MA: Harvard University Press.

Formosa, Paul (2013), 'Is Kant a Moral Constructivist or a Moral Realist?' *European Journal of Philosophy* 21: 170–96.

Frankena, William K. (1958), 'Obligation and Motivation in Recent Moral Philosophy', in Melden (ed.) 1958: 40–81.

Galvin, Richard (2009), 'The Universal Law Formulas', in Hill (ed.) 2009: 52–82.

Galvin, Richard (2010), 'Rounding up the Usual Suspects: Varieties of Kantian Constructivism in Ethics', *Philosophical Quarterly* 61: 16–36.

Garner, Richard T. (1990), 'On the Genuine Queerness of Moral Properties and Facts', *Australasian Journal of Philosophy* 68: 137–46.

Gaut, Berys (1997), 'The Structure of Practical Reason', in Cullity and Gaut (eds) 1997a: 161–88.

Geiger, Ido (2007), *The Founding Act of Modern Ethical Life: Hegel's Critique of Kant's Moral and Political Philosophy*. Stanford, CA: Stanford University Press.

Geiger, Ido (2010), 'What Is the Use of the Universal Law Formula of the Categorical Imperative?' *British Journal for the History of Philosophy*, 18: 271–95.

Gibbard, Alan (1999), 'Morality as Consistency in Living: Korsgaard's Kantian Lectures', *Ethics* 110: 140–64.

Ginsborg, Hannah (1998), 'Korsgaard on Choosing Nonmoral Ends', *Ethics* 109: 5–21.

Glock, Hans-Johann (ed.) (2003), *Strawson and Kant*. Oxford: Oxford University Press.

Grayling, A. C. (1992), 'Transcendental Arguments', in Dancy and Sosa (eds) 1992: 506–9.

Green, T. H. (1866), 'The Philosophy of Aristotle', *North British Review*, 45: 105–44, reprinted in Green 1885–8c: III, 49–91.

Green, T. H. (1874–5), 'General Introduction to Vol 1' and 'Introduction to the Moral Part of the *Treatise*', in David Hume, *A Treatise of Human Nature*, edited by T. H. Green and T. H. Grose (London: Longmans Green, 1874–5), I, 1–299, II, 1–71; reprinted in Green 1885–8c: I, 1–371.

Green, T. H. (1885–8a), 'Lectures on the Philosophy of Kant', in Green 1885–8c: II, 1–157.

Green, T. H. (1885–8b), 'Lectures on the Principles of Political Obligation', edited by R. L. Nettleship in Green 1885–8c: II, 334–553, reprinted in Green 1986: 13–193.

Green, T. H. (1885–8c), *The Works of T. H. Green*, edited by R. L. Nettleship. London: Longmans Green.

Green, T. H. (1986), *Lectures on the Principles of Political Obligation and Other Writings*, edited by Paul Harris and John Morrow. Cambridge: Cambridge University Press: 13–193.

Green, T. H. (2003), *Prolegomena to Ethics*, new edition with introduction by David O. Brink. Oxford: Oxford University Press.

Griffin, James (1992), 'The Human Good and the Ambitions of Consequentialism', *Social Philosophy and Policy* 9: 118–32.

Griffin, James (1996), *Value Judgement: Improving our Ethical Beliefs*. Oxford: Oxford University Press.

Guyer, Paul (ed.) (1992), *The Cambridge Companion to Kant*. Cambridge, Cambridge University Press.

Guyer, Paul (2000), *Kant on Freedom, Law and Happiness*. Cambridge: Cambridge University Press.

Guyer, Paul (2011), 'Kantian Perfectionism', in Lawrence and Jost (eds) 2011: 194–214.

Hammer, Espen (ed.) (2007), *German Idealism: Contemporary Perspectives*. London: Routledge.

Hardimon, Michael (1994), 'Role Obligations', *Journal of Philosophy*, 91: 333–63.

Hare, John E. (2000a), 'Kant on Recognizing our Duties as God's Commands', *Faith and Philosophy* 17: 459–78.

Hare, John E. (2000b), 'Kant's Divine Command Theory and its Reception within Analytic Philosophy', in Phillips and Tessin (eds) 2000: 263–77.

Hare, John E. (2001a), *God's Call: Moral Realism, God's Commands, and Human Autonomy*. Grand Rapids, MI: William B. Eerdmans.

Hare, John E. (2001b), *The Moral Gap: Kantian Ethics, Human Limits, and God's Assistance*, paperback edition. Oxford: Oxford University Press.

Hare, John E. (2009), *God and Morality: A Philosophical History*. Oxford: Wiley-Blackwell.

Hare, R. M. (1963), *Freedom and Reason*. Oxford: Oxford University Press.

Hart, H. L. A. (1958), 'Legal and Moral Obligation', in Melden (ed.) 1958: 82–107.

Hegel, G. W. F. (1892–96), *Lectures on the History of Philosophy*, translated by E. S. Haldane and Frances H. Simson, 3 volumes. London: K. Paul, Trench, Trübner; reprint edition. Lincoln, NE: University of Nebraska Press, 1995.

Hegel, G. W. F. (1948), *Early Theological Writings*, translated by T. M. Knox. Philadelphia, PA: University of Pennsylvania Press.

Hegel, G. W. F. (1969–71), *Theorie Werkausgabe: Werke in zwanzig Bänden*, edited by Eva Moldenhauer and Karl Markus Michel. Frankfurt: Suhrkamp.

Hegel, G. W. F. (1975), *Lectures on the Philosophy of World History: Introduction*, translated by H. B. Nisbet. Cambridge: Cambridge University Press.

Hegel, G. W. F. (1977), *Phenomenology of Spirit*, translated by A. V. Miller. Oxford: Oxford University Press.

Hegel, G. W. F. (1991a), *The Encyclopaedia Logic: Part I of the Encyclopaedia of the Philosophical Sciences*, translated by T. F. Geraets, W. A. Suchting, and H. S. Harris. Indianapolis, IN: Hackett.

Hegel, G. W. F. (1991b), *The Philosophy of Right*, translated by H. B. Nisbet. Cambridge: Cambridge University Press.

Hegel, G. W. F. (1999), *Political Writings*, translated by H. B. Nisbet. Cambridge: Cambridge University Press.

Heller, Thomas C., Morton Sosna, and David E. Wellbery (eds) (1986), *Reconstructing Individualism: Autonomy, Individuality and the Self in Western Thought*. Stanford, CA: Stanford University Press.

Henrich, Dieter (1994), 'The Concept of Moral Insight into Kant's Doctrine of the Fact of Reason', in his *The Unity of Reason: Essays on Kant's Philosophy*, edited by Richard Velkley. Cambridge, MA: Harvard University Press, pp. 55–87.

Herman, Barbara (1993), *The Practice of Moral Judgment*. Cambridge, MA: Harvard University Press.

Hill, Thomas E. (1992), *Dignity and Practical Reason in Kant's Moral Theory*. Ithaca: Cornell University Press.

Hill, Thomas E. (ed.) (2009), *The Blackwell Guide to Kant's Ethics*. Oxford: Wiley-Blackwell.

Hills, Alison (2008), 'Kantian Value Realism', *Ratio* 21: 182–200.

Hooker, Brad (2000), 'Moral Particularism: Wrong and Bad', in Hooker and Little (eds) 2000: 1–22.

Hooker, Brad, and Margaret Little (eds) (2000), *Moral Particularism*. Oxford: Oxford University Press.

Horn, Christoph, and Dieter Schönecker (eds) (2006), *Groundwork for the Metaphysics of Morals*. Berlin: Walter de Gruyter.

Horton, John (1992), *Political Obligation*. Atlantic Highlands, NJ: Humanities.

Horton, John (2006), 'In Defence of Associative Political Obligations', Parts One and Two, *Political Studies*, 54: 427–43 and 55: 1–19.

Hoy, David Couzens (1989), 'Hegel's Critique of Kantian Morality', *History of Philosophy Quarterly*, 6: 207–32.

Hoy, David Couzens (2009), 'The Ethics of Freedom: Hegel on Reason as Law-Giving and Law-Testing', in Westphal (ed.) 2009: 153–71.

Hume, David (1965), 'Of Suicide', in MacIntyre (ed.) 1965: 297–306.

Hume, David (1975), *An Enquiry Concerning Human Understanding* in *Enquiries Concerning Human Understanding and Concerning the Principles of Morals*, 3rd edition, edited by L. A. Selby-Bigge, revised by P. H. Nidditch. Oxford: Oxford University Press.

Hutcheson, Francis (1755), *A System of Moral Philosophy in Three Books*, 2 volumes. Glasgow: Foulis.

Hyman, John, and Helen Stewart (eds) (2004), *Agency and Action*. Cambridge: Cambridge University Press.

Illies, Christian (2003), *The Grounds of Ethical Judgement*. Oxford: Oxford University Press.

Irwin, T. H. (1984), 'Morality and Personality: Kant and Green', in Wood (ed.) 1984: 31–56.

Irwin, T. H. (2004), 'Kantian Autonomy', in Hyman and Stewart (eds) 2004: 137–64.

Irwin, T. H. (2007), *The Development of Ethics: A Historical and Critical Study; Volume I: From Socrates to the Reformation*. Oxford: Oxford University Press.

Irwin, T. H. (2008), *The Development of Ethics: A Historical and Critical Study; Volume II: From Suarez to Rousseau*. Oxford: Oxford University Press.

Irwin, T. H. (2009), *The Development of Ethics: A Historical and Critical Study; Volume III: From Kant to Rawls*. Oxford: Oxford University Press.

James, William (1975–88), *The Works of William James*, edited by Frederick H. Burkhardt, Fredson Bowers, and Ignas K. Skrupskelis, 19 volumes. Cambridge, MA: Harvard University Press.

James, William (1992–2004), *The Correspondence of William James*, edited by Ignas K. Skrupskelis and Elizabeth M. Berkeley with the assistance of Bernice Grohskopf and Wilma Bradbeer, 12 volumes. Charlottesville, VA: University Press of Virginia.

Johnson, Robert N. (2007), 'Value and Autonomy in Kantian Ethics', in Shafer-Landau (ed.) 2007: 133–48.

Jost, Lawrence, and Julian Wuerth (eds) (2011), *Perfecting Virtue*. Cambridge: Cambridge University Press.

Kain, Patrick (1999), 'Self-legislation and Prudence in Kant's Moral Philosophy', PhD dissertation, Notre Dame University.

Kain, Patrick (2004), 'Self-Legislation in Kant's Moral Philosophy', *Archiv für Geschichte der Philosophie* 86: 257–306.

Kain, Patrick (2006), 'Realism and Anti-Realism in Kant's Second *Critique*', *Philosophy Compass* 1: 449–65.

Kant, Immanuel (1900–), *Kants gesammelte Schriften*, edited by the Royal Prussian (later German, then Berlin-Brandenberg) Academy of Sciences. Berlin: Georg Reimer, later Walter de Gruyter.

Kant, Immanuel (1996a), *Practical Philosophy*, translated and edited by Mary J. Gregor. Cambridge: Cambridge University Press.

Kant, Immanuel (1996b), *Religion and Rational Theology*, translated and edited by Allen W. Wood and George di Giovanni. Cambridge: Cambridge University Press.

Kant, Immanuel (1997), *Lectures on Ethics*, edited by Peter Heath and J. B. Schneewind, translated by Peter Heath. Cambridge: Cambridge University Press.

Kant, Immanuel (1998), *Critique of Pure Reason*, translated by Paul Guyer and Allen Wood. Cambridge: Cambridge University Press.

Kant, Immanuel (2000), *Critique of the Power of Judgment*, translated by Paul Guyer and Eric Matthews. Cambridge: Cambridge University Press.

Kant, Immanuel (2007), *Anthropology, History, and Education*, edited by Günter Zöller and Robert B. Louden. Cambridge: Cambridge University Press.

Kant, Immanuel (2011), *Groundwork of the Metaphysics of Morals: A German–English Edition*, translated by Mary McGregor and revised by Jens Timmermann. Cambridge: Cambridge University Press.

Kemp Smith, Norman (1920), 'The Present Situation in Philosophy', *The Philosophical Review* 29: 1–26.

Kerstein, Samuel J. (2002), *Kant's Search for the Supreme Principle of Morality*. Cambridge: Cambridge University Press.

Klein, Alexander (2015), 'Science, Religion, and "The Will to Believe"', *HOPOS: The Journal of the International Society for the History of Philosophy of Science* 5(1): 72–117 .

Korsgaard, Christine M. (1996a), *Creating the Kingdom of Ends*. Cambridge: Cambridge University Press.

Korsgaard, Christine M. (1996b), *The Sources of Normativity*, with G. A. Cohen, Raymond Geuss, Thomas Nagel, and Bernard Williams, edited by Onora O'Neill. Cambridge: Cambridge University Press.

Korsgaard, Christine M. (1998), 'Motivation, Metaphysics, and the Value of the Self: A Reply to Ginsborg, Guyer, and Schneewind', *Ethics* 109: 49–66.

Korsgaard, Christine M. (1999), 'Self-Constitution in the Ethics of Plato and Kant', *The Journal of Ethics* 3: 1–29.

Korsgaard, Christine M. (2008a), 'Introduction', in her *The Constitution of Agency: Essays on Practical Reason and Moral Psychology*. Oxford: Oxford University Press, pp. 1–23.

Korsgaard, Christine M. (2008b), 'Realism and Constructivism in Twentieth-century Moral Philosophy', reprinted in her *The Constitution of Agency: Essays on Practical Reason and Moral Psychology*. Oxford: Oxford University Press, pp. 302–26.

Korsgaard, Christine M. (2008c), 'The Normativity of Instrumental Reason', reprinted in her *The Constitution of Agency: Essays on Practical Reason and Moral Psychology*. Oxford: Oxford University Press, pp. 27–68.

Korsgaard, Christine M. (2009), *Self-Constitution: Agency, Identity, and Integrity*. Oxford: Oxford University Press.

Krasnoff, Larry (2004), 'Pythagoras Enlightened: Kant on the Effect of Moral Philosophy', in Brender and Krasnoff (eds) 2004: 133–53.

Kraut, Richard (1992), 'In Defense of Justice in Plato's *Republic*', in Kraut (ed.) 1992: 311–37.

Kraut, Richard (ed.) (1992), *The Cambridge Companion to Plato*. Cambridge: Cambridge University Press.

Lafont, Cristina (2004), 'Moral Objectivity and Reasonable Agreement: Can Realism be Reconciled with Kantian Constructivism?' *Ratio Juris* 17: 27–51.

Lamont, W. D. (1934), *Introduction to Green's Moral Philosophy*. London: Allen & Unwin.

Langton, Rae (2007), 'Objective and Unconditional Value', *Philosophical Review* 116: 157–85.

Larmore, Charles (1996), *The Morals of Modernity*. Cambridge: Cambridge University Press.

Larmore, Charles (2008), *The Autonomy of Morality*. Cambridge: Cambridge University Press.

Leibniz, G. W. (1706), 'Opinion on the Principles of Pufendorf', translated in Leibniz 1988, pp. 64–75.

Leibniz, G. W. (1988), *Political Writings*, second edition, translated and edited by Patrick Riley. Cambridge: Cambridge University Press.

Lenman, James, and Yonatan Shemmer (eds) (2012), *Constructivism in Practical Philosophy*. Oxford: Oxford University Press.

Levinas, Emmanuel (1969), *Totality and Infinity: An Essay in Exteriority*, translated by Alphonso Lingis. Pittsburgh, PA: Duquesne University Press.

Lo, Ping-cheung (1981), 'A Critical Reevaluation of the Alleged "Empty Formalism" of Kantian Ethics', *Ethics* 91: 181–201.

Locke, John (1975), *An Essay Concerning Human Understanding*, edited with an introduction by P. H. Nidditch. Oxford: Oxford University Press.

Løgstrup, K. E. (1938), 'Pligt eller ansvar', *Kirken og Tiden* 14: 206–17.

Løgstrup, K. E. (1997), *The Ethical Demand*, translated by Theodore Jensen and Gary Puckering, revised with an introduction by Hans Fink and Alasdair MacIntyre. Notre Dame, IN: University of Notre Dame Press.

Løgstrup, K. E. (2007), *Controverting Kierkegaard*, partially translated by Susan Dew in Kees van Kooten Niekerk (ed.), *Beyond the Ethical Demand*. Notre Dame, IN: University of Notre Dame Press, pp. 49–82.

Louden, Robert B. (2000), *Kant's Impure Ethics: From Rational Beings to Human Beings*. Oxford: Oxford University Press.

Luther, Martin (1930), *Secular Authority: To What Extent It Should be Obeyed*, translated by J. J. Schindel in *Works of Martin Luther*. Philadelphia, PA: A. J. Holman.

Luther, Martin (1961), 'Preface to the Epistle of St Paul to the Romans', translated by Bertram Lee Woolf in *Martin Luther: Selections from his Writings*, edited by John Dillenberger. Garden City: Anchor Books, pp. 19–34.

McDowell, John (1994), *Mind and World*. Cambridge, MA: Harvard University Press.

McDowell, John (1998a), 'Are Moral Requirements Hypothetical Imperatives?' reprinted in his *Mind, Value, and Reality*. Cambridge, MA: Harvard University Press, pp. 77–94.

McDowell, John (1998b), 'The Role of *Eudaimonia* in Aristotle's Ethics', reprinted in his *Mind, Value, and Reality*. Cambridge, MA: Harvard University Press, pp. 3–22.

McDowell, John (2000), 'Towards Rehabilitating Objectivity', in Brandom (ed.) 2000: 109–22.

MacIntyre, Alasdair (ed.) (1965), *Hume's Ethical Writings*. New York: Collier Books.

MacIntyre, Alasdair (2007), 'Human Nature and Human Dependence: What Might a Thomist Learn from Reading Løgstrup?' in Andersen and Niekerk (eds) 2007: 147–66.

McManus, Denis (ed.) (2004), *Wittgenstein and Scepticism*. London: Routledge.

McNaughton, David (2002), 'An Unconnected Heap of Duties?' reprinted in Stratton-Lake (ed.) 2002: 76–91.

Mander, W. J. (2011), *British Idealism: A History*. Oxford: Oxford University Press.

Martin, Wayne (2009), 'Ought But Cannot', *Proceedings of the Aristotelian Society* 109: 103–28.

Melden, A. I. (ed.) (1958), *Essays in Moral Philosophy*. Seattle: University of Washington Press.

Mill, J. S. (1972), *Utilitarianism*, in *'Utilitarianism', 'On Liberty', and 'Considerations on Representative Government'*, edited by H. B. Acton. London: J. M. Dent.

Misak, Cheryl (2011), 'American Pragmatism and Indispensability Arguments', *Transactions of the Charles S. Peirce Society* 47: 261–73.

Misak, Cheryl (2013), *The American Pragmatists*. Oxford: Oxford University Press.

Moggach, Douglas (2011), 'Post-Kantian Perfectionism', in Moggach (ed.) 2011: 179–202.

Moggach, Douglas (ed.) (2011), *Politics, Religion, and Art: Hegelian Debates*. Evanston, IL: Northwestern University Press.

Murdoch, Iris (1970), *The Sovereignty of Good*. London: Routledge.

Murphy, Mark C. (2011), *God and Moral Law: On the Theistic Explanation of Morality*. Oxford: Oxford University Press.

Nagel, Thomas (1996), 'Universality and the Reflective Self', in Korsgaard 1996b: 200–9.

Neiman, Susan (1994), *The Unity of Reason*. Oxford: Oxford University Press.

Neuhouser, Frederick (2000), *Foundations of Hegel's Social Theory: Actualizing Freedom*. Cambridge, MA: Harvard University Press.

Newlands, Samuel, and Larry M. Jorgensen (eds), *Metaphysics and the Good: Themes from the Philosophy of Robert Merrihew Adams*. Oxford: Oxford University Press.

Newman, John Henry (1907), *Parochial and Plain Sermons*, new impression. London: Longmans, Green, and Co.

Nicholson, Peter P. (1990), *The Political Philosophy of the British Idealists: Selected Studies*. Cambridge: Cambridge University Press.

Niekerk, Kees van Kooten (2007), 'The Genesis of K. E. Løgstrup's View of Morality as a Substitute', in Andersen and Niekerk (eds) 2007: 55–84.

Nietzsche, Friedrich (1974), *The Gay Science*, translated by Walter Kaufmann. New York: Vintage Books.

Norman, Richard (1983), *The Moral Philosophers: An Introduction to Ethics*. Oxford: Oxford University Press.

Nozick, Robert (1981), *Philosophical Explorations*. Oxford: Oxford University Press.

Nussbaum, Martha (2000), 'Why Practice Needs Ethical Theory: Particularism, Principle, and Bad Behaviour', in Hooker and Little (eds), 2000: 227–55.

O'Hagan, Timothy (1987), 'On Hegel's Critique of Kant's Moral and Political Philosophy', in Priest (ed.) 1987: 135–59.

O'Hear, Anthony (ed.) (2004), *Modern Moral Philosophy*. Cambridge: Cambridge University Press.

O'Hear, Anthony (forthcoming), *Mind, Self and Power*. Cambridge: Cambridge University Press.

O'Neill, Onora (1989), *Constructions of Reason*. Cambridge: Cambridge University Press.

Parfit, David (2006), 'Normativity', in Shafer-Landau (ed.) 2006: 325–80.

Paton, H. J. (1967), *The Categorical Imperative*, 6th edition. London: Hutchinson.

Patzig, Günther (1959), 'Der Gedanke eines Kategorischen Imperatives', *Archiv für Philosophie* 6: 82–96.

Peirce, Charles Sanders (1992a), *The Essential Peirce*, edited by Nathan Houser and Christian Kloesel, 2 volumes. Bloomington and Indianapolis, IN: Indiana University Press.

Peirce, Charles Sanders (1992b), 'The Fixation of Belief', in Peirce 1992a: I, 109–23.

Peirce, Charles Sanders (1992c), 'Some Consequences of Four Incapacities', in Peirce 1992a: I, 28–55.

Phillips, D. Z., and Timothy Tessin (eds) (2000), *Kant and Kierkegaard on Religion*. New York: Palgrave Macmillan.

Pigden, Charles R. (1990), 'Ought-Implies-Can: Erasmus, Luther and R. M. Hare', *Sophia* 29: 2–30.

Pink, Thomas (2014), 'Law and the Normativity of Obligation', *Jurisprudence* 5: 1–28.

Pink, Thomas (forthcoming), 'Power, Scepticism and Ethical Theory', in O'Hear (ed.) (forthcoming).

Pippin, Robert B. (2005), 'Postscript: On John McDowell's Response to "Leaving Nature Behind"', in his *The Persistence of Subjectivity: On the Kantian Aftermath*. Cambridge: Cambridge University Press, pp. 206–20.

Price, Richard (1948), *A Review of the Principal Questions in Morals*, edited by D. D. Raphael. Oxford: Oxford University Press.

Prichard, H. A. (2002a), 'Does Moral Philosophy Rest on a Mistake?' in his *Moral Writings*, edited by Jim MacAdam. Oxford: Oxford University Press, pp. 7–20.

Prichard, H. A. (2002b), 'Duty and Interest', in his *Moral Writings*, edited by Jim MacAdam. Oxford: Oxford University Press, pp. 21–49.

Prichard, H. A. (2002c), 'Green: Political Obligation', in his *Moral Writings*, edited by Jim MacAdam. Oxford: Oxford University Press, pp. 226–52.

Prichard, H. A. (2002d), 'Kant's *Fundamental Principles of the Metaphysic of Morals*', in his *Moral Writings*, edited by Jim MacAdam. Oxford: Oxford University Press, pp. 50–76.

Prichard, H. A. (2002e), 'Moral Obligation', in his *Moral Writings*, edited by Jim MacAdam. Oxford: Oxford University Press, pp. 163–225.

Priest, Stephen (ed.) (1987), *Hegel's Critique of Kant*. Oxford: Oxford University Press.

Pufendorf, Samuel (1672), *The Two Books of the Elements of Universal Jurisprudence* [*Elementorum jurisprudentiae universalis libri duo*], translated by William Abbott Oldfather. Oxford: Oxford University Press, reprinted 1931.

Pufendorf, Samuel (1688), *On the Law of Nature and Nations* [*De jure naturae et gentium*], translated by C. H. Oldfather and W. A. Oldfather. Oxford: Clarendon Press, reprinted 1934.

Pufendorf, Samuel (2003), *The Whole Duty of Man, According to the Law of Nature*, edited by Ian Hunter and David Saunders. Indianapolis, IN: Liberty Fund.

Putnam, Ruth Anna (ed.) (1997), *The Cambridge Companion to Kant*. Cambridge: Cambridge University Press.

Rauscher, Frederick (2002), 'Kant's Moral Anti-Realism', *Journal of the History of Philosophy* 40: 477–99.

Rawls, John (1980), 'Kantian Constructivism in Moral Theory', *Journal of Philosophy*, 77: 515–72.

Rawls, John (1993), *Political Liberalism*. New York: Columbia University Press.

Rawls, John (2000), *Lectures on the History of Moral Philosophy*. Cambridge, MA: Harvard University Press.

Raz, Joseph (1975), *Practical Reason and Norms*, second edition. Oxford: Oxford University Press.

Raz, Joseph (1986), *The Morality of Freedom*. Oxford: Oxford University Press.

Reath, Andrews (2006a), 'Agency and Universal Law', in his *Agency and Autonomy in Kant's Moral Theory: Selected Essays*. Oxford: Oxford University Press, pp. 196–230.

Reath, Andrews (2006b), 'Autonomy of the Will as the Foundation of Morality', in his *Agency and Autonomy in Kant's Moral Theory: Selected Essays*. Oxford: Oxford University Press, pp. 121–72.

Reath, Andrews, and Jens Timmermann (eds) (2010), *Kant's Critique of Practical Reason: A Critical Guide*. Cambridge: Cambridge University Press.

Regan, D. H. (2002), 'The Value of Rational Nature', *Ethics* 112: 267–91.

Rescher, Nicholas (1987), *Ethical Idealism: An Inquiry into the Nature and Function of Ideals*. Berkeley, CA: University of California Press.

Ridge, Michael (2012), 'Kantian Constructivism: Something Old, Something New', in Lenman and Shemmer (eds) 2012: 138–58.

Riley, Patrick (1983), *Kant's Political Philosophy*. Totowa, NJ: Rowman and Littlefield.

Ritchie, D. G. (1891), *The Principles of State Interference*. London: Swan Sonnenschein.

Rödl, Sebastian (2013), 'Why Ought Implies Can', in Timmons and Baiasu (eds) 2013: 42–56.

Rorty, Richard (1991), 'Solidarity or Objectivity?' reprinted in his *Objectivity, Relativism, and Truth: Philosophical Papers Volume 1*. Cambridge: Cambridge University Press, pp. 21–34.

Rorty, Richard (1999), 'Trotsky and the Wild Orchids', reprinted in his *Philosophy and Social Hope*. London: Penguin, pp. 3–22.

Rorty, Richard (2000), 'Response to Michael Williams', in Brandom (ed.) 2000: 213–19.

Rorty, Richard (2006), 'Pragmatism as Anti-Authoritarianism', in Shook and Margolis (eds) 2006: 257–67.

Rorty, Richard (2007), 'Kant vs. Dewey: The Current Situation of Moral Philosophy' reprinted in his *Philosophy as Cultural Politics: Philosophical Papers Volume 4*. Cambridge: Cambridge University Press, pp. 184–202.

Ross, David (2002), *The Right and the Good*, edited by Philip Stratton-Lake. Oxford: Oxford University Press.

Scanlon, T. M. (1998), *What We Owe to Each Other*. Cambridge, MA: Harvard University Press.

Schiller, Friedrich (1962), 'Über Anmut und Würde', in *Nationalausgabe der Werke Schillers*, XX. Weimar: Böhlau.

Schiller, Friedrich (1967), *On the Aesthetic Education of Man in a Series of Letters*, translated by E. M. Wilkinson and L. A. Willoughby. Oxford: Oxford University Press.

Schiller, Friedrich (2003), 'Kallias or Concerning Beauty: Letters to Gottfried Körner', translated by Stefan Bird-Pollen, in J. M. Bernstein (ed.), *Classical and Romantic German Aesthetics*. Cambridge: Cambridge University Press, pp. 145–84.

Schiller, Friedrich (2005), 'On Grace and Dignity', translated by Jane V. Curran in *Schiller's 'On Grace and Dignity' in its Cultural Context*. Rochester, NY: Camden House.

Schmidtz, David (2007), 'Because It's Right', in Black and Tiffany (eds) 2007: 63–96.

Schneewind, J. B. (1986), 'The Use of Autonomy in Ethical Theory', in Heller, Sosa, and Wellbery (eds) 1986: 64–75.

Schneewind, J. B. (1992), 'Autonomy, Obligation, and Virtue: An Overview of Kant's Moral Philosophy', in Guyer (ed.) 1992: 309–41.

Schneewind, J. B. (1998a), 'Korsgaard and the Unconditional in Morality', *Ethics* 109: 36–48.

Schneewind, J. B. (1998b), *The Invention of Autonomy: A History of Modern Moral Philosophy*. Cambridge: Cambridge University Press.

Schneewind, J. B. (ed.) (2003), *Moral Philosophy from Montaigne to Kant*. Cambridge: Cambridge University Press.

Schneewind, J. B. (2010a), 'Moral Problems and Moral Philosophy in the Victorian Period', reprinted in his *Essays on the History of Moral Philosophy*. Oxford: Oxford University Press, pp. 42–61.

Schneewind, J. B. (2010b), 'No Discipline, No History: The Case of Moral Philosophy', reprinted in his *Essays on the History of Moral Philosophy*. Oxford: Oxford University Press, pp. 107–26.

Schnoor, Christian (1989), *Kants kategorischer Imperativ als Kriterium der Richtigkeit des Handelns*. Tübingen: J. C. B. Mohr.

Schopenhauer, Arthur (1988), *Sämtliche Werke*, edited by Arthur Hübscher. Mannheim: F. A. Brockhaus, vols 1–7.

Schopenhauer, Arthur (2009), *The Two Fundamental Problems of Ethics*, translated and edited by Christopher Janaway. Cambridge: Cambridge University Press.

Schwaiger, Clemens (2009), 'The Theory of Obligation in Wolff, Baumgarten, and the Early Kant', in Ameriks and Höffe (eds) 2009: 58–76.

Sciaraffa, Stefan (2011), 'Identification, Meaning, and the Normativity of Social Roles', *European Journal of Philosophy* 19: 107–28.

Selden, John (1892), *The Table Talk of John Selden*, edited by Samuel Reynolds. Oxford: Clarendon Press.

Sensen, Oliver (2009), 'Dignity and the Formula of Humanity', in Timmermann (ed.) 2009: 102–18.

Sensen, Oliver (2013), 'Kant's Constructivism', in Bagnoli (ed.) 2013: 63–81.

Shafer-Landau, Russ (2003), *Moral Realism: A Defence*. Oxford: Oxford University Press.

Shafer-Landau, Russ (ed.) (2006), *Oxford Studies in Metaethics, Volume 1*. Oxford: Oxford University Press.

Shafer-Landau, Russ (ed.) (2007), *Oxford Studies in Metaethics, Volume 2*. Oxford: Oxford University Press.

Shafer-Landau, Russ (ed.) (2008), *Oxford Studies in Metaethics, Volume 3*. Oxford: Oxford University Press.

Shell, Susan Meld (2009), *Kant and the Limits of Autonomy*. Cambridge, MA: Harvard University Press.

Shook, John R., and Joseph Margolis (eds) (2006), *A Companion to Pragmatism*. Oxford: Blackwell.

Sidgwick, Henry (1902), *Lectures on the Ethics of T. H. Green, Mr Herbert Spencer and J. Martineau*. London: Macmillan.

Sidgwick, Henry (1907), *The Methods of Ethics*, 7th edition. Indianapolis, IN: Hackett.

Simmons, A. John (2001), *Justification and Legitimacy*. Cambridge: Cambridge University Press.

Singer, Marcus George (1963), *Generalization in Ethics*. London: Eyre & Spottiswoode.

Sinnott-Armstrong, Walter (1984), '"Ought" Conversationally Implies "Can"', *The Philosophical Review* 93: 249–61.

Skidmore, James (2002), 'Skepticism about Practical Reason: Transcendental Arguments and their Limits', *Philosophical Studies* 109: 121–41.

Skorupski, John (1998), 'Rescuing Moral Obligation', *European Journal of Philosophy* 6: 335–55.

Skorupski, John (2006), 'Green and the Idealist Conception of a Person's Good', in Dimova-Cookson and Mander (eds) 2006: 47–75.

Skorupski, John (2011), 'Ethics and the Social Good', in Wood and Hahn (eds): 434–68.

Smith, Michael (1994), *The Moral Problem*. Oxford: Blackwell.

Smith, Steven B. (1989), *Hegel's Critique of Liberalism*. Chicago: University of Chicago Press.

Stern, Robert (2000), *Transcendental Arguments and Scepticism*. Oxford: Oxford University Press.

Stern, Robert (2003), 'On Strawson's Naturalistic Turn', in Glock (ed.) 2003: 219–33.

Stern, Robert (2004), 'Does "Ought" Imply "Can"? And Did Kant Think It Does?' *Utilitas* 16: 42–61.

Stern, Robert (2007a), 'Freedom, Self-Legislation and Morality in Kant and Hegel: Constructivist vs Realist Accounts', in Hammer (ed.) 2007: 245–66.

Stern, Robert (2007b), 'Transcendental Arguments: A Plea for Modesty', *Grazer Philosophische Studien* 74: 143–61.

Stern, Robert (2009), *Hegelian Metaphysics*. Oxford: Oxford University Press.

Stern, Robert (2012), *Understanding Moral Obligation: Kant, Hegel, Kierkegaard*. Cambridge: Cambridge University Press.

Stern, Robert (2014), 'Darwall on Second-Personal Ethics', *European Journal of Philosophy* 22: 321–33.

Stratton-Lake, Philip (1996), 'In Defence of the Abstract', *Bulletin of the Hegel Society of Great Britain* 33: 42–53.

Stratton-Lake, Philip (2000), *Kant, Duty and Moral Worth*. London: Routledge.

Stratton-Lake, Philip (ed.) (2002), *Ethical Intuitionism: Re-Evaluations*. Oxford: Oxford University Press.

Stratton-Lake, Philip (2002a), 'Introduction', in Stratton-Lake (ed.) 2002: 1–28.

Stratton-Lake, Philip (2002b), 'Introduction', in Ross 2002: ix–1.

Strawson, Galen (2010), *Freedom and Belief*, revised edition. Oxford: Oxford University Press.

Strawson, P. F. (1982), 'Freedom and Resentment', in Watson (ed.) 1982: 59–80.

Street, Sharon (2008), 'Constructivism about Reasons', in Shafter-Landau (ed.), 2008: 207–46.

Street, Sharon (2010), 'What is Constructivism in Ethics and Metaethics?' *Philosophy Compass* 5: 363–84.

Stroud, Barry (1968), 'Transcendental Arguments', *Journal of Philosophy* 65: 241–56.

Suarez, Francisco (1612), *On Laws and God the Lawgiver* [*De legibus, ac deo legislatore*], translated by Gwladys L. Williams, Ammi Brown, and John Waldron, in his 1944, vol. II, pp. 3–646.

Suarez, Francisco (1944), *Selections from Three Works of Francisco Suarez*. Oxford: Oxford University Press.

Superson, Anita M. (2009), *The Moral Skeptic*. Oxford: Oxford University Press.

Teichmann, Roger (2008), *The Philosophy of Elizabeth Anscombe*. Oxford: Oxford University Press.

Tenenbaum, Sergio (2012), 'The Idea of Freedom and Moral Cognition in *Groundwork III*', *Philosophy and Phenomenological Research* 84: 555–89.

Timmermann, Jens (2003), 'Sollen und Können: "Du kannst, denn du sollst" und "Sollen impliziert Können" im Vergleich', *Philosophiegeschichte und logische Analyse* 6: 113–22.

Timmermann, Jens (2006), 'Value without Regress: Kant's "Formula of Humanity" Revisited', *European Journal of Philosophy* 14: 69–93.

Timmermann, Jens (2007), *Kant's 'Groundwork of the Metaphysics of Morals': A Commentary*. Cambridge: Cambridge University Press.

Timmermann, Jens (ed.) (2009), *Kant's 'Groundwork of the Metaphysics of Morals': A Critical Guide*. Cambridge: Cambridge University Press.

Timmons, Mark, and Sorin Baiasu (eds) (2013), *Kant on Practical Justification: Interpretative Essays*. Oxford: Oxford University Press.

Urmson, J. O. (1975), 'A Defence of Intuitionism', *Proceedings of the Aristotelian Society* 75: 111–19.

Wallace, R. J. (2006), 'Normativity and the Will', reprinted in his *Normativity and the Will*. Oxford: Oxford University Press, pp. 71–81.

Watkins, Eric and William Fitzpatrick (2002), 'O'Neill and Korsgaard on the Construction of Normativity', *The Journal of Value Inquiry* 36: 349–67.

Watson, Gary (1982), *Free Will*. Oxford: Oxford University Press.

Watson, Gary (2007), 'Morality as Equal Accountability: Comments on Stephen Darwall's *The Second-Person Standpoint*', *Ethics* 118: 37–51.

Westphal, Kenneth R. (2003), 'Objective Gültigkeit zwischen Gegebenem und Gemachtem: Hegels kantischer Konstruktivismus in der praktischen Philosophie', *Jahrbuch für Recht und Ethik* 11: 177–98.

Westphal, Kenneth R. (ed.) (2009), *The Blackwell Guide to Hegel's 'Phenomenology of Spirit'*. Oxford: Wiley-Blackwell.

Willaschek, Marcus (2006), 'Practical Reason: A Commentary on Kant's *Groundwork of the Metaphysics of Morals* (GMS II, 412–417)', in Horn and Schönecker (eds) 2006: 121–38.

Willaschek, Marcus (2010), 'The Primacy of Practical Reason and the Idea of a Practical Postulate', in Reath and Timmermann (eds) 2010: 168–96.

Williams, Bernard (1981a), 'Moral Luck', in his *Moral Luck*. Cambridge: Cambridge University Press, pp. 20–39.

Williams, Bernard (1981b), 'Persons, Character and Morality', in his *Moral Luck*. Cambridge: Cambridge University Press, pp. 1–19.

Wittgenstein, Ludwig (1998), *Culture and Value*, edited by G. H. von Wright, revised edition. Oxford: Blackwell.

Wolf, Jakob (2007), 'A Response to Hans Reinders's "Donum or Datum?"', in Andersen and Niekerk (eds) 2007: 207–15.

Wolf, Susan (2009), 'Moral Obligations and Social Commands', in Newlands and Jorgensen (eds) 2009: 343–67.

Wolff, Christian (1751), *Vernünftige Gedancken von Gott, der Welt und der Seele des Menschen*, reprinted Ann Arbor, MI: UMI, 2005.

Wood, Allen W. (ed.) (1984), *Self and Nature in Kant's Philosophy*. Ithaca and London: Cornell University Press.

Wood, Allen W. (1990), *Hegel's Ethical Thought*. Cambridge: Cambridge University Press.

Wood, Allen W. (1998), 'Review of Korsgaard *Creating the Kingdom of Ends*', *Philosophical Review* 107: 607–11.

Wood, Allen W. (1999), *Kant's Ethical Thought*. Cambridge: Cambridge University Press.

Wood, Allen W. (2008), *Kantian Ethics*. Cambridge: Cambridge University Press.

Wood, Allen W., and Songsuk Susan Hahn (eds) (2011), *Cambridge History of Philosophy in the Nineteenth Century*. Cambridge: Cambridge University Press.

Index